T0305339

Patent Valuation

Founded in 1807, John Wiley & Sons is the oldest independent publishing company in the United States. With offices in North America, Europe, Australia, and Asia, Wiley is globally committed to developing and marketing print and electronic products and services for our customers' professional and personal knowledge and understanding.

The Wiley Finance series contains books written specifically for finance and investment professionals as well as sophisticated individual investors and their financial advisors. Book topics range from portfolio management to e-commerce, risk management, financial engineering, valuation and financial instrument analysis, as well as much more.

For a list of available titles, visit our web site at www.WileyFinance.com.

Patent Valuation

Improving Decision Making through Analysis

WILLIAM J. MURPHY,
JOHN L. ORCUTT,
PAUL C. REMUS

John Wiley & Sons, Inc.

Published by John Wiley & Sons, Inc., Hoboken, New Jersey.
Published simultaneously in Canada.

For general information on our other products and services or for technical support, please contact our Customer Care Department within the United States at (800) 762-2974, outside the United States at (317) 572-3993 or fax (317) 572-4002.

Wiley also publishes its books in a variety of electronic formats. Some content that appears in print may not be available in electronic books. For more information about Wiley products, visit our web site at www.wiley.com.

Library of Congress Cataloging-in-Publication Data:
Murphy, William J. (William Joseph), 1949-
  Patent valuation : improving decision making through analysis / William J. Murphy, John L. Orcutt, Paul C. Remus.—1
    p. cm.—(Wiley finance series)
  Includes bibliographical references and index.
  ISBN 978-1-118-02734-9 (hardback); ISBN 978-1-118-22213-3 (ebk);
ISBN 978-1-118-26082-1 (ebk); ISBN 978-1-118-23590-4 (ebk)
  1. Patents—Valuation. 2. Decision making. 3. Patents—Accounting. I. Orcutt, John L. II. Remus, Paul C., 1945- III. Title.
  HF5681.P3M87 2012
  657'.4—dc23   2012005831

10 9 8 7 6 5 4 3 2 1

Contents

Preface

We have a very simple goal with this book: to help inventors, entrepreneurs, executives, technology acquirers, technology managers, lawyers, judges, and anyone else who is part of the patenting process to make better patent decisions. Most readers of a book titled *Patent Valuation* are likely to appreciate that patented inventions are important. So, we are going to skip over the typical introduction to an intellectual property book that tells readers about the importance of intellectual property—in particular, patents—in a knowledge-based world. We assume that readers already know that patented inventions provide the foundation for modern economies and for many of the world's most successful companies.

What many readers may not fully appreciate, however, is a more subtle but equally important reality that stems from two related concepts. First, making informed decisions about the creation, management, and defense of patented inventions can distinguish competitive success (and significant wealth creation) from competitive failure (and economic waste). For patents to achieve their value-generating potential, numerous actors performing a variety of functions need to make multiple decisions. For example, inventors need to decide which research projects to pursue and how much to invest in the research project. If a patentable invention results from the research project, the inventor needs to decide whether to patent the invention and, if the answer is to patent, how much to invest in prosecuting the patent. Decisions then need to be made about patent management. Should the patent holder use the invention, transfer it to a third party, or do both? If the patent holder seeks to transfer some, or all, of its patent rights, how should the transfer be structured and at what price? Overlaying all these decisions are equally important litigation decisions. Should the patent holder sue a potential infringer (and how much should it spend on the litigation)? At what price should the patent holder settle? When should an alleged infringer settle a potential lawsuit, and when should it defend? As the societal importance of patents continues to increase, so, too, does the importance of wisely making each of these various patent decisions (and thousands more related decisions).

The second concept is that patent decisions can be significantly improved by recognizing that they can be quantified, compared, and evaluated. In short, patents and their related decisions can be valued and are implicitly valued even if that valuation frequently goes unnoticed. Through an attentive and disciplined thought process, valuation allows a decision maker to determine the course of action that provides the most advantageous outcome. Despite its acceptance in other business settings, valuation has been slow to develop as a wide-ranging decision-making tool for patents. One reason (and probably the most powerful reason) for this failure to systematically employ valuation analysis to guide patent decisions is the common misperception that patent valuation is too difficult. Because most patent decision makers believe that valuing patents is an inherently difficult exercise, they often believe that it is foolhardy to invest much energy into valuation unless it is absolutely required, such as when licensing a set of patent rights. Such thinking could not be more misguided. On the one hand, it fails to appreciate the extent to which valuing patents can improve patent decisions. Moreover, the idea that patents are overly difficult to value is simply wrong. One of the most fundamental premises of this book is that intelligent valuation skills are accessible to, and should be used by, each of the various decision makers in the patent process. This book provides narrative descriptions of the various topics, illustrative cases, step-by-step valuation techniques, user-friendly procedures and checklists, and an abundance of examples that help to make patent valuation an understandable decision-making tool that can be deployed throughout an organization.

OUTLINE OF THE BOOK

This book is organized into three parts. Part One examines the foundations for patent valuation and decision making. Chapter 1, "Valuation Basics," presents an overview of valuation and its role in decision-making processes. Chapter 2, "Patent Basics," provides a review of patent law basics. Because patent rights—separate from the underlying use of a patented invention—are central to an invention's ability to generate value, it is critical to understand those rights when valuing a patent. Chapter 3, "Valuation Analysis to Improve Patent Decision Making," provides an overview of the wide range of patent decisions that can benefit from valuation analysis and examines decision-making strategies that help to guide how much valuation analysis to conduct in a particular situation. With real-world applications in mind, this chapter also explains how valuation techniques can help to inform decision making without becoming tedious, overly burdensome endeavors. Chapter 4, "Disassembly," explains how the basic task of disassembling a valuation problem into its component parts can often be the most crucial step for generating a useful valuation. Disassembly helps the valuator to identify the individual factors that collectively generate the overall value of the item being valued, generate a better understanding of those individual factors and how they interact to generate value, organize the information so that it can be dealt with in a manageable way, and identify and eliminate extraneous information that is not important to the valuation process. This chapter also demonstrates how to incorporate disassembly techniques into patent valuation analyses.

Part Two provides the fundamental tools needed to value patents. Chapter 5, "Preparing for the Valuation," details the preparatory work that should be done before launching into a thorough valuation exercise. Chapter 6, "Income Methods: Discounted Future Economic Benefits Analysis," describes the basic discounted future economic benefits (DFEB) model for valuing patents. Chapter 7, "Advanced Income Methods: Incorporating the Value of Future Decision Opportunities," seeks to expand on the basic DFEB model to incorporate the value of future decision opportunities. The basic DFEB model does not fully capture future flexibility and choices that are embedded in patents, but more advanced techniques (such as real options theory and decision trees) do. Chapter 7 explores the theoretical and practical applicability of these advanced techniques. Chapter 8, "Market Methods," analyzes a number of the market methods that are used to value patents. This chapter also explains the strengths and weaknesses of these methods and how they can be effectively employed. Chapter 9, "Cost Methods," explains the core cost methods for valuing patents and demonstrates how to make practical use of them.

Part Three presents specific, practical scenarios that benefit from patent valuation. Chapter 10, "Pricing Patent Licenses," examines how to structure and price patent licenses. One of the most critical times for valuing a set of patent rights is when patent rights are being transferred voluntarily, and licenses are the most common method for such transfers. Chapter 11, "Patent Infringement Damages," provides an overview of U.S. law for calculating damages in patent infringement cases. The consequences of infringement litigation can be very material to a party, which makes understanding how patent damage awards are computed important to intelligent decision making in numerous litigation and nonlitigation patent settings. The potential net returns from bringing a lawsuit as well as the potential net costs from being sued for infringement should factor into a multitude of patent decisions. Chapter 12, "Unlocking the Potential Value within Patents," considers the latent, capital-generation potential that exists within patents. Unlocking the potential value of patent assets to access investment capital is critical to the creation and growth of entrepreneurial firms. This chapter describes a number of emerging methods for extracting this potential value from patents and explains the intersection between traditional valuation analysis and these emerging practices. Chapter 13, "Valuation in Patent-Based Tax-Planning Strategies," explores patent-based tax-reduction strategies and explains the role of valuation in these strategies.

Acknowledgments

We could not have completed this project without our colleagues at the Intellectual Property Valuation Institute (IPVI), which is part of the Franklin Pierce Center for Intellectual Property at the University of New Hampshire School of Law. Our IPVI colleagues, in particular Gordon Smith and Professor Susan Richey, have provided us invaluable assistance and insights throughout the book-writing process. We have also received substantial support from UNH Law Assistant Professors Jon Cavicchi and Tom Hemstock, who are two of the best law librarians in the world.

During our work on this book, we have had a number of talented research assistants who have provided us with thoughtful and generous assistance in researching and editing the book. They include Jeremy Barton, Jacki Lin, Ian Mullet, Sarah Rogers, and Joseph Young.

The various decision trees that we provide in this book were developed using TreeAge Pro. We would like to thank TreeAge Software, Inc. of Williamstown, Massachusetts (www.treeage.com) for providing us with a complimentary license to construct the decision trees for this book.

The authors would also like to thank Professor Ray Friel of the law faculty at the University of Limerick, Ireland, for his welcome advice and encouragement. The authors would also like to thank the law faculty at University College Cork, Ireland, who sacrificed the 2011 eLaw Summer Institute, an unexpected occurrence that fortuitously provided some much needed time for Bill to work on this book.

Finally, and most important, we want to thank our families and friends for their support. Bill would like to thank his family, in particular Tyler and Kristen Murphy, who have had to listen to more about patent valuation than any two college students should. John would like to thank his wife, Corinne, and his children, Xavier, Alexandre, and Morgane, for all the sacrifices they made to allow him to work on this book. John particularly wants to thank Morgane, who became a regular at his office while he worked on various drafts of the book and provided him with constant support and motivation. Everybody at UNH Law misses not having her around as much. Paul would like to thank his wife, Ann, and his children, Amy, Dana, and Jeb, for their encouragement and support. Paul would like to extend an additional thank-you to Amy and Dana, two lawyers, who put up with his seemingly unending hypothetical questions.

Patent Valuation

Foundations for Patent Valuation and Decision Making

CHAPTER 1

Valuation Basics

One cannot make an informed decision without valuation. By definition, decisions require choosing between alternative courses of action. Putting aside for a moment what *value* actually means, a reasonable decision maker will seek the alternative that provides the best value. If a firm is considering whether to buy an asset, it will want to determine the asset's value to the firm and compare it with the acquisition cost. If a firm is choosing between business strategies or financing strategies, it will want to pursue the strategy that provides the most value to the firm. The realization that informed decisions require valuation is well understood in many business settings. You would be hard pressed to find a competent corporate finance manager who does not rely on valuation as the primary decision making tool.

Despite its acceptance in other business settings, valuation has been slow to develop as a wide-ranging decision-making tool for patents. In the patent context, valuation analyses tend to be conducted only when absolutely required. If a company is about to license its patent rights to a third party, for example, or needs a damages estimate for an infringement lawsuit, a value obviously must be placed on the patent rights. Consciously valuing the potential patent rights at other times is much less common. In effect, thoughtful valuation efforts are limited to when money is about to change hands on the patent rights or when an asset value needs to be placed on the books for tax planning or accounting purposes. Using valuation to make patent decisions in other circumstances, however, remains the exception rather than the rule. Twenty or thirty years ago, when patents tended to be less critical to firms' success, it may have been permissible for companies to take a cavalier approach to valuing patents and making patent decisions. That is no longer the case. Today's successful manager, scientist, attorney, or governmental official involved with patents is constantly asked to make decisions, and that decision-making process can be significantly improved by understanding and using valuation analyses. Consider just a few of the common patent-related decisions that firms face on a daily basis:

- Which R&D project should the firm pursue?
- Should the firm obtain a patent?
- In which countries should the firm obtain a patent?
- How broadly should the firm's lawyers draft the patent's claims?
- How should the firm manage its patent portfolio?
- Should the firm sue a possible infringer?
- How should the firm respond to a threat of an infringement suit?
- How should the firm monetize a patent?

For those decision makers who purposefully or inadvertently try to avoid valuation analyses, their avoidance efforts will not be successful. Every decision involves a value judgment (the option chosen is better than the options not chosen), whether the decision maker appreciates it or not. When a company decides to prioritize one research and development (R&D) project over another, for example, the company has valued the winning R&D project higher than the other. When a company decides to settle a patent infringement suit, the company has valued the settlement alternative higher than the litigation alternative. Therefore, the choice is not whether to conduct a valuation analysis. Rather, the choice is whether to employ an intelligent valuation analysis that helps to inform the decision or to employ a sloppy process that ignores such valuable information.

Valuation has traditionally had a limited role in the patent context because it is perceived to be so complex and uncertain that the effort is not worth the information it generates. We could not disagree more with that line of thinking. This book is based on two foundational principles that we hope to prove throughout the text: (1) Reasonable valuation estimates can be generated for patents that significantly improve all aspects of patent decision making, and (2) conducting useful patent valuations is not that difficult. In fact, patent valuation skills can be made generally accessible to most actors in the patent industry and thereby improve decision making throughout the entire patent process.

In this chapter, we

- Explain what is meant by *value*.
- Provide a general overview of the valuation process and what it can accomplish.
- Explain the importance of identifying exactly what is being valued: the invention, the patent rights, or both?

- Examine some common misconceptions about valuation that obscure the ultimate benefits of the exercise.
- Provide an overview of the three fundamental valuation approaches (income, market, and cost).
- Consider limitations on rationality in valuation and decision-making exercises.

WHAT IS VALUE?

A valuation analysis seeks to determine an asset's value. Most of us have an intuitive appreciation of what is meant by *value*: It refers to the benefits that come from the asset. The unifying benefit patents provide is the cash flow that patent rights help to generate. Why do firms buy, sell, or otherwise make decisions about patent rights? There are many specific reasons, but the overarching rationale that links each patent decision is the firm's desire to generate economic benefits. By their nature, most firms are profit-driven entities. Whether or not mandated by law (e.g., in the case of corporations[1]), the fundamental purpose for most business firms is to generate profits. A firm's decisions to accumulate, use, transfer, enforce, or defend patent rights are therefore driven by the ability for that decision to generate "net" economic benefits—economic benefits that exceed related costs—that enhance the firm's economic position. Thus, a patent valuation analysis is an attempt to measure the net economic benefits that come from a firm's patent-related decisions.

How do patent rights help the rights holder to generate the net economic benefits that are the source of value? That is a topic we will cover throughout this book. For now, note that there are two choices: Economic benefits can be either direct or indirect.

1. **Direct economic benefits:** Patent rights can create a direct cash flow stream for the rights holder that could not be earned without those rights. For example, holding the patent rights may allow the rights holder to generate extra profits that stem from excluding competitors.
2. **Indirect economic benefits:** Patent rights can also generate indirect economic returns for the rights holder. Namely, the patent rights can (1) save money for the rights holder by reducing or eliminating certain negative costs and (2) indirectly help the rights holder to generate cash flow streams (e.g., a patent can signal R&D strength that helps the patent holder to raise investment capital and build other business lines).

On occasion, patents can also generate noneconomic benefits (see Box 1.1).

BOX 1.1: INSTRUMENTAL VERSUS INTRINSIC VALUE

In this book, we will generally focus on instrumental value. Patents have value as instruments of commerce that provide rights holders with certain economic benefits (both direct and indirect). Because patents are typically held by companies and other commercial actors, the instrumental value of patents is the dominant focus for most rights holders.

It should not be forgotten, however, that patents may also have intrinsic value for some rights holders. Many inventors are driven to patent by the possibility of financial gain, but some pursue patents for their intrinsic value. Intrinsic value includes noneconomic rewards such as the prestige, personal achievement, or feeling of accomplishment that comes from having a patent. For such an inventor, a patent can be a symbol of inventiveness or achievement, even if it does not create any real value in commerce. This intrinsic value of patents may help to explain why so many patents are pursued each year that generate no economic returns to the inventor.

Finally, value is a relative concept. The exact same asset will generate very different future economic benefits—and therefore very different values—depending on who possesses it and how it is deployed. Assume that a small start-up company develops a patented pharmaceutical drug that affects blood-flow circulation. This drug can be used as an effective treatment for two different health conditions: (1) It can help to treat pulmonary arterial hypertension (PAH), and (2) it can help to treat male erectile dysfunction (ED). The start-up company has strong research capabilities, but weak marketing and distribution capabilities. If the start-up keeps the patent and tries to market and distribute the drug itself, profits (and therefore the patent's value) would likely be low. If the start-up decides to license the drug's patent rights to a large pharmaceutical company to market and distribute the drug, profits (and therefore the patent's value) would likely be much higher. The same patent rights would have two very different values depending on who holds them. The same can be said for how the patent rights are deployed. Assume that the start-up licenses the drug's patent rights to the large pharmaceutical company, which is deciding how to market the drug. It could market the drug primarily as a PAH treatment or primarily as an ED treatment. To complete the hypothetical example, it turns out that the ED market is much larger than the PAH market and would generate more profits. Again, the same patent rights would have two different values, but this time deployment (rather than who holds the rights) would be the variable that changes value.

It is this relative nature of value that allows markets to develop. That different parties value an item differently is what encourages the exchanges that are the driving principle of markets. See Chapter 8 for a discussion of markets and their effect on patent valuation.

THE VALUATION PROCESS

How should value be determined? There are an almost infinite variety of possibilities; some are logical and reasonable, some not. No matter what method is used to measure value, however, the foundation of each valuation assessment is a translation exercise (see Figure 1.1). The valuation process takes a complex, ever-changing, and messy reality and translates it into a simplified, numerical measurement (see Box 1.2) or value result. In the case

FIGURE 1.1 The Foundation of Valuation Assessments Is a Translation Exercise

BOX 1.2: USING NUMBERS IN VALUATION ANALYSES

Using numbers is one of the most important, but also one of the most inexact, parts of any valuation exercise. Numbers are themselves the result of a translation exercise. They are a simplified representation of some complex reality that a valuator hopes to capture (such as the profits that will flow from the patent next year). This translation of complex reality into a number (or a range of numbers) is a simplification process. Although some information is lost in any simplification process, the objective is to employ simplification methods that retain as much critical information as possible without the burden of superfluous or distracting information. When all the available simplification methods risk significant information loss, the valuator needs to be aware of and consider the risk of lost information when interpreting the results of any valuation analysis.

1. Collect information inputs   2. Use selected methodology   3. Interpret results

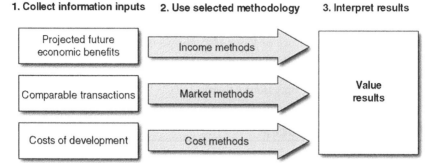

FIGURE 1.2 Valuation Analysis Is a Function of Three Basic Variables:
(1) Information Inputs, (2) Valuation Methodologies, and (3) Interpretation of
the Value Result

of patents, the value result will usually be expressed in terms of money
because patent valuation analyses attempt to measure the net economic
benefits (direct and indirect) that come from patents.

Conducting a valuation analysis is a function of three basic variables
(see Figure 1.2): (1) the information inputs (measurements of the complex
and messy reality), (2) the valuation methodology that translates these
inputs into a value result, and (3) the interpretation of the ensuing value
result. This combination of variables is why most valuation commentators
describe valuation as a combination of both art and science. The science
part of valuation is the logical and consistent application of reasonable
valuation methodologies. The art side, however, tends to be just about
everything else. The gathering of information variables and the interpretation of the value result require significant subjective judgments. What
information will be collected and what ignored? How will missing information be addressed? How will uncertainty, probable future outcomes, and
new information learned in the future be incorporated into the analysis?
Finally, what does the value result really mean?

By their very nature, patents can pose particular information input
challenges for valuators. Uncertainties about the legal strength of the patent
or the underlying technical and commercial viability of the invention make
information gathering even more subjective for patents than for many asset
classes. These challenges are compounded by the unique nature of patents
and the lack of robust patent trading markets. As a result, patent valuation
can be more weighted toward the art, rather than the science, side of the
spectrum.

IDENTIFYING THE SUBJECT MATTER OF THE VALUATION

One of the first steps in any valuation exercise is to identify clearly the item to be valued. For a patent valuation, the valuator must clarify what the term *patent* means in the context of that specific exercise. The problem stems from the multiple meanings that are commonly ascribed to the term, be it for the invention use, the patent rights, or both.

Invention Use, Patent Rights, or Both?

Sometimes the term *patent* is used to describe the economic use of the patented invention (see Box 1.3). At other times it is used to describe some of or all the intellectual property rights that come with a patent (e.g., it could be used to describe a single claim or embodiment or could focus on the totality of rights associated with the patent). And sometimes it is used to describe both the invention use and the patent rights collectively.

BOX 1.3: USE OF THE PATENTED INVENTION: PATENTED ARTICLE VERSUS PATENTED PROCESS

When considering the commercial use of a patented invention, there are two possibilities:

1. A product in the marketplace that results from the patented invention.
2. The use of the patented invention to do something.

Sometimes the product is the subject of the patent (in the words of the U.S. Patent Code, a patented article) so that both possibilities are combined. Sometimes, however, the patent is for a process (a patented process), and the use of that process may result in an unpatented product. For example, suppose that a company has discovered a new way to manufacture chopsticks that lowers its production costs by 30 percent. The ultimate product is not directly patentable because chopsticks were invented thousands of years ago. Instead, the company would be obtaining a patent on its new process to make chopsticks. Although a patent notice marking is not required on nonpatented articles that result from a patented process,[2] the chopsticks produced from the

(continued)

(continued)
patented process could be labeled with a notice of the patented process.
For a patented article, a patent notice marking is required so as to give
constructive notice of the patent to avert innocent infringement and
preserve certain remedies should infringement occur.

Although the underlying invention use and the patent rights are two
distinct value-generating assets, there are times when accurately separating
them can be difficult and not worth the bother. In those instances, the valuator may choose to conduct a *combined* invention use plus patent rights
valuation. Venture capitalists (VCs) provide a classic example of this combined approach. When evaluating the investment potential for a start-up
company, VCs tend not to separate the value of the individual patent rights
from the commercial application of the patented invention; rather, they are
much more likely to value the profit-generation capacity of the company as
a whole. A one-, two-, or three-patent-product start-up will be valued in the
aggregate on its ability to generate future profits, and the VC is unlikely to
conduct separate valuations for each of the patent-right/invention-use assets
that make up the company. The VC combined approach is not unreason-
able, but it is not always ideal. Even in the context of a VC investment, failing to distinguish the invention use's value from the patent rights' value can
result in both the VC and the start-up missing important information about
the start-up's overall value. Consider the following two possibilities:

1. What if the patent is declared invalid or its scope is narrowed?
2. What if the patent rights remain in force, but use of the invention is no
   longer commercially viable?

Neither of these possibilities is all that uncommon, which means that
both the VC and the start-up could benefit from incorporating such possibilities into their decision-making processes. Let us take a look at them one at
a time.

**Possibility 1: Invention Use May Have Commercial Value Even If the Patent
Rights Do Not**   What happens to the value of the VC's investment in the
start-up if the patent is declared invalid or its scope is narrowed (such as
when one of the patent's claims is invalidated)? It does not mean that the
value of the invention covered by such patent rights will be completely

eliminated. The invention use may remain valuable and continue to generate profits. Use of an invention does not require a patent to generate value. Unpatented inventions can be commercialized and generate profits through a variety of traditional commercialization practices and techniques that do not depend upon patent rights. Losing the patent rights will almost certainly decrease the profits, but that does not mean that the profits will decline to zero.

Understanding the stand-alone value for the use of the invention can help to inform both the VC and the start-up. If the stand-alone value for the invention use is substantial, the risk associated with the investment should be lower and could also suggest that the technology company should incorporate a nonexclusive patent licensing strategy into its business plan. If the stand-alone value of the invention use is minimal, the importance of the patent rights is highlighted and allows the parties to concentrate their due diligence on the strength of those rights.

Possibility 2: Patent Rights May Have Commercial Value Even If the Invention Use Does Not It is also possible that the invention use will lose its commercial value during the life of the patent. For example, one of the start-up's competitors may develop an improvement that reduces the commercial viability of the original invention. In that setting, the start-up may lose interest in the prior commercial use of the invention itself. The patent rights in the original invention could remain valuable, however, because to make and sell its improvement the competitor may need to license the start-up's patent.

Decoupling the Value of the Invention Use from the Value of the Patent Rights

There is no single method for decoupling the commercial value of the invention use from the value of the associated patent rights. How to decouple will depend on a host of factors, including the valuation technique employed and the track record of the invention and the patent rights. Even if the valuator does not formally decouple the invention's value from the patent rights' value, she should still keep in mind that the value of the patent rights is separate from the value of the invention use. That insight alone can sharpen the valuation effort. Take, for example, the typical VC combined valuation approach discussed above. Box 1.4 demonstrates how simply recognizing the separateness of the invention use's value from the patent rights' value can, with little additional work, help the VC to generate a more useful valuation analysis.

BOX 1.4: IMPROVING VC'S COMBINED APPROACH BY RECOGNIZING SEPARATENESS OF INVENTION USE'S VALUE FROM PATENT RIGHTS' VALUE

Let us assume that a VC is considering investing in a start-up company that sells one primary product. That product is covered by three patents, each of which is held by the start-up. The VC conducts a valuation analysis for the start-up company as a whole and comes up with a valuation range for the company between $75 million and $150 million. Some of the positive observations and assumptions that drove the valuation range include:

- A strong track record of the start-up's management team.
- The start-up's strong sales and distribution channels that provide a competitive advantage vis-à-vis competitors.
- The growth of the market for the start-up's product.
- The ability to charge a premium price for the next few years because the market is currently underserved.

On the negative side, the claims for the three patents were drafted broadly and bear significant risk of being invalidated if challenged.

Understanding the separate value for the invention use and the patent rights can help to inform the VC's valuation of the start-up as follows:

- The use of the invention is what is driving the start-up's value, not the value of the patent rights. The ability of the start-up to generate future cash flows is primarily a function of the growing market, the lack of current competitors, and the start-up's ability to beat future competitors through sound business practices.
- Therefore, the weak nature of the patent rights should not detract too much from the start-up's value.

VALUATION MISCONCEPTIONS

There is a danger in any book on valuation that the early introduction and discussion of mathematical concepts and techniques can obscure the subjective nature of valuation analysis. As a consequence, it is probably useful at the beginning to dispel a number of misconceptions that can interfere with valuation analysis and its ability to improve decision making.[3]

Misconception 1: Valuation Analysis Can Only Be Conducted by Experts

Although an expert valuation appraisal is beneficial or even indispensable at times, total abdication of the exercise to an outside expert is unwise. Expert assistance can be critical to a robust valuation analysis, but overreliance on experts diminishes the merit of the exercise. Valuation exercises are highly dependent on the quality of the inputs that feed the particular valuation methodology. More often than not, these inputs do not come from the expert valuator, but instead come from the actor who needs the valuation to guide a particular decision. A user who understands the limits and implications of the inputs used to feed her chosen valuation method will be better suited than others to interpret and employ the resulting valuation effectively.

The reason this particular valuation misconception persists stems from a misunderstanding of the valuation process, a failure to appreciate the benefits of hands-on involvement in the exercise, and reluctance by many to operate in areas where they are afraid they do not have sufficient training or expertise. One objective of this book is to demystify the valuation process. As the reader will see, most techniques are within the understanding of anyone with a willingness to learn and an open mind. Perhaps it is the unsettling realization that the valuation process is not an exact science that drives many to the authority of an expert who provides a feeling of reassurance in the face of this uncertainty. Rather than fear the uncertainty, it is more sensible to participate in the art of the process and develop an understanding of the strengths and weaknesses of the resulting value. Likewise, an understanding of the science part of valuation—such as which valuation models work best in which situations or what is required to apply a certain model to the available inputs correctly—gives the ultimate user a greater appreciation of the limits of the value result and a healthy skepticism regarding its relationship to some definitive truth.

Misconception 2: The Output from the Valuation Analysis—the Value Result—Is More Important Than the Valuation Process

The valuation process involves using valuation methods to translate the complex and messy reality surrounding the item to be valued into a usable and comparable value result. When most people think of valuation, they think of the number that comes out of the translation process; they think of the value result. That is unfortunate because it both overstates the power of the translation process and underappreciates the insightful knowledge that comes from performing the translation process. The translation process does not generate a perfect representation of the item being valued. The quality of that translation process will be dependent on the wisdom of the valuation method chosen, the quality of the input data, and the ability of the translator to interpret the results of the valuation exercise. In short, the quality of the value result is entirely dependent on the quality of the process that generated the result.

It is also important to remember that valuation is a uniquely context-sensitive undertaking, and a valuation calculated in one set of circumstances and at a certain point in time is unlikely to be appropriate for a different set of circumstances at another point in time. Without an appreciation for both the process and the context of that particular valuation, the value result is likely to be misunderstood.

Misconception 3: The More Quantitative and Mathematical the Approach, the More Accurate the Value Result

Quantitative models and consistent application of mathematics provide powerful valuation tools. When considering how to improve valuation analysis, the focus is frequently on increasing the sophistication of the valuation methodology with more quantitative and mathematical approaches. Increasing that sophistication can be beneficial, but the benefits will be lost if the inputs feeding the methodology are overly inaccurate. Some of the common information inputs can be measured and definitively obtained from the real world, but most of the inputs—particularly for the income methods (see Chapters 6 and 7)—come from the art side of the ledger and involve considerable subjective interpretation. What will the market be for the patented product in 10 years? How much pricing power will the patent provide to its holder? How easy (or how difficult) will it be for competitors to invent around the patent? This type of information—which is critical to running an income-based valuation analysis—has a subjective element that frequently overwhelms the ability to develop a precise numerical representation. Unless the accuracy of the inputs is also addressed, increasing the sophistication of the methodology to translate those inputs into a value result will not substantially improve the fidelity of that result. One can think of it as an example of the *garbage in, garbage out* principle. The quality of the value result is no greater than the quality of the inputs, no matter how sophisticated the quantitative manipulation.

Misconception 4: A Valuation Analysis Must Generate a Precise Result to Be Beneficial

The misconception that a valuation analysis must generate a precise result to be beneficial is one of the more difficult misconceptions to overcome because it seems so counterintuitive. The reality is that consumers of valuation analysis can easily become overly fixated on the precision of the valuation analysis. Valuation, however, is an inherently inexact undertaking. First, valuation analysis is by nature a relative exercise that does not lead to a single, absolutely correct determination of an asset's value. The value of an asset is not a fixed inherent property, but instead is dependent on the circumstances surrounding the asset. Who owns the asset and what usage that owner intends for the asset, for example, will significantly affect the asset's value. Second, the very function of valuation analysis will always involve a high level of imprecision. Valuation analysis is fundamentally about predicting the future. In other words, the value of a commercial asset, including a patent, stems from its ability to generate positive economic benefits (e.g., profits) in the future. Valuing commercial assets therefore requires predicting the extent of those future economic benefits, and predicting the future will always entail a substantial amount of error.

The inherent imprecision of valuation analysis does not mean the exercise is useless, but it does mean that decision makers need to learn how to use and interpret valuation analysis thoughtfully. In Chapters 3 and 4, we discuss in detail the decision-making improvements that can come from imprecise, but still useful, valuation analysis.

Misconception 5: There Is a Magic Bullet Method for Determining the Value of a Patent

Consumers of valuation services may be led to believe that there is a single, best method for determining the value of a patent. Perhaps this misconception is an expected consequence when there are so many valuation consultants who have a specific valuation methodology to sell. Perhaps it is the product of an overemphasis on the science side of valuation, with its mathematical formulas and calculations, and an underappreciation of the art side of valuation, where future projections, risk assessments, and substantial uncertainty exist. One thing that will be abundantly clear to readers of this book, however, is that there are a variety of methods for valuing a patent. Each method has its advantages and limitations, and there is no single, magic bullet valuation method.

THE THREE BASIC VALUATION METHODOLOGIES

The three basic valuation methodologies are income methods, market methods, and cost methods. Sometimes different names are used or some new valuation methodology is claimed, but all valuation methodologies can be traced back to these three fundamental approaches to valuation analysis. What differentiates the three methodologies is the source of information inputs each uses to generate a valuation result (see Figure 1.3). Income methods seek to measure directly the future economic benefits that will flow from a given asset. Income methods are forward-looking exercises in that the valuator *looks ahead* and uses projections of future benefits as the data for the model. Market methods seek to determine the value of an asset by reference to how other buyers and sellers have valued the same or similar assets. With a market method, the valuator *looks around* and uses contemporaneous market transactions as the data for the model. Finally, cost methods seek to determine value by using some measurable cost for the asset as a proxy for value. Cost methods are backward-looking exercises in that the valuator *looks behind* and uses historical costs as the data for the model.

The following brief overview of the basic methods (see Table 1.1) is meant to provide readers with a cursory understanding of the economic foundation for each approach. Each method is also the subject of a later chapter (or in the case of the income methods, chapters) that will provide a detailed explanation of the method, its strengths and weaknesses, and how to use the method to value a patent.

Income Methods

Income methods attempt to measure the net economic benefits that will come from the asset being valued. The most common form of income

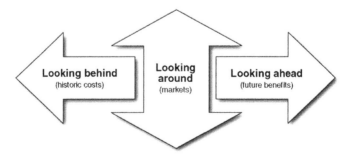

FIGURE 1.3 The Three Valuation Methods Use Three Different Types of Information Inputs

TABLE 1.1 Overview of the Three Methods

	Income Methods	Market Methods	Cost Methods
Focus of the approach	Measure the future economic benefits that will flow from a given asset	Consider how other buyers and sellers have valued the same or similar assets	Use some measurable cost for the asset as a proxy for value
Common examples of the method	Discounted future economic benefits (or discounted cash flow) analysis Real options analysis	Competitive exchange methods ▪ Auctions ▪ Less formal competitive exchanges Comparable transactions ▪ Valuation ratios ▪ Industry royalty rates Other methods ▪ Shadow pricing ▪ Surrogate valuation measures ▪ Stated preference methods	Cost of development Cost of reasonable alternative

Source: This table was inspired by a figure on the traditional valuation methods produced by Heinz Goddar and Ulrich Moser, "Traditional Valuation Methods: Cost, Market and Income Approach" in *The Economic Valuation of Patents: Methods and Applications,* eds. Federico Munari and Raffaele Oriani (2011), 111.

method involves projecting the asset's future net economic benefits—which will usually be expressed in terms of free cash flow or net profits—and then adding up the various benefits. Because these benefits will be received over time, a discount needs to be applied to take into account, among other things, the time value of money and the risk that actual benefits will be less than anticipated. The most common form of income method is referred to as a discounted cash flow (DCF) analysis, a term used because the analysis focuses on the future free cash flow that is projected for the valued asset. In this book, however, we do not use the DCF nomenclature, but instead refer to the standard discount method as a discounted future economic benefits (DFEB) analysis. We believe that DFEB analysis is more descriptive of the overall valuation approach that a valuator should take because free cash flow is not the only relevant measurement of future net economic benefits. Whether one uses the term DFEB or DCF, this income method tries to determine how much a firm should pay today for net economic benefits it may receive in the future. The DFEB method is the subject of Chapter 6.

One limitation of traditional net present value calculations using the DFEB method is their failure to capture future flexibility and choices. Patents provide their holders with the option to make informed choices in the future. Having those options can be extremely valuable and can also be difficult to incorporate into a standard, linear DFEB analysis. There have been a few attempts to incorporate the value of future flexibility into patent valuation analysis. The approach that has garnered the most attention has been the *real options* approach, but it is not the only viable one. Incorporating the value of future decision opportunities into a patent valuation analysis will be the subject of Chapter 7.

Market Methods

As a valuation tool, market methods seek to determine the value of an asset by using the wisdom and experience of self-interested buyers and sellers. The self-interested buyers and sellers can employ any number of valuation techniques to determine the value of a given transaction. The market then helps to aggregate the findings of these individual determinations. There are two core market methods for valuing assets:

1. **Competitive exchange:** The market of potential buyers is identified and encouraged to compete for the purchase of the asset, which helps to identify who ascribes the highest value to the asset. In effect, the seller polls the market to determine what buyers are currently willing to pay for the asset being valued.
2. **Comparable transactions:** The value of an asset is determined by looking at the range of prices paid in past or current transactions for similar assets. The value stems from the premise that a reasonable buyer "would not pay more for property than it would cost to purchase a comparable substitute."[4] Furthermore, if the comparable transaction took place in the past, it is assumed that the information derived from that past transaction remains relevant for the transaction under review.

In addition to these two core methods a number of derivative market techniques for valuing assets can be employed. Market methods are the subject of Chapter 8.

Cost Methods

Cost methods can be boiled down to this simple statement: The cost of an asset tells you something useful about its value. Despite their simplicity (or more likely because of their simplicity), cost methods tend to be the most widely criticized of the three types of valuation methods. Cost methods do not appear to make any effort to measure an asset's future net economic benefits, which makes them an easy target for criticism. When used for valuing patent rights, there are two primary cost methods:

1. **Cost of development:** A patent should be worth at least the amount it cost to develop the patented technology and obtain (and maintain) the patent rights.
2. **Cost of reasonable alternatives:** An economically rational technology acquirer will not pay more for a patent than the cost of a reasonable alternative technology.

There is a tendency to lump both of these cost methods together and criticize their validity as useful valuation tools. Such criticisms, however, are overbroad and can be misguided. The cost of reasonable alternatives method, for example, can be a surprisingly useful valuation tool. Cost methods are the subject of Chapter 9.

Interrelationship of the Three Basic Methods

Although the three basic methods are typically discussed as three wholly distinct valuation approaches, they are not, in fact, completely independent of one another. Business valuation experts Shannon Pratt, Robert Reilly, and Robert Schweihs provide the following explanation of the interrelationship of the three basic methods in the context of valuing a business:

> *The income approach requires some kind of a rate of return at which to discount or capitalize the income. The forces of the market drive these rates. All comparative valuation approaches relate some market value observation to either some measure of a property's ability to produce income or to some measure of the condition of its assets. The [cost] approach uses depreciation and obsolescence factors that are based, to a certain extent, on some measure of market values of assets.*[5]

The same interrelationship applies when using the three basic methods to value patents.

LIMITATIONS ON RATIONALITY IN VALUATION AND DECISION-MAKING EXERCISES

One more concept needs to be taken into account when considering valuation basics. In the past few decades, a revolution in cognitive science has changed our perceptions of how people act in economic circumstances. Described under various titles such as behavioral economics, neuroeconomics, or cognitive economics, the new research on the human thought process recognizes that people are often not the rational, utility-maximizing economic decision makers that classic economics once postulated.[6]

Most of the models discussed in this book assume a rational decision maker, and that rationality becomes part of the model. Recent research into real-world decision makers and the human mind reveals that humans are often not rational, but are subject to a variety of biases that arise from perception or context.[7] One of the best known biases that effects valuation decisions is risk aversion.[8] Risk aversion is a well-recognized trait in humans that demonstrates a systematic preference to avoid the uncertainty of a potentially larger reward in favor of a more certain one. When asked whether they would prefer $1 million guaranteed or a 75 percent chance to win $1.4 million, most people prefer the former choice even though the probability weighted value of the latter is greater (it is worth $1,050,000). Fortunately, there are a number of techniques for incorporating a person's degree of risk aversion into the valuation analysis, and we will cover one of those techniques, decision trees, in Chapter 4.

Another human bias that has been shown to affect patent decisions is the endowment effect, the name given to the observed phenomenon that individuals tend to value an item that they possess more than a comparable item that they do not possess, but wish to acquire. The endowment effect was first observed by researchers through a series of "willingness to accept" versus "willingness to pay" experiments.[9] In those experiments, subjects were demanding much more to give up something they already owned in comparison to how much they would pay to acquire the same item. This effect can cause distortions when a market price is being negotiated between the patent owner and a potential patent licensee or buyer.

As our understanding of human bias and irrationality increases so has our ability to incorporate these rationality deviations into our decision-making models.

REFERENCES

Damodaran, Aswath. 1994. *Damodaran on Valuation: Security Analysis for Investment and Corporate Finance*. New York: John Wiley & Sons.

Damodaran, Aswath. 2001. *The Dark Side of Valuation: Valuing Old Tech, New Tech, and New Economy Companies*. Upper Saddle River, NJ: Prentice Hall.

Kahneman, Daniel, Jack Knetsch, and Richard Thaler. Dec. 1990. "Experimental Tests of the Endowment Effect and the Coase Theorem." *Journal of Political Economy* 98: 1325.

Knetsch, Jack, and J. A. Sinden. 1984. "Willingness to Pay and Compensation Demanded: Experimental Evidence of an Unexpected Disparity in Measures of Value." *Quarterly Journal of Economics* 99: 508.

Koller, Tim, Marc Goedhart, and David Wessels. 2010. *Valuation: Measuring and Managing the Value of Companies*. 5th ed. Hoboken, NJ: John Wiley & Sons.

Munari, Federico, and Raffaele Oriani, eds. 2011. *The Economic Valuation of Patents: Methods and Applications*. Cheltenham, UK: Edward Elgar.

Murphy, William J. 2007. "Dealing with Risk and Uncertainty in Intellectual Property Valuation and Exploitation." In *Intellectual Property: Valuation, Exploitation, and Infringement Damages, Cumulative Supplement*, edited by Gordon V. Smith and Russell L. Parr, 40–66. Hoboken, NJ: John Wiley & Sons.

Neil, D. J. 1988. "The Valuation of Intellectual Property." *International Journal of Technology Management* 3: 31.

Plous, Scott. 1993. *The Psychology of Judgment and Decision Making*.

Pratt, Shannon, Robert Reilly, and Robert Schweihs. 2000. *Valuing a Business: The Analysis and Appraisal of Closely Held Companies*. 4th ed. New York: McGraw-Hill.

Simon, Herbert. Feb. 1955. "A Behavioral Model of Rational Choice." *Quarterly Journal of Economics* 69: 99.

Smith, Gordon V., and Russell L. Parr. 2005. *Intellectual Property: Valuation, Exploitation, and Infringement Damages*. Hoboken, NJ: John Wiley & Sons.

Thaler, Richard, ed. 1993. *Advances in Behavioral Finance*. Princeton, NJ: Princeton University Press.

Tversky, Amos, and Daniel Kahneman. 1981. "The Framing of Decisions and Psychology of Choice," *Science* 211: 453.

NOTES

1. *See e.g., Dodge v. Ford Motor Co.*, 170 N.W. 668 (Mich. 1919).
2. *Wine Railway Appliance Co. v. Enterprise R. Equipment Co.*, 297 U.S. 387 (1936) (cited with approval in *Bandag, Inc. v. Gerrard Tire Co., Inc.*, 704 F.2d 1578 (Fed. Cir. 1983)).
3. We are admirers of Prof. Aswath Damodaran's work on investment valuation. In his book *Damodaran on Valuation*, Damodaran starts with a number of myths about valuing financial investments. See Aswath Damodaran, *Damodaran on Valuation: Security Analysis for Investment and Corporate Finance*, 2–4. Similar approaches have been used by other valuation authors. We have borrowed that approach for this section on valuation misconceptions.
4. Gordon V. Smith and Russell L. Parr, *Intellectual Property: Valuation, Exploitation, and Infringement Damages* (2005), 169.

5. Shannon Pratt, Robert Reilly, and Robert Schweihs, *Valuing a Business: The Analysis and Appraisal of Closely Held Companies*, 4th ed. (2000), 46.

6. The beginning of the revolution can perhaps be traced to Herbert Simon's 1955 groundbreaking paper (for which he won the 1978 Nobel Prize in economics) that introduced the concepts of bounded rationality and satisficing as an alternative to maximizing. See Herbert Simon, "A Behavioral Model of Rational Choice," *Quarterly Journal of Economics* 69 (February 1955): 99.

7. For an entertaining (and growing) list of cognitive biases, the reader is invited to examine (and perhaps contribute) http://en.wikipedia.org/wiki/List_of_cognitive_biases.

8. Paradoxically, research indicates that although people may tend to avoid risks, once they have experienced a loss they may adopt risk-seeking behavior so as to eliminate the loss. Amos Tversky and Daniel Kahneman, "The Framing of Decisions and Psychology of Choice," *Science* 211 (1981): 453.

9. See e.g., Daniel Kahneman, Jack Knetsch, and Richard Thaler, "Experimental Tests of the Endowment Effect and the Coase Theorem," *The Journal of Political Economy* 98 (December 1984): 1325; and Jack Knetsch and J. A. Sinden, "Willingness to Pay and Compensation Demanded: Experimental Evidence of an Unexpected Disparity in Measures of Value," *The Quarterly Journal of Economics* 99 (1984): 508.

CHAPTER 2

Patent Basics

Since the dawn of history, inventive societies have proven to be more successful than other societies. Inventive capacity, not physical might or natural resource advantages, is the biggest factor in determining which societies will flourish and which will decline. In today's knowledge-based world, inventions have become more important than ever. The creation and commercialization of new technologies is the driving force behind sustainable economic growth and social prosperity. New technologies create new products, new markets, new processes for doing business, and even entirely new industries. Economic success—whether at the company level or the country level—requires a continuous stream of inventions and the conversion of these new ideas into usable products and services.

Patents play a unique and increasingly important role in the invention process and the effect of inventions in society. Commercially useful inventions tend to be the result of a complex, multifactor process involving many actors (see Figure 2.1 for one example of an inventive process). A typical inventive process usually involves the following actors and activities:

- Inventors conduct early-stage research to develop a useful concept.
- Developers take the useful concept and (a) create working prototypes that prove the commercial usefulness of the concept and (b) complete product development.
- Production and distribution capacity for the new product or service is developed.
- If the new product or service proves successful, the production and distribution capacity is expanded.
- Each step requires funding.

By providing enforceable and transferable property rights in an invention, patents drive each step of the invention process. The ability to obtain a patent motivates the researcher to conduct the early-stage research and to

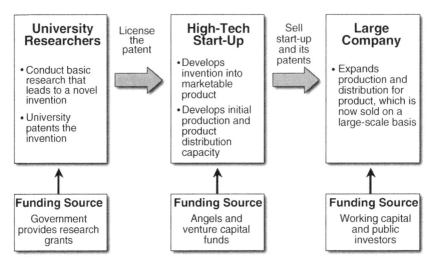

FIGURE 2.1 A Simplified Example of a University-Centric Inventive Process

seek various sources of capital (such as venture capitalists or companies) to help fund the effort. Patents also encourage the development effort needed to transform the inventive concept into a commercially useful product or service, and once again the funding of that effort. Building production and distribution capacity and selling the technology to third parties are also encouraged and facilitated by patents.

The increasing economic importance of patents can be shown through a number of metrics. Figure 2.2 shows the increase in worldwide patent applications filed from 1991 to 2008, and Figure 2.3 shows the increase in patent applications filed in the United States over that same period. Finally, Figure 2.4 shows the number of patent cases filed each year in U.S. district courts since 2000. During that period, the average number of patent cases filed each year has been just under 2,600.

Because patent rights—separate from the underlying use of the invention (see Chapter 1)—are central to an invention's ability to generate value, it is critical to understand those rights when valuing a patent. The grant, utility, and enforceability of a patent, for example, are all driven by the legal rules of the relevant patent system. Those legal rules are a primary determinant of the patent's economic value. This section will focus on the bundle of legal rights that come with a patent. Patent law is very complex and requires an understanding of a vast array of laws, regulations, and court decisions. To make things more complicated, patent protection is provided on a country-by-country basis, which means that country-specific variations in patent law need to be understood and addressed.

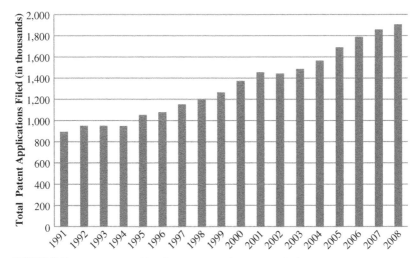

FIGURE 2.2 Rise in Worldwide Patent Applications Filed, 1991–2008
Source: WIPO Statistics Database, June 2010.

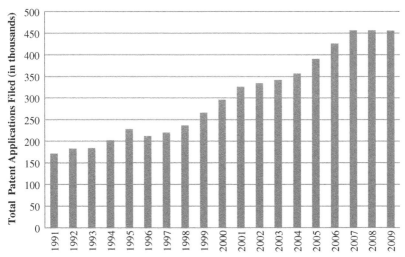

FIGURE 2.3 Rise in Patent Applications Filed in the United States, 1991–2009
Source: WIPO Statistics Database, June 2010.

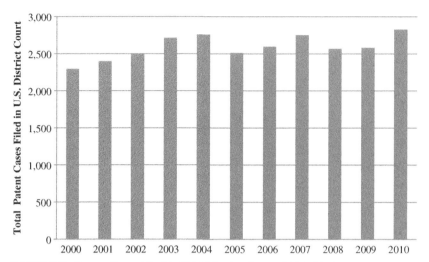

FIGURE 2.4   Patent Cases Filed in U.S. District Court, 2000–2010
Source: Intellectual Property Litigation Clearinghouse.

In this chapter, we

■ Provide a plain-English review of patent law basics.
■ Focus on U.S. patent law and briefly explain how a U.S. patent holder interacts with the broader international community.

WHAT IS A PATENT?

The United States Constitution gives Congress the power to "promote the progress of science in the useful arts by securing for limited times to authors and inventors the exclusive right to their respective writings and discoveries."[1] In 1790, Congress exercised this power by enacting the United States' first federal patent statute. This statute, and subsequent laws, authorizes what are commonly called utility patents. Utility patents protect useful inventions that are new and unobvious, such as machines, devices, chemical compositions, and manufacturing processes. A utility patent gives its holder the right to exclude others from making, using, or selling the patented invention in the United States for a term of 20 years from the date of the patent application. A patent owner may file a civil lawsuit for infringement against anyone who, without authority, makes, uses, or sells the patented invention.

Utility patents are what most people think of when the subject of patents comes to mind, but there are three other types of patents. One other type of patent, a provisional patent, can be used as a stepping-stone to a utility patent. A provisional patent requires much less formality than a utility patent, and as a result, it can be filed more quickly and cheaply than a utility patent. A provisional patent acts as a placeholder for a utility patent. If a utility patent application is filed within one year of the filing of a provisional patent application, the utility patent application dates back to the date of the provisional patent application.

The last two types of patents are design patents and plant patents. They cover subject matter that is not covered by a utility patent. A design patent may be used for a design that is ornamental and primarily nonfunctional. A plant patent may be used to protect only an asexually reproduced, distinct, and new plant variety, such as a flowering plant or fruit tree.

Rights Granted by Patents: The Right to Exclude

A patent grants its holder certain rights for a 20-year term starting from the date of the patent application. The most basic right that comes with a patent is the right to exclude others from "making, using, offering for sale, or selling the invention throughout the United States and if the invention is a process . . . the right to exclude others from . . . importing into the United States, products made by that process."[2] Patent rights fundamentally involve a negative rather than a positive right:

- A **negative right** entitles the right holder to stop someone else from doing something.
- A **positive right** entitles the right holder to do something.

A patent holder has the right to exclude others from performing certain acts with respect to the patented invention. A patent does not confer on its holder any positive rights to make, use, or sell the patented invention. This distinction between positive and negative rights is best explained by an example. A first inventor invents and obtains a patent on a three-legged stool, as illustrated in Figure 2.5. (We realize that a stool is not a patentable invention, but for purposes of illustrating the difference between positive and negative rights, a simple object like a stool provides a convenient example.) After using the stool and developing a backache, a second inventor invents and obtains a patent on an improvement, a three-legged stool with a back, as illustrated in Figure 2.6. The second inventor may exclude others from making, using, or selling the improved stool, but she may not make, use, or sell the improved stool herself. If the second

FIGURE 2.5   Three-Legged Stool

inventor were to make, use, or sell the improved stool, she would infringe the patent of the first inventor. In short, an inventor has no right to infringe another's patent simply because she has a patent covering an improved product or process.

As previously stated, patent rights are provided on a country-by-country basis, which means that the rights are limited to boundaries of

FIGURE 2.6   Improvement
on the Three-Legged Stool

the granting country. For a U.S. patent, the patent rights apply only in the United States.

Subject Matter of Patents

Section 101 of the U.S. Patent Act specifies subject matter eligibility for a patent as follows:

> *Whoever invents or discovers any new and useful process, machine, manufacture, or composition of matter, or any new and useful improvement thereof, may obtain a patent therefor. . . .*[3]

The inclusion of improvements means that patents are not just for momentous, historic discoveries. Typically, a company will not only patent new products, but also improvements on existing products to fence in its product line.

In addition to improvements, section 101 lists four more categories of patentable subject matter. The first category is a process, which consists of a method or a procedure, typically a method for making something or a method for using something. A process includes a new use of a known process, machine, manufacture, or composition of matter. The other three categories of patentable subject matter—machine, manufacture, or composition of matter—are generally things. Courts have held that these categories, when taken together, can cover "anything under the sun that is made by man."[4]

Despite the broad construction of the patentable subject matter concept, courts have created three exclusions to patentable subject matter: laws of nature, natural phenomena, and abstract ideas. It would be contrary to the purpose for patents—to promote scientific progress—if one could patent laws of nature and prohibit others from using them. The same can be said about the natural phenomenon exclusion, the application of which is the subject of much debate. For example, courts have reached different conclusions on whether a human gene isolated outside of the human body is a natural phenomenon or whether it has been changed enough by its isolation so that it is no longer a natural phenomenon.

There is even more debate on the question of when a process is just an abstract idea. The upsurge in the number of business-method patent applications raised the question of whether most of them were just descriptions of abstract ideas. The United States Supreme Court's *Bilski v. Kappos*[5] decision rejected the notion that the machine-or-transformation test is the sole test of patentability for a process claim. The machine-or-transformation test allows an inventor to demonstrate that a process claim is patentable by showing that the claim is tied to a particular machine or by showing that the claim transforms an article. If the machine-or-transformation test were the sole test of patentability for a process claim, the field of process claims would have been greatly narrowed.

Procedure to Obtain a Patent

To obtain a patent, the inventor (or inventors if more than one) must file a timely patent application with the United States Patent and Trademark Office (PTO). The patent application must describe and precisely claim the invention, as will be discussed in more detail below. The PTO assigns each application to an examiner with experience and expertise in the relevant area of technology. The examiner determines whether the invention described in the application complies with the legal requirements for patentability: utility, novelty, nonobviousness, and certain other formalities. If the examiner makes an unfavorable decision, she issues an office action rejecting all or some of the claims in the application. The inventor then has an opportunity to amend the application to remove the grounds for rejection or to argue that the grounds for rejection are inappropriate. If the examiner reaches a favorable decision, she allows the claims in the application, and, in due course, the PTO issues a patent. See Figure 2.7 for a diagram of the typical patenting process.

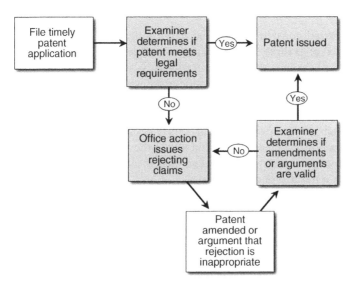

FIGURE 2.7 Diagram of the Typical Patenting Process

Inventors

It is important to identify correctly the inventors described in a patent application. If someone is named as an inventor who is not an inventor or if an inventor is omitted, and if the mistake is not corrected, any resulting patent can be invalidated. If one thinks of the invention as a solution to a problem, which solution is described in the claims (see discussion of claims further on), the question of inventorship boils down to who contributed to the solution of the problem as described in the claims.

The contributions of multiple inventors need not be equal. On the other hand, the contribution of an inventor must be more than suggesting a desired result (rather than a means to accomplish the result) or following instructions from someone else (rather than contributing to the concept of the invention).

Bars to Patents

Section 102 of the U.S. Patent Act sets forth certain bars to an inventor obtaining a patent. In general, the bars are meant to ensure that, if there are multiple patent applications describing the same invention, the inventor who is the *first to invent* is the one who obtains the patent. For the most part, the bars address actions by others that would prevent an inventor from obtaining a patent.

Section 102(b) also addresses certain actions by an inventor that will prohibit her from obtaining a patent on her own invention.

> *The invention was patented or described in a printed publication in this or a foreign country or in public use or on sale in this country more than one year prior to the date of the application for patent in the United States.*[6]

An inventor may destroy her own chances of obtaining a patent if she makes a public disclosure of the invention or she offers it for sale for more than the 1-year grace period before filing a patent application.

The United States has been the only country in the world to grant a patent to the first-to-invent inventor. Every other country grants a patent to the *first-to-file* inventor, the first inventor to file a patent application on the subject invention. As of March 16, 2013, however, the United States will become a first-to-file country as a result of the America Invents Act. Section 102 still maintains a one-year grace period wherein the first inventor to disclose the invention publicly has one year to file a patent application.

ANATOMY OF A PATENT

When the PTO issues a patent, it takes the patent application filed by the inventor, with amendments made during the prosecution of the application, retypes it in the PTO's format, and issues it as a patent. The patent application and the subsequent patent are divided into three main sections: specification, drawings, and claims.

Specification

The specification is a plain-English description of the invention. It is generally divided into four parts:

1. Here is the problem that existed.
2. Here are the attempts to solve the problem that were inadequate.
3. Here is how my invention solves the problem.
4. Here is a detailed description of how my invention works.

Drawings

All patents include some type of drawings to assist a reader in understanding the invention described in the patent. If the patent is for a machine, it is generally a schematic drawing of the machine with the parts labeled with numbers that are also used in the text of the specification. If the invention is a process, the drawing is often a flowchart with steps labeled with numbers that are also used in the specification.

Claims

The section at the end of a patent contains the claims. The legal definition of the invention is set forth in the claims. The claims are, in effect, similar to a deed for real estate in that they set the legal boundaries of the invention. An independent claim, one that stands alone, may, for example, describe an apparatus as having a housing. A subsequent dependent claim, one that adds to an independent claim and is dependent on that independent claim, could refer to the housing as being plastic.

Each of the numbered claims is a separate definition of the invention. As an example, an independent claim for the three-legged stool described earlier might read as follows:

I claim a stool comprising a seat and three legs.

The specific features described are called limitations. A patent is infringed when another invention has all the limitations in one of the claims of the patent. That the other invention may have additional features, such as another leg for a total of four legs, is not relevant to whether the invention infringes the patent.

Inventors typically ask that claims describe their inventions very specifically. For example, an inventor might draft an independent claim for the three-legged stool to read as follows:

I claim a stool comprising a plastic seat and three metal legs.

A stool made entirely of wood, for example, would not infringe these claims because it has neither a plastic seat nor metal legs.[7] The more specific the claim, the easier it is not to infringe. Therefore, an experienced patent drafter will try to draft at least some of the claims as broadly as possible. If claims are too broad, however, they may include other inventions already patented by others. For example, an independent claim that might be too broad (because it would cover any preexisting patented chair, stool, or sling) for the three-legged stool might read as follows:

I claim a support with one or more legs on which to sit.

The inventor and the patent drafter therefore try to strike a proper balance between drafting claims that are too narrow and claims that are too broad. Claims drafting has a major effect on the value of the patent rights. If the claims are too narrow, substantial value will be left on the table as other parties will be able to invent around the patent more easily. If too broad, however, the claim may be invalidated in a subsequent proceeding.

CRITERIA FOR A PATENT

To qualify for a patent, an invention needs three characteristics. It must be useful, novel, and nonobvious.

Utility

Section 101 of the U.S. Patent Act requires that the invention be "useful" to be patentable. This requirement is easy to meet. The invention does not need to be superior to existing technology; it need only be operable and capable of providing some benefit to humanity. To illustrate the low threshold for utility typically required by the PTO, Janice Meuller in her patent treatise *An Introduction to Patent Law* cites the example of U.S. Patent No. 5,457,821 (see Box 2.1), which is a patent for a hat in the

BOX 2.1: U.S. PATENT NO. 5,457,821

US005457821A

United States Patent [19]

Kiefer

[11] **Patent Number:**	**5,457,821**
[45] **Date of Patent:**	**Oct. 17, 1995**

[54] HAT SIMULATING A FRIED EGG

[76] Inventor: **Raymond D. Kiefer**, 105 Shady La., Spring City, Pa. 19475

[21] Appl. No.: **199,950**

[22] Filed: **Feb. 22, 1994**

[51] **Int. Cl.^{6}** **A42B 1/00**
[52] **U.S. Cl.** 2/195.1; 2/171; 2/195.2; D2/872
[58] **Field of Search** 2/171, 175.1, 195.1, 2/195.2, 195.3, 195.4; D2/865, 869, 872, 873, 874, 876, 879, 882, 884, 886, 893

[56] **References Cited**

U.S. PATENT DOCUMENTS

D. 170,061 7/1953 Maxwell et al. D2/886

D. 267,285 12/1982 Lipschutz D2/872

FOREIGN PATENT DOCUMENTS

292451 6/1928 United Kingdom 2/195.3

Primary Examiner—Diana Biefeld
Attorney, Agent, or Firm—Frederick J. Olsson

[57] **ABSTRACT**

A novelty hat in the form of a baseball cap has a yellow colored dome shaped top and a white colored brim, the outer periphery of which is irregular and part of which projects outwardly to form a visor. On the head of the wearer the hat makes the visual impression of a fried egg.

2 Claims, 2 Drawing Sheets

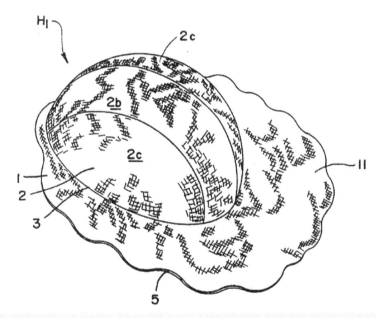

FIGURE 2.8 A Patent for a Hat in the Shape of a Fried Egg
Source: United States Patent and Trademark Office.

shape of a fried egg.[8] To support the utility of the invention, the inventor's description explained that the hat "finds utility, for example, as an attention-getting item in connection with promotional activities at trade shows, conventions, and the like."[9] The PTO examiner found that the hat invention complied with the utility requirement, and the patent was issued on October 17, 1995.

The inventions that tend not to meet the utility requirement are inoperable inventions. Classic examples of such inoperable, and therefore useless, inventions include perpetual motion machines,[10] time machines, and the like.

Novelty

Section 101 also requires an invention to be "new." This "new," or "novelty," requirement means that the invention must not have been described previously in a single source. An invention fails to meet the novelty test only if all the elements of the invention are present in another invention described in a single prior art reference. This rule precludes combining multiple references to describe an invention in full.

Nonobviousness

Related to the novelty requirement is the requirement that the invention be nonobvious. Section 103(a) provides that a patent may not be obtained

> *if the differences between the subject matter sought to be patented and the prior art are such that the subject matter as a whole would have been obvious at the time the invention was made to a person having ordinary skill in the art to which said subject matter pertains.*[11]

Courts have had great difficulty in defining the line between what is obvious and what is not. In essence, the rule is meant to stop someone from patenting small improvements that would be obvious to anyone working in the field. Many countries have similar criteria. For example, Japan and many European countries require an inventive step.

A patent examiner may combine prior art references to show that someone skilled in the art would have known these references and used common sense to combine them for an obvious improvement. The problem here is that many things are, in hindsight, obvious even though they were not at the time the invention was made. In addition to technical considerations, an inventor may use nontechnical considerations—such as commercial success and satisfaction of long-felt need—to show that an invention was not obvious at the time it was made.

TRANSFERRING PATENT RIGHTS

Once an inventor has obtained a patent, the next question is how to commercialize the invention. The inventor may retain the patent and proceed to commercialize the invention herself. This process, however, requires the inventor to invest the capital to produce and distribute the new product and to have the time and expertise for commercialization. It also requires the inventor to assume the risk of the invention not being a commercial success. Many inventors are unable, or unwilling, to make these investments or take these risks. In such situations, the inventor may look to transfer all or part of her interest in the patent to another party.

Assignments

The simplest method for transferring a patent is for the patent holder to assign it. An assignment is simply patent parlance for the sale of the patent. The assignor (seller) transfers all rights in the patent to the assignee (buyer). It is possible to assign an existing patent, a pending patent application, or even the rights to a future invention that an inventor may later develop. It is common practice, for example, for employers in R&D-centric industries to require employees to enter into invention assignment agreements that pre-assign their patent rights to future work-related inventions.

A rights holder can also mortgage her patent rights in connection with borrowing money, which involves a specific type of assignment. Mortgaging a patent involves a patent holder borrowing money and conditionally assigning the patent rights to the creditor until the debt has been repaid. Once the debt is repaid, ownership of the patent rights reverts to the original patent holder. See Chapter 12 for a detailed discussion of patents as collateral.

Licenses

A middle ground for a rights holder, between retaining and assigning all rights to a patent, is to license the patent. Unlike assignments, patent licenses do not transfer patent ownership to another. Whereas an assignment (with the exception of a conditional assignment in connection with a mortgage) serves as an irrevocable sale of patent rights, a license serves as a lease. A patent license is a contractual agreement whereby a licensor grants permission to use a set of patent rights to a licensee during a specified period in exchange for a specified payment.

Exclusive versus Nonexclusive Licenses Because licenses are contractual agreements, the specific terms of a license can be structured in just about any manner that the licensor and licensee can imagine. One issue that all licenses must address, however, is the nonrival nature of patent rights. Goods can be purely rival, purely nonrival, or lie somewhere in between. A purely rival good is one whose use (or consumption) by one person prevents others from using it at the same time. A hammer is often used as an example of a rival good. If one person is using the hammer, nobody else can simultaneously use that hammer. A purely nonrival good is one that can be used by one person and that use does not prevent others from using that same good at the same time.

Patents are nonrival. The use of the knowledge contained within the patent by one person does not prevent others from simultaneously using that knowledge. The nonrival nature of patents means that the patent holder needs to decide how to license the patent rights. Does the patent holder want to license the rights to a single party or take advantage of the nonrivalry and license the rights to multiple parties? Licenses are grouped into two broad categories, depending on how that question is answered:

1. **Exclusive licenses:** The patent owner promises to provide one or more patent rights to one party and nobody else. The exclusive license can cover the entire patent, or it can be limited to cover a specific geographic region, field of use, or both.
2. **Nonexclusive licenses:** The patent owner promises to provide one or more patent rights to multiple parties and does not promise any exclusivity to any single licensee.

Reduced to the most basic level, exclusive licenses are used when the licensor wants to provide patent rights to a single party, and nonexclusive licenses are used when the licensor wants to provide patent rights to multiple parties.

Tailoring the License A patent license, whether exclusive or nonexclusive, can cover the entire patent or be limited in any number of ways. Typical limitations include the following:

- **Manner of use limitations:** The license can grant permission to use the patent rights for certain usages (e.g., using the patented technology to run tests), but not others (e.g., selling the patented technology).

- **Geographic limitations:** The license can limit permission to use the patent rights to a specific geographic area (e.g., the license grants permission to practice the patent in California only).
- **Field of use limitations:** The license can limit permission to use the patent rights to a specific field of use (e.g., the license grants permission to the licensee to manufacture and use patented parts in home appliances, but not for use in commercial applications).
- **Transfer limitations:** The license can restrict, or prohibit, the licensee from transferring the patent rights to another.

Deciding Whether to License or Assign

Licenses are far more common than assignments. The popularity of licenses is almost certainly due to the specific features of licenses and the greater flexibility they provide compared to an assignment. Table 2.1 provides a comparison of licenses and assignments along a number of their more critical features. If the rights holder wants to take advantage of the nonrival nature of patent rights and simultaneously transfer them to multiple transferees, the license option provides the obvious solution.

TABLE 2.1 Comparison of Licenses and Assignments along Select Features

	Licenses	Assignments
Ability to take advantage of nonrival nature of patent rights	Nonexclusive licenses have unlimited ability Exclusive licenses have limited ability based on the rights granted in the license	Not available
Nature of transfer	Title remains with rights holder Transfer is revocable	Title passes to transferee Transfer is irrevocable
Formal requirements	None	Must be in writing to be enforceable
Standing to sue	Nonexclusive licensees have no standing to sue for patent infringement Exclusive licensees have standing to sue for patent infringement, but may be required to join the patent holder to the lawsuit	Assignee has standing to sue for patent infringement

When a patent holder wishes to sell the patent, that sale will typically be structured as an exclusive license rather than an assignment. The flexibility of a license, and the fact that a licensor retains some control over the patent, makes licensing more appealing than outright assignments to patent holders.

Payment Methods for Patent-Right Transfers

There are no restrictions on the payment methods that can be used to assign or license a set of patent rights. Such payment methods can be as creative as the parties wish them to be. Common payment methods for patent-right transfers include the following:

- A recurring royalty payment that is based on the economic benefits the transferee generates from the patent rights.
- A one-time payment at the time of transfer.
- A partial up-front payment at the time of transfer coupled with a recurring royalty payment.
- An equity interest in the transferee.
- The employer's agreement to hire the employee (in the case of an employee invention assignment agreement).

See Chapter 10 for a detailed discussion of payment methods for patent licenses and their valuation.

NATIONALITY OF A PATENT

It is important to remember that patent protection is done on a country-by-country basis. An invention is not protected in any given country unless a patent is issued by the patenting authority in that country. Treaties among most countries, however, facilitate patent applications in the various countries.

Paris Treaty

As discussed previously, in the United States, an inventor must file a patent application within one year of publicly disclosing her invention or be barred from obtaining a patent. In most other countries, a patent application must be filed prior to public disclosure; if not, the inventor is barred from obtaining a patent. The Paris Treaty mitigates this requirement. It provides that if an inventor files a patent application in any country that is a signatory to the Paris Treaty, she has one year to file an application in any other country that is a signatory, and the second application will date back to the date of the first application. For example, if an inventor files an application in the United States and then publicly discloses her invention, she may still file applications in other countries that are signatories to the Paris Treaty. If she files within one year of the U.S. application, the applications in the other countries will date back to the U.S. application and thus predate the public disclosure.

Patent Cooperation Treaty

The Patent Cooperation Treaty (PCT) is essentially a way to defer for 30 months the major costs of obtaining patent protection in other countries. To comply with the PCT, a PCT application must be filed within one year of filing a U.S. application. The inventor then has 30 months from the date of the U.S. application to file with the other countries in which she would like patent protection. During the 30 months, the inventor may have an indication of how successful her invention will be and obtain royalty payments to help with the costs of entering the other countries.

REFERENCES

Chisum, Donald. Updated through 2011. *Chisum on Patents*. Newark, NJ: Matthew Bender.

Fusco, Stefania. 2009. "Is *In re Bilski a Déjà Vu?*" *Stanford Technology Law Review*1.

Meuller, Janice. 2006. *An Introduction to Patent Law*. 2nd ed. New York: Aspen Law & Business.

Romer, Paul M. 1990. "Endogenous Technological Change." *Journal of Political Economy* 98: S71.

Schecter, Roger E., and John R. Thomas. 2004. *Principles of Patent Law Concise Hornbook Series*. St. Paul, MN: West.

Stanford Encyclopedia of Philosophy. Available at http://plato.stanford.edu/.

NOTES

1. U.S. Constitution, article I, section 8, clause 8.
2. 35 U.S.C. sec. 154.
3. 35 U.S.C. sec. 101.
4. *Diamond v. Chakrabarty*, 447 U.S. 303, 309 (1980), quoting S.Rep. No. 1979, 82d Cong., 2d Sess., 5 (1952); H.R.Rep. No. 1923, 82d Cong., 2d Sess., 6 (1952). Footnote 6 of *Diamond v. Chakrabarty* decision further explains that the "anything under the sun" language was used by P. J. Federico, who was a principal drafter of the 1952 recodification of the Patent Act of 1952. In

testimony about the 1952 act, Federico explained that "Under section 101 a person may have invented a machine or a manufacture, which may include anything under the sun that is made by man. . . ." Hearings on H.R. 3760 before Subcommittee No. 3 of the House Committee on the Judiciary, 82d Cong., 1st Sess., 37 (1951).

5. 130 S.Ct. 3218 (2010)
6. 35 U.S.C. sec. 102(b).
7. The doctrine of equivalents, which is beyond the scope of this discussion, may mitigate this result in certain limited circumstances.
8. Janice Meuller, *An Introduction to Patent Law*, 2nd ed. (2006) 196–198.
9. Ibid., 196.
10. For a recent example of a perpetual motion machine that was denied a patent under section 101, *see Newman v. Quigg*, 877 F.2d 1575 (1989).
11. 35 U.S.C. sec. 103(a).

CHAPTER 3

Using Valuation Analysis to Improve Patent Decision Making

Everybody would like to make better decisions, but what exactly does that mean? Entire disciplines have been developed—with decision theory and its various outgrowths being the most obvious—to study the human decision-making process and to generate better results. The goal of these pursuits is to help decision makers identify the best decision among competing but uncertain choices. One of the more critical insights that stems from decision theory is the recognition that choices can be quantified and thereby compared with one another on an apples-to-apples basis.

Every decision involves a value determination. When one alternative is chosen over another, the decision maker has, either consciously or subconsciously, valued the chosen decision higher than the competing choices. If a firm decides to obtain a license for patent A rather than patent B, the firm has determined that a license for patent A is more valuable to the firm than a license for patent B (see Figure 3.1). Expressed as an equation, we can say that the value of a patent A license is greater than the value of a patent B license.

As a practical matter, making a direct comparison of one item to another can be challenging. It frequently requires comparing a complex array of judgments, many of which will be highly uncertain. If the decision maker is faced with multiple choices at once, making direct comparisons quickly becomes unmanageable. To avoid the unwieldy nature of direct comparisons, most valuation exercises replace direct comparisons with an equivalency exercise. Instead of directly comparing license A with license B, the decision maker will determine the value for the licenses in terms of a quantifiable, common measurement—usually money—and then make an apples-to-apples comparison based on the common measurement (see Figure 3.2). If the firm determines that license A provides a net benefit of $3 million whereas license B provides a net benefit of $2 million, the choice of license

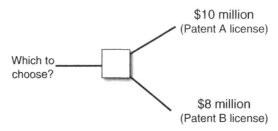

FIGURE 3.1 Choosing between Patent Licenses

A over license B is now clear. If the situation involves more choices (such as pursuing license C or using a nonpatented technology), those choices can also be calculated in dollars and easily compared with the choice of license.

Valuation analysis is particularly beneficial for patent decisions. As the societal importance of patents continues to increase, so too does the importance of making sound patent decisions. Today's successful manager, scientist, attorney, or governmental official involved with patents is constantly asked to make decisions, and that decision-making process can be significantly improved by recognizing that decisions can be quantified, compared, and evaluated. A fundamental premise of this book is that intelligent valuation skills are accessible to, and should be used by, each of the various decision makers in the patent process.

In this chapter, we

▨ Provide an overview of the wide range of patent decisions that can benefit from valuation analysis.

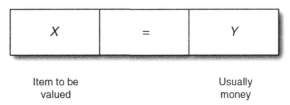

FIGURE 3.2 Valuation as an Equivalency Exercise

- Examine common decision-making strategies and consider how those strategies provide guidance on how much valuation analysis to conduct in a particular situation.
- Explain how valuation techniques can help to inform decision making without becoming tedious, overly burdensome endeavors.
- Introduce a patent decision auditing system that can be used to prioritize patent decisions.

PATENT DECISIONS

Patents have the ability to create enormous value. For patents to achieve their value-generating potential, however, numerous actors performing a variety of functions need to make multiple decisions (see Figure 3.3). Improving the outcome from this complex matrix requires improving

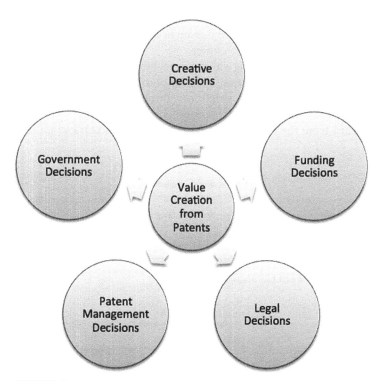

FIGURE 3.3 Distribution of Functions and Decisions Needed to Create Value from Patents

decision making throughout the process. The first step to making such improvements is to identify the various decisions with some precision. If an actor does not recognize that she is making a crucial decision that could be improved by valuation analysis, there is little hope to improve the decision making. Once the various actors have a better appreciation of the various decisions on which they can improve—frequently with very little cost or effort—the valuation tools that are provided in Part Two of this book become much easier to implement.

Creative Decisions

Some of the earliest patent-related decisions stem from the creative process, and these decisions can lead inventors to create valuable inventions that are worthy of patent protection. When faced with competing projects, for example, a researcher needs to decide which research projects to pursue. Figure 3.4 sets forth a common scenario in which the researcher must decide between competing projects. Making that choice can be extremely difficult, but if the researcher is able to place a value on each project (see Figure 3.5), the decision regarding which project to pursue becomes much clearer. Here, project B is by far the most attractive choice.

Although we will be explaining valuation techniques in Part Two, it is worth noting here that such valuation techniques are not limited to purely tangible, economic interests. The valuation amounts in Figure 3.5, for example, do not need to be limited to economic profits that the researcher can expect to earn from the project. The valuation amounts can include any

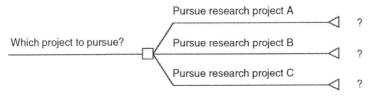

FIGURE 3.4 Deciding between Competing Projects

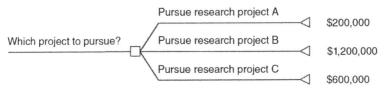

FIGURE 3.5 Placing a Value on the Competing Projects

number of intangible benefits to the researcher, such as greater prestige or greater pleasure that the researcher may garner from one project versus another. Other common creative decisions that could benefit from some type of valuation analysis include the following:

- How should research funding be spent?
- For whom should the researcher work?
- In what geographic region should the researcher conduct the research?
- Should the research be conducted on a collaborative basis with other researchers? If the answer is yes, then how should the collaborative relationship be structured? How should the fruits of the research be shared among the various collaborators?

Funding Decisions

In a 2009 interview conducted by PricewaterhouseCoopers' Intellectual Property Media Group, a Siemens executive explained, "If you cannot value your IP [intellectual property], you cannot prioritize your research and development."[1] Funding decisions are an area where formal valuation analysis is not uncommon. Because funding decisions require the making of an investment, funding organizations recognize the importance of valuation analysis. Generally speaking, the funding organization will pursue the project with the greatest projected return on investment (ROI). For Figure 3.6, the funding organization should obviously fund project A rather than projects B or C. Project A's ROI projection is significantly higher than each of the other options.

Legal Decisions

The law and choices relating to the law significantly affect patent rights throughout the potential life of a patent. Legal decision making plays a major role in whether a rights holder is creating or destroying patent value. Unfortunately, lawyers have been slow to incorporate valuation analysis

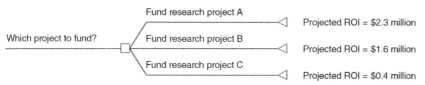

FIGURE 3.6 Deciding Which Research Project to Fund

into their decision making, which makes legal decisions one of the richest areas for improvement.

Protecting the Intellectual Property   Choosing whether or not to seek a patent for the invention is one of the most fundamental legal decisions for an inventor. In developing an intellectual property protection strategy, the inventor needs to decide whether to patent the invention, maintain the invention as a trade secret, or use a combined patent plus trade secret strategy. The patent versus trade secret decision has long been described as an either/ or scenario: Either obtain a patent or obtain a trade secret. There are pros and cons to each approach that can be valued and can thereby better inform the decision (see Box 3.1). A third choice is often overlooked: the option of combining patent protection for an invention with trade secret protection. Karl Jorda has long advocated for this combined intellectual property management approach. Jorda explains that the "best policy and practice is to obtain patents as the centerpiece in an intellectual property portfolio and maintain trade secrets as underpinnings for patents to protect unpatentable collateral know-how and show-how."[2]

BOX 3.1: COMMON FACTORS FOR CHOOSING BETWEEN PATENT AND TRADE SECRET PROTECTION

Patent protection is preferable when

- The inventor wishes to license the technology to third parties.
- The invention is easy to reverse engineer.
- The use of the invention will require public disclosure of its underlying secrets.
- Competitors are developing a comparable invention.
- The inventor (or her product) could benefit from the extra credibility that results from a patent.

Trade secret protection is preferable when

- The inventor does not intend to license the technology to third parties.
- The invention is difficult to reverse engineer and is easy to keep secret.
- The costs of obtaining and maintaining a patent are greater than the benefits that will come from the invention.

Prosecuting the Patent Patent prosecution is an inherently complex process punctuated with many major and minor decisions. Each decision carries with it a variety of possible outcomes and risks and therefore could be improved with valuation analysis. Box 3.2 provides an inventory of some of the most common decisions involved with prosecuting a patent. One of the more critical patent prosecution decisions will be the inventor's choice on how to respond to the patent office's first office action. Under U.S. patent law, an office action is an official written communication from a U.S. Patent and Trademark Office (PTO) examiner that explains the PTO's views on a pending patent application. If the office action rejects some of the patent application's claims, the inventor will need to decide how to respond. Abandoning or narrowing the problematic claims will increase the chance of the patent being issued, but could also significantly decrease the value of the issued patent. This type of decision would greatly benefit from a thoughtful valuation analysis.

BOX 3.2: INVENTORY OF COMMON DECISIONS WHEN PROSECUTING A U.S. PATENT

1. Initial decisions
   - How broadly to draft the claims
2. Decisions immediately after filing
   - Whether to file a Patent Cooperation Treaty application
   - Whether to request nonpublication of the patent application
3. Decisions after first office action
   - How to deal with claims that are rejected by the patent examiner (e.g., amend, argue, cancel, or abandon the rejected claims)
4. Communicating with the patent examiner
   - Interviewing the patent examiner to discuss rejected claims
5. Final office action
   - Whether to file a request for continued examination for rejected claims
6. Turning to the court system
   - Whether to appeal rejected claims to the Board of Patent Appeals and Interferences (BPAI)

(continued)

(continued)
- If the claim is rejected by the BPAI, whether to appeal to the United States Court of Appeals for the Federal Circuit (CAFC)
- If the claim is rejected by the CAFC, whether to seek certiorari from the U.S. Supreme Court

Source: Jacki Lin, "Risk Analysis for Patent Prosecution," University of New Hampshire Law Student White Paper Series (copy on file with authors) (2011).

Litigation Management   Lawsuits are an integral part of the patent system. Whether it is a lawsuit to enforce a licensing agreement or a patent infringement suit, litigation provides patent holders with their most fundamental enforcement tool. The most obvious application for valuation analysis in the litigation context is to calculate potential damages in a patent infringement lawsuit (see Chapter 11). Calculating damages, however, is only one of many possible applications for valuation analysis. Litigation involves a host of decisions for the parties on both sides of the lawsuit, and each decision can benefit from valuation analysis. To illustrate this concept, consider a company that has been sued for patent infringement. The plaintiff has offered to settle the suit for $1 million. How should the defendant and its lawyers decide whether to accept the settlement offer? One approach could be for the defendant to identify its alternatives to the settlement decision and place a value on each alternative (see Figure 3.7). The defendant can

FIGURE 3.7   Deciding Whether to Accept a Settlement Offer

then employ the valuation techniques from Part Two of this book to value each alternative and choose the most valuable one.

Other common litigation decisions that would benefit from valuation analysis include the following:

- Whether to bring a lawsuit.
- How much to invest in bringing or defending a lawsuit.
- Determining venue for the lawsuit.
- Who to include as defendants.
- Whether to appeal a negative decision.

Patent Management Decisions

Like any other asset, patent rights need to be managed so as to maximize their potential economic benefits. At the most obvious level, commercialization strategies need to be developed. Should the patent holder practice the patent itself, assign the patent to a third party, license the patent to a third party, or do some combination of each of these options? Presumably, the patent holder will want to pursue the most valuable commercialization strategy. Beyond these most basic commercialization decisions are a host of more subtle but equally important patent management decisions. Such decisions include the following:

- Should the patent holder create an intellectual property holding company to hold and commercialize the patent? See Chapter 13 for a discussion of the intellectual property holding companies and the potential tax advantages that may come from that strategy.
- Should the patent holder collateralize the patent? See Chapter 12 for a discussion of patent collateralization.
- Should the patent holder pursue additional improvement patents?
- Should the patent holder continue to pay maintenance fees on a patent or allow the patent to lapse?

Government Decisions

When thinking about patents and the actors most in need of valuation analysis, there is a tendency to focus on certain obvious actors. Inventors, technology companies, technology buyers and sellers, technology funders, and patent litigants immediately come to mind as parties who need valuation analysis. One party that is frequently left off the list, however, may actually be the most critical for an overall society's ability to create and extract value from patents. That frequently forgotten party is the government, and it may be the party most in need of valuation analysis.

The government plays numerous roles in the patent system. Most important is that the government establishes the rules. If creating patentable inventions and generating value from them is viewed as a game, patent laws and regulations are the primary rules for that game. What can be patented? What is required to obtain a patent? What property rights come with owning a patent? What remedies are available to a patent holder who believes that her patent is being infringed? These rules of the game have a profound effect on the behavior of the various players in the game. It should not be controversial to suggest that the goal of government rule makers is to encourage clearly defined optimal behavior. In the case of patents, the laws and regulations ought to encourage the creation and commercialization of more inventions and to increase the public inventory of knowledge. Optimal behavior is encouraged by establishing rewards for desirable behavior (inventors who follow the patent rules obtain property rights) and punishments for deviant behavior (patent infringers are subject to various sanctions).

Developing laws and regulation is very analogous to making an investment. With an investment, the investor commits money based on her forecasts of future economic benefits that will result from the investment. Valuation analysis can (and should) be used by the investor to forecast and place a value on those future economic benefits. Valuation analysis can (and should) be used in a similar way to shape legal rule making, with the analysis simply focused on measuring a slightly different outcome. As noted above, the primary goal of laws and regulations is to encourage beneficial behavior and deter undesirable behavior. That behavior may or may not have a tangible economic effect, but laws and regulations are always aimed at influencing behavior. The valuation analysis could therefore seek to forecast the potential behavioral outcome from the laws and regulations and the costs and benefits associated with that outcome. Rather than have political arguments drive the process, government rule makers should rely more heavily on valuation analysis to guide their rule-making function.

MAXIMIZING, OPTIMIZING, AND SATISFICING: HOW MUCH TO INVEST IN VALUATION ANALYSIS

Few disagree with the principle premises of this book: that patenting and the patent system involve numerous decisions and that most of those decisions would benefit from valuation analysis. Where we meet resistance is not with the concept of valuation, but instead with its practical application. How do you practically implement valuation into basic decision making? It is one thing to take the time to conduct a valuation when faced with a patent infringement lawsuit or when patent rights are being transferred, but broadly employing valuation analysis to make decisions may appear too burdensome. There are two primary reasons valuation analysis may appear too onerous for general use in broader decision making:

1. Belief that valuation analysis is extremely complicated and expensive to perform and requires valuation experts to do it properly.
2. Recognition that valuation analyses are likely to be inexact and flawed.

As we demonstrate throughout this book, the first concern is simply wrong. While expert guidance and assistance can be beneficial, most valuation techniques are within the understanding of anyone with a willingness to learn and an open mind. The second concern tends to be the more problematic one. Because valuation is an inherently inexact undertaking— valuation analyses never lead to a single, absolutely correct determination of an asset's value—many will ask what is the point of spending resources to obtain a valuation determination that is almost certainly wrong. This line of thinking, however, is misguided. The problem with the second concern is that it fails to appreciate the breadth of strategies that can be employed for making decisions and thereby fails to appreciate the decision-making improvements that can come from inexact, but still useful, valuation analyses. There are three well-recognized, logical strategies for making decisions:

1. **Maximizing strategy:** The decision maker tries to identify the option that will provide the *best* possible outcome—as defined by subjectively defined preferences (such as profit maximization)—and ignores (largely)[3] the costs for obtaining the information needed to reveal the best outcome.
2. **Optimizing strategy:** The decision maker would like to pursue the best possible option, but recognizes the need to account for the direct and opportunity costs associated with decision making. The decision maker will seek the best possible option until the costs for seeking a better option become too high, at which point she will settle for the best identified strategy, with the understanding that a better option may be out there and discoverable if information costs for identifying the best possible option were free.
3. **Satisficing strategy:**[4] The decision maker establishes a threshold for what is a *good enough* outcome. Once the decision maker identifies an option that will produce a good enough outcome, the search for better options ends and the good enough option is taken.

Parties, of course, remain free to pursue less logical, less disciplined, or less well-informed decision-making strategies, but presumably few parties would consciously choose to employ a clearly flawed strategy. Clearly flawed strategies result from the party not appreciating the flaw or not realizing that a better strategy exists.

Appreciating that there is a range of decision-making strategies helps to place the benefits from valuation analyses into context and guide a decision maker on how much to invest in such analyses. Valuation analysis is not a one-size-fits-all endeavor. There is no single approach to valuing decision alternatives. Moreover, there is no single approach for how much to invest in a particular valuation effort or what level of accuracy is required for the effort to be worthwhile. For some decisions, the valuation effort needs to be quite extensive and extremely accurate to be useful. For other decisions, a less extensive and less accurate effort could still be extremely beneficial to the decision maker. Figure 3.8 provides a graphic illustration of one method for deciding how extensively to pursue valuation analysis for a particular decision. The x-axis represents the importance of the decision, and the y-axis represents the ease with which useful valuation information can be obtained. Those two variables, when combined with the three logical decision-making strategies, should motivate a reasonable decision maker

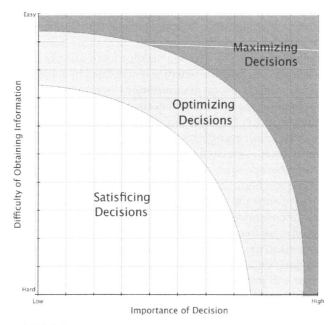

FIGURE 3.8 The Ideal Decision-Making Strategy for a Particular Patent-Valuation Effort

to make the following strategic choices about how much to invest in valuation analysis.

1. **Maximizing as the preferred strategy:** With a maximizing strategy, the decision maker will not be concerned with information-gathering costs and will obtain as much information as possible so as to make the best possible decision. If the decision is very important and the ease of obtaining information is low, the decision maker should be prepared to perform extensive valuation analysis with little concern about its cost. The typical criticisms of the maximizing approach—that it can be wasteful by producing redundant or overlapping information—should be outweighed by the importance of getting the decision right and the ease of obtaining the information.

   Maximizing is likely to be the preferred strategy in settings such as major patent-infringement litigation (e.g., bet-the-company litigation for the defendant) and the sale of a patent-based start-up company. In both cases, the decision maker should have easy access to much of the relevant valuation information, and the decision may be the firm's last truly meaningful decision. In a bet-the-company litigation, the defendant may go out of business if it loses the lawsuit. For a start-up sale, the transaction may be the equivalent of a liquidation event for the firm's owners.

2. **Optimizing as the preferred strategy:** With an optimizing strategy, the decision maker continues to seek the best possible option, but understands that there may be a need to rely on a more restricted amount of information. The difference between maximizing and optimizing is really just a matter of degree, with the optimizer paying closer attention to cost-benefit analysis when determining whether to extend the valuation analysis. Optimizing becomes the preferred strategy as the importance of the decision decreases and the difficulty in obtaining useful valuation information increases. The decreasing importance of the decision undermines the justification for wasting resources on the information-gathering effort. In addition, as the cost of information increases, the chance that extra valuation analysis will be wasteful also increases.

   With the exception of bet-the-company litigation or the sale of a patent-based start-up, optimizing will be the preferred strategy for most important decisions. Major funding decisions, major patent portfolio acquisition decisions, decisions to establish patent transfer-pricing strategies, and major licensing transactions, among many other examples, are all likely to favor an optimizing strategy. Valuation analysis will be critical to the decision-making process, but the decision maker should remain sensitive to cost-benefit implications of the analysis.

3. **Satisficing as the preferred strategy:** At first glance, the satisficing strategy may seem intuitively less attractive than maximizing or optimizing. By definition, the decision maker does not try to find the best possible option, but instead sets a search limit that causes her to settle for the first option that is satisfactory. Nobel Prize–winning economist Herbert Simon is credited with developing the concept of satisficing as a decision-making strategy. Simon took aim at neoclassic economic theory, which "assumes that the decision maker has a comprehensive, consistent utility function, knows all the alternatives that are available for choice, [and] can compute the expected value of utility associated with each alternative."[5] Simon reasoned that the human mind has only a limited capacity for formulating and making complex decisions and offered a more realistic vision of economic actors that he called "bounded rationality." Human decision makers still need to make decisions, but they must do so with "egregiously incomplete and inaccurate knowledge about the consequences of actions."[6] Simon explained that a satisficing strategy is well adapted for this world of bounded rationality. Box 3.3 provides an everyday example of a satisficing strategy to illustrate the concept.

BOX 3.3: AN EVERYDAY EXAMPLE OF A SATISFICING STRATEGY: BUYING A MOBILE PHONE

The nearly universal use of mobile phones means that most of us have experience with having to decide what phone to buy with which plan. Classical economic theory postulates that consumers are utility maximizers who weigh out all the phone and plan alternatives and then select the best combination when matched against all the selection criteria. That is not the technique most of us use when making this decision. The myriad phone plans offered by the various phone companies are sufficiently complex and numerous that it is highly unlikely that the normal consumer would spend the time and energy to collect the data, much less analyze it. Throw in the accompanying phone equipment decision and it is not surprising that consumers use some technique other than a maximizing strategy to make their decision.

The decision technique that most of us normally use is a satisficing one. We first determine a manageable number of key selection criteria, such as does the plan have coverage in certain geographic areas, will it easily allow communication with friends and family, does it permit use

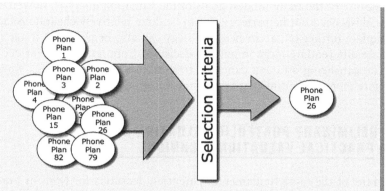

FIGURE 3.9 Choosing a Phone and Plan with a Satisficing Strategy

of the desired phone, and does it meet certain cost parameters. We then search the multiplicity of phone and plan options until we find one that satisfies this selection criteria screen, at which point we are likely to stop investigating any further (see Figure 3.9). Maybe a better option is out there, but the one we found is good enough. Can any of us truly say that we are 100 percent confident that the phone and plan combination we ultimately select is the absolute best? Of course not, because most of us believe that the time and effort necessary to make that determination would not be worth it.

In terms of patent valuation, the satisficing strategy becomes preferred when the importance of the decision and the cost for obtaining useful valuation information do not justify an optimizing strategy. The decreased importance of the decision and the high information costs should force the decision maker to face the reality of her resource and cognitive limitations. A decision needs to be made, and the existing limitations mean that it will almost certainly be imperfect. Instead of throwing resources at the decision, a satisficing decision maker can save those resources for more important decisions or lower information cost decisions, but still preserve a satisfactory outcome.

Satisficing is the preferred strategy for any decision that does not justify an optimizing strategy. When most people think about patent valuation, they think about maximizing scenarios (such as valuing patent rights for a major patent-infringement litigation), but maximizing scenarios actually make up only a tiny minority of patent decisions. The vast majority of patent decisions are best served by a satisficing strategy. Namely, the decision can be improved by conducting minimal, but thoughtful, valuation analysis.

Because of the more modest goals of the valuation analysis, however, such analysis need not be perfect and can be done relatively cheaply. As we will explain further on, a satisficing strategy can also be used as a triage tool to help differentiate more important decisions from less important decisions. The satisficing strategy can help to establish which decisions warrant a more thorough optimizing or maximizing approach.

PRELIMINARY PORTFOLIO VALUATION AUDIT: A PRACTICAL VALUATION TECHNIQUE

Many of the most fundamental patenting decisions for firms or organizations with substantial patent portfolios involve prioritizing individual patents within the portfolio. A firm's patent portfolio can generate significant value for the firm, but it almost certainly requires managing the portfolio so as to achieve that positive result. Portfolio management can generate value for a firm in many ways:

- By identifying valuable patents that are inadequately protected and increasing their protection.
- By identifying valuable patents that are not being fully monetized.
- By identifying patents with values that no longer justify paying maintenance fees.

The first step to managing a large patent portfolio is to conduct some form of triage to decide which patents should receive immediate attention. Ideally, the firm will want to address its most valuable patents first, but how should the firm make that determination? Conducting a complete valuation of each patent in an extensive portfolio is likely to be too onerous, too time consuming, and too expensive for most firms to consider. Complete valuations may be possible for a few patents, but to deal with the overall portfolio a cheaper method will almost certainly be required. We like a technique that we refer to as a preliminary portfolio valuation (PPV) audit to conduct the initial triage. This audit is not meant to establish definitive values for the various patents, but instead to identify inexpensively three broad categories for patent management within the portfolio based on an assessment along two separate dimensions: (1) the strategic importance of the patent and (2) the strength of the legal relationship to the patent. By using the PPV audit, the patent portfolio manager can quickly identify

- Patents that are strategically important, but have inadequate legal protection and require immediate attention.

- Patents in which the strategic importance and existing legal protection are in balance and do not require special attention at this time.
- Patents in which the strategic importance does not justify the current level of legal protection and may represent a potential waste of the organization's resources and assets unless the strategic importance can be increased.

By broadly classifying the patents in a portfolio using the PPV audit, an action plan is developed and a more refined valuation analysis can be strategically deployed on a targeted and more manageable group of patents. The power of a PPV audit is not limited to its ability to disassemble the portfolio management problem, but also stems from its ability to reassemble the information thoughtfully. The value of a patent is a function of both its commercial qualities and its legal qualities and requires an analysis of both to develop a reasonable estimate. Unfortunately, most firms use either a patent attorney or a businessperson to manage their patent portfolios, which can result in biased analysis. If the portfolio is managed by a patent attorney, there is a significant risk that any portfolio analysis will overemphasize the legal aspects of the issue. Specifically, the patent attorney will be most concerned with inadequately protected patents, even if those patents are not very strategically important to the firm. If the portfolio is managed by a businessperson, the opposite bias is likely. The businessperson is likely to be most concerned with the strategically important patents without appreciating potential legal dangers. The PPV audit makes it easy for the firm's legal and business agents to both contribute to the analysis and to combine their collective wisdom.

Mechanics of a PPV Audit

The value of a patent depends on an analysis of both its legal and business elements. Factors that affect legal value include the legal strength and breadth of the patent claims, how the courts are currently interpreting patents of this type, and the practices of the United States and foreign patent offices. On the business side, important factors include the future potential market, foreseeable competitors, possible alternatives to the patented technology, and general economic conditions. The problem is how to consider and incorporate an assessment of all these factors into a simple and relatively inexpensive valuation exercise to prioritize the patents under management. As a reminder, the goal is not to establish a highly accurate valuation of each patent; rather, the goal is to provide a facile, inexpensive valuation that is good enough as a first cut to triage patents into a few different categories for further attention.

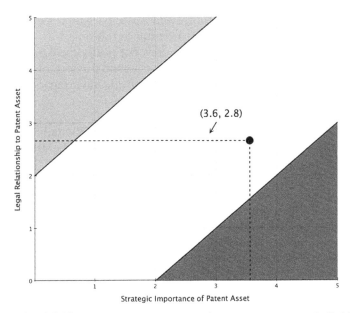

FIGURE 3.10   Plotted Point on a PPV Chart Representing an Individual Patent Asset

One way to generate a good enough valuation is to conduct a PPV audit. The PPV audit reduces the various business and legal dimensions associated with a particular patent to x and y coordinates that can then be plotted on a two-axis chart (see Figure 3.10). The PPV audit allows the valuator to plot a point (or bubble, if another measured dimension is added)[7] for each identified patent asset.

The PPV audit can be reduced to a four-step process.

1. **Identify the patents:** The first step is to develop a clear picture of the firm's portfolio and then identify each of the firm's patent assets.
2. **Determine the strategic importance of the patent assets:** The next step is to evaluate the strategic importance of each of the firm's identified patent assets. Generally speaking, this task involves specifying the firm's various business strategies and identifying those individual patents that are necessary to pursue those strategies. For patents that do not have an obvious fit with the firm's existing business strategies, this task requires determining whether such patents will become valuable for future strategies or are valuable to third parties. There is no single method for reducing these strategic evaluations into a number that can be plotted on

Strategic Importance Factor	Weight (0–1)	x	Score (0–5)	=	Calculated Factor Value
Enhances competitive position	0.4	X		=	
Lowers production costs	0.2	X		=	
Improves product characteristics	0.1	X		=	
Provides marketing advantage	0.2	X		=	
Compliments other products	0.1	X		=	

Total of weights must add up to 1.0

Add all calculated factor values and plot on *x*-axis ⟶

FIGURE 3.11 Determine the Strategic Importance Factors and Weightings

the PPV audit chart. One simple method is to prepare a uniform score sheet that requires two steps.

a. **Develop a uniform score sheet that applies to each patent.** Identify the factors that make patents strategically important for that particular firm. Figure 3.11 provides an example. The factors listed in the figure are illustrative and will not apply to every firm. To obtain more information from the exercise, we recommend weighting the importance of the factors rather than treating all factors as equal. The combined weights of all the factors must add up to 1 (or 100 percent) (see Figure 3.11). The uniform score sheet will be used for all the firm's patents so that apples-to-apples comparisons can be made among patents assets in the portfolio.

b. **Score each patent.** Use the score sheet to score each patent asset on a 0-to-5 scale for each strategic importance factor (see Figure 3.12). Each factor score is multiplied by that factor's weight to yield a factor value. All the factor values are added up to yield a single strategic importance value for the patent asset being examined. This value will be the x value on the PPV audit chart.

The process of discussing and determining the weights and scores for a firm's patent assets is, in and of itself, a highly useful endeavor. We recommend against delegating this task to outside experts, although their assistance may be helpful. These discussions lead to a deeper understanding and appreciation on the part of the firm's decision

Strategic Importance Factor	Weight (0–1)	X	Score (0–5)	=	Calculated Factor Value
Enhances competitive position	0.4	X	3	=	1.2
Lowers production costs	0.2	X	4	=	0.8
Improves product characteristics	0.1	X	4	=	0.4
Provides marketing advantage	0.2	X	5	=	1.0
Compliments other products	0.1	X	2	=	0.2

Total of weights must add up to 1.0

Add all calculated factor values and plot on *x*-axis ⟶ | 3.6 |

FIGURE 3.12 Example of a Completed Strategic Importance Score Sheet

makers about the relevant factors that affect value. Such understanding and appreciation are not captured as effectively if the task is performed by someone removed from the ultimate decision-making activities.[8]

3. **Determine the firm's legal relationship with the patent assets.** The firm's legal relationship to each patent asset must also be evaluated. The process is similar to that used to assess strategic importance.

   a. **Develop a uniform score sheet that applies to each patent.** The legal relationship score sheet is generally developed with the help of legal counsel. The score sheet should include the legal relationship factors that affect the certainty of control the firm possesses over each patent asset (see Figure 3.13). As with the strategic importance score sheet, the legal relationship factors should be weighted, with the combined weights adding up to 1 (or 100 percent).

   b. **Score each patent.** Use the score sheet to score each patent asset on a 0-to-5 scale for each factor (see Figure 3.14). Each factor score is multiplied by that factor's weight to yield a factor value. All the factor values are added up to yield a single legal relationship value for the patent asset being examined that will be the *y* value on the PPV audit chart.

4. **Plot the PPV audit chart and evaluate the findings.** Once the portfolio of patent assets is plotted on the valuation chart, guidance for action and decision making is made clearer. For example, using the chart in Figure 3.15 it is apparent that patent asset 7 requires attention (legal or otherwise) to strengthen the company's relationship to the asset. By

Legal Relationship Factor	Weight (0–1)	x	Score (0–5)	=	Calculated Factor Value
Survived legal challenge	0.4	x		=	
Broad claims	0.2	x		=	
No blocking patents	0.1	x		=	
Patent covers critical competitive elements	0.2	x		=	
No close prior art	0.1	x		=	

Total of weights must add up to 1.0

Add all calculated factor values and plot on *x*-axis ⟶ ☐

FIGURE 3.13 Determine Legal Relationship Factors and Weightings

contrast, patent asset 1 is overprotected, indicating that valuable resources have been wasted on it. Using this chart, management can quickly identify strategically important patent assets to which the company has an inadequate legal relationship as well as patent assets that are legally overprotected.

Legal Relationship Factor	Weight (0–1)	x	Score (0–5)	=	Calculated Factor Value
Survived legal challenge	0.4	x	2	=	0.8
Broad claims	0.2	x	4	=	0.8
No blocking patents	0.1	x	2	=	0.2
Patent covers critical competitive elements	0.2	x	3	=	0.6
No close prior art	0.1	x	4	=	0.4

Total of weights must add up to 1.0

Add all calculated factor values and plot on *x*-axis ⟶ 2.8

FIGURE 3.14 Example of a Completed Legal Relationship Score Sheet

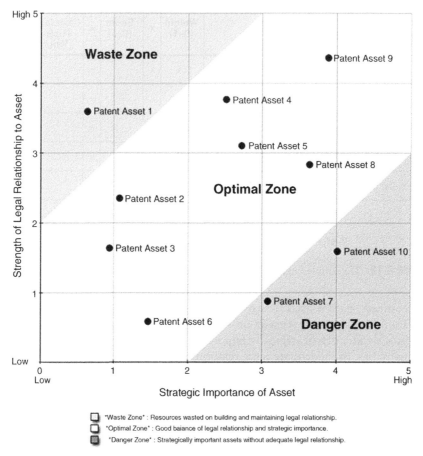

FIGURE 3.15 A Completed PPV Audit Chart

The PPV audit chart in Figure 3.15 contains two shaded areas that can be useful indicators for management action. The shaded zone in the lower right of the chart represents what we call the danger zone. Any patent asset that is determined by the PPV audit exercise to reside in this zone requires immediate management attention; the chart tells us that the patent asset in question has a strategic importance that is not commensurate with its legal relationship. The PPV audit chart identifies which patents to focus on and what needs to be done: strengthen the legal relationship.

On the other hand, the shaded zone in the upper left of the chart represents what we call the waste zone. Patent assets that fall in this area have legal relationships that exceed their strategic importance, indicating that resources were spent on securing or protecting the legal relationship in excess of the economic benefits expected from the asset. This situation presents the patent manager with a more complicated future course of action. Some patent assets in the waste zone should receive a lower priority and should not receive additional resources. For others in the waste zone, the best course of action may be to invest resources to improve the assessed strategic importance of the asset. The PPV factor chart gives the patent manager a list of factors on which to concentrate. If there is little prospect that the patent asset will ever develop as an important strategic asset for internal use, there may be an outside market for the patent that would provide a significant cash flow.

REFERENCES

Bernstein, Peter. 1998. *Against the Gods: The Remarkable Story of Risk.* New York: John Wiley & Sons.

Hadjiloucas, Tony, and Mark Haller. 2009. "Intellectual Asset Deals and Decisions: Are You Building or Destroying Value?" *Intellectual Asset Management Magazine—IP Value 2009.* 34.

Jorda, Karl. 2008. "Patent and Trade Secret Complementariness: An Unsuspected Strategy." *Washburn Law Journal* 48: 1.

Lin, Jacki. 2011. "Risk Analysis for Patent Prosecution." UNH Law Student White Paper Series (copy on file with authors).

Raiffa, Howard. 1968. *Decision Analysis: Introductory Lectures on Choices under Uncertainty.* Reading, MA: Addison-Wesley Publishing.

Simon, Herbert. 1956. "Rational Choice and the Structure of the Environment." *Psychological Review* 63: 129.

Simon, Herbert. 1959. "Theories of Decision-Making in Economics and Behavioral Science." *American Economic Review* 49: 253.

Simon, Herbert. 1997. *An Empirically Based Microeconomics.* Cambridge, UK: Cambridge University Press.

Skinner, David. 1999. *Introduction to Decision Analysis: A Practitioner's Guide to Improving Decision Quality.* 2nd ed. Gainesville, FL: Probabilistic Publishing.

Watson, S. R., and R. V. Brown. 1978. "The Valuation of Decision Analysis." *Journal of the Royal Statistical Society—Series A* 141: 69.

Vermeule, Adrian. 2005. "Three Strategies of Interpretation." *San Diego Law Review* 42: 607.

NOTES

1. Tony Hadjiloucas and Mark Haller, "Intellectual Asset Deals and Decisions: Are You Building or Destroying Value?" *Intellectual Asset Management Magazine—IP Value 2009* (2009): 34.

2. Karl Jorda, "Patent and Trade Secret Complementariness: An Unsuspected Strategy," 48 *Washburn Law Journal* 1 (2008): 1.
3. In economic theory, the maximizing strategy is typically described as having a decision maker who *completely* ignores the costs for obtaining information. The decision-maker will be described as a "simple-minded maximizer" who will continue to search for all possible information with zero recognition of the costs involved with obtaining information. See, e.g., Adrian Vermeule, "Three Strategies of Interpretation," *San Diego Law Review* 42 (2005): 607. We find the theoretical formulation of the maximizing strategy to be too extreme to be terribly useful. In the world of valuation, nobody would *completely* ignore information-gathering costs. As a result, we describe the maximizing strategy as having a decision maker who *largely* ignores the costs of obtaining information because we do believe that there are times when more extreme information-gathering efforts are useful and should be distinguished from an optimizing strategy.
4. "A decision-making strategy that aims for a satisfactory or adequate result, rather than the optimal solution. This is because aiming for the optimal solution may necessitate needless expenditure of time, energy, and resources. The term "satisfice" was coined by American scientist and Noble-laureate Herbert Simon in 1956." Satisficing. Dictionary.com. *Investopedia.com*. Investopedia Inc. www.investopedia.com/terms/s/satisficing.asp#axzz1k7PFe1xc (accessed: January 21, 2012).
5. Herbert Simon, *An Empirically Based Microeconomics* (1997), 17.
6. Ibid.
7. The standard PPV audit exercise generates a point (x,y) that is plotted on a chart with two measured dimensions (usually strategic importance as the x-axis and strength of legal relationship as the y-axis). It is possible to visually represent an additional dimension by using bubbles instead of points, where the bubble diameter captures the extra dimension. One extra dimension that can be helpful in the PPV audit is to have the bubble diameter reflect the estimated (or calculated) value of the plotted patent, which provides the decision maker with a visual cue that careful attention needs to be paid to the larger bubbles (i.e., more valuable patents).
8. The importance of the process of evaluation, as opposed to just the resulting value, was the subject of the first two valuation misconceptions given in Chapter 1: Valuation analysis can only be conducted by experts; and The output from the valuation analysis—the value result—is more important than the valuation process.

CHAPTER 4

Disassembly

The task of disassembling a valuation problem into its component parts is often the most crucial step for generating a useful valuation. The separation of any inquiry into its critical elements, which are then individually assessed and subsequently reassembled in a logical and consistent manner, is a well-recognized analytical technique. Nowhere is it truer than with a valuation exercise.

Reduced to its core, valuation analysis has three elements:

1. Information inputs.
2. Valuation techniques that translate the information inputs into value results.
3. Interpretation of the value results.

Much of the work to improve valuation analysis focuses on improving valuation techniques. Developing more quantitative models that apply sophisticated mathematical methodologies gives an appearance of rigorous analysis and numerical certainty. In reality, a valuation technique's benefit (no matter how sophisticated the technique) remains dependent on the quality of the information inputs (see Figure 4.1). The valuation technique simply translates the information inputs into a value result. If the information inputs are highly inaccurate, the value result will be highly inaccurate.

If valuators had perfect information, valuation analyses would generate few challenges. The perfect information would be plugged into a reasonable valuation method that would generate an easy-to-interpret valuation result. Take the example of a standard discounted future economic benefits (DFEB) analysis (see Chapter 6), which attempts to measure the net economic benefits that will come from the asset being valued. If the valuator had perfect information about (a) the free cash flows that will come from the asset and (b) the discount rate that is needed to account for the time value of money, determining the value of the asset would be extremely simple. Of course, the

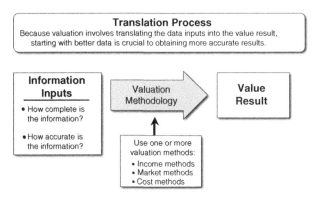

FIGURE 4.1 The Translation Process Is Sensitive to the Quality of the Data

valuator will not have such perfect information and instead will face a number of information problems, including the following:

- What are the various sources, both direct and indirect, for the future free cash flows?
- What will the amount and timing of the free cash flows from each source be?
- What are the most significant risks to achieving those outcomes? What will the market be for the patented product in 10 years? How much pricing power will the patent provide to its holder? How easy (or how difficult) will it be for competitors to invent around the patent?
- What are the multiple pathways (both currently known and not yet known) that can be pursued to generate economic benefits from the asset?
- What will the inflation rate during the future period that is being evaluated be?

Using the same DFEB method, a valuator who does a better job of addressing these questions will generate a more accurate valuation result. The valuator who better reduces information problems will improve the accuracy of the data being evaluated, the value result, and the interpretation of the value results.

One of the most useful ways to improve information inputs in the valuation context is through a process of disassembly. Disassembling a valuation task into its component parts helps the valuator to identify more clearly the separate information inputs that will affect the value result and to better assess the effect of each input, thereby increasing the likelihood that no significant element is overlooked. In addition, by breaking down a complex, multifaceted valuation task into more readily understood and assessed elements, the selection of the most appropriate technique to reassemble the components becomes more manageable. The disassembly process itself can be disassembled into a three-step process:

1. **Disassemble** the valuation problem into its individual parts.
2. **Apply focused logic** and analytical rigor to each part.
3. **Reassemble** the individual parts back into a coherent solution that can be evaluated at the aggregate level.

This disassembly process helps the valuator to identify the individual factors that collectively generate the overall value of the item being valued, generate a better understanding of those individual factors and how they interact to generate value, organize the information so that it can be dealt with in a manageable way, and identify and eliminate extraneous information that is not important to the valuation process.

In this chapter, we

- Look at decision trees as a disassembly (and reassembly) tool for patent valuations.
- Explain how to use disassembly techniques to develop higher-quality data for patent valuations.
- Consider how disassembly can be used to improve a valuator's ability to interpret the input data used in a patent valuation as well as the results that come from a patent valuation.

DISASSEMBLY AND DECISION TREES

One of the most powerful tools for disassembling, analyzing, and reassembling patent problems is a decision tree. Decision trees, which get their name from the graphic representation of the technique that resembles a tree on its side, use diagrams to force the valuator to disassemble the item (or decision) being valued and to analyze each component part carefully. Decision trees can be used to improve patent valuation analysis and patent decision making in a variety of valuation settings. In this book, for example, we use decision trees in a number of settings: to develop or improve the accuracy of profit or cash-flow projections for a DFEB analysis, as a method to incorporate into a valuation analysis future choices that may become available, to determine whether to accept a lawsuit settlement, and to examine the wisdom of various patent-based tax-reduction strategies. And these applications are just a few of the possibilities.

FIGURE 4.2 Standard Graphical Conventions for Decision Trees

Decision-Tree Components and Conventions

Decision trees (also referred to as probability trees) use a treelike graphical model for mapping potential event outcomes. The model consists of nodes and branches that connect the nodes. There are three different kinds of nodes used in a decision tree (see Figure 4.2):

1. Decision (or choice) nodes, usually shown as squares or rectangles.
2. Uncertainty (or chance) nodes, shown as circles.
3. Outcome (or consequence) nodes, shown as triangles.

Decision trees help to highlight the best choice (or most likely outcome) among possible alternatives. There are five steps to constructing a decision tree:

1. Identify the constituent parts of the decision or valuation exercise.
2. Specify the subsequent decisions and uncertainties that flow from the initial decision.
3. Determine the probabilities for each future uncertainty.
4. Predict the value for each alternative decision and outcome path.
5. Perform the necessary rollback calculations to reassemble the constituent elements back to a value result.

Constructing a Decision Tree

The easiest way to explain the steps in constructing a decision tree is through an example. Let us assume that a company (Acme) has been sued for patent infringement. Acme has received an offer from the plaintiff to dismiss the lawsuit if Acme pays the plaintiff $1 million. In effect, Acme's valuator needs to determine the cost of the lawsuit and whether paying $1 million to make that lawsuit go away provides good value to Acme.

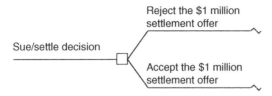

FIGURE 4.3 Graphical Representation of the Settle or Continue Lawsuit Problem

Step 1: Identify the Constituent Parts of the Decision or Valuation Exercise In this simple example, Acme has two alternatives (see Figure 4.3):

1. Accept the settlement and the lawsuit ends.
2. Reject the settlement and the lawsuit continues.

Step 2: Specify the Subsequent Decisions and Uncertainties That Flow from the Initial Decision If Acme accepts the offered settlement, there is no further uncertainty for that alternative. As a result, that branch of the decision tree would end. For the other branch, where Acme rejects the settlement, there is continued uncertainty with two immediate potential consequences:

1. The lawsuit continues to trial and reaches a verdict.
2. Acme receives a new settlement offer and eventually settles the dispute.

Adding these consequences to our example gives us the decision tree in Figure 4.4.

Step 3: Determine the Probabilities for Each Future Uncertainty Because we have identified two potential consequences in our example, the decision tree

FIGURE 4.4 Insert the Initial Consequences

FIGURE 4.5 Determine the Probability for Each Uncertainty Node

now requires us to assign a probability estimate to each (see Figure 4.5). Let us assume that we assess the chance that Acme will receive further settlement offers and eventually settle the dispute at 75 percent. Because the consequence branches must add up to 100 percent, the probability that the case reaches a verdict will be 25 percent.

Neither the *reach verdict* nor the *accept new settlement* offer alternative ends the uncertainty for the respective branch. As a result, a further uncertainty node must be added to each of those two branches. In other words, we need to continue each branch by repeating steps 1 through 3. For the reach verdict branch, Acme can either win or lose the lawsuit. Let us assume that Acme has a 60 percent chance of winning the suit. That leaves a 40 percent chance that Acme will lose the suit. For the accept new settlement offer alternative, there are three potential consequences: Acme may receive a lower offer, a higher offer, or the same $1 million offer. Let us assume that the probabilities for the three alternatives are 40 percent, 30 percent, and 30 percent, respectively.

Step 4: Predict the Value for Each Alternative Decision and Outcome Path The next step is to predict the outcome values for each path we have identified. For the reach verdict alternative, let us assume a single possible damage award of $5 million. In addition to the damage award, Acme forecasts that it will cost $250,000 to litigate the matter to conclusion regardless of whether it wins or loses the suit. For the accept new settlement offer alternative, let us assume a single possible lower offer of $500,000 and a single possible higher offer of $2 million. In addition to the settlement offer, Acme forecasts that it will cost $100,000 in legal fees until this subsequent settlement is reached. Adding all these consequences to our example gives us the decision tree in Figure 4.6.

FIGURE 4.6 Insert the Consequences and Eventual Outcomes

Step 5: Perform the Necessary Rollback Calculations to Reassemble the Constituent Elements Back to a Value Result

The final step is to perform the necessary calculations to make the original determination. Does paying $1 million to make the lawsuit go away provide Acme with good value? In decision tree parlance, this process is referred to as rolling back the tree. What occurs is that the decision-tree program (or an individual with pen and paper, if unassisted by technology) starts with the final projected outcomes and works back to the original inquiry (usually right to left), assessing each decision and uncertainty node along the way. For uncertainty nodes, the mathematical method is to take the probability estimate on the branch and multiply it by the outcome associated with that branch.[1] The values for each of the uncertainty branches are added together (because the total of the probabilities should add up to 100 percent), and a value for the uncertainty node is produced. The value also becomes the input value for any subsequent calculations involving that particular node.

For embedded decision nodes (decisions that are projected to take place at a future time), the process is to assess each decision branch according to a predetermined selection criterion: Either select the decision that has the maximum value or minimum value, depending on the decision maker's preference. The process of calculation and assessment continues until the uncertainty and decision nodes are reduced to the original decision with values presented for each of the decision pathways.

For our Acme example, we can take the projected possible outcomes and probabilities to develop a complete decision (see Figure 4.7) and generate a weighted average calculation (or expected value) for the cost of rejecting the $1 million settlement offer (see Box 4.1). The cost of rejecting the lawsuit projects to be almost $1.5 million, which means that Acme should probably decide to accept the $1 million settlement offer. Rejecting the offer will cost Acme roughly $500,000.

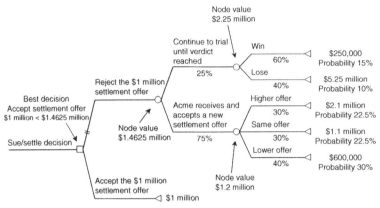

FIGURE 4.7 Complete Decision Tree for the Acme Example

BOX 4.1: COST OF REJECTING THE $1 MILLION SETTLEMENT OFFER: WEIGHTED AVERAGE CALCULATION

Outcome	First Node Probability (Reach Verdict or Subsequently Settle)	Second Node Probability: (1) Win v. lose or (2) Settlement Outcome	Combined Probability	Projected Outcome	Expected Value of Outcome
Win at trial	25%	60%	15%	* $ 250,000 =	$ 37,500
Lose at trial	25%	40%	10%	* $5,250,000 =	$ 525,000
Settle for higher amount	75%	30%	22.5%	* $2,100,000 =	$ 472,500
Settle for same amount	75%	30%	22.5%	* $1,100,000 =	$ 247,500
Settle for lower amount	75%	40%	30%	* $ 600,000 =	$ 180,000
Weighted average calculation (expected value)				=	$1,462,500

Using the basic building blocks described in this section, decision trees of great complexity can be constructed. The strength of the analysis is that what may appear to be an impossibly complex problem can, through careful consideration of the various subelements, yield insights not otherwise obtainable or obvious. Decision trees require valuators to (1) disassemble problems into their component parts, (2) analyze the component parts, and

(3) reassemble those parts back into a holistic treatment of the problem. This methodical approach to problem solving can significantly improve valuation analysis. In addition, decision trees provide a very useful tool for dealing with uncertainty, or at least explicitly including uncertainty into the valuation (or decision-making) activity. Because uncertainty is frequently the most challenging part of any valuation (or decision-making) activity, that function of decision trees is extremely important.

Sometimes decision makers resist decision tree analysis by claiming that they are unable to delineate the problem in sufficient detail or that they cannot specify the required inputs regarding probability assessments for uncertainty nodes or projected consequences for outcome nodes. As the relatively simple Acme example demonstrates, even a basic disassembly of the decision problem, coupled with very rough estimates regarding uncertainties and outcomes, is better than relying on an unarticulated hunch because the exercise requires using the best, if not perfect, information that the decision maker has. If an estimate in the tree is nothing more than a wild guess, it will at least be included as the current best estimate, and that guess can be noted for a subsequent sensitivity analysis (see Chapter 6) to help determine how accurate the estimate has to be to change the decision that is based on the guess.

USING DISASSEMBLY TO DEVELOP HIGHER-QUALITY DATA

The calculations involved in most valuation methodologies are generally not that challenging. What is challenging is developing the data needed for the calculations. Valuators therefore need usable mechanisms for collecting and understanding the data necessary to run a valuation analysis. Disassembly provides a particularly useful mechanism for that effort.

Common Information Problems

In an ideal world, valuators would have easy access to perfect information about the items that they are valuing. Such an ideal situation never exists, however, which requires valuators to cope with a number of common information problems. Four of the more substantial information problems are the following:

1. Missing information.
2. Disorganized information (the overwhelming nature of the information makes it difficult to process and appreciate).

3. Noise (irrelevant or inaccurate information that increases, rather than decreases, information problems).
4. Aggregation distortion (aggregating the information masks additional information or insights contained in the component data parts).

Because of the unique and complex nature of patents, each of these information problems can be particularly acute when trying to conduct a patent valuation (see Box 4.2).

BOX 4.2: INFORMATION PROBLEMS IN THE PATENT-VALUATION SETTING

1. Missing information
   - Projected net economic benefits from the patent
   - Appropriate discount rate
   - Pricing from comparable patent transactions
   - Risk of infringement lawsuits
   - Risk that the patent (or some of its claims) will be invalidated

2. Disorganized information
   - Developing reasonable net economic benefit projections, which requires understanding a vast array of business, technical, and legal factors
   - Evaluating litigation risk, which requires understanding the strengths of the case, the tendencies of the other party, the proclivity of the court, and the probable outcome of the remedies proceedings

3. Noise
   - Headline deal value announcements (see Chapter 8)

4. Aggregation distortion
   - Industry royalty rates (without access to individual deal information) (see Chapters 8 and 10)
   - Making patent management decisions based on the aggregate value of the patent portfolio (without a reasonable understanding of the value of the individual patents that make up the patent portfolio)
   - Failure to understand that a particular patent monetization path is superior to another

Disassembly Can Help to Reduce the Information Problems

Disassembly can help to address each of the four fundamental information problems. A favorite example of the power of disassembly is not a patent example but rather comes from one of the great scientists of the twentieth century, Enrico Fermi. Fermi, one of the founding fathers of atomic energy research, won the Nobel Prize in physics in 1938. He used the power of disassembly to develop reasonably accurate estimates to what appeared to be unanswerable questions. The most famous Fermi question is one he liked to ask his science and engineering students about piano tuners. Fermi would ask his students, without allowing them to use any external information sources, to estimate the number of piano tuners in Chicago. Of course one could hire an army of surveyors to locate and count each piano tuner, but that would be extremely expensive. In fact, the cost of that effort would almost certainly be higher than the value of the information being sought. Fermi demonstrated how a simple process of disassembly would allow the students to generate a reasonable enough estimate at almost no cost. The inquiry starts by determining the component parts of the answer. What are the basic factors that determine the number of piano tuners in a given city? The most significant factors are likely to be the following:

- Number of households in Chicago
- Number of households that are likely to own a piano
- Frequency of piano tuning
- Number of pianos that a piano tuner can tune in a year

Rather than try to solve the overall problem of how many piano tuners are in Chicago, students were instructed to resolve the more manageable disassembled problems.

- How many households are in Chicago? We could resolve that question by taking the current population of Chicago (roughly 3 million, including the immediate suburbs) and divide it by the average number of people who live in a household (roughly four per household), which gives us 750,000. We could then estimate that there are roughly 600,000 to 900,000 households in Chicago.
- How many households are likely to own a piano? The students could conduct a quick poll of how many of their families own a piano. Let us say the number is 1 in 2. These university students are likely to be from more affluent families than the general population, so we may want to

reduce that estimate of 1 in 2 to 1 in 4 or 1 in 5. We now have an estimate of roughly 120,000 to 225,000 pianos in Chicago.

- How often are pianos tuned? One student explains that the standard
  recommendation is to tune a piano every six months. It is doubtful that
  most piano owners are that diligent, so let us estimate that pianos will
  be tuned once per year on average.

- How many pianos can a piano tuner tune in a year? Tuning a piano
  takes roughly two hours, which means that a piano tuner can tune between three and four pianos in 1 day. Assuming that piano tuners work
  five days per week for 49 weeks per year (two weeks are eliminated for
  vacation and 1 week for holidays), that leaves 245 working days per
  year. We can estimate that a piano tuner can tune between 735 and 980
  pianos per year. To make the numbers easier to manage, we can round
  that estimate to between 750 and 1,000 pianos per year.

With that disassembled information, we can estimate that the number
of piano tuners in Chicago should be between 120 (120,000 pianos ÷
1,000 piano tunings per year per tuner) and 300 (225,000 pianos ÷ 750
piano tunings per year per tuner). This estimate of 120 to 300 is not a perfect answer, but consider how far we progressed. When most people are
posed the piano tuners question, their immediate response is, "There is no
way that I can answer that question." This disassembly exercise, however,
proves that this question is not unknowable. Instead, the information can be
estimated with reasonable accuracy at little cost and with little effort simply
by disassembling the problem.

Using Disassembly to Generate Forecasts and Estimate Discount Rates

One of the most powerful uses of disassembly is to help to generate cash-
flow or profit projections for a set of patent rights. Chapter 6 explains how
to use disassembly to improve the forecasting function. Disassembly is also
very useful for estimating discount rates, which we cover in Chapter 6.

Sample Disassembly Exercise to Develop Seemingly Incalculable Data

To provide a concrete example of disassembly's usefulness for generating
data, we want to provide a sample analysis. For this example, we will use
disassembly to generate data that may seem at first glance to be incalculable.

Background Information for the Hypothetical Example   A researcher at a
university (University) developed a new technology (let us call it the

Device). University's technology transfer office needs to decide whether to pursue a patent for the Device. The technology transfer office has the following information about the science and business landscape for the Device:

Science Landscape for the Device

- There are existing technological alternatives to the Device. There is one dominant alternative (the Dominant Technology), which has already been patented, and it is a better technology and already widely used. There are a few low-price alternatives to the Dominant Technology, and the Device could serve as another low-price alternative.
- The Device does not require much further development to be a viable commercial product.

Business Landscape for the Device

- The patent rights to the Dominant Technology are held by a company (the Dominant Technology Company).
- A number of companies are trying to compete with the Dominant Technology Company. They are all low-cost technology producers and are not capable of competing at more sophisticated levels. Individually, none of these companies is particularly strong, but collectively they are a significant economic player.
- None of these low-cost technology companies has ever licensed technology from a university, and none appears to be prepared to do so now.

With that background information, should University pursue a patent for the Device?

Disassembly Analysis   To answer that question, we suggest that University's technology transfer office start by drawing a map of the decision on whether or not to patent (see Figure 4.8). That decision map should disassemble the decision into its component parts.

If direct economic benefits (see Chapter 1 for the definitions of direct and indirect economic benefits) were University's only concern, the analysis would be fairly simple. The analysis could be as simple as: *If the net present value of the future net cash flows from the patent rights for the Device is greater than the net present value of obtaining and maintaining those patent rights, patenting would be the economically rational decision.* As we can see from the decision map, however, there are also indirect economic benefits that University should consider. Not patenting may better capitalize on those indirect economic benefits. How do we account for this balance

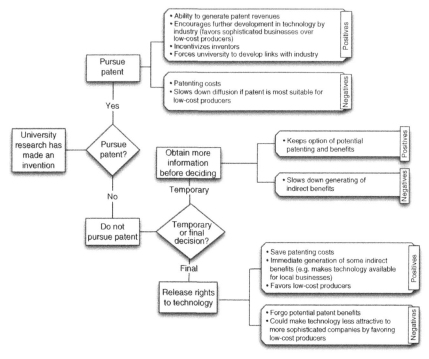

FIGURE 4.8   Map of a Decision Whether to Patent

between direct and indirect economic benefits? Let us try a simple disassembly exercise.

**First: Identify the Direct Benefits That May Come from Obtaining a
Patent**   The first step to valuing a benefit is to identify it. The valuator
should begin by identifying the various benefits that may come from obtaining a patent. Because receiving direct cash-flow streams tends to be quite
popular among rights holders, it usually makes sense to start with the direct
benefits. In the case of University, the decision map identifies only a single
direct benefit, which would be the royalties from licensing the patent.

**Second: Identify the Indirect Benefits That May Come from Obtaining a
Patent**   The valuator should then identify the indirect benefits of patenting.
The list of indirect benefits indicated on the decision map is much longer
than the list of direct benefits. To understand the indirect benefits, it is useful to understand University's function and motivations. Unlike many institutions, universities tend not to be pure profit maximizers. Instead, the core

mission for most universities is to contribute to society by creating and distributing knowledge. Most universities wish to generate more revenues, but they will also frequently turn down revenue-generating opportunities if such opportunities unduly interfere with their ability to create and distribute knowledge that betters society. For public universities, serving as a catalyst for local economic development may also be core to their mission.

In the case of University, the decision map identifies the following indirect benefits:

- Ability of the patent to help local businesses be more competitive.
- Ability of the patent to incentivize University researchers to conduct future research.
- Ability of the patent to attract future researchers to University.
- Ability of the patent to improve University's relationship with industry.

Third: Quantify the Direct and Indirect Benefits That May Come from Obtaining a Patent   In our experience, most university technology transfer offices lack the expertise or resources to conduct elaborate quantification exercises, but they are staffed with thoughtful professionals who know their business quite well. Moreover, if the office is trying to determine whether or not to patent an invention, the invention is probably not a clear winner and most likely has only modest potential. All told, this setting is perfect for using a satisficing strategy (see Chapter 3) to make the decision. There are limited resources available to obtain information to improve the decision, and there is little need for making a perfect decision. Obtaining *good enough* information will already greatly improve decision making.

One inexpensive quantification tool is to assemble a team of knowledgeable individuals who are familiar with the Device technology and the local economy to make relative assessments on the direct and indirect benefits. Specifically, each member of the team could be asked to do the following:

- **For each direct benefit:** Identify its percentage of the overall direct benefits and determine on a scale of 1 to 5 (with 5 being best) how substantial each direct benefit will be.
- **For each indirect benefit:** Identify its percentage of the overall indirect benefits and determine on a scale of 1 to 5 (with 5 being best) how substantial each indirect benefit will be.

Let us assume that the Device resulted in the findings in Table 4.1. Figure 4.9 represents those same results graphically.

TABLE 4.1   University's Direct and Indirect Benefits of Obtaining a Patent on the Device

	Direct Benefit			Indirect Benefits			
	Direct Benefit (%)	Weight	Total Effect		Indirect Benefits (%)	Weight	Total Effect
Royalties	100%	1	1	Patent will help local businesses	50%	1	0.5
				Patent will incentivize University inventors	25%	2	0.5
				Patent will attract future University researchers	10%	1	0.1
				Patent will improve relationships with industry	15%	2	0.3
Total			1	Total			1.4

Out of a possible score of 10, patenting the Device generates a benefit score of only 2.4. Patenting the Device generates such minimal benefits that not patenting the technology appears to be the better decision. This type of analysis can help to identify easy decisions that require no further analysis as well as more difficult decisions that likely need further analysis. For example, University could establish the following guidelines on whether to pursue a patent:

- If the invention receives a benefit score of less than 3, it will definitely not be patented.
- If the invention receives a benefit score of more than 6, it will definitely be patented.
- If the invention receives a benefit score between 3 and 6, further analysis will be done.

Even though the Device would be an automatic deny under the above criteria (since it received a 2.4 benefit score from obtaining a patent), Table 4.2 provides the Device's score if the technology is not patented. Table 4.2 helps to confirm that the decision not to patent is the correct decision as the Device generates a 3.6 benefit score from not obtaining a patent.

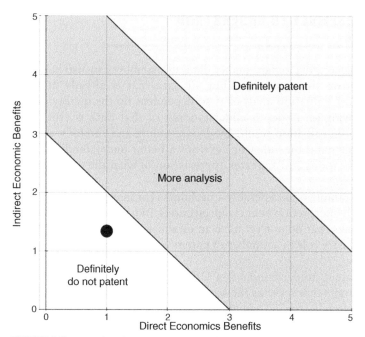

FIGURE 4.9 Graphical Representation of University's Direct and Indirect Benefits of Obtaining a Patent on the Device

TABLE 4.2 University's Direct and Indirect Benefits of Not Obtaining a Patent on the Device

Direct Benefit				Indirect Benefits		
	Direct Benefit (%)	Weight	Total Effect		Indirect Benefits (%)	Weight	Total Effect
Royalties	0%	N/A	0	Released technology will help local businesses	80%	4	3.2
				Released technology will incentivize University inventors	10%	1	.1
				Released technology will attract future University researchers	0%	N/A	N/A
				Released technology will improve relationships with industry	10%	3	.3
Total			0	Total			3.6

N/A = not applicable.

USING DISASSEMBLY TO UNDERSTAND DATA BETTER

In addition to generating higher-quality data, disassembly can also help valuators to improve their understanding of data that is already at their disposal. Because valuation analysis is so dependent on the quality of the input data, having an in-depth understanding of that data is crucial to understanding the valuation result. By disassembling and carefully analyzing the available data, the valuator develops a better understanding of its limits and implications and a greater appreciation of what the valuation result actually means.

A classic example of disassembly's usefulness for interpreting data is in connection with interpreting financial projections, in particular sales projections for products that do not yet have an established track record. Projections play a primary role in a number of patent valuation settings:

- When a patent holder conducts a DFEB analysis, the projected cash flows or profits that serve as the basis for the DFEB are the single most important variable for the valuation analysis.
- When a patent holder conducts royalty-rate negotiations with a potential licensee, the sales forecasts for the patent-related item will be crucial to the licensor maximizing financial returns.
- When a venture capitalist is trying to value a patent-based start-up, the basis of the valuation will be the start-up's profit projections.

In Chapter 6, we will explain in detail how to develop these types of projections, but for now we want to talk about what to do with projections that have been developed by somebody else. Let us assume that a patent holder is considering licensing the patent through an exclusive license and has two potential licensees. Each licensee is offering a royalty rate of 5 percent of net sales of the patented product, so the deciding factor for the patent holder should be which licensee is likely to generate the most net sales.[2] To begin to make that determination, the patent holder should require each potential licensee to provide a set of financial projections that cover the period of the potential license. The potential licensees have an incentive to exaggerate the net sales projections, so the patent holder should take their projections with a grain of salt and analyze them. Because of the multitude of factors that will affect future sales, disassembling the projections into their component parts allows for a much better understanding of the degree of uncertainty associated with the overall net sales projections. Depending on the specific context of the patented product, a variety of business, technical, and legal factors may all affect the ability of a potential licensee to

BOX 4.3: SELECT FACTORS THAT MAY AFFECT A LICENSEE'S SALES PERFORMANCE

Business Issues
- Has the licensee conducted a marketing study to guide its projections?
- From a business standpoint, how defensible is the licensee's business model?
- How strong are the licensee's sales and marketing capabilities?
- How defensible are the licensee's distribution channels?
- How strong are the licensee's production capabilities?
- Does the licensee have a cost advantage in its production model?
- What are the licensee's other products, and how does the licensed technology fit into the licensee's existing product portfolio?

Technical Issues
- What is the licensee's R&D capability?
- Will the licensee be able to conduct any development or follow-up research work to ensure continuing success of the licensed technology vis-à-vis competing technologies?
- Does the licensee have the technical strength to figure out how to incorporate the licensed technology into other products that it sells?

Legal Issues
- Is the licensed technology a probable target for infringement suits? If the answer is yes, is the licensee well suited to handle such suits (e.g., does the licensee have a strong patent portfolio that will allow it to enter into cross-licensing agreements)?
- Is the licensee able to manage any foreseeable regulatory hurdles?
- Does the licensee have the legal capabilities to structure, when appropriate, efficient legal relationships to distribute the licensed technology efficiently?

generate future sales of the patented product. Box 4.3 provides a list of some of the more common business, technical, and legal factors that could help a licensor to predict better the future sales performance of potential licensees.

Analyzing these various factors requires expertise in a variety of disciplines, and it can be very difficult to find any one individual who has all the necessary expertise to conduct that valuation. In addition to disassembling the overall valuation problem, we also recommend disassembling tasks and assigning them to various experts to analyze. Specifically, we frequently recommend that parties that are conducting significant valuation analyses establish a valuation team to address the problem. The valuation team should consist of individuals with complimentary expertise for analyzing the valuation problem. A common mix of experts for a valuation team would include a business expert experienced in finance, a business expert experienced in commercializing the relevant technology, a technology expert who is familiar with the relevant technology, and an intellectual property/business attorney.

If a valuation team is used, the following is a simple five-step approach for disassembling the licensee's proffered sales projections.

1. Identify the factors that could affect the licensee's ability to meet its sales projections.
2. Assign each factor to the valuation team member with the relevant expertise.
3. Analyze the various factors individually.
4. Once the individual factors have been analyzed, reconvene the valuation team to analyze the factors collectively.
5. Adjust the forecasted net sales based on the valuation team's assessment.

REFERENCES

Damodaran, Aswath. 1994. *Damodaran on Valuation: Security Analysis for Investment and Corporate Finance*. New York: John Wiley & Sons.

Gompers, Paul, and Josh Lerner. 2001. *The Money of Invention—How Venture Capital Creates New Wealth*. Boston: Harvard Business School Press.

Hubbard, Douglas. 2010. *How to Measure Anything: Finding the Value of "Intangibles" in Business*. 2nd ed. Hoboken, NJ: John Wiley & Sons.

Munari, Federico, and Raffaele Oriani, eds. 2011. *The Economic Valuation of Patents: Methods and Applications*. Cheltenham, UK: Edward Elgar.

Murphy, William J. 2007. "Dealing with Risk and Uncertainty in Intellectual Property Valuation and Exploitation." In *Intellectual Property: Valuation, Exploitation, and Infringement Damages, Cumulative Supplement*, edited by Gordon V. Smith and Russell L. Parr, 40–66. Hoboken, NJ: John Wiley & Sons.

Neil, D. J. 1988. "The Valuation of Intellectual Property." *3 International Journal of Technology Management* 31.

Obituary. Nov. 29, 1954. "Enrico Fermi Dead at 53; Architect of Atomic Bomb." *New York Times*.

Pratt, Shannon, Robert Reilly, and Robert Schweihs. 2000. *Valuing a Business: The Analysis and Appraisal of Closely Held Companies.* 4th ed. New York: McGraw-Hill.

Raiffa, Howard. 1968. *Decision Analysis: Introductory Lectures on Choices under Uncertainty.* Reading, MA: Addison-Wesley Publishing.

Skinner, David. 1999. *Introduction to Decision Analysis: A Practitioner's Guide to Improving Decision Quality.* 2nd ed. Gainesville, FL: Probabilistic Publishing.

Smith, Gordon V., and Russell L. Parr. 2005. *Intellectual Property: Valuation, Exploitation, and Infringement Damages.* Hoboken, NJ: John Wiley & Sons.

NOTES

1. In this example, the outcomes are expressed in dollars, but anything that can be expressed as a numerical value can be used.

2. This statement is a bit overbroad. Because of the time value of money and the greater risk associated with sales in later years, the patent holder should be looking at both the total amount of net sales and when those net sales will be generated. Net sales that are generated sooner will be more valuable than net sales generated later. See Chapter 6 for a discussion of discount rates.

Patent Valuation
Techniques

Preparing for the Valuation

Before launching into a detailed valuation exercise, a valuator should do a fair amount of preparatory work. This work involves analyzing the legal rights that make up the patent being valued. As we explained in Chapter 2, patents are a multifaceted property interest that involves a complex bundle of legal rights. Understanding which rights are involved with a particular patent and how those rights are to be employed is crucial to understanding what value can be generated from the patent. Immediately launching into some form of income, market, or cost method of valuation analysis without first considering the following fundamental questions will almost certainly lead to an inaccurate valuation or incomplete analysis:

1. What exactly is being valued: the use of the invention, the patent rights, or both?
2. What are the specific legal characteristics of the patent rights being valued?
3. How will the patent rights be used?

We addressed the first question (does the valuation cover the use of the invention, the patent rights, or both) in Chapter 1. This chapter covers the remaining two questions.

In this chapter, we

- Explain how the bundle of rights that come with a patent affect its value.
- Explore the alternative uses that can be made of a patent because different usages can generate very different values for a patent.

UNDERSTANDING THE BUNDLE OF LEGAL RIGHTS

The work required to value a patent bears many resemblances to the work that should go into any type of property valuation. Take, for example, a classic real estate appraisal. Most real estate appraisal checklists will remind the appraiser to determine the following:

- What is the ownership interest that is being valued?
- What is the description of the property being valued?
- Are there any encumbrances on the property rights?
- What are the characteristics of the neighborhood surrounding the property?

For patents, a similar exercise needs to be done. Although the questions are formulated slightly differently than for real estate and the focus of the inquiries is largely about understanding a complex web of legal rights, the essence of the exercise is the same. Box 5.1 provides a comparison of the standard real estate appraisal preliminary work questions and the corresponding analysis that is required for a patent valuation. This chapter examines each of these patent-valuation preliminary questions and explains how to incorporate such information into a patent-rights valuation analysis.

BOX 5.1: SIMILARITIES BETWEEN THE PRELIMINARY WORK REQUIRED FOR A REAL ESTATE APPRAISAL AND THAT REQUIRED FOR A PATENT VALUATION

Real Estate Appraisal	Patent Valuation
Ownership interest in the property	
1. Does the "owner" possess valid title to the property? ✓ Can the chain of title be established? 2. What type of property ownership does the party have? ✓ Is the interest fee simple (absolute title to and possession of the land)? ✓ Is the interest leased fee (a third party has a lease right to the property)? ✓ Is the interest a leasehold estate (it is the lessee's interest in the property that is being valued)?	1. Does the "owner" possess a valid interest in the patent? ✓ Is the patent still in force? ✓ Are there any potential invalidity challenges, such as obviousness, lack of novelty, enablement of best mode defects, or filing errors? ✓ What is the remaining life of the patent? ✓ Can the chain of title be established?

3. Is there any co-ownership of the property?

2. What type of patent ownership does the party have?
   ✓ Does the party own the patent? If yes, is the patent subject to any existing license agreements?
   ✓ Is the party the licensee? If yes, is the license exclusive or nonexclusive?
3. Are there any joint owners?
   ✓ Are necessary assignments properly completed?

Description of the property

1. What is the description of the real property?
   ✓ What are the property's boundaries (e.g., what are the property's metes and bounds)?
   ✓ What does the property include within its boundaries?

1. What is the description of the patent rights?
   ✓ What are the "claims" for the patent?

Encumbrances on the property rights

1. Are there any liens against the property?
2. Are there any restrictions on the owner's right to exclude?
   ✓ Are there any easements?

1. Are there any liens against the patent?
2. Are there any restrictions on the patent owner's right to exclude?
   ✓ Did the government fund the research for the invention?
   ✓ Are there any "shop rights"?
   ✓ Are there any compulsory license requirements?

Understanding the neighborhood

1. How do neighboring pieces of property affect the value of the property?

1. How do neighboring patent rights affect the value of the patent?
   ✓ Are there blocking patents?
   ✓ Are there synergistic patents?

OWNERSHIP INTEREST IN THE PATENT

As with real estate valuations, questions about the ownership interest in a patent involve three issues. It is necessary to determine whether the owner possesses a valid interest in the patent, what the type of ownership is, and if there are any joint owners.

Does the "Owner" Possess a Valid Interest in the Patent?

There is no point in valuing a patent unless a valid ownership interest in the patent can be established. Is the patent still in force? Are there any potential invalidity challenges to the patent? What is the remaining life of the patent? Can a chain of title be established to show that the current holder of the patent rights has proper title to those rights?

Is the Patent Still in Force?

One of the first inquiries that a valuator should undertake is to determine whether the relevant patent is still in force. Just because a patent was granted does not mean that it remains in force. The simplest way for a patent to lose force is failure to pay the required maintenance fees (also referred to as renewal fees or patent annuities). The economic premise behind maintenance fees is to discourage the maintenance of dormant and low-value patents. If the patent is not worth paying the maintenance fee, which is typically not very high, the patent holder will abandon the patent and allow the knowledge covered by the patent to enter the public domain. Most developed countries have some type of maintenance fee system.

In the United States, maintenance fees are required for utility patents, but not for design and plant patents (see Chapter 2 for a discussion of the different types of U.S. patents). Maintenance fees for utility patents must be paid to the U.S. Patent and Trademark Office (PTO) within $3\frac{1}{2}$, $7\frac{1}{2}$, and $11\frac{1}{2}$ years from the date that the patent was granted[1] (see Table 5.1). U.S. patent law allows for a 6-month grace period for paying a maintenance fee, although a late payment surcharge is then added to the maintenance fee.[2] If the maintenance fee and surcharge (if applicable) have not been paid by the expiration of the grace period, the patent will expire at the end of that grace period.[3] If a patent has expired due to failure to pay maintenance fees, limited options do exist to revive the patent.[4] A maintenance fee analysis should be done for each country or jurisdiction covered by the patent right that is being valued.

Potential Invalidity   Throughout the world, a large number of patents are incorrectly granted by patent examiners each year. These patents should have been denied, for example, because the invention was obvious or lacked novelty, the inventor did not satisfy the enablement or best

TABLE 5.1 U.S. Patent Maintenance Fees for Utility Patents

Due Date (Measured from Grant Date)	Maintenance Fee		Grace Period	Grace Period Surcharge		Expiration Date (Measured from Grant Date)
	Standard	Small Entity		Standard	Small Entity	
3½ years	$1,130	$ 565	6 months	$150	$75	4 years
7½ years	$2,850	$1,425	6 months	$150	$75	8 years
11½ years	$4,730	$2,365	6 months	$150	$75	12 years

Source: U.S. Patent and Trademark Office.

mode requirement, or the patent application was not filed within the 1-year grace period (see Chapter 2 for a discussion of the requirements for a valid patent). Although granted patents are presumed to be valid,[5] these incorrectly granted patents risk invalidity challenges from third parties that may decide to

- Request a reexamination of the patent, which could result in the patent being limited or declared invalid.
- Infringe the patented technology and seek to limit or invalidate the patent at trial if challenged.

When valuing a patent right, the valuator should have an understanding of the patent's reexamination and litigation history. If the presumed value of the patent right is sufficiently high, it may be worthwhile to conduct a prior art search to estimate the probability that a subsequent infringement case will be brought and the probability that such a case would be successful.

Remaining Life of the Patent If the patent remains in force, the valuator should determine its remaining life. For most of its history, the United States measured its patent terms from the date the patent was issued. That changed, however, in 1995. For patents filed after June 8, 1995, the potential duration for a patent is 20 years from the date the patent application was filed. For patents in force on, or issued on applications filed by, June 8, 1995, the potential duration for the patent is the greater of 20 years from the date of filing or 17 years from the date the patent was granted. For patent rights that involve foreign patent protection, a review of the relevant duration law for each country or jurisdiction covered by the patent right should be conducted.

The remaining life of the patent places a quasi cap on the premium pricing that may flow from a patent's exclusivity rights. Alternative

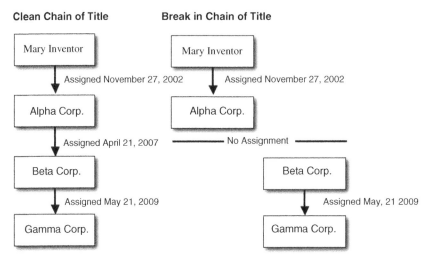

FIGURE 5.1 Chain of Title

technologies, however, will frequently extinguish that premium pricing long before the expiration of the patent.

Establishing Chain of Title Like other forms of property, proving ownership of a patent right requires establishing a chain of title. In the United States, initial patent ownership (title) is granted by the federal government when it issues the patent. That ownership interest may be assigned (see Chapter 2) to subsequent parties who then become the owners of the patent. To establish ownership, the current patent owner must be able to document each assignment from the original patent to the current ownership (see Figure 5.1).

In theory, documenting the chain of title should be relatively easy. Initial patent ownership is easy to document, and each assignment should be recorded with the patent office and therefore be easy to prove. In the United States, however, such recordation is optional and not mandatory. Moreover, the PTO does not confirm the accuracy of the assignment, so an inaccurate assignment could be recorded. Assignees, however, do have a substantial incentive to properly record the assignment because the U.S. Patent Act provides that

> *an assignment, grant or conveyance shall be void as against any subsequent purchaser or mortgagee for a valuable consideration, without notice, unless it is recorded in the Patent and Trademark Office within three months from its date or prior to the date of such subsequent purchase or mortgage.*[6]

What Type of Patent Ownership Does the Holder Have?

Once it is determined that the patent right remains valid and the chain of title can be established, the next step is to determine what type of patent ownership interest is being valued. Is the relevant patent right owned or licensed? If it is licensed, what type of license is it? What the rights holder can do is largely defined by the type of ownership interest in the patent. Ignoring co-ownership rights for the moment (which will be discussed immediately below), there are three broad categories of ownership interest that a holder may have in a patent: (1) owner; (2) exclusive licensee; or (3) nonexclusive licensee.

Owned Patents   The simplest form of ownership is to own the patent. For valuation purposes, owned patents can be divided into two categories: (1) those that are not subject to any existing license agreements (absolute patents) and (2) those that are subject to existing license agreements (encumbered patents). In the case of absolute patents, the valuator can focus on the absolute potential of the patent without concern for restrictions that prior license agreements may have placed on the patent. In determining the highest valued use for the patent, any legal usages can be considered. With encumbered patents, the valuator must take into account the various contractual obligations that are associated with the patent. These existing license agreements are not inherently good or bad for the valuation (see Box 5.2), but instead must be examined on a case-by-case basis.

BOX 5.2: TYPICAL POSITIVE AND NEGATIVE ASPECTS FROM EXISTING LICENSE AGREEMENTS

Typical Positive Aspects
- May produce predictable cash flow from the patent that helps to reduce uncertainty about the value of the patents.

Typical Negative Aspects
- May be at below-market royalty rates that depress future cash flows from the patents.
- May impose unfavorable restrictions on the future use of the patent that prevent the current or future holders from employing the highest valued use of the patent.

Licensed Patents   As we explained in Chapter 2, there are two types of patent licenses:

1. **Exclusive licenses:** The patent owner promises to provide one or more patent rights to one party and nobody else. The exclusive license can cover the entire patent, or it can be limited to cover a specific geographic region, field of use, or both.
2. **Nonexclusive licenses:** The patent owner promises to provide one or more patent rights to multiple parties and does not promise any exclusivity to any.

A patent license, whether exclusive or nonexclusive, can cover the entire patent or be limited in any number of ways. Typical limitations include manner of use limitations, geographic limitations, field of use limitations, and transfer limitations. These limitations allow the patent holder to tailor the bundle of rights associated with the patent to suit the particular needs of individual licensees. For example, if one licensee does not value the rights to use the patent in a particular field of use, those rights can be excluded from the license and instead licensed to another licensee who values those rights and is willing to pay for them. In this way, the patent holder can develop an ideal mix of licenses that generates the most value. Sometimes that will mean providing a single license for the complete bundle of patent rights, whereas at other times it will mean dividing up the patent rights into multiple patents (see Figure 5.2).

Joint Owners

In addition to the obvious patent owner, there may be joint owners of the patent that could substantially alter its value. U.S. patent law requires that the inventor, or a party authorized by the inventor, make the patent application. If someone is named as inventor who is not an inventor or if an inventor is omitted and the mistake is not corrected, any resulting patent can be invalidated. Determining who should be listed as an inventor can be challenging, in particular for inventions that result from large research teams or collaborative research projects. Who is the inventor when multiple employees for a firm all work together to develop the invention? To address this issue, employers in research and development- (R&D) centric industries typically require employees to enter into invention assignment agreements that pre-assign their patent rights to future work-related inventions. Failure to obtain such invention assignment agreements can materially affect the value of the patent for the employer firm. Under U.S. patent law,

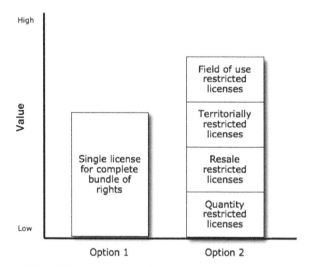

FIGURE 5.2   Increasing Value by Division

employee inventors are co-owners of the resulting patent and, as such, have the right to "make, use, offer to sell, or sell the patented invention within the United States, or import the patented invention into the United States, without the consent of and without accounting to the other owners."[7] In short, joint owners have the right to exploit the patent, including licensing it to third parties, without having to pay anything to the other joint owners absent an agreement to the contrary.

DESCRIPTION OF THE PATENT RIGHTS

With real estate, the boundaries of the real property rights are set forth by the deed's description of the property (such as metes-and-bounds descriptions of the property). The same principle applies for patents. The claims section of the patent (see Chapter 2) provides the description of the property rights in the invention that are conveyed by the patent. The breadth of the claims will define the breadth of the exclusivity rights. When valuing a patent, particular attention should be paid to the claims (see Figure 5.3). If the claims are drafted narrowly, their economic benefit potential will be more restricted. At the same time, the invalidation risk for the patent will be lower because there is less of a chance that the claims are impermissibly overbroad. If the claims are drafted broadly, the economic potential will be greater, but the invalidation risk will also be greater.

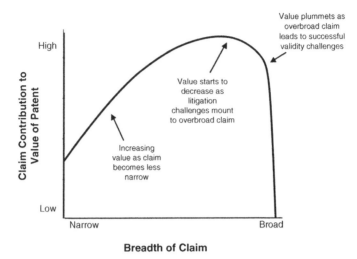

FIGURE 5.3   Narrow versus Broad Claims

ENCUMBRANCES ON THE PATENT RIGHTS

An encumbrance is a claim against the title of property held by someone other than the owner. Encumbrances on the patent rights include liens and restrictions on the right to exclude.

Liens

With real estate, the encumbrance is most often created by a mortgage loan and is held by a bank (or its subsequent transferees). Similarly, patents may have encumbered titles that are created when patent holders contract with creditors to provide the patent as collateral for a debt. To protect its interest in the collateral, a creditor needs to establish a valid claim against the collateral that will take precedence over other potential claimants. To do so, an asset encumbrance system needs to have a public notice system so the creditor can determine if there are prior pledges against the property, or liens, that could interfere with the creditor taking control of the collateral should default occur. Likewise, a creditor taking a security interest in an asset must give notice to the public that the asset is now encumbered by the security interest, or lien, so as to ensure priority of that interest over subsequent third-party creditors.

In the United States, security interests in personal property (which includes intellectual property as a generic category) are governed by individual state laws based on Article 9 of the Uniform Commercial Code (UCC),[8] unless preempted by federal law. Unfortunately, there is some uncertainty as to where and how to file, what constitutes notice of a security interest, who has priority, and what property is covered by a security interest. Article 9 sets out a comprehensive scheme for the regulation of security interests in personal property and fixtures. Under the legal framework of Article 9, a security interest is an encumbrance and is divorced from title to the underlying property. The situation is somewhat complicated because Article 9 does not adequately address issues relating to security interests in general intangibles involving the UCC's step-back provisions. The step-back provisions apply when the parties' substantive rights are governed by a federal statute or when a federal statute provides for a national system of registration or specifies a place of filing different from the UCC.[9] This issue can develop when one creditor files a conditional assignment at the PTO attempting to use a particular patent asset as collateral and another creditor attempts to create a security interest under the UCC in a state. When such a conflict arises for a patent asset, the priority is resolved in favor of the state UCC filing.[10] For a more extensive discussion regarding security interests involving patents, see Chapter 12.

Restrictions on the Right to Exclude

A few legal doctrines may restrict the patent holder's exclusivity rights and thereby reduce the value of the patent rights. Three of the more common such doctrines are the following:

1. **Government-funded research:** The government accounts for a significant percentage of R&D spending throughout the world. In the United States, for example, the government accounts for more than 20 percent of U.S. R&D expenditures annually.[11] As the invention's funder, the government may have certain rights in the invention, such as a nonexclusive, royalty-free license to practice inventions resulting from the funded research.
2. **Shop rights:** When an employee, during working hours and using her employer's resources, conceives and develops an invention that she later patents, the employer is entitled to a nonexclusive right to practice the invention.[12] These so-called shop rights are not transferable to an unrelated party, except in the case of a sale of the employer's business as a whole.[13] Despite the shop rights, the employee's rights to license or assign the patent are not restricted.[14]
3. **Compulsory licenses:** Patent laws in many countries (typically developing countries) call for compulsory, fixed-price patent licenses for certain inventions that affect public health and safety. Compulsory licensing, when implemented, tends to involve pharmaceutical patents.

UNDERSTANDING THE PATENT RIGHTS' NEIGHBORHOOD

Everyone has heard the adage that the three most important things about real estate are "location, location, location." Not surprisingly, real estate valuations are heavily influenced by the quality of the surrounding neighborhood. A good neighborhood can boost the value of a piece of property, whereas a bad neighborhood depresses it. The same concept applies to patent valuations. The value of a set of patent rights can be heavily influenced by the property rights that surround the patent. Throughout this book, our discussion of patent valuation tends to focus on valuing the rights associated with a single patent rather than a portfolio of related patents. We do that to keep the valuation concepts as simple as possible. Commercially valuable products, however, frequently involve a complex web of separate patent rights rather than a single patent operating in isolation. There may be *blocking* patents that could significantly detract from the value of the patent right. There may also be *synergistic* patent rights that could significantly enhance the value of the patent right. Understanding this web of patent rights is critical to understanding the value of each patent right in the web.

Blocking Patents

A blocking patent is a patent that blocks a rights holder on a different patent from exploiting the different patented invention without a license to the blocking patent. To understand the concept of blocking patents, one needs to understand that patents do not provide an *affirmative* right to make, use, or sell the patented invention (a patent does not provide the right to practice the patented invention). Instead, a patent provides a *negative* right to exclude others from making, using, or selling the invention.[15] See Chapter 2 for a description of the exclusionary rights that come with a patent. Therefore, having a patent does not automatically provide the rights holder with a freedom to operate in some particular use of the patent. An existing patent, with its own rights to exclude others, may block the desired use. When there are a lot of separately owned blocking patents covering a particular product, a patent thicket is said to exist.

A patent search should be conducted to help determine whether any blocking patents exist. Accurately identifying blocking patents allows the valuator to make two key determinations. First, the valuator can determine if there is an alternative economic path for the blocked patent. The rights holder may be able to work around the potentially blocking patents. Second, the valuator can determine the viability of obtaining a license to the blocking patent. In either case, dealing with the blocking patent will involve costs that should be subtracted from the stream of future economic benefits that are projected from the blocked patent.

Synergistic Patent Rights

The mirror image of blocking patents is a synergistic portfolio of patent rights. A group of related patent rights may be worth more in the aggregate when held in a single portfolio (or controlled in a single pool) than if held separately by different owners. By combining a patent right (the relevant patent) with a portfolio of synergistic patents, blocking patent problems may be eliminated for both the relevant patent and the other patents in the portfolio and thereby may raise the value for each of the patents. A patent right that is held as part of a synergistic portfolio may have a very different value than if held in isolation. In many cases, it will be necessary to value the *patent family* in addition to the individual patent.

At times, competitors may seek to pool their patents into a single patent pool. One of the more famous patent pools is the Manufacturers Aircraft Association (MAA). In early 1917, the U.S. government was concerned that a patent thicket in the aircraft industry was retarding the development of aircraft by U.S. companies. With the United States preparing to enter World War I, there was concern that this lack of development would prevent U.S. war planes from competing with their European counterparts. To remedy this situation, Congress created the MAA and encouraged the feuding aircraft manufacturers to join. The MAA members contributed their major aircraft patents to a pool controlled by the MAA and entered into cross-licenses with the other members at fixed rates. The MAA put a stop to more than a decade of crippling patent litigation in the U.S. aircraft industry and allowed for American aircraft development to resume. More recent examples include patent pools for MPEG-2 technology and for MP3 and DVD players to help ensure interoperability of the devices. Patent pools, if not structured properly, could violate antitrust law, and the Federal Trade Commission has forced some patent pools to dissolve.

EXPLOITING THE PATENT RIGHTS

The final preliminary issue that a valuator should address before attempting a patent valuation is how the rights holder intends to exploit those rights. When valuing an asset, it is necessary to understand the purpose for which that asset is intended. Value is a relative concept. The exact same asset will generate very different future economic benefits—and therefore very different values—depending on who possesses it and how it is deployed. That same principle applies to patents. It is therefore important to understand who the rights holder is and how the rights holder intends to exploit the patent. How are the patent rights going to help the patentee to generate positive economic benefits? At their core, patent rights are a form of commercial asset. Patent rights can be particularly valuable commercial assets, but they are still commercial assets. That means that their value fundamentally comes from their ability to generate positive economic benefits, which can be direct or indirect.

1. **Direct economic benefits:** Patent rights can create a direct cash flow stream for the rights holder that could not be earned without those rights. For example, holding the patent rights may allow the rights holder to generate extra profits that stem from excluding competitors.
2. **Indirect economic benefits:** Patent rights can also generate indirect economic returns for the rights holder. Namely, the patent rights can (1) save money for the rights holder by reducing or eliminating certain negative costs and (2) indirectly help the rights holder to generate cash flow streams (e.g., a patent can signal R&D strength that helps the patent holder to raise investment capital and build other business lines).

For this section, we provide a general overview of why patentees obtain patents. Also included is how that general motivation should shape the valuation analysis of the relevant patent rights.

Direct Economic Benefits

Patent rights generate direct cash flows for patentees through market power, litigation revenues, and licensing and assignment revenues. Each of these ways provides direct economic benefits.

Incentive Theory: Exercising Market Power   The classic explanation for why patentees pursue patent rights is commonly referred to as the incentive theory. The potential for extra profits that stem from a patent's exclusivity rights provides the incentives needed for creating, producing, and disseminating inventions. For economic actors to consistently invest in the inventive process—whether that involves creating something new or improving what already exists—they must believe that they will be able to capture the returns from those efforts. Unlike traditional economic activities, however, the output of the inventive process is not an easily protectable good or service; rather, it is knowledge. Knowledge suffers from a problem that economists refer to as free riding. It is inherently difficult to prevent others from copying knowledge, which makes it challenging for inventors to capture the full value of their inventive efforts. Competitors can copy the invention and unfavorably skew the supply-and-demand balance. Moreover, by avoiding development costs, free riders can enjoy a substantial cost advantage over the inventor when selling the inventions and therefore profitably sell the invention at a lower price than the inventor can match. In effect, inventors are punished for engaging in the inventive process.

Societies have long sought to remedy this free-rider problem for inventors and to establish incentive structures that maximize the creation, production, and dissemination of inventions among their people. In prerevolutionary France, for example, the French Acadamie des Sciences used public funds to award monetary prizes to inventors whose inventions received the approval of the Academie's judges. Under that type of system, a group of experts (or judges) sought to reward the inventions that they believed would be the most successful. Over the last few hundred years, such expert-driven models have lost out to a very different reward system for inventions (see Box 5.3). Today, most countries around the world try to encourage inventions in a more indirect and market-based fashion by providing inventors with the opportunity to obtain a patent.

Patents evidence a set of economic rights that societies have decided to award to inventions. More specifically, a patent provides its holder, for a limited period of time, with the right to exclude others from making, using, or selling a new, nonobvious invention. Rather than try to predict the eventual success of a given invention, patents provide inventors with the opportunity to earn monetary rewards over time through the actual commercial success of their invention based on the temporary right to exclude that comes with a patent. Experts do not pick which inventions will be—or more precisely which inventions the experts *think* will be—the winners at the outset. Choosing the winners is left to the actual consumers of the invention, who pick the winners based on their decision to purchase, or not, the patented inventions.

BOX 5.3: ENGLISH STATUTE OF MONOPOLIES

The U.S. patent law system can trace its origins to 1624 and the English Statute of Monopolies. The Statute of Monopolies helped to limit the royal prerogative to grant economic monopolies to useful inventions and innovations. Interestingly, the Statute of Monopolies is also viewed as one of the foundations of competition (or antitrust) law and the preference for markets rather than state (or crown) control over commerce.

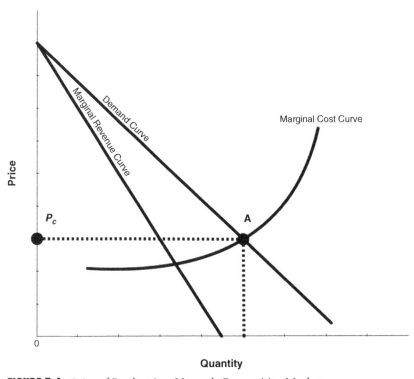

FIGURE 5.4 Price of Product in a Normal, Competitive Market

Under the incentive theory, the economic value of the patent rights (as opposed to the value of the invention's use) stems from the extra profits that can be generated by excluding others from exploiting the invention. In a normal, competitive market, the price for a given product or service will be roughly equal to the marginal cost for producing the good or service. Competition from alternative producers of the good or service will squeeze out any excess profits and eventually drive the price to the marginal cost of production (or the equilibrium price) (see Figure 5.4). If a firm tries to price the product above the equilibrium price, customers will simply purchase the product from a lower-priced competitor and the firm that raised its price will lose customers.

Absent patent rights, inventions are subject to the same competitive forces as other products or services. Competition will force the price at which an invention can be sold to the marginal cost of production. Patent rights, however, change the normal competitive scenario by reducing the level of competition and allowing a patentee to price the invention above

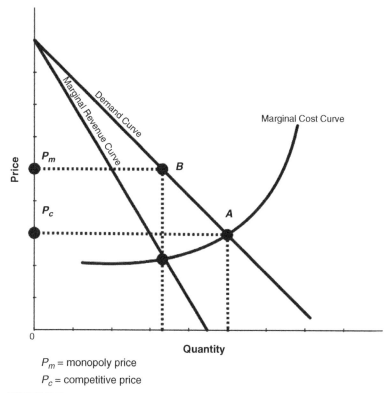

P_m = monopoly price
P_c = competitive price

FIGURE 5.5 Market Power That Comes from Patent Rights

the normal equilibrium price. Patent rights provide the patentee with what economists refer to as market power. A firm has market power when it can raise the price of its product or service and not lose its customers to competitors. Market power allows the patentee to charge a price for the invention above the cost of production and thereby earn extra profits (see Figure 5.5). Because patent rights allow the patentee to exclude others from making or distributing the same invention, the competition that drives the price to the marginal cost of production can be reduced.

When valuing the patent rights for an invention under the classic incentive theory, the valuator is trying to calculate the value of the extra profits that come from excluding competitors. This market power results when the patent confers some degree of monopoly power on the owner. Not surprisingly, patents are commonly described as providing the patentee with a monopoly. What the owner receives, however, is more accurately termed a *property* monopoly, as distinguished from an *economic* monopoly.

One with a property monopoly has the exclusive right to control access to the asset (e.g., you have a property right to exclude people from entering your car), but that exclusive right to control access may not confer any economic power.

An economic monopoly results when that property monopoly yields a competitive advantage. For example, you happen to own the only car in town and can therefore charge higher fees to drive your neighbors around. Related back to patents, the patent owner has a right to exclusively practice the invention (a property monopoly), but does not necessarily obtain any economic power from that exclusivity. When a firm has an economic monopoly, the firm has little to no competition and therefore serves as the only viable source for a particular product or service. Because there are no competitors to take its customers, a party with economic monopoly power can aggressively price its product or service.

A patent seldom provides the patentee with complete economic monopoly power over a market. In most cases, the patentee will have a property monopoly to practice the invention, but technical and economic substitutes for the invention will exist and serve as competitors for the patentee, thus limiting the scope of any economic monopoly. The patent only prevents competitors from using the invention; it does not prevent competitors from using substitute products or services to try to capture customers if the patentee's pricing becomes too aggressive. Lauren Stiroh and Richard Rapp provide the following description of this phenomenon:

> A pharmaceutical firm may patent a new chemical entity that is distinctly different from other molecules. If . . . that product treats a condition for which there are many other adequate treatments, the patent is likely to confer little, if any market power. If, on the other hand the drug treats a condition that heretofore had no cure, then the patent is likely to confer substantial market power.[16]

Nonpracticing Entity Strategies   Many patentees do not practice their patented inventions. These nonpracticing entities (NPEs) do not generate profits by producing or selling the inventions covered by their patents. Instead, they generate passive income from their patents either by licensing the patent rights to other parties to practice the invention or by bringing lawsuits that claim infringement of their patent rights. Although a bit oversimplified, we find it useful to divide NPEs into two broad categories based on how they use their patent rights.

Litigation Revenue Model: Patent Trolls   At their worst, NPEs can act as a form of patent bully who use their patents—including some overbroad patents that probably should not have been granted in the first place—and the high cost of defending against a patent infringement lawsuit to coerce companies into paying royalty payments. In such cases, the NPE is not obtaining a patent to create value, but instead wants the patent rights so as to impose a tax on those who are trying to use the technology to benefit society. By much of the media, and some academics, these coercive NPEs have been ingloriously given the label of patent trolls. For purposes of this section, we will use a more polite term for these litigious-minded NPEs and refer to them as patent licensing and litigation companies (PLLCs).

In the case of PLLCs, the value of the patent rights does not come from market power. For PLLCs, patent rights will frequently generate value based on the cost of defending against a patent infringement lawsuit. In a typical scenario, the PLLC will acquire patents, frequently from smaller inventors, and thereby develop a patent portfolio (the Portfolio). The PLLC will then contact companies to advise them that they are infringing one or more patents in the Portfolio and offer the potential infringers the opportunity to license the patents. The price for the license can be pegged at an amount that is less than the cost of defending the infringement suit, or at a more aggressive amount that includes the expected costs and potential damages at risk. In the former situation, the PLLC tries, at a minimum, to obtain a license fee based on the nuisance value of the infringement suit. The nuisance value of an infringement suit is equal to

$$CL_\Delta - DR$$

where CL_Δ = cost of litigation for defendant

DR = discount rate from CL_Δ that PLLC must provide to defendant to motivate defendant to enter into a license agreement with PLLC rather than fight the infringement lawsuit

It is economically rational for the PLLC to bring an infringement suit whenever the nuisance value of the suit is greater than PLLC's cost of litigation. The value of PLLC's patent rights will derive primarily from the licensing profits it generates from pursuing this strategy. The licensing profits will be equal to the sum of licensing revenues minus PLLC's costs for obtaining those revenues (e.g., attorney's fees) and maintaining the patent rights. This value proposition helps to explain the pattern of behavior of the typical PLLC. The PLLC will simultaneously pursue its strategy against a significant number of defendants. Defendants who agree to settle early are provided a steeper discount rate when the strength of the PLLC's infringement case is less clear and the resources the PLLC has to pursue the matter are fewer. In effect, the early settlers help both to test the strength of the PLLC's case (the PLLC can experiment with different theories and tactics) and to fund a more vigorous pursuit of the case going forward.

The above analysis focuses on the value of a patent right that has already been specifically identified for infringement litigation. When trying to determine the purchase price that a PLLC should pay for patents that it is thinking about adding to its portfolio, the valuation exercise needs to be adjusted to include the various uncertainties that the PLLC will face.

Licensing or Assignment Revenue Model Although criticisms against NPEs are quite common, they tend to overgeneralize the role of NPEs. NPEs, in fact, cover a wide range of patentees beyond PLLCs that includes universities, highly innovative high-technology start-up companies, and companies with patent portfolios that are so substantial that they simply cannot practice all of the inventions in their portfolio. There are a number of socially beneficial reasons for an NPE to obtain a patent but decide not to practice it. Specialization, and the efficiency that it produces, provides one of the most powerful reasons. Adam Smith, in his classic *Wealth of Nations*, was the first to formally identify the efficiency benefits that stem from specialization. Using the now famous pin-making example, Smith noted the incredible benefits that can come from the division of labor:

> *To take an example, therefore, from a very trifling manufacture; but one in which the division of labour has been very often taken notice of, the trade of the pin-maker. . . . One man draws out the wire, another straights it, a third cuts it, a fourth points it, a fifth grinds it at the top for receiving the head; . . . and the important business of making a pin is, in this manner, divided into about eighteen distinct operations, which, in some manufactories, are all performed by distinct hands, though in others the same man will sometimes perform two or three of them. I have seen a small manufactory of this kind where ten men only were employed, and where some of them consequently performed two or three distinct operations. . . . Those ten persons . . . could make among them upwards of forty-eight thousand pins in a day. Each person, therefore, making a tenth part of forty-eight thousand pins, might be considered as making four thousand eight hundred pins in a day. But if they had all wrought separately and independently, and without any of them having been educated to this peculiar business, they certainly could not each of them have made twenty, perhaps not one pin in a day; that is, certainly, not the two hundred and fortieth, perhaps not the four thousand eight hundredth part of*

FIGURE 5.6 Invention Process Includes Three Distinct Operations

what they are at present capable of performing, in consequence of a proper division and combination of their different operations.[17]

In the above passage, Smith describes how specialization can help to improve the physical manufacturing of goods, but his specialization insight goes well beyond the realm of physical manufacturing and applies equally to the invention process. Just as pin making can be divided into a number of distinct operations, so too can the process for creating and commercializing inventions. At the broadest level, the invention process can be divided into three very distinct operations (see Figure 5.6):

1. The research that leads to the creation of the invention.
2. The development work that transforms the basic invention into a commercially viable product or service.
3. The commercial distribution of the product or service.

A single entity—even if that entity is a corporation that consists of multiple individuals—may not have the ability to perform all three of the basic invention operations efficiently (or even competently), but it may be very good at one of the operations. Universities and high-technology start-up companies, for example, are frequently very good at the invention-creation operation, but not necessarily at the commercial development or distribution operations. In such a scenario, the inventing entity may logically evaluate its competitive strengths and weaknesses and choose to focus solely on the invention-creation operation. Mechanically, the inventing entity will patent its inventions and then license out—or in some cases assign—the technology and related know-how to other entities that possess the commercial development or commercialization capabilities that the inventing entity lacks.

Even firms that tend to practice their patents may find occasions where licensing the patent provides a better economic outcome. A common example of this outcome occurs when the patent covers a broad range of uses, in which case the patentee may not have the expertise to manufacture and distribute patented products in each field of use. For example, a medical device company may have invented a patented device that allows for manipulation of image pixels that makes mammograms more easily readable. The medical device company may want to practice that invention in the area of mammography. That same invention, however, may also be valuable in the area of satellite imagery, weather imagery, or any number of other image-related applications. Developing the manufacturing and distribution capabilities that are needed to pursue these additional markets may be cost-prohibitive for the medical device company. Licensing the technology to existing companies in these additional markets may be a more valuable strategy.

For NPEs that are pursuing a true licensing-based (as opposed to a litigation-based) revenue model, the approach to valuation should be similar to the approach taken under the incentive theory. If the valuator is trying to value the patent rights that are to be licensed, the focus of the valuation exercise should be approximating the market power that is associated with those patent rights. More specifically, the valuator should identify the range of potential licensees and determine the value of the market power that would be transferred to the probable licensee(s).

Indirect Economic Benefits

Patent rights can also generate positive economic returns for patentees in a number of indirect ways. Rather than generate a positive cash flow stream directly from the patent rights, the rights may allow the patentee to lower its costs for doing business or may tangentially improve the patentee's economic interests in some other manner. This section focuses on four of the more common indirect economic benefits that stem from patent rights: cross-licensing, preemptive patenting, signaling firm strength, and increasing the liquidity of technological information.

Cross-Licensing   A popular strategy that firms use to generate indirect economic returns is to develop a large portfolio of patents that can be used defensively. The patentee uses its portfolio to improve its bargaining leverage in both cross-licensing deals and patent infringement suits. The basic strategy is simple enough. When firm A needs to secure a license from firm B (including when firm A is faced with an infringement lawsuit from firm B), firm A can negotiate a better price with firm B if firm A owns one or more patents that firm B needs. Carl Shapiro provides the following general description of cross-licensing:

> *Cross licenses are the preferred means by which large companies clear blocking patent positions amongst themselves. Based in part on work I have done on behalf of Intel, I can report that broad*

cross licenses are the norm in markets for the design and manufacture of microprocessors. For example, Intel has entered into a number of broad cross licenses with other major industry participants, such as IBM, under which most of each company's vast patent portfolio is licensed to the other. Furthermore the companies generally agree to grant licenses to each other for patents that will be issued several years into the future, typically for the lifetime of the cross licensing agreement. Often these cross licenses involve no running royalties, although they may involve balancing payments at the outset to reflect differences in the strength of the two companies' patent portfolios as reflected in a patent pageant, and/or the vulnerability of each to an infringement action by the other.[18]

The desire to develop a cross-licensing arsenal appears to have been a major motivator for Microsoft's patent acquisition strategy over the last few decades. As Anthony Miele writes:

In 1993, Microsoft only held 24 patents and was struggling with IBM over software licensing. When the two companies could not come to terms, IBM wielded a portfolio of over 1,000 patents as a strong-arm tactic to get Microsoft to the table. Analysts said Microsoft eventually had to ante up an estimated $20–30 million in patent and licensing fees. In the wake of this, Bill Gates told financial analysts "Our goal is to have enough patents to be able to take and exchange intellectual property with other companies." As of October 2000, Microsoft held 1,391 patents.[19]

By 2008, Microsoft's patent portfolio had increased to roughly 8,500 patents.[20]

Google's 2011 effort to acquire Motorola is an example of just how far the cross-licensing strategy has come. In August 2011, Google announced that it would be acquiring Motorola for $12.5 billion to "supercharge the Android ecosystem."[21] Industry commentators suggest that one of the big motivators for the deal was Google's desire to obtain Motorola's portfolio of roughly 12,500 issued patents (some sources indicate the number could be as many as 17,000 issued patents) and 7,500 pending patents. Microsoft, Apple, and Oracle, among others, have filed numerous patent infringement lawsuits against Google for its Android operating system and against various Android original equipment manufacturers. Google can use Motorola's massive patent portfolio to better combat these lawsuits and improve its leverage in negotiating settlements.

Unlike the direct cash flow strategies discussed above, the cross-licensing strategy does not provide the patentee with a new cash flow stream. Instead, the cross-licensing strategy is a cost-saving strategy that provides a firm with the ability to lower the cost of its patent licensing expenses. Stated simply, a potential patent licensee should seek to obtain a patent for cross-licensing purposes when

$$CP < R^*P$$

where CP = cost of developing/obtaining a patent and adding it to the patent portfolio
   R = reduction in licensing fee that patent licensors will provide to the licensee as a result of patents that the licensee holds that could be used against the licensors
   P = probability of obtaining reduction in licensing fee

This valuation analysis can be done at the individual patent level or be done more broadly across a group of patents. There is also a final point on cross-licensing: It can present a number of antitrust issues. The Federal Trade Commission and the Antitrust Division of the Department of Justice have brought a number of cases against cross-licensors.[22] The risk of antitrust proceedings should be factored into any cross-licensing valuation analysis.

Preemptive Patenting   A patent permits the exclusion of others from practicing an invention, and, as such, the patent rights have the potential to be anticompetitive. The function of a patent is to prevent others from practicing a particular invention. In most cases, the inventor's motivation for obtaining these anticompetitive rights is to preserve the inventor's right to practice the invention or to preserve that right for its licensees or assignees. In some cases, however, the inventor obtains a patent with the intention of preventing that invention from ever being practiced by anyone. The patent is obtained defensively to prevent competitors from obtaining similar patents and to raise the costs for competitors to enter into a given market.

For an established firm, having a patent on its preferred product or process provides only limited market power. Competitors will seek to develop technical substitutes for the invention and use those substitutes to compete against the established firm. To try to prevent that competition, the established firm may seek to obtain preemptive (or defensive) patents for the substitute inventions before its competitors so as to foreclose having to compete against those substitute inventions. In some cases, the established firm does not even have to obtain the preemptive patent. Simply signaling to the market its intention to obtain preemptive patents may be enough to dissuade some competitors from seeking substitute inventions.

When valuing a preemptive patent, the economic benefit from the patent will be its ability to increase the market power for another product or service. Obtaining a preemptive patent should be attractive when

$$CP < IMP$$

where CP = the cost of developing or obtaining a patent and adding it to the patent portfolio
IMP = the expected increase in market power from foreclosing competition from a substitute invention

As was the case for cross-licensing, this preemptive patenting valuation analysis can be done at the individual patent level or more broadly across a group of patents.

Signaling Firm Strength   To thrive, companies must succeed in a variety of different competitive contexts. A company must compete to obtain customers for its products or services, it must compete to obtain managers and employees to run the venture, and it must compete to obtain the financial resources that are needed to create and grow the company. A company may also need to compete to develop strategic partnerships and obtain assistance from various third parties (e.g., obtain talented legal counsel). Questions about the quality of the company are at the heart of each of these competitive contexts.

- **Competition for customers:** How good are the company's products or services?
- **Competition for managers and employees:** How good are the career opportunities offered by the company?
- **Competition for financial resources:** How profitable will the company be?
- **Competition for strategic partners and third-party assistance:** Is the company worth working with?

For high-quality companies, resolving this information gap makes it easier to compete in each of these contexts. If the company is able to convincingly communicate its quality to customers, managers and employees, financing sources (e.g., investors), and strategic partners and third parties, the company should be better able to obtain each of these resources. For newer, high-technology companies with unproven products or services and an unproven track record, this information gap can be particularly challenging. As a result, many start-up companies seek mechanisms that will favorably shape outsiders' impressions about the company's quality. Getting a high-quality venture capital firm to invest in the start-up company, for example, can be a powerful signal to the outside world of the start-up's quality.

Obtaining patents may help technology companies, in particular start-ups, to signal their quality to the outside world. David Hsu and Rosemarie Ziedonis studied the ability of patenting to affect investors' perceptions about start-ups positively.[23] They looked at the signaling value of patents for 370 U.S. semiconductor device start-ups that were "founded between 1975 and 1999 and that received at least one round of venture financing by September 2005."[24] Their study found that patenting can positively affect investor perceptions of start-ups in a number of ways. Specifically, they found that patent application stock improves investor valuation estimates for start-ups and that this signaling effect is greatest in early financing rounds and when the investor is a prominent venture capital fund. Their findings also suggest that "having larger patent application stocks increases both the likelihood of sourcing initial capital from a prominent VC and of achieving liquidity through an initial public offering."[25]

For valuation purposes, the valuator should seek to determine whether a patent, or group of patents, provides the patentee with any of these intangible benefits.

Common Theme Links Each of the Various Rationales

Each of the patenting strategies discussed in this section helps the patentee to generate positive economic results and boost the patentee's overall profitability. Because the positive economic results are generated in different ways depending on the intended usage of the patent, the valuator needs to be prepared to adjust how to measure the value of the patent rights. If the patentee intends to use the patent under the incentive theory, the valuator will be valuing the market power—the extra profits—that come from the patent rights. If the patentee intends to use the patent for cross-licensing purposes, the patent can still help to improve the patentee's profitability. The patent simply helps in a different way. In the case of a cross-licensing rationale, the patent helps to improve profitability by decreasing the patentee's licensing costs. What the valuator needs to measure to value the patent rights will therefore depend on the patentee's strategy for holding the patent rights. Table 5.2 provides a breakdown of reasons for holding a patent and how the valuator should approach each strategy.

TABLE 5.2 Patentee's Strategy for the Patent Shapes the Valuation Analysis

Patent Strategy	What the Valuator Should Measure
Direct economic benefit strategies	
Practicing entity incentive theory	Value of the market power
Litigation revenue model	Nuisance value of the patent infringement litigation
Licensing or assignment revenue model	Value of the market power in the hands of the licensee(s)
Indirect economic benefit strategies	
Cross-licensing	Value of the ability to reduce licensing costs
Preemptive patenting	Value of the increased market power for the firm's other products or services
Signaling firm strength	Value of the intangible benefits that come from signaling technological strength to the outside world

Finally, a patentee can pursue multiple patent strategies with a single patent. For example, it is not uncommon for a patentee to (1) seek to practice the invention for certain markets, (2) license the patent for other markets, (3) use the patent as part of its defensive portfolio of patents, and (4) use the patent to signal R&D strength to potential customers, investors, or strategic partners. In such a case, the valuator needs to be prepared to value each of the various usages of the patent and combine them to generate an overall value for the patent rights.

REFERENCES

Association of University Technology Managers (AUTM). *U.S. Licensing Activity Surveys—FY 2005–2009.*

Bakos, Tom. July/Aug. 2005. "Valuing Innovation, Invention, and Patents." *Contingencies* 27.

Bessen, James, and Michael Meurer. Winter 2008–2009. "Of Patents and Property." *Regulation* 18.

Cromley, J. Timothy. Nov. 2004. "20 Steps for Pricing a Patent: To Value an Invention You Have to Understand It." *Journal of Accountancy* 31.

"End Patent Wars of Aircraft Makers; New Organization Is Formed, Under War Pressure, to Interchange Patents. BIG ROYALTIES TO BE PAID Wright and Curtiss Interests Each to Receive Ultimately $2,000,000—Increased Production Predicted. Payment of Royalties. Increased Production Predicted." Aug. 7, 1917. *New York Times.*

Gilbert, Richard. 2004. "Antitrust for Patent Pools: A Century of Policy Evolution."2004 *Stanford Technology Law Review* 3.

Gilbert, Richard, and David Newbery. 1982. "Preemptive Patenting and the Persistence of Monopoly." 72 *American Economic Review* 514.

Google, Inc. Aug. 15, 2011. *Current Report on Form 8-K.*

Graham, Stuart, and Ted Sichelman. 2008. "Why Do Start-Ups Patent?" 23 *Berkeley Technology Law Journal* 1063.

Guellec, Dominique, Catalina Martinez, and Pluvia Zuniga. 2009. "Pre-Emptive Patenting: Securing Market Exclusion and Freedom of Operation." *OECD STI Working Paper 2009/8.*

Heller, Michael. 2008. *The Gridlock Economy: How Too Much Ownership Wrecks Markets, Stops Innovation, and Costs Lives.* New York: Basic Books.

Hsu, David, and Rosemarie Ziedonis. 2007. "Patents as Quality Signals for Entrepreneurial Ventures." Paper presented at DRUID Summer Conference 2007.

Kramer, Michael. 2007. "Valuation and Assessment of Patents and Patent Portfolios through Analytical Techniques." 6 *John Marshall Review of Intellectual Property Law* 463.

Miele, Anthony. 2001. *Patent Strategy: The Managers Guide to Profiting from Patent Portfolios.* New York: John Wiley & Sons.

Munari, Federico, and Raffaele Oriani, eds. 2011. *The Economic Valuation of Patents: Methods and Applications.* Cheltenham, UK: Edward Elgar.

Murphy, William. 2002. "Proposal for a Centralized and Integrated Registry for Security Interests in Intellectual Property." 41 *IDEA* 197.

Organisation for Economic Co-operation and Development. Vol. 2008/2. *Main Science and Technology Indicators.*

Orcutt, John, and Hong Shen. 2010. *Shaping China's Innovation Future: University Technology Transfer in Transition.* Cheltenham, UK: Edward Elgar.

Patel, Nilay. Aug. 15, 2011. "What Is Google's Patent Strategy?" *Washington Post.*

Pitkethy, Robert. 1997. "The Valuation of Patents: A Review of Patent Valuation Methods with Consideration of Option Based Methods and the Potential for Further Research." *Judge Institute Working Paper* 21/97.

Pretnar, Bojan. 2003. "The Economic Impacts of Patents in a Knowledge-Based Market Economy." 34 *International Review of Intellectual Property and Competition Law* 887.

Schecter, Roger E., and John R. Thomas. 2004. *Principles of Patent Law, Concise Hornbook Series.* St. Paul, MN: West.

Shapiro, Carl. 2001. "Navigating the Patent Thicket: Cross Licenses, Patent Pools, and Standard Setting." In *Innovation Policy and the Economy*, Vol. 1. edited by Adam Jaffe, Josh Lerner, and Scott Stern, 119–150. Cambridge, MA: M.I.T. Press.

Smith, Adam. 1776. *An Inquiry into the Nature and Causes of the Wealth of Nations.* Chicago: University of Chicago Press (reprinted in 1976).

Stiroh, Lauren, and Richard Rapp. 1998. "Modern Methods for the Valuation of Intellectual Property." 532 *Practicing Law Institute/Patent* 817.

Sudarshan, Ranganath. 2008–2009. "Nuisance-Value Patent Suits: An Economic Model and Proposal." 25 *Santa Clara Computer and High Technology Law Journal* 159.

NOTES

1. 37 C.F.R. sec. 1.362(d).
2. 37 C.F.R. sec. 1.362(e).
3. 37 C.F.R. sec. 1.362(g).
4. 37 C.F.R. sec. 1.378.
5. 35 U.S.C. sec. 282.
6. 35 U.S.C. sec. 261.
7. 35 U.S.C. sec. 262.
8. The original version of the Uniform Commercial Code was promulgated in 1951 and first enacted in Pennsylvania in 1953. That first version rejected the title concept underlying prior conditional sales and chattel mortgage law. UCC sec. 9-202 (1951 Official Version). By contrast, the federal recording system provided to handle patent assignments under section 261 of the Patent Act has stayed essentially unchanged since 1870. See The Patent Act of 1870, ch 230, 16 Stat. 198-217 (1870).
9. Under the language of Revised Article Nine, eligibility for a filing deferral requires that the displacing federal statute have "requirements for a security interest's obtaining priority over the rights of a lien creditor." [U.C.C. [Revised] § 9-311(a)(1)]. This language is narrower than the former "partial step-back" in old Article Nine [U.C.C. § 9-302(3)(a) (1995)]. As of January 1, 2006, Revised Article Nine has been adopted in every state.
10. The leading case on the relationship between §261 of the Patent Act and Article Nine is *In re Cybernetic Services, Inc.*, 252 F.3d 1039, 59 U.S.P.Q.2d (BNA) 1097, 44 U.C.C. Rep. Serv. 2d 639 (9th Cir. 2001), cert. denied, 534 U.S. 1130, 122 S. Ct. 1069, 151 L. Ed. 2d 972 (2002). In *Cybernetic Services*, the Ninth Circuit affirmed a decision that had upheld the Article Nine "perfection" of a security interest in the debtor's patented data recorder against a challenge brought by the debtor's bankruptcy trustee under §544(a)(1) of the Bankruptcy Code.
11. OECD (Vol. 2008/2), *Main Science and Technology Indicators.*
12. *United States v. Dubilier Condenser Corp.*, 289 U.S. 178 (1933).
13. *Lane & Bodley Co. v. Locke*, 150 U.S. 193 (1893).
14. *United States v. Dubilier Condenser Corp.*, 289 U.S. 178 (1933).
15. 35 U.S.C. sec. 271(a).
16. Lauren Stiroh and Richard Rapp, "Modern Methods for the Valuation of Intellectual Property," *PLI/Pat 817* 532 (1998): 820.
17. Adam Smith, *An Inquiry into the Nature and Causes of the Wealth of Nations* (1776), 5 (Dent, London, 1910).
18. Carl Shapiro, "Navigating the Patent Thicket: Cross Licenses, Patent Pools, and Standard Setting" in Adam Jaffe, Josh Lerner, and Scott Stern, (eds.), *Innovation Policy and the Economy*, vol. 1 (2001), 129–130.
19. Anthony Miele, *Patent Strategy: The Managers Guide to Profiting from Patent Portfolios* (2000), 40.
20. Stuart Graham and Ted Sichelman, "Why Do Start-Ups Patent?" *Berkeley Tech. L.J.* 23 (2008): 1063, 1077.

21. Google, Inc. *Current Report on Form 8-K* (August 15, 2011).
22. See Richard Gilbert, "Antitrust for Patent Pools: A Century of Policy Evolution," *Stanford Technology Law Review* (2004), 3.
23. David Hsu and Rosemarie Ziedonis, "Patents as Quality Signals for Entrepreneurial Ventures," paper presented at DRUID Summer Conference 2007.
24. Ibid., 15.
25. Ibid., 1.

CHAPTER 6

Income Methods: Discounted Future Economic Benefits Analysis

Why do firms buy, sell, or otherwise make decisions about patent rights? There are many specific reasons, but the overarching rationale that characterizes each patent decision is the firm's desire to generate economic benefits. By their nature, most firms are profit-driven entities. Whether or not mandated by law (e.g., in the case of corporations[1]), the fundamental purpose for most business firms is to generate profits. A firm's decisions to accumulate, use, transfer, enforce, or defend patent rights are therefore driven by the ability for that decision to generate net economic benefits— economic benefits that exceed related costs—that enhance the firm's economic position. A patent valuation analysis is therefore an attempt to measure the net economic benefits that come from a firm's patent-related decisions.

Valuations based on income methods are considered to be the most theoretically sound valuation approach for commercial assets, including patents, because income methods attempt to measure the net economic benefits that drive a firm's asset decisions. For example, if a firm is considering buying an asset that will generate $1,000 worth of present-valued net economic benefits, the firm should value the asset at $1,000 and be willing to pay up to that amount to acquire the asset. If a firm already owns an asset and is considering a new use for the asset that will generate $500 worth of present-valued net economic benefits, the firm should value this new use at $500 and be willing to invest up to that amount to pursue the venture.

Income methods attempt to measure the net economic benefits that will come from the asset being valued. The most common form of income method involves projecting the asset's future net economic benefits—which will usually be expressed in terms of free cash flow or net profits—and then adding up the various benefits. Because these benefits will be received over time, a discount needs to be applied to take into account, among other things, the time value of money and the risk that the benefits that are ultimately received are less than anticipated. We can reduce this concept to a concise valuation statement:

Valuing commercial assets involves approximating the present value of the future net economic benefits that the firm will derive from the asset.

Said even more simply:

How much is a firm willing to pay today for net economic benefits that it may receive in the future?

Although frequently more complex than the typical commercial asset, patents follow the same fundamental valuation principle as other business assets. Namely, patents can generate future streams of net economic benefits for their holders and decisions to acquire, exploit, or sell patents are driven by these benefits. Income methods therefore also offer the most theoretically sound approach to valuing patents. The most common form of income method is referred to as a discounted cash flow (DCF) analysis, a term used because the analysis focuses on the future *free cash flow* that is projected for the valued asset. In this book, however, we do not use the DCF nomenclature, but instead refer to the standard discount method as a discounted future economic benefits (DFEB) analysis. We believe that DFEB analysis is more descriptive of the overall valuation approach that a valuator should take because free cash flow is not the only relevant measurement of future net economic benefits (see Box 6.1). No one measurement is ideal in all situations, and the valuator should employ the net economic benefit measurements that are most relevant for the rights holder's particular needs. Whether one uses the term DFEB or DCF, this income method tries to determine how much a firm should pay today for net economic benefits it may receive in the future.

BOX 6.1: FREE CASH FLOWS AND OTHER NET ECONOMIC BENEFITS

Free cash flow (or net cash flow to equity) is the traditional measurement used in a DFEB calculation. Free cash flow calculates the cash that can be paid to the firm's equity shareholders after all expenses (operating or otherwise) have been paid and after taking into account the reinvestment of funds back into the firm. A common way to calculate free cash flow is

FCF = net income (after tax)
+ noncash charges (e.g., amortization and depreciation)
− net capital expenditures − changes in net working capital
+ changes in long-term debt

In addition to free cash flow, a valuator may decide to use a number of income measurements for the DFEB analysis. Three of the more common alternatives are the following:

- **Net income (after tax):** The firm's earnings after operating expenses, write-offs, interest expenses, depreciation charges, and taxes have been deducted
- **Pretax income:** The firm's earnings after operating expenses, write-offs, interest expenses, and depreciation charges have been deducted, but before taxes have been deducted
- **Operating profit:** The firm's earnings after operating expenses have been deducted

When choosing the specific income measurement for the DFEB analysis, the valuator needs to be careful to apply a discount rate that is appropriate for that specific income measurement.

In this chapter, we

- Provide the basic arithmetic for a DFEB analysis.
- Provide a framework for developing the reasonable projections of future economic benefits that are the basis of a DFEB analysis.
- Explain the role of discount rates and how to use them effectively in a DFEB analysis.
- Examine the weaknesses involved in a DFEB analysis and explain how to manage those weaknesses.
- Explain how to make practical use of this inherently imprecise valuation tool.

BASIC ARITHMETIC OF THE DISCOUNTED FUTURE ECONOMIC BENEFITS ANALYSIS

For even the most math-challenged individuals, the arithmetic for a DFEB analysis is relatively simple. It may look a bit complicated at first glance, but we promise that it does not involve any math skills beyond using exponents (repeated multiplication of the same number by itself). Let us start with the basic formula for a DFEB analysis:

$$PV = EB_0 + \frac{EB_1}{1 + r_1} + \frac{EB_2}{(1 + r_2)^2} + \frac{EB_3}{(1 + r_3)^3} + \cdots + \frac{EB_n}{(1 + r)^n}$$

where
PV = present value
EB = economic benefit
$EB_{1,2,3,etc.}$ = economic benefit in the first, second, third (and so on) periods of the stream of benefits
EB_n = economic benefit in the last period of the stream of benefits
$r_{1,2,3,etc.}$ = discount rate in the first, second, third (and so on) periods

Note: The above formula applies the end-of-year discounting convention rather than the midyear discounting convention. The difference between the two conventions is discussed next.

The DFEB calculation is an easy valuation tool to understand. The current values of the patent's future net economic benefits are just added together (see Box 6.2).

BOX 6.2: ADDING UP THE PRESENT VALUE OF THE FUTURE NET ECONOMIC BENEFITS

Assumptions
- The patent right used in this example will generate net economic benefits for five years.
- The example measures the net economic benefits at yearly intervals, but more (or less) frequent measurements could be made.

	Future Year					
	1	**2**	**3**	**4**	**5**	**Total**
Projected net economic benefits from the patent right	$1.0 million	$1.5 million	$2.0 million	$1.5 million	$1.0 million	
Discount rate	12%	15%	18%	20%	20%	
Present value	$0.9 million	$1.1 million	$1.2 million	$0.7 million	$0.4 million	$4.3 million

The math behind this calculation is

$$\underset{\text{Year 1}}{\frac{\$1\text{ million}}{1.12}} + \underset{\text{Year 2}}{\frac{\$1.5\text{ million}}{1.15^2}} + \underset{\text{Year 3}}{\frac{\$2.0\text{ million}}{1.18^3}} + \underset{\text{Year 4}}{\frac{\$1.5\text{ million}}{1.20^4}} + \underset{\text{Year 5}}{\frac{\$1.0\text{ million}}{1.20^5}} = \underset{\text{PV}}{\$4.3\text{ million}}$$

Over the next five years, the patent right holder projects that it will receive $7 million of net economic benefits, but the present value of that stream of net economic benefits is only about 60 percent of that amount.

Focus Is on Net Economic Benefits

Although the valuator has some flexibility in deciding which economic benefits it wishes to measure with a DFEB analyses (see Box 6.1), the analysis should focus on some form of net economic benefit (the economic benefits that are left after subtracting the costs for generating those benefits). The ultimate objective of a DFEB analysis is to determine whether the investment needed to accumulate, exploit, or sell the patent rights will be justified by the returns from that activity (or those activities). If the analysis is done using gross economic benefits (such as revenues or gross profit), the investment needed to obtain the benefit is left out of the analysis. A DFEB analysis of a gross measurement provides information on the amount of gross benefits that can be generated, but tells the valuator nothing about the investment required to obtain those benefits and whether that investment is justified by the expected return on such investment.

Terminal Value

A DFEB is meant to measure all the future net economic benefits that are projected to flow from a particular venture. In some cases, the venture will

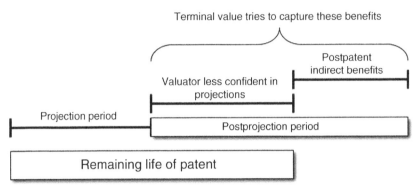

FIGURE 6.1   Role of Terminal Value in Patent

have a fixed duration and the valuator can confidently project the net economic benefits for the duration of the venture. For example, a potential
licensee seeks to license the patent rights for an invention for three years,
after which the licensee intends to abandon the venture completely. In that
scenario, the valuator should be able to project the net economic benefits for
all three years of the project.

In many cases, however, the valuator will not be able to project the future net economic benefits for the entire life of the venture confidently. That
conclusion may seem counterintuitive, at first glance, because patent rights
have a fixed duration. Why is the valuator not able to project the economic
benefits for the remaining life of the patent rights confidently? There are two
primary reasons that task may prove challenging for the valuator and therefore require an adjustment to the DFEB calculation (see also Figure 6.1).

1. **There is a long remaining life for the patent rights.** It is difficult to make
   reasonable, informed projections more than a few years into the future.
   If the remaining life for the patent rights extends too far into the future,
   those rights may extend further than the valuator's ability to project net
   economic benefits confidently. For example, new uses and markets for
   the patent may develop years after the valuation exercise. Looking too
   far ahead, it also becomes more difficult for the valuator to project such
   things as competing technologies that may reduce the value of the
   patent.
2. **Some indirect benefits extend beyond the life of the patent.** The bulk of
   the economic benefits that come from the patent rights will be earned
   during the life of the patent. Some benefits, however, may extend
   beyond the life of the patent and beyond the ability of the valuator to

make confident projections. For example, the exclusivity provided by the patent may allow the rights holder to achieve market dominance in the technology that will provide net economic benefits (such as goodwill or cost savings due to economies of scale) beyond the life of the patent. Dolby provides a nice illustration of this concept; it was able to transfer the consumers' perceptions regarding the patented product's advantages into a trademark (Dolby®) that has the potential to live long beyond the life of the original patent.

In either case, the valuator needs a mechanism to bring closure to the projections while still being able to capture the future net economic benefits that may take place beyond the projection period. This closure process is referred to as estimating the terminal value for the venture. The valuator will project (and discount) net economic benefits for those future periods for which she feels confident in her projections. The valuator will then conclude the DFEB calculation with a terminal value that approximates the value of the patent rights from the end of the projection period until that time when the patent rights no longer produce any net economic benefits. The formula for the DFEB analysis with a terminal value is

$$PV = EB_0 + \frac{EB_1}{1 + r_1} + \frac{EB_2}{(1 + r_2)^2} + \frac{EB_3}{(1 + r_3)^3} + \cdots + \frac{EB_n}{(1 + r)^n} + \frac{\text{terminal value}_n}{(1 + r)^n}$$

Developing the terminal value is itself a valuation analysis, although a relatively rudimentary one because of the high input uncertainty. Developing a terminal value is an example of a satisficing valuation method (see Chapter 3). As the projections extend further into the future and the uncertainty surrounding the inputs needed to develop those projections increases, a *good enough* valuation method is probably all that can reasonably be expected (see Figure 6.2).

Traditional Terminal Value Calculations Are Not Ideal for Patent Valuations
There are a few traditional methods for calculating terminal value in the context of valuing a company (as opposed to valuing patent rights). Unfortunately, these traditional methods do not translate well to patent valuations. Two of the most common methods are the stable growth rate method and the terminal multiple method.

1. **Stable growth method:** Sometimes referred to as the Gordon growth method, this method assumes that the company will settle into a constant growth rate and grow at that rate forever. The formula for the Gordon growth method is

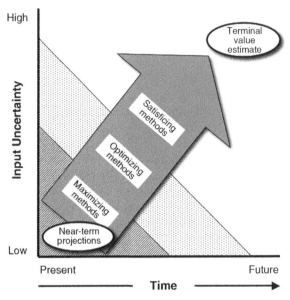

FIGURE 6.2 Developing the Terminal Value Is a
Satisficing Method

$$
\text{terminal value} = \frac{\begin{array}{c}\text{final projected period of net economic benefits}\\ \times (1 + \text{stable, long-term growth rate})\end{array}}{(\text{discount rate} - \text{long-term growth rate})}
$$

This constant growth rate in perpetuity is not appropriate for valuing patent rights because the patent rights will not continue in perpetuity. By extending the net economic benefits in perpetuity, the
Gordon growth method dramatically overvalues the terminal value of
the patent rights.

2. **Terminal multiple method:** This method takes a financial metric from
   the company's final projection period and applies it to an acceptable
   valuation multiple. For example, the valuator may take the company's
   earnings per share for the final projected period and multiply it by a
   price-to-earnings ratio for comparable companies to determine a market value of the company in that future period. Theoretically, the terminal multiple method could be used to calculate the terminal value for
   patent rights. The valuator could, for example, try to identify market-
   based multiples for comparable patents. Maybe comparable patents are
   being sold at a multiple of 15 × current year pretax profits. The valuator could take the last year of projected pretax profits for the patent

being valued and multiply it by 15 to obtain the terminal value. In practice, however, the terminal multiple method is next to impossible to use for patents. To begin with, there is a lack of readily accessible, disclosed market transactions for patent rights (see Chapter 8). Without access to such market transactions, comparable multiples cannot be identified. Even if market transactions for patent rights were available, identifying sufficiently comparable patents (comparable technology, comparable breadth of claims, comparable number of years left on the patent) would also be very challenging and would likely require such significant adjustments to permit an apples-to-apples comparison that the exercise would likely be pointless.

Performance Possibilities Method: Patent-Specific Approach to Calculating Terminal Value Because traditional methods for calculating terminal value do not work well for patent rights, we suggest taking the following approach, which we refer to as the performance possibilities method. The performance possibilities method recognizes the exponentially increasing difficulty in projecting net economic benefits the farther out in the future one goes. Rather than try to come up with a complex equation that will likely be rendered meaningless by the inaccuracy of its inputs, our preference is to use a visual exercise to help the valuator with the terminal value issue. Figure 6.3 provides five curves that represent probable performance possibilities for a patent's postprojection period:

1. Net economic benefits rise to plateau.
2. Net economic benefits increase and then fall.
3. Net economic benefits remain relatively constant.
4. Net economic benefits continue to rise at an increasing rate.
5. Net economic benefits steadily decline.

We recommend that the valuator use Figure 6.3 to project which of the five outcomes is the most likely for the given set of patent rights being valued. The valuator can use the insights from the curve to continue the net economic benefit projections for the remaining life of the patent and to determine if any indirect benefits are likely to extend beyond the patent's life. For example, if the valuator believes that possibility 3 is the most likely outcome, she can extend the final projected period of net economic benefits for the remainder of the patent's life. If the valuator believes that possibility 5 is the most likely outcome, she can apply a steady decrease in net economic benefits to the final projected period.

Because the uncertainty of the terminal value years will be much greater than for the early projected years of the DFEB analysis, the valuator should

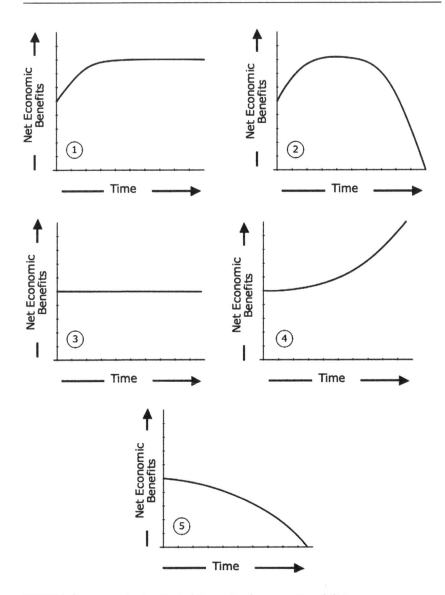

FIGURE 6.3 Postprojection Period Patent Performance Possibilities

consider increasing the discount rate for these further-out years. The valuator should also consider using some of the analytical methods that are discussed later in this chapter and in Chapter 7, such as decision-tree analysis, to help improve the quality of the projections.

GARBAGE IN, GARBAGE OUT: THE CHALLENGES LAY IN THE INPUTS, NOT THE MATH

Conducting a DFEB analysis for patent rights requires the valuator to develop two inputs:

1. Projections (by period) of the net economic benefits that are anticipated from the patent right.
2. The discount rate for each of the projected net economic benefit receipts.

The arithmetic for a DFEB valuation is not overly challenging. What is challenging is developing sufficiently accurate inputs to make the DFEB calculation meaningful. While the clean mathematical calculations of a DFEB analysis can convey an aura of precision, the quality of the analysis is entirely dependent on the quality of the inputs that are used in the calculation.[2] If the inputs are substantially wrong, the answer that comes from the DFEB analysis will be substantially wrong (see Figure 6.4).

The quality of the projected net economic benefits is particularly important because those projections tend to have a greater mathematical effect on the DFEB calculation than the discount rate (see Box 6.3). The uncertainty surrounding the amount and timing of the future economic benefits is a more crucial problem to resolve than whether the discount rate should be a few percentage points higher or lower.[3] If the economic benefit projections are substantially wrong, the DFEB analysis will not provide much useful insight into the value of the patent right.

Unfortunately, predicting the future is an inherently difficult exercise that will always entail a substantial amount of error. Approximating the

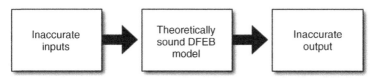

FIGURE 6.4   Garbage In, Garbage Out Principle Applies to DFEB Analyses

BOX 6.3: DFEB ANALYSIS IS MORE SENSITIVE TO INACCURATE BENEFIT PROJECTIONS THAN TO INACCURATE DISCOUNT RATES

The greater sensitivity of a DFEB analysis to inaccurate benefit projections is very easy to demonstrate. The following is a simple DFEB analysis for 5 years of cash flows.

	Future Year					
	1	2	3	4	5	Total
Projected free cash flows	$20.0 million	$30.0 million	$40.0 million	$30.0 million	$20.0 million	
Discount rate	20%	20%	20%	20%	20%	
Present value	$16.7 million	$20.8 million	$23.1 million	$14.5 million	$8.0 million	$83.2 million

What if the free cash flow projections were wrong? Let us assume that the discount rate was correct but that the free cash flow projections overestimated the future results.

- If the actual free cash flow is 10 percent less per year, the present value for the cash flow stream will be reduced by 10 percent to $74.8 million.
- If the actual free cash flow is 20 percent less per year, the present value for the cash flow stream will be reduced by 20 percent to $66.5 million.
- If the actual free cash flow is 30 percent less per year, the present value for the cash flow stream will be reduced by 30 percent to $58.2 million.

What if the discount rate was wrong? Now let us assume that the free cash flow projections were correct, but that the discount rate was too low.

- If the discount rate should have been 22 percent per year (a 10 percent increase), the present value for the cash flow stream will be reduced by 4.4 percent to $79.5 million.

- If the discount rate should have been 24 percent per year (a 20 percent increase), the present value for the cash flow stream will be reduced by 8.5 percent to $76.1 million.
- If the discount rate should have been 26 percent (a 30 percent increase), the present value for the cash flow stream will be reduced by 12.3 percent to $73.0 million.

present value of the future stream of net economic benefits offers the most theoretically sound approach to valuation, but the inherent imprecision involved with developing the inputs means that a DFEB analysis is likely to have a large error rate. This large error rate does not mean that a DFEB analysis has little value, but it does mean that a user of a DFEB analysis needs to understand the limitations of the analysis. A DFEB analysis can provide valuable information, but it cannot be relied on to provide 100 percent accurate answers.

PROJECTING FUTURE NET ECONOMIC BENEFITS

With the inherent real world inaccuracy of the DFEB method in mind, much of the value of a DFEB analysis is the thoughtful discipline that it should require of a valuator to develop the inputs, in particular the economic benefit forecasts. As we explain throughout this book, one of the keys to better patent valuations is recognizing the power of disassembly. Disassembling the matter into its component parts and applying focused logic and analytical rigor to each part can dramatically improve the understanding and assessment of the projections. Once the separate components have been assessed, they need to be reconstituted into a coherent solution that can be evaluated at the aggregate level.

Identifying Sources of Economic Benefits

The starting point for a DFEB analysis is to determine the various types of future economic benefits that a rights holder anticipates (or should anticipate) from the patent rights. The rights holder can pursue a number of different strategies to generate these benefits. Consider the following strategies and economic benefits (many of which are discussed in detail in Chapter 5):

Common strategies to generate direct cash flow from the patent rights

- Practice the patented invention and extract extra profits based on the patent's exclusivity rights (exercise market power).

- License the patent and generate royalties.
- Assign the patent and collect the proceeds from the assignment.
- Allege others have infringed the patent rights and, when successful, generate royalties or settlement payments.
- Securitize the patents and collect the proceeds from the securitization.

Less direct economic benefits that may flow from the patent rights

- Accumulate a portfolio of patents to improve the rights holder's leverage in cross-licensing negotiations and thereby reduce its licensing costs.
- Protect the firm's technological advantage by obtaining preemptive patents.
- Increase the rights holder's goodwill by signaling technological strength to potential investors, employees, customer, and strategic partners.
- Increase the liquidity of the rights holder's technological information.
- Generate marginal cost savings from (1) increased production levels or (2) improved technology.
- Achieve market dominance in the technology beyond the life of the patent.

There are many ways to generate economic benefits from a patent right. These items are only a partial representation.

Scope of the Inquiry   One of the valuator's first tasks is to understand the goal of the intended valuation exercise. Different goals may necessitate the valuator to be more or less expansive in identifying ways the patent rights could generate economic benefits. For example, if the valuation goal is to determine the wisdom of pursuing a specific opportunity—such as whether to bring a patent infringement suit or whether the rights holder should pay the maintenance fee for the patent—it may not be necessary for the valuator to take an expansive look at all the possible ways that the holder can profit from the patent rights. In such cases, the best approach would be for the valuator to focus entirely on the specific opportunity that is being considered.

If, however, the valuation goal is to determine generally the value of the patent rights—such as when deciding whether to purchase or assign the rights—the valuator does need to take an expansive look at the potential sources of benefits that could flow from the patent rights. In addition to identifying the ways in which the holder currently intends to generate economic benefits, the valuator should also seek the other plausible ways that the holder could generate economic benefits from its patent rights. The more expansive look at the potential sources of benefits can also serve as a valuable tool to help firms with their patent management strategies. The exercise forces firms to think strategically about their patents and, in many cases, will help the holder to realize that its current usage of a set of patent rights may not be the highest-valued strategy.

Isolating Market Power   Most of the sources of economic benefits are relatively easy to isolate for forecasting purposes. Once the source is identified, it is not overly challenging to identify how much of the benefit should be attributed to the patent. Take, for example, the proceeds from licensing the patent rights. The net benefit will be the cash inflow of royalty payments minus the related cash outflow.

Some sources of economic benefits, however, can be difficult for the valuator to isolate to run a DFEB analysis. One of the more difficult benefits to isolate is the extent of the market power that can be attributed to the patent rights, as opposed to the use of the invention (see Chapter 1). One method for isolating market power is to define market power as the difference between the current (or projected) profit margin and the normal profit margin for comparable, nonpatented technology.[4] In equation form,

$$\text{market power} = \begin{matrix}\text{current (or projected)} \\ \text{profit margin}\end{matrix} - \begin{matrix}\text{normal profit margin for comparable,} \\ \text{nonpatented technology}\end{matrix}$$

It should be pointed out that the premium pricing advantage that comes from patent protection tends not to be constant. Instead, the pricing advantage is likely to decrease over time as competing technologies enter the market to challenge the rights holder's patented technology. Market power projections that do not include this pricing advantage erosion should be examined with particular care.

Don't Forget the Indirect Benefits   Generally speaking, identifying the sources (whether existing or potential) for direct cash flow streams that may flow from a patent is not very complicated. It may require pointing out an option that was not otherwise obvious to the holder—"Have you thought about licensing your patent to a third party with a China strategy?"—but once a party begins to look for new direct sources of cash flow, they tend to be easy to identify.

We find the bigger challenge to be identifying the indirect benefits. They are harder to find for a few reasons. First, they tend to be less obvious and therefore require more thoughtful inquiry to identify. Second, and maybe of equal importance, the indirect benefits can be much more difficult to quantify than direct cash flow streams. Some valuators may avoid identifying indirect benefits (or ignore those that are identified) because they do not know how to quantify these benefits. Ignoring indirect benefits is a misguided approach that can lead to poor patent decisions. Chapter 4 provides an example of how to incorporate indirect economic benefits into a patent valuation analysis. That example also provides a useful technique for quantifying indirect benefits.

Forecasting the Future Economic Benefits

Once the sources of benefits have been identified, the amount and timing of the benefits from each source need to be forecast. We address both certain and uncertain benefits.

Start with the Certain Benefits   Not all future economic benefits are highly uncertain. In fact, it is common that some of the future revenues and costs that will be associated with a set of patent rights are highly certain and can be calculated with confidence. Revenues and costs which are already locked in by contract (e.g., fixed licensing revenues from existing licensing agreements) or that are predetermined by law (e.g., patent maintenance fees) or convention (e.g., depreciation) can be forecasted with a very high level of certainty.

Addressing the Uncertain Benefits   Much, if not most, of the future economic benefits, however, will not be as easy to project as the certain benefits. It is these less certain future economic benefits that require what we think of as true forecasting.

Revenue-Centric Models   There are a number of ways to build a set of net economic benefit projections. A common method is to forecast revenues for the relevant time period and build the projections down from that top-line figure. Once the projected revenues have been established, the valuator develops the relevant costs for that level of revenue production, which leads to the ultimate net economic benefits. In many cases, the costs are simply calculated as a percentage of the forecasted revenues (see Box 6.4), which causes the revenue forecasts to drive the math for the entire projection exercise.

BOX 6.4: EXAMPLE OF A REVENUE-CENTRIC SET OF PROJECTIONS

When a projection exercise starts, it can feel like an overwhelming challenge to develop all the projections. This five-year set of forecasts shows, however, that only a few inputs may drive the projection model. In this example, units sold and price per unit provide the total revenue, which then drives the rest of the projection model. With the exception of the initial overhead expenses, the rest of the costs and expenses are calculated as a percentage of total revenue.

	Year 1	Year 2	Year 3	Year 4	Year 5
Revenue					
Units sold	0	1,000	5,000	10,000	50,000
Price per unit	$0	$300	$240	$180	$150
Total revenue	$0	$300,000	$1,200,000	$1,800,000	$7,500,000
Manufacturing costs					
As % of sales	0%	90%	75%	65%	55%
Estimated costs	$0	$270,000	$900,000	$1,170,000	$7,500,000
Gross profit	$0	$30,000	$300,000	$630,000	$3,375,000
Standard overhead expenses					
General and administrative at 10% of total revenue	$0	$30,000	$120,000	$180,000	$750,000
Sales at 12% of total revenue	$0	$36,000	$144,000	$216,000	$900,000
Marketing at 3% of total revenue	$0	$9,000	$36,000	$54,000	$225,000
Total standard overhead expenses	$0	$75,000	$300,000	$450,000	$1,875,000
Initial overhead expenses					
Research & development	$100,000	$100,000	$0	$0	$0
Manufacturing engineering	$50,000	$50,000	$0	$0	$0
Regulatory costs	$50,000	$0	$0	$0	$0
Initial promotions	$25,000	$0	$0	$0	$0
Salesperson training	$10,000	$0	$0	$0	$0
Total initial overhead expenses	$235,000	$150,000	$0	$0	$0
Pretax profits	($235,000)	($195,000)	$0	$180,000	$1,500,000

Cost-Centric Models   Although revenue-centric projections tend to be common, projections that focus on cost reductions are also employed. Net economic benefits can stem from revenue growth that exceeds the corresponding costs or they can stem from reducing costs. Commentators Gordon Smith and Russell Parr point out that "a cost saving can be just as profitable as an increase in sales revenue, and many technology innovations produce such an economic benefit."[5] Smith and Parr cite the following examples for how intellectual property (including patent rights) can reduce costs:

- Reduction in the amount of raw materials used.
- Substitution of lower-cost materials without sacrifice of quality or product performance.
- Increases in the amount of production output per unit of labor input.
- Improved quality that reduces product recall.
- Improved production quality that reduces waste or finished product rejects.
- Reduced use of electricity and other utilities.
- Production methods that control the amount of wear and tear on machinery and thereby reduce the amount of maintenance costs and production downtime for repairs.
- Elimination of manufacturing steps and the machinery investment previously used in the eliminated process.
- Reduction or elimination of effluent requiring environmental treatment.[6]

The cost savings approach can be a pure cost savings approach (the patent rights are only projected to reduce costs and have no influence on revenues) or a combined revenue growth and cost savings approach (the patent rights are projected to both influence revenues and reduce costs). With the pure cost savings approach, the valuator will take the existing revenue projections and use the insights about the patent rights to adjust the cost savings during the projection period. With the combined approach, the valuator will need to adjust both the revenue and cost projections based on the characteristics of the patent rights.

Developing the Revenue or Cost Forecasts to Drive the Projection Model   The key to building the projection model is therefore to come up with the revenue forecasts (in the case of a revenue-centric model; see Figure 6.5) or cost forecasts (in the case of a cost-centric model). Numerous methods have been developed to forecast the revenue or cost inputs. These various methods can be conveniently grouped into two broad categories of approaches:

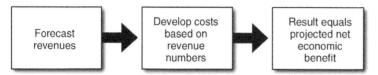

FIGURE 6.5   Converting Revenue Forecasts into Net Economic Benefits

1. Extrapolation of future results from historical trends.
2. Develop projections based on analytical analysis.

Extrapolating Future Performance from Historical Patterns: Past as Prologue   One of the most commonly used techniques for developing revenue or cost forecasts is to extrapolate future performance from historical patterns. In effect, you look behind yourself to see forward (the past is prologue). Securities analysts, who tend to be some of the highest-profile forecasters, provide a classic example of the historical approach. Securities analysts commonly use historical performance to generate forecasts for the public companies they follow. The three most common historical extrapolation methods are (1) model prior period, (2) regression analysis, and (3) model growth patterns.

Model Prior Period   The model prior period approach is as simple as it sounds. The valuator takes a prior operating period that represents a normal (not extraordinary) outcome. The valuator then projects that normal, prior period forward at a reasonable growth rate. Let us assume that a patented product generated $500,000 in sales last year and $400,000 the year before that. It turns out that last year's sales were inflated by a one-time, $90,000 contract. Without that contract, last year's sales for the product would have been $410,000, which is in line with prior sales periods. The valuator could then take $410,000 as the starting point. In this particular case, the valuator believes the patented product's market is fairly mature. The valuator therefore projects a growth rate for the next three years of 3 percent per year, which results in revenue forecasts of $422,300, $434,969, and $448,018 for the next three years.

Regression Analysis   A regression analysis is only slightly more complex than the model prior period approach. With a typical linear regression analysis, historical results are analyzed to determine a venture's historical growth pattern. More specifically, a line of best fit is drawn through the historical data points. The slope of the line of best fit is then used to extend the growth pattern forward. Today, conducting a linear regression analysis is a relatively simple endeavor. Numerous software programs (including

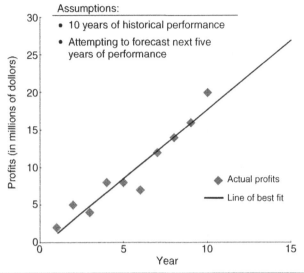

Historical Data (profits in millions of dollars)										
Year	1	2	3	4	5	6	7	8	9	10
Forecasted profits	2	5	4	8	8	7	12	14	16	20

Projected Results Based on Line of Best Fit (profits in millions of dollars)					
Year	11	12	13	14	15
Forecasted profits	20	21	23	25	27

FIGURE 6.6   Linear Regression Analysis

Microsoft Excel) allow the valuator to conduct such analyses. Figure 6.6 provides a linear regression example.

Model Growth Patterns   With early-stage technologies, there are seldom any meaningful historical results from which future results may be extrapolated. In those cases, surrogate data, such as model growth patterns for similar technologies, can be used to develop the future growth performance pattern. Model growth patterns are an outgrowth of product life-cycle theory. Product life-cycle theory was popularized in the 1950s and 1960s and is based on the premise that new products tend to follow a similar four-stage pattern.

1. **Introduction:** The product will generate low sales volume and growth until customers become aware of it.

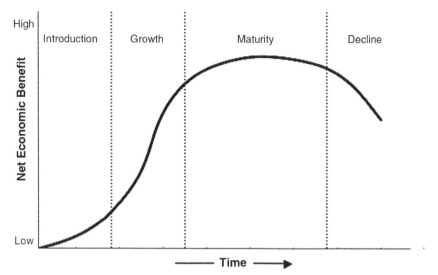

FIGURE 6.7   Classic S-shaped Product Life-Cycle Curve

2. **Growth:** If customers embrace the product, it will experience rapid growth as it moves to fill the demand that is not being met by existing products.
3. **Maturity:** The market for the product will eventually saturate, and the sales curve will plateau.
4. **Decline:** The sales curve will ultimately decline because superior substitutes will be developed to displace the original product.

Instead of developing future forecasts based on the product's particular historical performance, the forecasts are based on the historical performance of comparable products. Figure 6.7 depicts the classic S-shaped product life-cycle curve.

Analysts have developed a number of variations to the classic S-shaped curve. Such variations include the Gompertz model, the Fisher-Pry model, the Pearl-Reed model, and the Bass model. These variations attempt to model more precisely product sales patterns in different settings.[7]

Problems with Historical Forecasting Methods   Extrapolating future performance from historical trends can prove quite challenging for patent rights. We want to focus on two problems in particular:

1. Lack of historical data.
2. Past performance is no guarantee of future results.

The first problem is obvious enough. If the valuator is conducting her valuation before the patent right has established meaningful historical data, there will be little to no useful information for extrapolating future performance. This situation is problematic because it is precisely at these early stages that a meaningful valuation is often most critical. The valuation may be needed to obtain critical early-stage funding, attract talented employees, or provide comfort to potential customers and strategic partners.

The second problem is less obvious, but potentially even more damaging. No matter how often the refrain is repeated—past performance is no guarantee of future results—it is a difficult concept for most people to truly appreciate. Warding against overreliance on simple extrapolation can be particularly difficult when there are many years of historical data from which to draw. The future trend line can appear so clear that it is difficult to appreciate how unreliable that trend may actually be. Consider Table 6.1, which provides annual Standard & Poor's 500 performance since 1951. Using the prior 10 or 20 years as a guide, one would think the next 1, 2, 5, or 10 years of performance would resemble somewhat closely that prior

TABLE 6.1　Ability of Historical Standard & Poor's 500 Returns to Forecast Future Returns

Time Period	Compound Annual Growth Rate	Next Year's Return	Compound Annual Growth Rate		
			Next 2 Years	Next 5 Years	Next 10 Years
1951–1960	16.05%	28.51%	8.02%	13.48%	8.24%
1951–1970	12.08%	14.54%	16.82%	3.24%	8.46%
1961–1970	8.24%				
1961–1980	8.35%	−5.33%	7.13%	14.64%	13.99%
1971–1980	8.46%				
1971–1990	11.19%	30.95%	18.70%	16.74%	17.59%
1981–1990	13.99%				
1981–2000	15.78%	−11.98%	−17.28%	0.45%	9.14%
1991–2000	17.59%				
1991–2010	9.14%	2.05%	N/A	N/A	N/A
2001–2010	1.31%				

N/A = not available.

Source: Moneychimp.

period. Shouldn't all that prior data provide clear guidance for the future? It turns out that the answer is a rather emphatic no. In each case, the next 1, 2, 5, or 10 years of performance are quite different from the prior 10- or 20-year experience.

The extrapolation of future performance from historical trends nevertheless remains alive and well in investment circles. As we explained earlier, securities analysts have a tendency to develop their financial forecasts based on extrapolation of historical trends. One of the most important of those financial forecasts is the current-year earnings of the companies they follow. Academic studies have shown, however, that securities analysts, as a class, are not accurate forecasters of company earnings.[8] In particular, these studies have shown that securities analysts have a tendency to substantially overestimate current-year earnings at the beginning of the year and then adjust them downwards toward actual earnings throughout the year. Analysts also have a tendency to be overoptimistic when projecting earnings growth rates.

None of this discussion is meant to suggest that historical trends are worthless for developing meaningful forecasts. We do, however, want to warn that blind reliance on historical data is not likely to generate sound projections.

DEVELOPING PROJECTIONS FROM ANALYTICAL ANALYSES

The ability of computers and specialized software to aid in the forecasting process, coupled with improved understanding of statistics and probabilities, has turned a number of highly sophisticated analyses into useful and accessible forecasting methods. One of the analytical methods that we find most effective for developing forecasts is the use of decision trees. In this section, we explain how decision trees can be used to develop intelligent forecasts. We also provide a detailed example for how to run such an analysis.

Decision-Tree Analysis

As we explained in Chapter 4, decision trees use the power of disassembly to account for the uncertainty involved with complex problems and to incorporate information from subsequent decisions. In the context of forecasts, decision trees require valuators to (1) disassemble the projection into its component parts, (2) analyze the component parts, and (3) reassemble those parts back into a holistic and usable projection. There are five steps to constructing a decision tree for developing a forecast:

1. Identify the constituent parts of the decision or projection exercise.
2. Specify the subsequent decisions and uncertainties that flow from the initial decision or starting point for the projection.
3. Determine the probabilities for each future uncertainty.
4. Predict the value for each alternative decision and outcome path.
5. Perform the necessary roll-back calculations to reassemble the constituent elements back to a usable projection.

To demonstrate how decision trees can be used to develop projections, let us use a hypothetical. Let us assume that a patent holder (Tech Co.) wants to forecast the direct net economic benefits it can generate from a patent. Tech Co. developed a new technology (the Device) and obtained a patent on the invention.

Step 1: Identify the Constituent Parts of the Decision or Projection Exercise   The first step in constructing a decision tree is to identify the constituent parts of the decision or projection exercise. To keep this example simple, let us assume that Tech Co. has four viable, but conflicting options: (1) license the patent right on an exclusive basis, (2) refrain from licensing the patent right and instead generate revenues by practicing the invention, (3) license the patent right on a nonexclusive basis to licensees and also generate revenues by practicing the invention, or (4) license the patent right on a nonexclusive basis and refrain from practicing the invention itself. See Figure 6.8 for the graphical representation of these decisions.

Because the four alternatives are mutually exclusive, the valuator should do a separate DFEB calculation for each alternative to rank them against one another. Presumably, Tech Co. will want to follow the most profitable strategy. For purposes of this example, we will focus solely on the "refrain from license and practice the invention" option. We begin by identifying exactly what we want to project. Let us assume that Tech Co. will be developing a revenue-centric set of projections, so the two most

FIGURE 6.8   Graphical Representation of Tech Co.'s Initial Choices

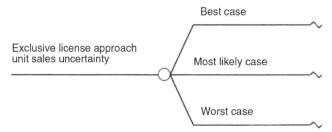

FIGURE 6.9 Insert the Initial Consequences: Best, Worst, and Most Likely Case Scenarios

important variables to forecast are the unit sales and price per unit for the Device. Again to keep this manageable, we will limit our example to projecting Device unit sales based on an expected price per unit. Price per unit, however, could be modeled as an additional uncertainty.

Step 2: Specify the Subsequent Decisions and Uncertainties That Flow from the Initial Decision or Starting Point for the Projection There is considerable uncertainty surrounding future unit sales for the Device with a wide range of potential consequences. A popular approach for making the range of potential consequences manageable is to establish best, worst, and most likely case scenarios for the forecast event. In the Tech Co. example, that means that the valuator will need to determine best, worst, and most likely Device unit sales for year 1 (see Figure 6.9).

Step 3: Determine the Probabilities for Each Future Uncertainty Once the range of outcomes has been developed, probabilities need to be assigned to each potential outcome (see Figure 6.10). It is not uncommon for valuators to struggle to come up with these probabilities. The probabilities provide a

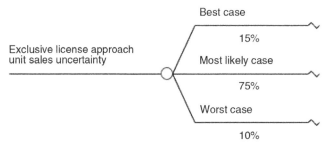

FIGURE 6.10 Determine the Probabilities for the Different Scenarios

precise number for a matter on which the valuator is likely to feel very uncertain. One technique for overcoming that hesitation is to have the valuator simply describe her uncertain feelings. Rather than start with a quantitative probability (e.g., there is a 20 percent chance that the best case scenario will occur), the valuator may wish to start by ascribing qualitative assessments to the different alternatives. Let us assume that the valuator makes the following qualitative assessments:

	Year 1
Best-case scenario	A reach
Most likely case scenario	Very likely
Worst-case scenario	Less likely to occur than the best case

Once the qualitative assessments are made, they tend to be relatively easy to convert into quantitative probabilities. Let us assume that the valuator translates the qualitative assessments as follows:

	Year 1*
Best-case scenario	15%
Most likely case scenario	75%
Worst-case scenario	10%

*The probabilities sum to 100 percent, which indicates that all outcomes have been considered for that year.

Step 4: Predict the Value for Each Alternative Decision and Outcome Path   The next step is to predict the year 1 unit sale forecasts. Let us assume the valuator comes up with the following range of forecasts:

	Net Royalties from Exclusive License Year 1
Best-case scenario	1,200
Most likely case scenario	600
Worst-case scenario	50

Figure 6.11 includes the year 1 unit sales forecasts. It is worth noting that steps 3 and 4 can be done in reverse depending on the preference of the valuator. Some valuators prefer starting with the value forecasts, which helps them to predict probabilities more confidently. Other forecasters prefer starting with the probabilities.

FIGURE 6.11 Insert the Consequences and Predict the Range of Unit Sales

Step 5: Perform the Necessary Rollback Calculations to Reassemble the Constituent Elements Back to a Usable Projection
The final step is to perform the necessary calculations. In decision-tree parlance, the calculation process is referred to as rolling back the tree. What occurs is that the decision-tree program (or an individual with pen and paper, if unassisted by technology) starts with the final projected outcomes and works back to the original inquiry (usually right to left), assessing each decision and uncertainty node along the way. The mathematical method is to take the numerical value in the far right chance node on the branch and multiply it by the probability from that chance node and each earlier chance node on the branch.[9] For our Tech Co. example, we can take the valuator's projected possible outcomes and probabilities and generate a weighted average calculation (or expected value) for year 1 unit sales (see Figure 6.12 and Box 6.5).

Redo Steps 2 through 5 for Each Successive Year
For our example, the valuator determines that year 1 sales are likely to impact year 2 sales. The valuator should then continue her work and generate a table of potential outcomes for year 2 along with probabilities (see Box 6.6).

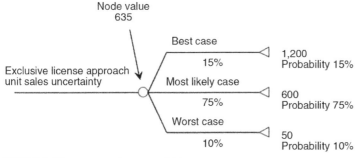

FIGURE 6.12 Projected Units Sold for Year 1

BOX 6.5: PROJECTED UNITS SOLD FOR YEAR 1: WEIGHTED AVERAGE CALCULATION

Best-case scenario	$1{,}200 * 15\% = 180$
Most likely case scenario	$600 * 75\% = 450$
Worst-case scenario	$50 * 10\% = 5$
Weighted average calculation (expected value)	$= 635$

BOX 6.6: PROJECTED UNITS SOLD FOR YEAR 2: POTENTIAL OUTCOMES AND PROBABILITIES

Year 1 Result	Year 2 Result	Projected Units Sold	Probability*
Best-case scenario	Best-case scenario	3,000	20%
Best-case scenario	Most likely case scenario	1,800	60%
Best-case scenario	Worst-case scenario	1,320	20%
			100%
Most likely case scenario	Best-case scenario	1,500	30%
Most likely case scenario	Most likely case scenario	900	50%
Most likely case scenario	Worst-case scenario	700	20%
			100%
Worst-case scenario	Best-case scenario	125	10%
Worst-case scenario	Most likely case scenario	75	60%
Worst-case scenario	Worst-case scenario	40	30%
			100%

*The probabilities sum to 100 percent for each year, which indicates that all outcomes have been considered for that year.

BOX 6.7: PROJECTED UNITS SOLD FOR YEAR 2: WEIGHTED AVERAGE CALCULATION

Year 1 Probability	Year 2 Probability	Combined Probability (Year 2 * Year 1)		Year 2 Projected Units Sold		
15%	20%	3%	*	3,000	=	90
15%	60%	9%	*	1,800	=	162
15%	20%	3%	*	1,320	=	40
75%	30%	22.5%	*	1,500	=	337.5
75%	50%	37.5%	*	900	=	337.5
75%	20%	15%	*	700	=	105
10%	10%	1%	*	125	=	1
10%	60%	6%	*	75	=	5
10%	30%	3%	*	40	=	1
Weighted average calculation (expected value)					=	1,079

With the information from Box 6.7, we can add year 2 to the decision tree (Figure 6.13) and generate a weighted average calculation (or expected value) for year 2.

The valuator would need to continue this exercise for each year in the DFEB model. Our two-year projections already include nine branches. A full analysis of the projected unit sales for the remaining life of the patent will likely require too many branches to easily manage without computer assistance. Although that may seem intimidating at first glance, there are numerous decision-tree software programs that can easily support such full analyses. Once the unit sales projections are completed, the valuator should do a similar analysis to project price per unit and the annual costs associated with generating Device revenues.

Dealing with Information Loss: Conducting Sensitivity Analyses on the Decision-Tree Analysis

Using numbers to represent the probability of future possible outcomes is one of the most important, but also one of the most inexact, parts of any valuation exercise. In each case, the complex realities that go into

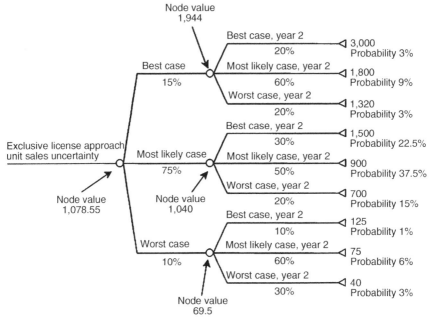

FIGURE 6.13 Projected Units Sold for Years 1 and 2

generating economic benefits from the patent are being distilled into a numerical representation that can be usefully employed in a valuation analysis and later measured for accuracy. This translation of the complexity of future outcomes into a number (or numbers) is a simplification process. The patent's possible future economic outcomes are simplified into a more convenient form for analysis. In any simplification process, some information is lost. The objective is to employ simplification methods that retain as much critical information as possible without the burden of superfluous or distracting information. When the only available simplification methods involve significant information loss, the valuator needs to take that into account when interpreting the valuation results.

One of the benefits of decision-tree analysis is that it forces the valuator to recognize that it is virtually impossible to anticipate all the possible future occurrences that will affect the future economic benefits that a patent right will generate. When using decision-tree analysis to project future economic benefits, the goal should be to logically account for as much future uncertainty as possible. One benefit of the technique is that it encourages, and provides a convenient mechanism for, valuators to collect more information and conduct extra scrutiny that may help to transform ambiguous uncertainty into quantifiable risk.[10]

One way to address the loss of information problem is to conduct a sensitivity analysis. A sensitivity analysis tests how sensitive the outputs in a mathematical model are to variations in the inputs. By breaking down the overall decision into its various component parts, the decision-tree process makes it relatively easy to perform sensitivity analyses by allowing the valuator to test the consequences of changing various inputs. In our earlier Tech Co. example, maybe the valuator is not entirely comfortable with the 15 percent/75 percent/10 percent probability assessment for year 1. The valuator can test how sensitive the projection is to these probability estimates by inserting a range of different probability assessments to see if different probabilities significantly change the outcome.[11] If, for example, a 5 percent/70 percent/25 percent or a 10 percent/70 percent/20 percent set of probability assessments does not significantly change the outcome, the valuator can be relatively confident and move ahead. If the changed inputs significantly alter the outcome, the valuator may wish to scrutinize the matter more carefully to see if more confident probabilities can be developed.

ESTIMATING THE DISCOUNT RATE

Once the net economic benefits have been projected, they need to be discounted back to present value. The standard method is to apply a discount rate to the future cash flows to derive their present value using the well-known formula

$$PV = \frac{FV}{(1 + r)^t}$$

where PV = present value
FV = future value
r = discount rate
t = period into the future

The discount rate is meant to approximate the rate of return that the investing party requires so as to invest in a given venture.

The Five Components of the Discount Rate

A number of methods are used to determine the discount rate. Some are loosely calculated and informal, and some more deliberate and sophisticated. When trying to determine the proper discount rate for a given DFEB calculation, one place to start is to disaggregate the discount rate into its

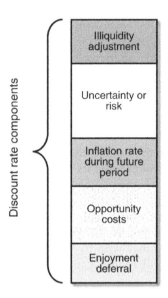

FIGURE 6.14   Five Components
of the Discount Rate

component parts. The discount rate has five component parts, each representing a different element that needs to be considered (see Figure 6.14): (1) enjoyment deferral, (2) opportunity costs, (3) inflation rate during the future period, (4) uncertainty (or risk), and (5) illiquidity adjustment. The preferred method for determining an appropriate discount rate is to assess each of the five components separately and then later recombine these five assessments to derive the rate.

Enjoyment Deferral   Let us begin with the enjoyment deferral component. This component, as the name suggests, attempts to capture the natural tendency of human beings, all other things being equal, to value the present more than the future. This perhaps obvious sentiment is captured in our common culture through statements like "a bird in the hand is worth two in the bush." To help illustrate this point, consider the following choice. You can have $10,000 today or $10,000 a year from now. Assuming no unusual circumstances, the logical choice is $10,000 today; even if we assume that the $10,000 payment a year from now is absolutely guaranteed, there is no inflation and there is no question of liquidity. Why would that be so?

Given a risk-free, inflation-free, totally liquid choice of $10,000 today or $10,000 a year from now, there are two reasons that taking the $10,000 today is the logical choice. Enjoyment deferral is the first reason. Deferring enjoyment produces a cost on the party who is being asked to make the deferral. Even if you bury the $10,000 in your backyard, where it earns no interest and is not being put to any productive use, there is always the potential to dig it up if necessary. This potential is not present if you defer receiving the $10,000. This potential or option has value.

Opportunity Costs   The second component is the cost of lost opportunities. There may be lost opportunities if you select $10,000 in one year. By delaying receiving the $10,000, any benefits that may arise during that one year by using the $10,000 in some productive manner are sacrificed. For example, earning interest from the $10,000 would be sacrificed. Another opportunity could be investments that would be missed or that would require borrowing. To the extent that there are forgone potential earnings or interest, use of the firm's weighted average cost of capital may be a logical rate for this component.

Inflation Rate during the Future Period   The third component represents a conversion for inflation. Consider again the choice between $10,000 today and $10,000 one year from now. Assuming an inflation rate of 4 percent, the $10,000 is worth only $9,600 at the end of the year. If the inflation rate remains constant, the $10,000 would be worth only $8,154 at the end of year 5. To the extent there is inflation, a conversion must be made to adjust the future dollar to account for the intervening inflation. At times, that adjustment may be minimal, but there have been economic periods when inflation has been substantial and required a correspondingly substantial adjustment.

Uncertainty or Risk   The fourth component addresses the uncertainty (or risk) surrounding the future performance of the venture. Projections of net economic benefits are simply that; they are just projections. Will the benefits that are ultimately received be less than anticipated? The uncertainty component is generally the most subjective, in particular for early-stage technologies (see below). Because DFEB calculations are usually limited to a small handful of projected earnings streams, this component is crudely used to represent any variability associated with future risk and uncertainty. For less certain earnings streams, a higher percentage is used for this component. For more certain earnings streams—for example, a known and relatively certain royalty stream from a patent—a much lower percentage would be used.

To the extent that a decision-tree type of valuation method is used to determine the future earnings stream, that analysis may itself have taken into account some (or most) of the uncertainty. If that is the case, uncertainty should constitute a lower percentage of the overall discount rate so as to avoid double-counting uncertainty in the DFEB calculation.

Illiquidity Adjustment The fifth, and final, component of the discount rate seeks to account for the risk that the future earnings may be illiquid or have impaired marketability. The liquidity of an asset refers to the ease with which its owner can convert it into cash. A highly liquid asset is one that has both a ready market for trading and is regularly traded in such volumes that an asset holder wishing to convert the asset into cash can do so quickly and at low transaction costs. An illiquid asset is the inverse. Illiquidity imposes a cost on the asset owner, and this final component seeks to quantify that cost.

The net economic benefits that tend to flow from patent rights tend to include a mix of both liquid and illiquid assets. Royalty and other cash streams tend to be highly liquid assets that may not require any illiquidity adjustment. Other benefits, however, may be highly illiquid and require an illiquidity discount, such as the resale value of the patent, the value of an infringement lawsuit, or increased goodwill by signaling technological strength.

Recombining the Five Components Once the five components have been determined, they should be recombined to determine an appropriate discount. Assume, for example, that the valuator makes the following determinations: enjoyment deferral = 1 percent, opportunity costs = 2 percent, inflation rate during the future period = 4 percent, uncertainty (or risk) = 18 percent, and adjustment for lack of liquidity = 2 percent. In that case, the discount rate would be 27 percent.

Discount Rates for Early-Stage Technologies

For early-stage technologies, the uncertainty (risk) component of the discount rate can be so large that it becomes the overriding element in determining the discount rate. For early-stage technologies, uncertainty surrounds almost all the critical aspects that will go into the patent rights' ability to generate an earnings stream. Consider just a few of the typical questions that tend to surround early-stage technology:

- Will the new technology work?
- Will customers want to use the technology?
- Even if the new technology has been well documented in the lab, how easily (and cost effectively) can it be commercialized?
- Will the firm be capable of both developing and executing a business plan to capitalize on the technology?
- Does the firm have sufficient funds to execute its business plan for the technology?
- How strong are the firm's patent rights?
- How will competing firms react to the new technology?

One of the more prominent sources of funding for earlier-stage technologies is venture capital firms. The modern venture capital industry originated in the United States in the mid-1940s and has since grown into a highly professionalized industry that annually invests multiple tens of billions of dollars around the world, with a particular focus on high-technology start-up companies. As we explained in Chapter 1, when venture capitalists evaluate the investment potential for a start-up, they tend not to separate the value of the individual patent rights from the value of the overall company. A one-, two-, or three-patent-product company will be valued in the aggregate on its ability to generate future net economic benefits. In conducting that valuation, the venture capitalists need to account for the increased risk of investing in earlier-stage technology. They tend to deal with the increased risk by grouping start-up companies into different development stages and favoring return rates (or discount rates) for each stage.[12] Table 6.2 provides an example of a common way to characterize the basic development stages for a start-up company, and Table 6.3 provides a sample range of return rates that a venture capital firm may charge at the various development stages.

TABLE 6.2 Development Stages for Start-up Companies

Development Stage	Description	How Long Venture Capitalists Expect to Hold Investment
Seed stage	The start-up is just getting started and is determining whether the business venture is worth pursuing. The technology is nascent, and a proven prototype has probably not yet been developed.	7 to 10 years
Early stage	The technology has been shown to work in the laboratory setting (and a prototype has likely been built), but the ability to commercialize the technology has not yet been proven. The start-up is probably still at the presales stage.	5 to 7 years
Intermediate stage	The technology is being sold and showing some commercial viability. The rapid sales expansion that characterizes start-ups, however, has not yet taken place.	3 to 5 years
Later (or expansion) stage	The start-up is relatively mature and has shown success at scaling up its business.	1 to 3 years

TABLE 6.3   Sample Rates of Return (ROR) That Venture Capital Firms May
Require

Development Stage	Annual ROR range
Seed stage	60–100+%
Early stage	40–70%
Intermediate stage	30–50%
Later (or expansion) stage	20–35%

Source: Based on a table in Gordon V. Smith and Russell L. Parr, *Intellectual Property: Valuation, Exploitation, and Infringement Damages* (2005), 292.

The venture capital ROR range can be used as guidance on an appropriate discount rate for earlier-stage technology. If the venture capital ROR range is employed, it will probably not be necessary to factor into the overall discount rate separate discounts due to enjoyment deferral, opportunity costs, inflation rate, or illiquidity. All those components are meant to be captured by the venture capital ROR range. In practical terms, the uncertainty component is so large that it overwhelms the mathematical significance of the other components so they are just folded in under the overall risk variable.

A Few Mechanical Considerations

We want to close the discount rate discussion by addressing three questions that frequently come up when running a DFEB analysis:

1. Should a constant discount rate be used to run the DFEB calculation, or should the valuator vary the discount rate by period?
2. Should the discount rate be applied at the end of each year or more frequently?
3. How do different earnings measurements (e.g., free cash flows versus net income versus pretax profits) affect the discount rate analysis?

Constant versus Variable Discount Rate   The constant versus variable discount rate question is asked frequently, and there is no definitive answer to the question. One explanation of the debate with regards to valuing companies is as follows:

> *The argument for varying [the discount rate] is that the investment risk may be greater—or less—later in the projection period than it is at the beginning of the projection period. This is a highly judgmental (and usually quite subjective) matter. Most commonly, analysts use a constant discount rate—reflecting the average amount of investment risk—throughout the projection period.*[13]

We believe that this summation applies equally to patent valuations as it does company valuations.

End-of-Year versus Midyear Discounting Convention   Should the valuator discount the earnings stream each year, or more frequently? The truly accurate answer would be to say that the discount rate should be applied each time that the firm receives a future net economic benefit. It would be unreasonably unwieldy to try to forecast each month or each week that a firm may receive a net economic benefit. As a result, two conventions—end-of-year and midyear discounting conventions—have been developed to make the discount process more manageable.

End-of-Year Discounting Convention   The end-of-year discounting convention assumes that the firm receives its net economic benefits once per year at the end of each year in the forecast. The discount rate is therefore applied at the end of each year in the forecast period. The DFEB formulas that we have been employing up to this point in the chapter have all followed the end-of-year discounting convention:

$$PV = EB_0 + \frac{EB_1}{1 + r_1} + \frac{EB_2}{(1 + r_2)^2} + \frac{EB_3}{(1 + r_3)^3} + \cdots + \frac{EB_n}{(1 + r)^n}$$

Midyear Discounting Convention   The midyear discounting convention assumes that the firm receives its net economic benefits once per year at the middle of each year in the forecast. This midyear assumption tries to approximate an even receipt of net economic benefits throughout the year. Mechanically, the midyear discounting convention requires the valuator to make the following adjustments to the standard DFEB formula:

$$PV = EB_0 + \frac{EB_1}{(1 + r_1)^{0.5}} + \frac{EB_2}{(1 + r_2)^{1.5}} + \frac{EB_3}{(1 + r_3)^{2.5}} + \cdots + \frac{EB_n}{(1 + r)^{n-0.5}}$$

Choosing between the Two Conventions   There is no definitive rule for when to apply one convention versus the other. The valuator should choose the convention that better approximates when net economic benefits will be received in the particular venture that is being analyzed. It should be noted, however, that using the midyear discounting convention will increase the present value calculation (see Box 6.8) because that convention assumes that the net economic benefits are received earlier by the firm.

Matching the Discount Rate to the Specific Earnings Measurement   Related to the discounting conventions issues is the problem of trying to match the discount rate to the specific earnings measurement used in the DFEB calculation.

BOX 6.8: MIDYEAR DISCOUNT CONVENTION RESULTS IN HIGHER PRESENT VALUE CALCULATION

Assumptions
- The patent right used in this example will generate net economic benefits for five years.
- The net economic benefits by future period are $20.0 million (year 1), $30.0 million (year 2), $40.0 million (year 3), $30.0 million (year 4), and $20.0 million (year 5).
- The discount rate is a constant 20 percent.

Present Value Using the End-of-Year Discount Convention

	Future Year					
	1	2	3	4	5	Total
Projected free cash flows	$20.0 million	$30.0 million	$40.0 million	$30.0 million	$20.0 million	
Discount rate using end-of-year discount convention	20%	20%	20%	20%	20%	
Present value	$16.7 million	$20.8 million	$23.1 million	$14.5 million	$8.0 million	$83.2 million

Present Value Using the Midyear Discount Convention

	Future Year					
	1	2	3	4	5	Total
Projected free cash flows	$20.0 million	$30.0 million	$40.0 million	$30.0 million	$20.0 million	
Discount rate using midyear discount convention	20%	20%	20%	20%	20%	
Present value	$18.3 million	$22.8 million	$25.4 million	$15.8 million	$8.8 million	$91.1 million

Most analyses on how to develop discount rates focus on how to develop discount rates for free cash flow because it lends itself perfectly to discount analysis. The purpose of the discount rate is to calculate the present value of the net economic benefits actually received by the firm. Of the earnings measurements that are typically used for a DFEB analysis (see Box 6.1), free cash flow is the only one that actually measures received benefits. The whole point of cash flow measurements is to track the firm's actual cash inflow and outflow. The other earnings measurements—such as net income (after tax), pretax income, and operating profit—do not track benefits that are actually received. Instead, they track benefits that have been earned, but not necessarily received. As a result, these other earnings measurements require higher rates for each component in the discount rate to account for any earned but not yet collected portion of that earnings measurement.

REFERENCES

Baker, Samuel. Aug. 2007. "Economics Interactive Tutorial." University of South Carolina, Arnold School of Public Health, Dept. of Health Services Policy and Management. http://hadm.sph.sc.edu/Courses/Econ/tutorials.html.

Clarkson, Gavin. 2001. "Avoiding Suboptimal Behavior in Intellectual Asset Transactions: Economic and Organizational Perspectives on the Sale of Knowledge." *Harvard Journal of Law and Technology* 14: 711.

Denton, F. Russell, and Paul Heald. 2003. "Random Walks, Non-Cooperative Games, and the Complex Mathematics of Patent Pricing." *Rutgers Law Review* 55: 1175.

Gray, William. 1993. "Inflation and Future Return Expectations." *Financial Analysts Journal* 49: 35.

Layne-Farrar, Anne, and Josh Lerner. Mar. 2006. "Valuing Patents for Licensing: A Practical Survey of the Literature." http://ssrn.com/abstract=1440292.

Matcher, David, David Simel, John Geweke, and John Feussner. 1990, "A Bayesian Method for Evaluating Medical Test Operating Characteristics When Some Patients' Conditions Fail to Be Diagnosed by the Reference Standard." *Medical Decision Making* 10: 102.

Metropolis, Nicolas. 1987. "The Beginning of the Monte Carlo Method." *Los Alamos Science* (Special Issue): 125.

Munari, Federico, and Raffaele Oriani, eds. 2011. *The Economic Valuation of Patents: Methods and Applications.* Cheltenham, UK: Edward Elgar.

Murphy, William J. 2007. "Dealing with Risk and Uncertainty in Intellectual Property Valuation and Exploitation." In *Intellectual Property: Valuation, Exploitation, and Infringement Damages, Cumulative Supplement,* edited by Gordon V. Smith and Russell L. Parr, 40–66. Hoboken, NJ: John Wiley & Sons.

Neil, D. J. 1988. "The Valuation of Intellectual Property." *International Journal of Technology Management* 3: 31.

Pitkethly, Robert. 1997. "The Valuation of Patents: A Review of Patent Valuation Methods with Consideration of Option Based Methods and the Potential for Further Research." Judge Institute, Working Paper WP 21/97.

Poltrorak, Alexander, and Paul Lerner. 2002. *Essentials of Intellectual Property.* New York: John Wiley & Sons.

Pratt, Shannon, Robert Reilly, and Robert Schweihs. 2000. *Valuing a Business: The Analysis and Appraisal of Closely Held Companies,* 4th ed. New York: McGraw-Hill.

Raiffa, Howard. 1968. *Decision Analysis: Introductory Lectures on Choices under Uncertainty.* Reading, MA: Addison-Wesley Publishing.

Schecter, Roger E., and John R. Thomas. 2004. *Principles of Patent Law, Concise Hornbook Series.* St. Paul, MN: West.

Skinner, David. 1999. *Introduction to Decision Analysis: A Practitioner's Guide to Improving Decision Quality.* 2nd ed. Gainesville, FL: Probabilistic Publishing.

Smith, Gordon V., and Russell L. Parr. 2005. *Intellectual Property: Valuation, Exploitation, and Infringement Damages.* Hoboken, NJ: John Wiley & Sons.

Stiroh, Lauren, and Richard Rapp. 1998. "Modern Methods for the Valuation of Intellectual Property." *Practicing Law Institute/Patent* 817: 532.

Yoo, Christopher. 2010. "Product Life Cycle Theory and the Maturation of the Internet." *Northwestern University Law Review* 104: 641.

Zhang, Shidi, Qiuju Huo, Dan Sun, Dongxu Wei, and Sihui Xu. June 25, 2011. "Profit Milestones and Changing Risks and Expected Returns of Venture Capital Projects: An Empirical Exploration Using Comparable Companies." http://ssrn.com/abstract=1814167.

NOTES

1. See, e.g., *Dodge v. Ford Motor Co.*, 170 N.W. 668 (Mich. 1919).
2. Shannon Pratt, Robert Reilly, and Robert Schweihs, *Valuing a Business: The Analysis and Appraisal of Closely Held Companies*, 4th ed. (2000), 154.
3. D.J. Neil, "The Valuation of Intellectual Property," *Int. J. Technology Management* 3 (1988): 31, 35.
4. This formula is adapted from the "royalty rate" formula in Gordon V. Smith. and Russell L. Parr, *Intellectual Property: Valuation, Exploitation, and Infringement Damages* (2005), 201–203.
5. Smith and Parr, *Intellectual Property*, 187.
6. Ibid., 187–188.
7. Ibid., 227–234 provides a detailed discussion of these variations and the mathematics for using such curves.
8. See Vijay Chopra, "Why So Much Error in Analysts' Earnings Forecasts?" *Financial Analysts Journal* (November/December 1998): 35; see also David Dreman and Michael Berry, "Analyst Forecasting Errors and Their Implications for Security Analysis," *Financial Analysts Journal* (May/June 1995): 30; David Dreman, *Contrarian Investment Strategies: The Next Generation* (1998), 91 (updating and reporting Dreman and Berry 1995).
9. In our example, the outcomes are expressed in terms of number of units, but anything that can be expressed as a numerical value can be used.
10. Chapter 7 discusses how to accommodate subsequently acquired information, including through Bayesian analysis, to improve projection accuracy.
11. When sensitivity is truly critical to the analysis, mathematical tools can be applied to help the valuator determine sensitivity. For an example of such mathematical tools, see William J. Murphy, "Dealing with Risk and Uncertainty in Intellectual Property Valuation and Exploitation," in *Intellectual Property: Valuation, Exploitation, and Infringement Damages, Cumulative Supplement,* edited by Gordon V. Smith & Russell L. Parr (2007), 48–50.
12. See e.g., Smith and Parr, *Intellectual Property*, 292.
13. Pratt, Reilly, and Schweihs, *Valuing a Business*, 159.

CHAPTER 7

Advanced Income Methods: Incorporating the Value of Future Decision Opportunities

One limitation of a linear, net present value (NPV) calculation using the discounted future economic benefits (DFEB) method (see Chapter 6) is its inability to capture future flexibility and choices. To better understand the valuation ramifications of failing to capture future flexibility and choices, consider the following example. A company has a promising project under way that may result in a patentable technology for an emerging commercial market. There are a number of uncertainties facing the decision makers, but they can be divided into two major categories:

1. Uncertainties about the viability of the technology.
2. Uncertainties about the emerging commercial market.

Both categories of uncertainties will significantly affect the valuation of a potential patent involving the technology under development. With a traditional DFEB method, valuators tend to use a rather blunt instrument for incorporating this uncertainty into the valuation analysis. The typical means for addressing the uncertainty is to determine and apply a suitably large discount rate to the expected cash flows. What is missing from this analysis, however, is that there are a series of flexible decision opportunities that stretch into the future. These decision opportunities will depend on facts that are not yet known but that will be known at the time each decision will need to be made. For example, the decision to continue investing in technology development a year from now may depend on how attractive the commercial market has become, which is something that is not currently known but will be more certain at the time of the future decision. If the market is hot, a decision to increase investment at that future time can be

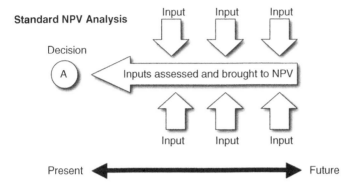

FIGURE 7.1   Standard, Linear NPV Analysis Struggles to Incorporate Future Choices

made. If the market has failed to develop, a decision to scale back or abandon the technology can be made at that later date and substantial costs can be saved.

Having an option to make a more informed choice in the future is extremely valuable. How to incorporate this option value into the valuation exercise can be difficult using a standard, linear NPV methodology (see Figure 7.1).

There have been a few attempts to incorporate the value of future flexibility into patent valuation analysis. The approach that has garnered the most attention has been the real options approach to valuing patents.[1] This approach seeks to include in patent valuation analysis the value associated with the rights holder's options to continue, abandon, or change its decisions regarding a patent. The real options approach has developed from the success of the financial options marketplace and the pioneering work in financial options valuation that was conducted by Fischer Black, Myron Scholes, and Robert Merton in the early 1970s. The resulting Black-Scholes option pricing model is widely used by investors to price financial options.

Broadly speaking, an option is a contractual right (without the obligation) to make some commercial decision. In the world of financial options, that typically means the right (without the obligation) to buy or sell a financial instrument or contract. Having the right, but not the obligation, to make that decision in the future when more information is available has value independent of the underlying asset and option methods seek to calculate that option value. Patents act like options in many ways, which makes the underlying premise of the Black-Scholes options pricing model applicable to patents (see Figure 7.2). There are major obstacles, however, in porting the Black-Scholes options pricing model to patent valuation that we discuss throughout this chapter. The result is that real options theory continues to be more theory than a practical valuation tool.

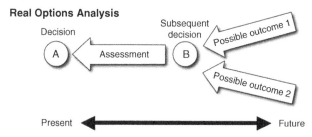

FIGURE 7.2 Real Options Analysis Tries to Incorporate the Option Value of Future Decisions

Although real options theory may have limited practical application, there are other ways to incorporate the value of future decision opportunities into a patent valuation analysis. One of the easiest and most effective ways for doing that is through the use of decision-tree analysis. When used as a valuation tool, decision trees are designed to incorporate more than just the current decision being made (such as what strategy should the firm pursue to monetize its patent). Decision trees can also include future decisions or choices that are expected and that may have an effect on the value of the current decision. Assessments about various possible future paths and probabilities may be captured in a decision tree analysis and valued. One of the more attractive features of the decision-tree method is its accessibility to a wide range of decision makers and decisions. The method can be conducted in an extremely complicated and precise manner or in a simple and rough manner with limited information. Even a simple and rough decision-tree valuation can provide useful insights about future decision opportunities and can be easily changed and expanded over time as new information becomes available.

In this chapter, we

- Describe how options work and how they generate value.
- Explain the concept of real options and why patents are a form of real option.
- Explore the theoretical and practical applicability of real option methods to patents.
- Examine how decision trees can help capture the embedded option value within patents.
- Consider other advanced analytical techniques, such as Monte Carlo analysis and Bayes' theorem and explain how they can be used to help value flexibility and uncertainty.

OPTION CONTRACTS AND THEIR VALUE

It is probably useful to start at a more basic level with a general explanation of options. We will then launch into discussions of real options and real option theory.

What Is an Option Contract?

When valuators refer to options, they are typically talking about option contracts. An option contract is an irrevocable offer to do something—frequently to sell or buy an asset—that becomes contractually binding if the holder of the option exercises the option and accepts the offer. The most common forms of options contracts are so-called calls and puts. A call option is an irrevocable offer by the issuer of the option to sell something to the option holder at a specified price for a specified time. The call option can cover financial instruments, real property, personal property, services, or anything else that can be the subject of a sales contract. Until the option holder decides to exercise the call option, she has no contractual obligation to purchase the subject matter of the call option. The result is that there is a discretionary period during which the option holder can decide whether or not to make the purchase. During that discretionary period, the option issuer is contractually obligated to sell the item or items if the option holder affirmatively decides to make the purchase. A put option is the inverse of a call option. With a put option, the option issuer is making an irrevocable offer to purchase something from the option holder at a specified price for a specified time.

The power of options has long been understood. One of the first recorded uses of an option contract comes from Aristotle in 332 B.C. Aristotle tells the story of an earlier philosopher, Thales of Miletus, who predicted a good olive harvest. Thales, who had little money at his disposal, contracted for the right (but not the obligation) to hire all the olive presses in Miletus and Chios,[2] which he determined would be in high demand should the predicted bumper crop materialize. His prediction was correct, and the relatively small sum he used to purchase the option to the olive presses generated a substantial profit that made Thales quite wealthy.

Generating Value from an Option Contract

A call option generates value for the option holder if the value of the underlying asset increases sufficiently (see Figure 7.3). Let us consider a simple example. Issuer sells 1,000 call options to Holder for $1 per option. The terms of the 1,000 call options are

subject matter	=	each option entitles the holder to purchase one share of Acme common stock
exercise price (or strike price)	=	$15.00 per share
exercise period	=	beginning today and running for five years from the date hereof
current stock price for Acme common stock	=	$8.00

The purchase generates a profit for Holder if Acme's common stock price rises above $16.00 per share. If Acme's stock price rises to $20 per share, for example, Holder could exercise the options and generate a profit of $4 per share:

$20/share	–	$1/share	–	$15/share	=	$4/share
(then current stock price)		(option purchase price)		(exercise price)		(profit per share)

With a put option, value is generated for the option holder if the value of the underlying asset decreases sufficiently.

Having the right, but not the obligation, to make a decision in the future when more information is available has value independent of the underlying decision. In our Acme example, the option holder is able to

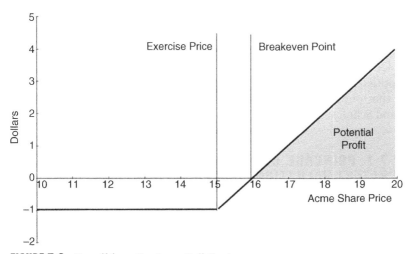

FIGURE 7.3 Payoff from Buying a Call Option

invest a relatively small sum to obtain the contractual right to a profit if certain favorable events occur, in this case having Acme stock price increase. If the stock price increases above the exercise price, the holder can make an informed decision to exercise the options. If the stock price never increases above the exercise price, the holder can make an informed decision not to exercise the options. It is this option value that advanced income methods seek to incorporate into patent valuation analysis.

Black-Scholes Options Pricing Model

For many years, investors bought and sold option contracts in the financial markets without having a particularly accurate or useful valuation technique. Some claimed success in this quest, such as the London broker named Charles Castelli. In 1877, Castelli published a book entitled *The Theory of Options in Stocks and Shares* that "concentrated primarily on the profits that could be made by the purchaser, and discussed only in passing how options were priced, noting that prices tended to rise in periods of what we would now call high volatility."[3] For the next 96 years, a wide variety of interest from many quarters—ranging from academics to adventurers looking for a market edge—struggled to find a reliable method to price options. That all changed in 1973 with the development of the Black-Scholes option pricing model.[4]

The groundwork for the Black-Scholes option pricing model was laid some 70 years earlier in *The Theory of Speculation*, the 1900 doctoral thesis of French mathematician Louis Bachelier, who was under the supervision of Henri Poincaré (who is now probably most famous for his contributions to what would later be known as chaos theory; see Box 7.1). Decades later, Bachelier's work caught the eye of a young MIT professor, Paul Samuelson, who in 1955 wrote a paper entitled *Brownian Motion in the Stock Market*. A year later, the doctoral thesis of A. James Boness at the University of Chicago entitled *A Theory and Measurement of Stock Option Value* put forth a model that anticipated some of the concepts found in the later work of Black and Scholes.

BOX 7.1: POINCARÉ, CHAOS THEORY, AND PATENT VALUATION

Given Poincaré's importance to the development of chaos theory and his contribution to what would latter evolve into real options theory, it is useful to remember chaos theory's lesson about increasingly interconnected and sufficiently complex and adaptive systems. Any predictive models examining complex and adaptive systems will ultimately be subject to initial condition sensitivity (commonly known as the butterfly effect). Will the increasingly complex patent valuation models meet the same fate as efforts to model the weather or the economy with ever more complicated models that include increasing numbers of interrelated inputs? Will we hit the limits of chaos theory—particularly when the models are needed most—during times of great volatility and uncertainty? Perhaps such a phase will eventually follow the application of real option theory to patent valuation, a phase where the insights of chaos theory will need to be embraced and incorporated into patent valuation models.

How to value these financial option contracts properly confounded analysts until 1973, when Fischer Black and Myron Scholes published a paper describing a method that has become widely known as the Black-Scholes option pricing model. There are five primary inputs that affect the value of a financial option contract to purchase stock:

1. $S =$ current price of the underlying stock.
2. $K =$ exercise price of the option (commonly referred to as the strike price).
3. $T =$ time until option expires.
4. $r =$ an estimate of the risk-free interest rate now and in the near future.
5. $v =$ an estimate of the volatility of the underlying stock's price.

The Black-Scholes formula then calculates the price for a stock call option contract as follows:

$$C = SN(d_1) - Ke^{(-rT)}N(d_2)$$

where $C =$ price of the call option
$N =$ cumulative standard normal distribution
$e =$ exponential function
$$d_1 = \frac{\ln(S/K) + (r + v^2/2)T}{v\sqrt{T}}$$
$$d_2 = d_1 - v\sqrt{T}$$

A comparable equation can be used to price a stock put option contact.
One of the key insights of the Black-Scholes options pricing model is that increased volatility in the value of the underlying asset increases the value of

the option. In hindsight, this observation may appear obvious, but its implication for patents is profound. If a patent can be characterized as possessing a type of option to partake in some future opportunity, the patent's embedded option value increases as the volatility in the underlying opportunity increases.

The greatest contribution of the Black-Scholes options pricing model was its ability to remove the difficult-to-measure risk element from the valuation calculation through the use of dynamic hedging.[5] With risk removed from the calculation, the first four components for the model were readily observable and the fifth component (future volatility) could be estimated. Because future volatility is by definition unknown, historical volatility is often used as an estimate or surrogate measure (see Chapter 8 for a discussion of the utility of surrogate measures).

The original option pricing model that Black and Scholes described was subsequently improved by the contributions of Robert Merton and Jonathan Ingerson to eliminate the original model's assumptions of no dividends, no taxes or transaction costs, and constant interest rates. The final result was an extremely robust valuation tool that was remarkably accurate when compared against long-term historical data. In 1997, Scholes and Merton won the Nobel Prize in economics for a new method to determine the value of derivatives. Black had died two years before and was therefore not eligible for the award.

REAL OPTIONS

A *real* option is an investment opportunity in which the option (but not the obligation) to make a future decision (such as buying or selling an asset) is embedded in the opportunity rather than contained in a separate financial contract. A real option exists when the investment opportunity has an unclear future, but also provides the decision maker with flexibility to defer decisions about that opportunity to a later date when more information may be available. A real-world example of a real option could be a package delivery business purchasing a fleet of flexible-fuel vehicles that run on either gasoline or a gasoline blend of up to 85 percent ethanol (E85).[6] That fleet would provide the business with a real option for purchasing either regular gasoline or a gasoline blend based on actual fuel prices in the future (see Figure 7.4). In addition, just like a financial option, the fleet's real option on fuel purchases would expire when the vehicles expire.

Call Options and Put Options

Real options are comparable to financial option contracts and include both real call options and real put options. With a real call option, the owner of

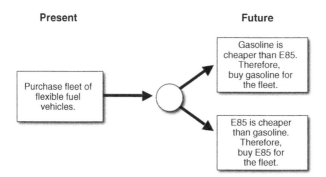

FIGURE 7.4   Example of a Real Option for Purchasing Fuel

the investment opportunity will have the option to make further investments in the opportunity. With a real put option, the owner of the opportunity will have the option to sell the opportunity.

Valuing Real Options with Financial Option Contract Methods

Having the right, but not the obligation, to make decisions about an investment opportunity in the future when more information is available has value independent of the underlying opportunity. Developing an accurate value for an opportunity that includes a real option therefore requires accounting for that option value. Lenos Trigeorgis and Scott Mason refer to this more accurate value as "extended NPV" and define it as[7]

$$\text{extended NPV} = \begin{array}{c} \text{basic NPV for} \\ \text{the opportunity} \end{array} + \begin{array}{c} \text{option values for the real options} \\ \text{that are embedded in the opportunity} \end{array}$$

To develop the extended NPV, the valuator could run a traditional DFEB analysis for the opportunity and then include the option values for the real options that are embedded in the opportunity. To determine these option values, the valuator will need to identify each real option and then, ideally, run some type of appropriate option pricing method to value the option. When a real option can be properly analogized to a financial option contract, the possibility exists that financial option contract valuation methods can be adapted for such real options. A starting point for running that analogy analysis is to compare the Black-Scholes inputs for valuing a call option to the specific real option. Box 7.2 provides a comparison of the five basic Black-Sholes inputs to a real option.

BOX 7.2: COMPARING A STOCK CALL OPTION TO A REAL OPTION

Information about Call Option Needed to Run a Black-Scholes Calculation	Real Option
1. Current price of the underlying stock	NPV of the cash flow that will result from the future decision
2. Exercise price of the option	Capital investment required to pursue the future decision
3. Time until option expires	Time when the future decision will expire (length of time the future decision can be deferred)
4. Estimate of the risk-free interest rate now and in the near future	Same
5. Estimate of the volatility of the underlying stock's price	Estimate of the volatility of the cash flow that will result from the future decision

This box is based on, and borrows liberally from, a table prepared by Raffaele Orinani and Luigi Sereno, "Advanced Valuation Methods: The Real Options Approach" in *The Economic Valuation of Patents: Methods and Applications*, ed. Federico Munari and Raffaele Oriani (2011), 143.

As Box 7.2 demonstrates, the Black-Scholes inputs can be matched to comparable real option information. The difficulty, however, is in coming up with sufficiently accurate estimates for those real option inputs to run a meaningful calculation. One of the strengths of the Black-Scholes method for financial options contracts is the relative ease with which the necessary inputs can be gathered and the reliability of that information (see Box 7.3). When it comes to real options, such convenient and reliable sources for the necessary information inputs may not exist.

VALUING PATENTS USING OPTION-PRICING INSIGHTS

Patents are embedded with real options. Researchers have modeled a number of different real options that exist within a patent.[8] Each of these real options, at its core, is an option to wait to make a decision until more

BOX 7.3: INFORMATION SOURCES FOR THE BLACK-SCHOLES INPUTS

Black-Scholes Inputs	Information Source
1. Current price of the underlying stock	Publicly disclosed stock market prices, which benefit from the market's wisdom
2. Exercise price of the option	Strike price will be listed in the financial contract
3. Time until option expires	Expiration date will be listed in the financial contract
4. Estimate of the risk-free interest rate now and in the near future	The Treasury bill rate is frequently used
5. Estimate of the volatility of the underlying stock's price	There are many techniques for estimating volatility, but they all depend on historic and recent trades in the specific stock, comparable stock, and the stock market in general

information becomes available. For valuation purposes, the two most relevant subcategories of this option to wait are the option to wait to use the patent (option to use) and the option to wait to enforce the patent's exclusive rights (option to exclude).

Patents and Real Options

If we disassemble real options into their core qualities, there are three:

1. The net economic benefits that may flow from the opportunity are uncertain and depend in part on future decisions by the option holder.
2. The current uncertainty that surrounds those future decisions decreases over time as more information becomes available.
3. The opportunity provides the decision maker with flexibility to defer decisions to a later date.

Those same three qualities are embedded in any given patent:

1. The net economic benefits that may flow from the patent are uncertain and depend in part on future decisions by the patent holder.

2. The current uncertainty that surrounds those future decisions decreases over time as more information becomes available.
3. The patent's right to exclude provides the patent holder with the ability to defer investment decisions about the patent until a later date.

Option to Use The ability to defer decisions about how to use the patented technology can generate significant value for a patent holder. To illustrate this point, consider the following example.[9] A firm (Acme) holds a patent with 17 years of remaining protection. Acme believes that commercializing the patented invention has a 30 percent chance of generating $1 million in annual profits for the life of the patent and a 70 percent chance of generating no profits. Acme will need to invest $4 million to pursue this opportunity. Based on these assumptions, Acme should not pursue the opportunity. The expected net benefits from the project (before discounting to present value) would be 30 percent of $17 million, or $5.1 million. Once those benefits are discounted back to present value (assume a 10 percent discount rate), the opportunity would generate an NPV of roughly $2.4 million, which would not justify the capital investment.

Just because the invention is not worth practicing today, however, does not mean that it will not be worth practicing in the future. Based on these facts, the firm could simply wait to commercialize the invention and continue to gather information about the commercialization opportunity. Let us assume that the firm continues to gather information and after one year, the uncertainty about the opportunity greatly decreases. Because the firm has waited one year, the potential profits from the opportunity will have decreased to $16 million (16 years times $1 million), but let us assume that the probability of success has increased to 80 percent. At this point, the opportunity looks very attractive for the firm as the expected net benefits from the project (before discounting to present value) would be 80 percent of $16 million, or $12.8 million. With a 10 percent discount rate, that would translate to an NPV for the commercialization opportunity of roughly $6.2 million, which justifies the $4 million capital investment. By allowing the firm to defer the commercialization decision for a year, the patent's embedded real option allows the net economic value of the commercialization opportunity to increase from $0 to $2.2 million.

This option to wait to use the patent can apply to any number of patent-related decisions. Licensing decisions, assignment decisions, decisions to market the patented technology in foreign markets, decisions to develop improvements to the invention, and decisions to renew the patent are all examples of future use decisions that may benefit from deferral. When analogizing a patent's option to use to financial option contracts, one can think of the option to use as a call option. The patent holder has the option to purchase the future opportunity.

Option to Exclude   The most basic right that comes with a patent is the right to exclude others from "making, using, offering for sale, or selling the invention."[10] To enforce this right, the patent holder can use the legal system to enjoin infringing activity and sue for damages caused prior to the injunction (see Chapter 11). Not surprisingly, some refer to this option to exclude as an "option to sue."[11] The right to exclude exists regardless of whether the patent holder has a meaningful right to use the invention, such as when an effective blocking patent exists (see Chapter 5).

The ability to defer a decision on whether to exercise this right to exclude another from practicing an invention can have value that can be captured under option analysis. The right to exclude can be modeled as the net present value of the cash flows that come from others *not* practicing the invention. Those cash flows may come, for example, from having greater pricing power on a patented product, from encouraging another party to license the patented technology or from potential patent damages awards. If the present value of exercising the right to exclude exceeds the cost of pursuing the exclusion, it makes economic sense to exercise the embedded option and pursue the exclusion. In some cases, the option to exclude has more value than the option to use.

The option to exclude can be modeled as a put option.[12] The patent holder has the option to sell cash flow from the patented technology in exchange for obtaining a damages award against an infringer (see Chapter 11).

Trying to Adapt Black-Scholes to Patents

Recognizing that real options are embedded within patents is one thing, coming up with a reasonable value for them is altogether another matter. One of the more popular attempts to value these embedded real options is by adapting the Black-Scholes options pricing model to the patent context. Although the Black-Scholes options pricing model has proven to be a highly effective valuation tool for securities-based option contracts, translating this success to patent assets remains largely theoretical. The reason that Black-Scholes is not widely used in the patent context is an input problem. The methodology of Black-Scholes is fine, but if you cannot generate sufficiently accurate inputs to feed the equation, the methodology loses much of its usefulness.

As we explained earlier in this chapter, a strength of the Black-Scholes method for financial options contracts is the relative ease with which the necessary inputs can be gathered and the reliability of that information.

When it comes to valuing the real options embedded within a patent, such convenient and reliable sources for the necessary information inputs may not exist. For example, one of the key inputs in the Black-Scholes options pricing model is the volatility of the underlying stock's price. Devising a reliable measure of this volatility for the Black-Scholes options pricing model (using an algorithm developed for real-time ballistic missile navigation corrections) was an inspired insight. In the patent context, the corresponding input would be the volatility of the cash flow that results from the future decision. Currently, there is nothing that constitutes a usable measurement for the cash flow volatility associated with an individual patent. In the financial options market, finding a consistently reliable measurement that anyone could extract from available data was a breakthrough discovery of the Black-Scholes options pricing model that eventually led to a Nobel Prize in economics. Finding a measurement of corresponding functionality for patents would be no less momentous.

USING DECISION TREES TO INCORPORATE THE VALUE OF A PATENT'S FUTURE DECISION OPPORTUNITIES

The benefit of the real options approach to valuing assets is that it requires the valuator to take account of the value of future decision opportunities that are embedded within the patent. Although the ability to practically use real options analysis has not yet caught up with its theoretical soundness, other techniques can be used to incorporate the value of these future decision opportunities. Decision trees (see Chapter 4) are one such technique. When used as a valuation tool, decision trees are designed to incorporate more than just the current decision being made. Decision trees can also include future decisions or choices that are expected and that may have an effect on the value of the current decision. Assessments about various possible future paths and probabilities may be captured in a decision-tree analysis and valued.

Decision-tree analysis and real options analysis each try to incorporate the value of future decision opportunities, but each uses a different technique. With decision-tree methods, the value of future decision opportunities is measured by requiring the user to make a current assessment of the probabilities associated with the future uncertainties and assess the future decision nodes in accordance with the currently delineated probabilities and expected consequences. Under the real options approach, this future uncertainty is incorporated into the valuation by a technique that attempts to value the flexibility directly.

For some who were introduced to decision trees in the past, the technique may have appeared too complicated for everyday use. Fortunately, that is no longer the case. Just as software programs such as Excel have made spreadsheet construction and assessment easier, so too has the emergence of robust decision-tree software made decision trees more readily accessible to decision makers. In addition, decision trees provide the decision maker with a relatively understandable framework to guide the disassembly of a complex evaluation task into discreet elements that will ultimately be presented in a comprehensible and easy to interpret visual and numerical format.

We do not want to create the impression that decision trees are problem free. They are not. As one can readily appreciate, decision-tree analysis is a powerful tool, but even a small amount of experimentation with the software and the technique exposes a potential problem; the decision tree quickly becomes unwieldy with so many uncertainty, decision, and terminal nodes that it becomes difficult to construct and evaluate. The tree becomes too "bushy" to manage. Fortunately, there are additional analytical techniques, and software incorporating them, that offer a solution to this problem. Analytical techniques that would not have been realistically useful without some method of automation are now available and can help the decision maker prune the decision-tree construction task into a more manageable affair. In this section, we focus on three of these analytical techniques:

1. The Monte Carlo technique to model thousands of possible future scenarios.
2. The inclusion of Markov chains to link various attributes in a manner that considers relational or transitional probabilities.
3. Incorporating new information through the use of Bayes' theorem and other approaches.

Monte Carlo Technique

When the future has a large number of random configurations, developing decision-tree models can be unwieldy and unduly complex. Monte Carlo techniques (see Box 7.4) can be an effective tool to help valuators to manage such situations. The Monte Carlo method uses random numbers and probability statistics to investigate complex systems. The technique uses statistical sampling to calculate approximate solutions to quantitative problems.

An illustrative example may be helpful. Suppose that a company has developed a patentable technology for pharmaceutical production. In

BOX 7.4: ORIGIN OF THE MODERN MONTE CARLO TECHNIQUE

Stanislaw Ulam, a Polish-born mathematician who worked for John von Neumann on the Manhattan Project in 1944 and Edward Teller on the hydrogen bomb in 1951, is credited with inventing the modern Monte Carlo technique in 1946. The first paper published using the term was written by Nicolas Metropolis and Ulam in 1949, with Metropolis reportedly coining the term.

Ulam was not the first person to recognize that statistical sampling could assist in solving quantitative problems, but he did recognize that the development of computers during World War II could make the process less difficult. To this end, he developed the statistical sampling computer algorithms.

modeling the future, assume that four sequential variables have been identified that are relevant to the value of the technology:

1. The breadth of the patent claims allowed by the Patent Office.
2. The scalability of the technology from prototype to full production.
3. The size of the market for the technology.
4. The regulatory approval of the technology by the appropriate governmental bodies.

Each of these four uncertainties could be assigned a finite number of potential outcomes, and a probability could be assigned to each. A decision tree using this approach, however, would grow limbs quickly as more potential outcomes are added and would rapidly become cumbersome. One solution is to use a Monte Carlo simulation technique. Instead of multiple, individual outcome branches that would be evaluated at each uncertainty node, an appropriate distribution of the possible outcomes at that node would be used. An outcome for each of the four uncertainties would be selected on a probability-weighted basis, which would constitute one run of the simulation. Thousands of runs would be calculated in this manner, each selecting an individual potential future scenario with differing assumptions regarding the outcomes of uncertain events. The runs are subsequently combined and are usually presented in the form of a frequency distribution (see Figure 7.5) to paint a more complete picture than would be possible if a single (even if most likely) future was used.

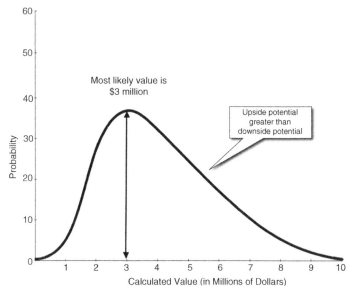

FIGURE 7.5 Sample Monte Carlo Frequency Distribution Result

Without the aid of computers, the use of the Monte Carlo technique would be impractical. Low-cost computing power and relatively easy-to-use software programs, however, have made this a widely available tool to assist decision makers. As with the DFEB analysis, the accuracy of the Monte Carlo technique is limited by the accuracy of the probabilities assigned and any estimate of the distribution of the potential scenarios.[13]

Information That May Be Derived from Monte Carlo Visuals One of the many advantages of the Monte Carlo technique is that it preserves and presents information to the valuator in a clear, visual way that might otherwise be lost. At various input points in the tree, the value for that particular node is selected from expected distributions according to the associated probabilities. In any tree, innumerable nodes can be assessed using the Monte Carlo technique, with the resulting value passed on to the next nodes as an input. Running the simulations thousands of times will result in distributions containing thousands of points that can be graphically displayed to the valuator. Consider, for example, the curve in Figure 7.6. This curve represents the distribution curve for the potential outcome from two different investment opportunities: opportunity A and opportunity B. Each investment opportunity presents a most likely value of $3 million. Does that mean that both opportunities are roughly the same? Absolutely not. When one looks at the kurtosis (the peakedness or flatness) and the skewness

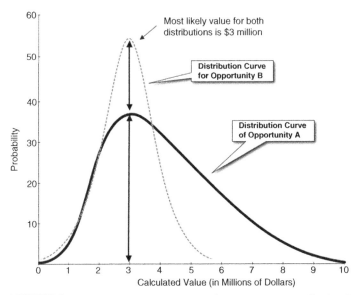

FIGURE 7.6   Comparing Two Monte Carlo Frequency Distribution Results

(asymmetry around the media) of the curves, the difference between the two opportunities should be obvious. Opportunity A, with its relatively flat shape and definite skew to the right, represents a much different value proposition than distribution B, with its normal bell curve centered on the $3 million mean value.

- Opportunity A has greater volatility, but the volatility in this case is primarily on the good side. Opportunity A provides a great deal of probable upside potential without any meaningful increase in downside risk.
- Opportunity B has very little volatility and provides a good deal of certainty that the outcome will be $3 million or very close to that number.

This extra information derived from the kurtosis and skew of the two opportunities may be lost to the valuator if not presented in this form.

Monte Carlo and Nonnormal Data Distributions   It appears that the distribution of patent valuations is not a normal, or Gaussian, distribution. Instead, patent valuations appear to follow either a power-law or log normal distribution. At one end of the spectrum is a large number of patents that have modest to nonexistent economic value. At the other end of the spectrum is a much smaller number of patents of enormous value; patents that allow the owner to control multibillion dollar markets. This nonnormal (or non-Gaussian) distribution is also undoubtedly true for many of the input elements that go into patent valuations.

A famous Italian economist, Vilfredo Pareto, is credited with discovering and discussing the first power law in 1897 when examining wealth distribution among individuals (it is now often called a Pareto or Bradford distribution). In the subsequent hundred years, power-law distributions have been found to be relatively common in the world of nature, but power-law explanations for data distributions in other fields has been increasing.[14] Log-normal distributions have an equally long history, with one of the earliest being the data associated with fruit fly inheritance uncovered in 1914. Both have similar attributes that can be important. The fascination with power-law and log-normal distributions in popular literature has increased of late, where the phenomenon is often referred to by the name of one of their most notable characteristics, the long or fat tail.

As a consequence, it is unlikely that extrapolations from statistical descriptions assuming a normal or Gaussian distribution will be a good fit with the real-world data that conform more closely to another type of distribution. A savvy decision maker will want to incorporate such insights into the valuation assessment. The good news is that most Monte Carlo simulations in decision-tree software permit the user to select a distribution that is different from what is usually the default (a normal or Gaussian distribution). This improved consideration of the probabilities surrounding unlikely, but not impossible, big consequence outcomes (what some call black swans) will help expose lurking surprises, both pleasant and unpleasant.

Use of Markov Chains in Patent Valuation

In 1909 the Russian mathematician Andrei Markov disclosed a theory of stochastic processes—processes involving the operation of chance—now commonly known as Markov chains. Although the use of decision trees to assist in a complex assessment of patent value might be attractive in the abstract, the practical limitations of determining all the various decision points and outcomes so as to construct the tree can be overwhelming. In situations where event timing is important, where critical events may happen more than once, or where risk is continuous over time, the use of techniques based on Markov chains can be helpful in making an otherwise immense assessment task more manageable.

Technically, a Markov chain consists of a sequence of chance events that are independent of one another, but where information regarding the probabilities of a particular event in the sequence depends on the value of a prior event in the sequence. In a process that can be described by a Markov chain, there are various states, and the process evolves from state to state at random. The evolution is said to be memoryless because the probability of moving from one state in the process to another is determined solely by the current state. In a Markov chain, the future is conditionally independent of the past. A common child's board game such as Chutes and Ladders, where the player's position is changed at each turn when a dice is thrown to determine a random number of steps to be taken from the current position, is an example of a type of Markov chain.

Another more complicated example is the famous random walk theory for stock prices from financial research. This theory, made popular by Princeton University economist Burton Malkiel in his book, *A Random Walk Down Wall Street*, claims that stock prices are not predictable but instead fluctuate randomly, which means that past movements or trends in the price of a stock cannot be used to predict its future movement. Even if the particular direction a stock price might take the next day is unpredictably random, the price (whether up, down, or unchanged) is more likely to be in the vicinity of the current price than some distant point, and this relationship can be expressed as a probability. Just as a wandering drunk may randomly stagger down the sidewalk, the location of the drunk's next step (although random) is related to the drunk's current position. In other words, it is more likely that the drunk's next location will be in the vicinity of the drunk's current position than some other random location on the sidewalk.

One way that a Markov Chain can be used by the patent decision maker to help model the future as part of a valuation exercise can be illustrated by the following example. Let us suppose that a firm (Acme) has just purchased a portfolio of 300 patents from a bankrupt firm (Beta). We can classify any patent in that portfolio into three distinct categories: (1) valid, (2) under attack or weakening, and (3) invalid. Acme's initial assessment is that 249 of the patents are valid, 51 are under attack or weakening, and none are currently in the invalid category. As the future unfolds, Acme knows that this particular mix will change. Each year, the term of some of the valid patents will move closer to expiration, others will be legally challenged, and others will become doubtful commercially. These patents will then pass into the under attack or weakening category. Of those in this second category, some will be able to withstand the challenges and return to the valid category, and some will not and will end up in the invalid category. Let's further assume that past experience, expert analysis, or a best-guess estimate informs Acme that 20 percent of the patents currently listed as valid will be challenged either by marketplace dynamics, legal attack, or normal term expiration and will move into the under attack or weakening category each year. Next, Acme has estimated that of the patents under attack or weakening 75 percent will withstand the challenges and return to the valid category, 15 percent will remain in the under attack or weakening category another year, and the remaining 10 percent will move into the invalid category during the same time frame. Once in the invalid category, it is assumed that there is no escape. The decision makers at Acme want to evaluate this patent portfolio over the next 10 years and want to include this information in the assessment.

Although it is possible to construct an elaborate decision tree that stretches out into the future that incorporates these uncertainties, we can use a Markov chain to help to model this set of related probability assessments more easily. Without the Markov chain and Markov matrix, a decision tree that attempted to model the evolution of our simple three-category patent portfolio in the conventional way would generate 3 branches for the first time period, 6 branches for the second period, 12 branches for the third period, 24 branches for the fourth period, and so on. It is easy to see that using the conventional decision tree approach without Markov chains would quickly become rather complex to use and very resource intensive.

Like the Monte Carlo technique discussed earlier, the use of a Markov chain with its predetermined states and transitional probabilities can greatly simplify the valuation or decision-making exercise. In most decision-tree software programs, the two techniques can be combined so that the runs in the Monte Carlo simulation can process a predefined Markov chain with its specified probabilities at a particular point in the process. By using these techniques, information estimates regarding the evolution of the patent categories can be readily included.

Adjusting Input Estimates Over Time: Incorporating New Information

When buying or selling a patent right or valuing patent rights for an infringement lawsuit, valuation is frequently a one-time exercise. If you are using the valuation exercise to improve intellectual property management, however, you should keep in mind the need to revisit your economic benefit projections and your discount rate estimates and adjust them over time as new information becomes available.

Simplest Approach   We will discuss below Bayes' theorem and its ability to improve probability analysis with new information. Bayes' theorem is a powerful tool, but because it can also be a bit intimidating to use for less mathematically inclined individuals, we want to start by providing the simplest approach to adjusting input estimates over time.

As we explained in Chapter 6, much of the value of a DFEB analysis is the thoughtful discipline that goes into the exercise. To conduct a DFEB analysis, the valuator needs to develop a detailed set of inputs. That exercise provides the firm with an explicit record of the assumptions that guided its ultimate decision. Let us use an example to illustrate the concept. Assume that a firm decided to exclusively practice its patented invention because the DFEB analysis projected $5 million of present-value pretax profits over the next seven years. That firm can revisit that decision during the seven-year period and evaluate the quality of the decision and determine what went right and what went wrong. Some probable areas of inquiry would be the following:

- Are unit sales meeting expectations?
- Is the price per unit meeting expectations?
- If the price per unit is not meeting expectations, is it because the patent is not providing the market power that was forecasted?
- If the patent is not providing the market power that was forecasted, what went wrong?

Because each of the questions started as a numerical projection and can be addressed, at least partially, with a numerical answer, the firm can concretely evaluate its original decision-making process and make adjustments for future, similar decisions. In addition, the firm can incorporate this new information to determine whether it should change course on its original decision. Firms miss out on a significant opportunity to improve their performance when they fail to take the time to reevaluate these types of decisions that lend themselves so perfectly to such analysis.

Bayesian Approach   There are many situations where new information or evidence is obtained and has to be combined with existing knowledge, beliefs, or estimates. Unfortunately, the average human mind is notoriously poor at performing this task correctly.[15] In these circumstances, the 300-year-old Bayes' theorem can make the difference between reasonable judgment and costly error. The widely used Bayes' theorem (or Bayes' revision) makes use of prior estimates of probability to revise assessments that an uncertain event will occur based on information obtained after the original probability estimates are made. Mathematically, Bayes' theorem is expressed as

$$P(B) \times P(A\backslash B) = P(A) \times P(B\backslash A) \quad \text{or} \quad P(A\backslash B) = \frac{P(A) \times P(B\backslash A)}{P(A)}$$

where $P(A) =$ probability of A
         $P(B) =$ probability of B
   $P(A\backslash B) =$ probability of A given B
   $P(B\backslash A) =$ probability of B given A

Thus, the probability of *B* times the probability of *A* given *B* is equal to the probability of *A* multiplied by the probability of *B* given *A*.

Named after eighteenth-century amateur mathematician Reverend Thomas Bayes, this technique has found its way into a variety of modern decision-making situations, from the algorithms in spam filters trying to determine if a particular email is legitimate or not,[16] to the interpretation of medical testing information.[17] It can also be used to help the decision maker to properly incorporate new information that may be obtained and assessed in light of prior uncertainty evidence. As a consequence, this powerful analytical tool is often included in commercially available decision-tree software.

The classic decision used to illustrate Bayes' theorem is derived from the television game show *Let's Make a Deal*. In this game, the contestant is shown three doors on stage, and hidden behind one is a fabulous prize. The other two doors hide objects of lesser value. The contestant selects one of the doors. Rather than open the selected door, the show's host opens one of the two doors not selected to reveal one of the two lesser objects. The host then asks the contestant if he or she would like to change his or her original selection to the other remaining door. Should the contestant make the switch? In other words, when presented with new information (the prize is not behind the door that the host has revealed), is the decision to switch to the other unopened door more valuable (a choice with a higher chance of exposing the sought-after prize) than a decision to stay with the original door choice?

Bayes' theorem tells us, counterintuitively, that the chance of winning the fabulous prize that is behind one of the two remaining unopened doors is improved if the contestant makes the switch. The normal intuition is that the choice between the two unopened doors is equal: namely, that there is a 50:50 chance that the prize is behind either door. Bayes' theorem is powerful precisely because our normal intuition about these probabilities is incorrect and that the actual probabilities are two in three and one in three in favor of the unopened door not previously selected (see Box 7.5). Again, modern software and ready access to computers makes inclusion of Bayes' theorem a relatively painless task that can provide better assessments of the risks and uncertainties involved in making projections and thereby better valuation analysis.

Decision analysis is replete with estimates regarding future probabilities. Although these probabilities represent the best estimates at the time they are made, additional information will become available as the future unfolds (just as the game-show host opens one of the previously closed doors and fixes with certainty that the now-opened door does not conceal the prize). This new information needs to be assessed properly. It is here

BOX 7.5: THE MATHEMATICAL PROBABILITIES FROM THE *LET'S MAKE A DEAL* EXAMPLE, OR WHY YOU SHOULD SWITCH FROM DOOR A TO DOOR C

At the beginning of the game, the probability that the prize is behind any given door is one in three, which can be expressed as $P(A) = 1/3$.

Now assume that you choose door A and that the host opens door B (to reveal a lesser prize). What are the probabilities for the various doors?

- The probability that the host opens door B if the prize were behind door A is 50:50, or one in two, which can be expressed mathematically as $P(\text{host opens B/A}) = 1/2$.
- The probability that the host opens B if the prize were behind B is zero (because the host always opens a losing door and never the one with the prize) and can be expressed as $P(\text{host opens B/B}) = 0$.
- The probability that the host opens B if the prize were behind C is 100 percent (because, once again, the host always opens a losing door) and can be expressed as $P(\text{host opens B/C}) = 1$.

Combining the above probabilities, we find that the probability the host opens door B is then $P(\text{host opens B}) = [P(A) \times P(\text{host opens B/A})] + [P(A) \times P(\text{host opens B/B})] + [P(A) \times P(\text{host opens B/C})]$, which is $1/6 + 0 + 1/3$. This result can be expressed as $P(B) = 1/2$.

Using Bayes' theorem, we can then figure out the probability that the prize is behind door A or C, given the host opening door B:

$$P(A \backslash \text{host opens B}) = P(A) \times \frac{P(\text{host opens B/A})}{P(B)} = \frac{1/3 \times 1/2}{1/2} = 1/3$$

$$P(C \backslash \text{host opens B}) = P(A) \times \frac{(P(\text{host opens B/C})}{P(B)} = \frac{1/3 \times 1}{1/2} = 2/3$$

In other words, the probability that the prize is behind door C given that the host opened door B is two in three compared with one in three for door A. It is to your advantage to switch from door A to door C.

that Bayes' theorem excels as a useful method to ensure that the decision maker will incorporate the new information in a logically consistent manner, thus preventing faulty analysis that will lead to mistaken decisions.

REFERENCES

Abramowicz, Michael. 2007. "The Danger of Underdeveloped Patent Prospects." *Cornell Law Review* 92: 1065.

Adamic, L. A., and B. A Huberman. 2000. "The Nature of Markets in the World Wide Web." *Quarterly Journal of Electronic Commerce* 1.

Black, Fischer, and Myron Scholes. 1972. "The Valuation of Option Contracts and a Test of Market Efficiency." *Journal of Finance* 27: 399.

Black, Fischer, and Myron Scholes. 1973. "The Pricing of Options and Corporate Liabilities." *Journal of Political Economy* 83: 637.

Cotropia, Christopher. 2009. "Describing Patents as Real Options." *Journal of Corporation Law* 34: 1127.

Denton, F. Russell, and Paul Heald. 2003. "Random Walks, Non-Cooperative Games, and the Complex Mathematics of Patent Pricing." *Rutgers Law Review* 55: 1175.

MacKenzie, Donald. Dec. 2003. "Bricolage, Exemplars, Disunity and Performativity in Financial Economics." *Social Studies of Science* 33: 831.

Marco, Alan. 2005. "The Option Value of Patent Litigation: Theory and Evidence." *Review of Financial Economics* 14: 323.

Merton, Robert. 1973. "The Theory of Rational Option Pricing." *Bell Journal of Economics* 4, no. 1: 141.

Merton, Robert. 1976. "Option Pricing When Underlying Stock Returns Are Discontinuous." *Journal of Financial Economics* 3: 124.

Metropolis, Nicolas, and Stanislaw Ulam. 1949. "The Monte Carlo Method." *Journal of the American Statistical Association* 44: 335.

Murphy, William J. 2007. "Dealing with Risk and Uncertainty in Intellectual Property Valuation and Exploitation." In *Intellectual Property: Valuation, Exploitation, and Infringement Damages, Cumulative Supplement*, edited by Gordon V. Smith and Russell L. Parr, 40–66. Hoboken, NJ: John Wiley & Sons.

Oriani, Raffaele, and Luigi Sereno. 2011. "Advanced Valuation Methods: The Real Options Approach." In *The Economic Valuation of Patents: Methods and Applications*, edited by Federico Munari and Raffaele Oriani, 141–168. Cheltenham, UK: Edward Elgar.

Perillo, Joseph. 2009. *Calamari and Perillo on Contracts*. 6th ed. St. Paul, MN: West.

Pitkethly, Robert. 1997. "The Valuation of Patents: A Review of Patent Valuation Methods with Consideration of Option Based Methods and the Potential for Further Research." Judge Institute, Working Paper WP 21/97.

Pitkethly, Robert. 2006. "Patent Valuation and Real Options." In: *The Management of Intellectual Property*, edited by Derek Bosworth and Elizabeth Webster, 268–292. Cheltenham, UK: Edward Elgar.

Poitras, Geoffrey. 2009. "The Early History of Option Contracts." In: *Vinzenz Bronzin's Option Pricing Models: Exposition and Appraisal*, edited by Wolfgang Hafner and Heinz Zimmerman, 487–518. Berlin: Springer-Verlag.

Raiffa, Howard. 1968. *Decision Analysis: Introductory Lectures on Choices under Uncertainty*. Reading, MA: Addison-Wesley Publishing.

Skinner, David. 1999. *Introduction to Decision Analysis: A Practitioner's Guide to Improving Decision Quality*, 2nd ed. Gainesville, FL: Probabilistic Publishing.

Schwarz, Eduardo, and Lenos Trigeorgis, eds. 2004. *Real Options and Investment under Uncertainty: Classical Readings and Recent Contributions*. Hong Kong: M.I.T. Press.

Trigeorgis, Lenos, and Scott Mason. 2004. "Valuing Managerial Flexibility." In *Real Options and Investment under Uncertainty: Classical Readings and Recent Contributions*, edited by Eduardo Schwarz and Lenos Trigeorgis, 47–60. Hong Kong: M.I.T. Press.

NOTES

1. Interestingly, one "real options" approach to valuing patents was granted a U.S. patent in 2005 (U.S. Patent No. 6,862,579).
2. To be more precise, Aristotle described the transaction as Thales paying "earnest-money" to secure the olive presses. Scholars have interpreted that clause to mean that Thales purchased an option to hire the presses in the future and that Thales was not contractually committed to use the presses later in the year. Geoffrey Poitras, "The Early History of Option Contracts," in *Vinzenz Bronzin's Option Pricing Models: Exposition and Appraisal*, edited by Wolfgang Hafner and Heinz Zimmerman (2009).
3. Donald MacKenzie, "Bricolage, Exemplars, Disunity and Performativity in Financial Economics," *Social Studies of Science* 33 (December 2003): 831, 836.
4. Fischer Black and Myron Scholes, "The Valuation of Option Contracts and a Test of Market Efficiency," *Journal of Finance* 27 (1972): 399. Although the 1972 paper in the *Journal of Finance* was the first published discussion of their theory, a paper that was subsequently published in 1973 (but was referenced in the 1972 paper that beat it to print) in the *Journal of Political Economy* is considered the landmark work. Fischer Black and Myron Scholes, "The Pricing of Options and Corporate Liabilities," *Journal of Political Economy* 81 (1973): 637.
5. Dynamic hedging to remove the risk component was a major contribution to the concept made by Robert Merton. Robert Merton, "The Theory of Rational Option Pricing," *Bell Journal of Economics* 4, no. 1 (1973): 141.
6. Christopher Cotropia, "Describing Patents as Real Options," *Journal of Corporation Law* 34 (2009): 1127, 1129.
7. Lenos Trigeorgis and Scott Mason, "Valuing Managerial Flexibility," in *Real Options and Investment under Uncertainty: Classical Readings and Recent Contributions*, edited by Eduardo Schwarz and Lenos Trigeorgis, Lenos (2004), 48.

8. Raffaele Oriani and Luigi Sereno, "Advanced Valuation Methods: The Real Options Approach" in *The Economic Valuation of Patents: Methods and Applications*, eds. Federico Munari and Raffaele Oriani (2011), 149–152.
9. Michael Abramowicz provides a similar example in Michael Abramowicz, "The Danger of Underdeveloped Patent Prospects," *Cornell Law Review* 92 (2007): 1065, 1076. Our example was motivated by Abramowicz's example.
10. 35 U.S.C. sec. 154.
11. See Oriani and Sereno, Luigi, "Advanced Valuation Methods," 150 and 152.
12. Ibid., 152.
13. Although many distributions would be expected to be normal, in some situations a log-normal or triangular distribution may be more accurate.
14. One type of power law distribution is Zipf's law, named after the Harvard linguistics professor George Kingsley Zipf, who was exploring the distribution of common word use in language in the 1940s. Another power-law example describes the population of towns and cities noticed by the German geographer Felix Auerbach in 1913. A majority live in cities and towns of relatively modest sizes, but there are some giant "outliers" such as New York City or Los Angeles that are so much larger than what would be expected if city size were a normal or Gaussian distribution.

    In 1999, two researchers at Xerox's Palo Alto Research Center were examining the distribution of website visitors using 120,000 AOL user logs. They discovered that the distribution was a power law function, with a small number of sites getting a large portion of web traffic and a large number of sites receiving much more modest visitor rates. L. A. Adamic and B. A. Huberman, "The Nature of Markets in the World Wide Web," *Quarterly Journal of Electronic Commerce* 1 (2000): 5–12.
15. As an example, the reader is invited to consider the *Let's Make a Deal* problem discussed later in this section.
16. The SpamBayes program, based on the work of software programmer Paul Graham (developer of the ARC dialect of the Lisp computer language and author of *Hackers and Painters: Big Ideas from the Computer Age*, O'Reilly Media, 2004) is an example.
17. For example, see David Matchar, David Simel, John Geweke, and John Feussner, "A Bayesian Method for Evaluating Medical Test Operating Characteristics When Some Patients' Conditions Fail to Be Diagnosed by the Reference Standard," *Medical Decision Making* 10 (1990): 102.

CHAPTER 8

Market Methods

Markets are one of the most powerful tools employed to value assets. The market is often referred to as the penultimate arbiter of value, and many assert that a market-derived price is the most accurate reflection of what something is worth. The power of a market comes from the ability of parties to exchange scarce resources. Most commonly, a seller will provide scarce goods or services in exchange for the buyer paying money. Through a process of self-interested negotiation, each party seeks to obtain a more valuable resource than it surrenders. The buyer and the seller thereby establish a *value* for the goods or services that are sold. In well-developed markets, information about previously agreed values is taken into account by other market participants, which can lead to the recognition of market prices for the goods or services being exchanged. It is true that a well-functioning market can produce a reasonable valuation for a particular good or service, but to properly evaluate what the market price or other market indications actually mean, the dynamics and conditions surrounding the market-derived value must be closely examined. The key to employing market methods is to understand their strengths and weaknesses and what they actually tell us about the value of a particular asset.

As a valuation tool, market methods seek to determine the value of an asset by using the wisdom and experience of self-interested buyers and sellers. The self-interested buyers and sellers can employ any number of valuation techniques to determine the value of a given transaction, and the market helps to aggregate the findings of these individual determinations. There are two core market methods for valuing assets:

1. **Competitive exchange:** The market of potential buyers is identified and encouraged to compete for the purchase of the asset, which helps to identify who ascribes the highest value to the asset. In effect, the seller polls the market to determine what buyers are currently willing to pay for the asset being valued.

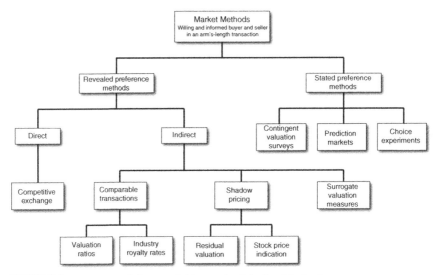

FIGURE 8.1 Diagram of Core and Alternative Market Methods

2. **Comparable transactions:** The value of an asset is determined by looking at the range of prices paid in past or current transactions for similar
assets. The value stems from the premise that a reasonable buyer
"would not pay more for property than it would cost to purchase a
comparable substitute."[1] Furthermore, if the comparable transaction
took place in the past, it is assumed that the information derived from
that past transaction remains relevant for the transaction under review.

In addition to these two core methods a number of derivative market
techniques for valuing assets can be employed (see Figure 8.1). Some of the
more common approaches will be analyzed in this chapter.

Market methods are regularly used to value patents. Although it is un-
deniable that patents pose particular challenges for market-based valuation
techniques, they remain an important and useful valuation tool for patents.
We will analyze a number of the market methods that are used to value patents. We will also explain the strengths and weaknesses of these methods
and how they can be effectively employed.

In this chapter, we

- Examine markets and their strengths and weaknesses with respect to
  patent rights.
- Explain the two core market methods and demonstrate how to make
  practical use of them.

- Examine some of the more common alternative market methods and once again demonstrate how to make practical use of them.

MARKETS AND PATENT RIGHTS

Standard economic theory explains that the collective actions of buyers and sellers will cause a market price to develop for a traded item. The market price, which is the point at which supply and demand converge, will represent the best estimate for the value of the traded item if the market is sufficiently competitive. Frequently cited characteristics for a competitive market are[2]

- There are numerous buyers and sellers.
- Free and immediate entry and exit for market participants exist.
- There is full and perfect knowledge for each buyer and seller.
- The traded items are homogeneous (or fungible).
- The market has no externalities.
- All buyers and sellers are utility maximizers.
- There are no external parties that are regulating the price, quality, or quantity in the marketplace.

The major U.S. public stock markets—e.g., the New York Stock Exchange (NYSE) and NASDAQ—provide a good example of competitive markets. For large, publicly traded companies such as Cisco, Google, and Intel, the most recent price obtained from a national stock exchange provides a powerful assessment of the value of a share of such company's stock. Millions of identical shares are traded between willing buyers and sellers each day (if not each minute) who are able to benefit from an extensive mandatory disclosure system that helps to inform each of these decisions. For a stockholder selling large-company stock through one of the major U.S. public stock markets, that sale will benefit from an effective competitive exchange process. For a stockholder (or other party) who simply wants an estimate of the value of the stock, the announced stock prices provide a reasonable estimate.

Active, competitive markets have proven difficult to assemble for patents.[3] For this chapter, we want to explain how the inherently unique nature of patents creates three fundamental problems for developing competitive markets:

1. **Information problems about the patent rights:** In practice, there are few publicly disclosed patent transactions that can be usefully employed for determining the market price for any particular patent right.

2. **Comparability problem:** Even when data on potentially comparable transactions is available, the unique nature of patents can make using such data particularly challenging to employ in a valuation analysis.

3. **Lack of convenient exchange institutions:** Although there have been a few attempts to establish formal markets for trading patent rights, such efforts have yet to generate much in the way of tangible progress. There are few meaningful institutions that support primary or secondary transactions in patent rights and nothing that is comparable to the market institutions that support securities transactions.

Even though the ingredients for a competitive patent market do not exist—and are not likely to exist anytime soon—it does not mean that market methods cannot be employed to value patent rights. Rather, it simply means that buyers and sellers have to work harder to employ the methods or have to accept that the valuation information generated may be less informative than it would be were the market more ideal.

Information Problems

Information is the lifeblood of a market. Accurate information about an economic opportunity facilitates proper market decisions. On the one hand, the buyer of the opportunity is properly informed about the merits of the particular opportunity as well as other available opportunities such that the buyer can allocate capital to the opportunities that are likely to generate the highest returns. On the other hand, the seller of the opportunity is properly informed about the value of the opportunity and the optimal timing and structure of the transaction so as to achieve the best price. In a perfect world, such information would be perfectly accurate and costless. Although no known market produces such perfectly accurate and costless information (see Box 8.1), markets with greater information problems will be less competitive than markets with fewer information problems. The information problems that surround patents are particularly acute and have proven to be a major obstacle to developing viable patent markets.

Uncertainty One information problem that affects patents is uncertainty about their future performance. Because many patents cover new technology with little to no commercial track record, the uncertainty about their future economic potential is extreme. Will the new technology function effectively? Will consumers embrace the technology? Will the

---

BOX 8.1: INFORMATION PROBLEMS ARE NOT UNIQUE TO PATENTS

The information problems that affect patents are not unique to patent markets. Understanding how other markets deal with these information problems could provide insights in how to improve patent markets over time. For example, consider the following:

- **Uncertainty:** Extreme uncertainty about future performance is a significant information problem for start-up company markets. Through repeat performance and particular expertise, however, specialized investors such as venture capital firms have learned to operate in this uncertain environment.
- **Asymmetric information:** Asymmetric information between corporate managers and shareholders plagues all corporate securities markets. Public securities markets address this problem with mandatory disclosure regimes, whereas private securities markets tend to address the problem with heightened disclosure duties.

---

technology be commercially scalable? The strength of the patent's legal rights (e.g., validity of claims) can also be highly uncertain. The acute uncertainty that accompanies most patents requires potential buyers of the patent rights to have a heightened level of technical, business, and legal expertise so as to make an intelligent purchase decision. As a result, the potential pool of buyers for a given set of patent rights will frequently be very shallow.

Asymmetric Information Another information problem that affects patents involves asymmetric information between the patent holder and the potential acquirer of the patent rights. Asymmetric information occurs when one party to a negotiated transaction has materially less accurate (or less complete) information than the other party. The patent holder will typically have much better information about the potential positives and risks involved with the patented technology than any potential buyer. To make matters worse, the patent holder's self-interest may cause her to exploit this information advantage to the detriment of any potential buyer. The patent holder is likely to emphasize the potential upside to a buyer while downplaying (or omitting) the negatives.

Where asymmetric information prevents buyers from being able to distinguish good (valuable) patents from bad (not valuable) patents, a classic *lemons problem* occurs.[4] In such a setting, buyers are likely to generate valuations that average together the good and bad patents to allow for a reasonable return. It means, however, that buyers will underpay for good patents (because they are judged average) and overpay for bad patents (because they are also judged average). Because good patents are penalized by this effect, holders of good patents should strive to differentiate their good patents from bad and average patents. If good patents cannot be differentiated, holders of good patents should be expected to leave the market because they will be disappointed with the price paid by buyers. Left unchecked, this lemons problem will cause bad patents to dominate the market because their holders will be the most motivated by the average price paid by buyers, thus jeopardizing the very existence of the market.

Lack of Publicly Disclosed Patent Transactions One of the greatest information problems for market-based patent valuation methods is the dearth of publicly disclosed patent transactions. There are few publicly disclosed patent transactions that can be used to inform market-based valuation analysis. Although it is not uncommon for companies to publicize major patent deals, seldom do such announcements reveal the detailed information needed to use the prior deal in a comparable transactions analysis. Many announcements fail to disclose any financial terms, and those that do report financial terms will almost always limit their disclosure to the "headline deal value,"[5] which is virtually useless for any meaningful comparable transaction analysis. The headline deal value might disclose, for example, a gross estimation of the potential value for the transaction that is derived solely for marketing purposes (such as to impress shareholders or customers of a company's financial strength). Royalty rates, payment structures, risk burdens, and meaningful deal terms that can have a substantial effect on the value of the transaction are seldom willingly disclosed.

When one of the parties to a patent transaction is a U.S. reporting company (e.g., listed on a national securities exchange such as the NYSE or NASDAQ), there is the possibility that the reporting company may be required to publicly file a copy of the assignment or license agreement with the Securities and Exchange Commission (SEC) as part of the company's ongoing disclosure requirements under federal securities law. Reporting companies must publicly file their "material contracts."[6] Although the definition of material contracts is actually quite narrow, it is broad enough to capture some significant patent transactions. Such public filings can be accessed through the SEC's EDGAR database (http://www.sec.gov)

provided that you know the name of the company that filed the patent as-signment or license agreement.

Unfortunately, even if a company has publicly filed a patent assign-ment or license agreement with the SEC, there is a good chance that the filing will not include the contract's all-important pricing informa-tion. Companies that are required to file a material contract have the option of seeking confidential treatment for information in the contract that could harm the company's competitive position.[7] It is common for the SEC to allow for specific pricing information to be redacted from the contract prior to filing. Such confidential treatment, however, does not last forever. The confidential treatment will be granted for a specific period of time (typically 1 to 10 years) that is meant to cover the useful life of the information for which protection is sought. Parties wishing access to the confidential information can make a Freedom of Informa-tion Act request to the SEC (see Box 8.2) to find out if the confidential-ity period has expired.

BOX 8.2: MAKING A FREEDOM OF INFORMATION ACT REQUEST TO OBTAIN CONFIDENTIAL PATENT LICENSE INFORMATION

The Freedom of Information Act (FOIA) is the federal government's version of a freedom of information law. FOIA allows individuals and organizations to request access to undisclosed federal agency records and information. Each federal agency has its own particular proce-dures for how it will receive a FOIA request. The procedures for how to make a FOIA request to the SEC can be found at www.sec.gov/foia/howfo2.htm.

In short, a FOIA request to the SEC must satisfy four basic requirements:

1. It must be in writing.
2. It must specifically cite FOIA.
3. It must reasonably describe the records requested.
4. It must indicate a willingness to pay any FOIA fees charged by the SEC.

There is no specific request form required, but the SEC does pro-vide a sample request form (http://www.sec.gov/foia/sample1.htm)

to make things easier. The written request must be sent to the SEC's FOIA office by any of the following means:

E-mail: foiapa@sec.gov

Fax: (202) 772-9337

Mail: 100 F Street NE, Mail Stop 2736, Washington, DC 20549

Sources: SEC website; 2010 U.S. Securities and Exchange FOIA Annual Report.

Comparability Problems

Even when data on potentially comparable transactions are available, the very nature of patents can make using such data particularly challenging in a valuation analysis. Both the unique nature of patent rights and the potential problems with industry royalty rates present challenges.

Unique Nature of Patent Rights   Patents should only be granted to inventions that are "novel."[8] In other words, each patent, by definition, should cover a unique invention, which makes finding true comparables all the more difficult. Valuations based on comparability analysis are easiest to conduct for commodity assets. A barrel of crude oil of a specified composition is the same as any other barrel of crude oil of the same composition. The price for one barrel of crude oil should therefore be the same as any other barrel. As the level of differences between the asset being valued and the comparable pool of asset transactions becomes greater, the more art that is required in conducting the comparable transactions analysis. For example, no two residential houses are perfectly identical (even if the floor plan is perfectly identical, the location has to be different by definition), and yet comparable home sale analysis is the dominant valuation method for residential real estate. The evaluator must consider the similarities and differences between the home being valued and the pool of comparable home sales and make adjustments accordingly.

For patent rights, however, the level of uniqueness is likely to be of a much more extreme level than for residential home sales. Consider just some of the various ways that one patent right may be very different from another:

- Quality of the technology.
- Quality of the patent and its claims.

- Quality of the license rights that are associated with the patent.
- Transferability (or nontransferability) rights associated with the patent.
- Suboptimal use of the comparable patent may have depressed its value

Industry Royalty Rates Are Not Comparable   In an attempt to compensate for the lack of available individual transaction data, parties will sometimes employ industry royalty rates (see Chapter 10). The parties to a license transaction, for example, may use industry royalty rates to help to determine the appropriate royalty rate for their specific transaction. Aggregate industry royalty rates, however, provide almost no guidance for any individual patent or transaction. Trying to compare an individual patent to an industry-wide selection of patents is next to impossible. As discussed in Chapter 7, it appears that the distribution of patent valuations is not a normal, or Gaussian, distribution. Instead, patent valuations appear to follow either a power-law or log-normal distribution. At one end of the spectrum will be a large number of patents that will have modest to nonexistent economic value. At the other end of the spectrum will be a much smaller number of patents of enormous value; patents that allow the owner to control multibillion dollar markets. As a result, it is not clear what the average royalty rate for an industry says about a single patent.

Lack of Convenient Exchange Institutions and the Need for Intermediaries

Markets, when they exist, provide a powerful valuation tool. Unfortunately, in the case of patent rights, formal markets to support primary and secondary transactions are largely nonexistent. There have been efforts to create such markets, with Ocean Tomo's effort to create a public market for patent rights as the highest profile effort (see discussion of Ocean Tomo later in this chapter), but none has yet to enjoy more than limited success. One of the major reasons for the absence of such a market is a lack of essential intermediaries to support it.

The role of intermediaries in a market is often overlooked. An intermediary is someone who facilitates the function of the market, but is not acting in the role of buyer or seller. Intermediaries develop to address problems that exist in a market (and as our previous discussion should demonstrate, patent markets have significant problems to address). For example, a long and impressive list of intermediaries has developed to improve the efficiency of public stock markets. These intermediaries, which include such market fixtures as investment banks, research analysts, public auditors, and mutual fund managers, help to reduce various information and agency problems that plague stock markets.

Many envision a market as a self-organizing entity that promptly emerges whenever there are buyers and sellers, but even the simple market-places of old required essential institutions (a place and time for the buyers and sellers to assemble) and intermediaries to function. For the simple barter markets of ancient times, local authorities began to police and regulate the market to deter thieves and protect the honest merchants. Where the distance between buyer and seller was great, chains of intermediaries emerged and helped to facilitate the acquisition of goods in far-off lands for eventual sale in the local marketplace. Courts and legal systems developed to enforce contracts and settle disputes. Bankers and moneylenders, shippers and caravan organizers, warehouse operators and dock workers all emerged to help develop and maintain the markets in goods that transformed human existence from one of local limitations to one of global reach.

The role of intermediaries in the information age marketplace for intangible products is even more essential. These intermediaries perform three vital functions:

1. Collect, analyze, and disseminate information.
2. Certify, value, and authenticate assets and activities.
3. Monitor and regulate transactions and participants.

Without these intermediaries, who often work behind the scenes, modern markets would cease to function, or, at least, they would function suboptimally. Failure to appreciate the necessity for intermediaries and the subsequent lack of maturity of critical intermediaries, we believe, is a primary reason for the failure of robust patent markets to develop.

COMPETITIVE EXCHANGE

Although employing market methods to value patents involves a number of challenges, their use should not be ignored. The competitive exchange method, for example, can be one of the simplest and most accurate methods for valuing a patent that is being transferred. A competitive exchange requires identifying and encouraging a market of potential buyers to compete for the patent, which helps to identify those who ascribe the highest value to the patent. In effect, the patent holder polls the market to determine what buyers are currently willing to pay for the patent. A competitive exchange, therefore, requires two essential elements:

1. A pool of interested buyers.
2. A mechanism for encouraging them to compete for the opportunity.

For many types of assets, a competitive exchange can be used by either the seller or the buyer. An asset seller can assemble a pool of interested buyers and encourage them to compete for the right to purchase the asset. An asset buyer, on the other hand, can assemble a pool of interested sellers and encourage them to compete for the right to sell the asset. When used by the seller, a competitive exchange helps the seller to determine the maximum price that buyers are willing to pay for the asset. When used by the buyer, it does the inverse and indicates the lowest price at which sellers are willing to part with the asset. Unlike income- or cost-based valuation methods, which seek to determine an intrinsic value of an asset, competitive exchanges are all about determining relative value. The goal of a competitive exchange is to determine the value that others (the bidders) place on the asset. Competitive exchanges are agnostic to the valuation methods employed by bidders and instead rely on the self-interest of those bidders to push the valuation to a point that is most favorable to the party holding the auction.

Competitive exchanges are particularly well suited for assigning or licensing patent rights (transfer outs). Because of the unique nature of patents, the ability for a buyer to use the competitive exchange structure is quite challenging. As a result, we will focus specifically on the ability of a patent holder to use the competitive exchange to transfer patents to potential buyers.

Auctions

Auctions are one of the more common forms of competitive exchange and are a standard valuation method. In the United States, for example, auctions account for a substantial amount of the economic activity of the federal government. The U.S. Treasury Department sells trillions of dollars of treasury securities each year through weekly, sealed-bid auctions. The federal government commonly uses various auction strategies to sell federal assets (e.g., sale of radio spectrum, sale of mineral rights, and sale of seized property) or to purchase assets with public funds (e.g., bidding for federal government contracts). Auctions are frequently used throughout the private and public sectors to make all sorts of purchase and sale decisions, from the most trivial to the most important. When a company decides to hold a holiday party, it is not uncommon to solicit bids for catering the party from a variety of caterers. When the board of directors of a large corporation decides that the corporation should be sold, it is very common to use an auction process to ensure the maximum sales price for the company. An auctioneer can employ a number of different auction models. Table 8.1 provides a summary of the some of the more common ones.

TABLE 8.1 Common Auction Models

Type of Auction	Description
English auction (also called standard auction)	The English auction is considered by most to be the standard form of auction. In an English auction, there is open bidding among the various competitors. The auctioned item ultimately goes to the highest bidder.
Japanese auction	A Japanese auction is a special variety of the English auction in which new bidders are not admitted after the auction starts. At each round, the price is raised; each bidder must then indicate whether he or she is still in or is dropping out (similar to a betting round in poker). When only one bidder remains, that bidder is the winner. When an electronic push button is used to facilitate the process of indicating each bidder's decision, these auctions are referred to as button auctions.
Blind, sealed-bid auction (also called Yankee auction)	The second most common auction is the blind, sealed-bid auction (sometimes called a Yankee auction) that is often employed in governmental contract activities. In the basic form of this auction, each buyer submits a bid without knowing what the other potential buyers have bid. As with the English auction, the winner is the bidder with the highest bid. When competitors are vying to provide a government contract, these auctions are conducted with a twist: The sellers are the bidders, and the winner is the person submitting the lowest bid. In other words, the successful bidder in such a sealed-bid contest for providing the service or item is the one that agrees to sell that service or item at the lowest price.
Dutch auction	In a classic Dutch auction, the auctioneer starts the auction with the announcement of a high opening price and the price starts descending until someone accepts one of the descending prices. This type of auction has the singular benefit of being

extremely fast and, unsurprisingly given this speed benefit, is used in the Dutch flower market to move vast quantities of perishable flowers each day.

Vickery auction (also called second-price, sealed-bid auction)

A lesser-known type of auction, but one that millions of people encounter the results of every day, is the Vickery auction. In this type of auction, bids are submitted simultaneously through sealed bids. As a consequence it is sometimes referred to as a second-price, sealed-bid auction because the amount paid by the successful bidder is the price submitted by the second-highest bidder. The highest bidder prevails but will be paying the price bid by the second-highest bidder. This type of auction was named after William Vickery, who won the Nobel Prize in economics in 1996 for his work in the area.

A Vickery auction may yield a higher price for a seller than an alternative type of auction because it is thought to encourage bidders to bid their maximum value for the item being auctioned rather than try to fathom a bid price that is slightly above the second-highest bidder, which might be the case in an English auction. Because the successful bidder will only have to pay what the second-highest bidder bid, there is no penalty for having a maximum value that greatly exceeds the next highest bidder because the high bidder will only be paying that lower second-highest bid price.

The Ocean Tomo/ICAP Patent Brokerage Auction Market Auctions for patent rights have lately received a lot of attention. Much of the focus has been on Ocean Tomo's efforts to create a trading market for patent rights. Ocean Tomo, an intellectual property merchant bank, is generally credited with the boldest effort to date to create a public market for patents. In April 2006, Ocean Tomo held the first of a series of live patent auctions that were meant to create a liquid market for patent asset sales. That first auction generated rather modest results. Approximately 400 patents were offered in 77 lots. Of the lots offered, 24 were sold for an aggregate total of roughly

$2.7 million.[9] Subsequent auctions generated comparable results. From spring 2006 through summer 2009, for example, Ocean Tomo held 10 auctions that generated about $115 million in sales (or $11.5 million per auction).[10] Proceeds for the first eight of these auctions generated an average of $176,000 per patent sold, and the tenth auction generated an average of $95,900 per patent sold.[11]

Ocean Tomo's auctions have tended to be structured as open outcry, English auctions. Interested bidders submit real-time bids in person or by proxy; or they may submit absentee bids in advance of the auction.[12] Prior to the fall of 2008, all winning purchases had to be paid for with a lump sum payment (see Chapter 10), but later auctions have allowed for more creative payment structures.[13] For patents that do not sell during the auction, private deals are sometimes negotiated after the auction.[14]

The volume of patents and revenue raised from Ocean Tomo's auctions were not insignificant, but the overall results fell short of expectations for the service. In June 2009, Ocean Tomo sold its patent auction business to ICAP Patent Brokerage. It appears that similar results have continued under ICAP Patent Brokerage's operation of the auctions.[15]

Other Examples   Despite the limited success of the Ocean Tomo/ICAP Patent Brokerage market, attempts to establish patent exchange markets have continued. A number of Internet-based patent exchanges, for example, have been attempted. Examples include IpAuctions.com, TAEUS Online Patent Exchange, Tynax, and Yet2.com. Patents are even being sold on eBay. Some of these Internet-based exchanges operate as true auctions, whereas others are more akin to matching services.

One of the most significant sources of patent auctions going forward may be the bankruptcy courts. Bankruptcy courts have long held debtor auctions of patent rights. The most significant patent-asset bankruptcy auction was the $4.5 billion sale of Nortel's patent portfolio (consisting of 6,000 patents) in 2011 to a consortium of bidders that included Apple, EMC, Ericsson, Microsoft, RIM, and Sony. With the general proliferation of patent assets in companies, we expect that patent portfolios will increasingly be among the most important assets for bankrupt companies. Moreover, the success of the Nortel patent auction should help to focus bankruptcy courts on the importance of these patent assets and ensure that they are managed with care by bankruptcy trustees and courts.

Less Formal Methods of Competitive Exchange

Formal auctions are not the only competitive exchange method that can be employed to value patent rights. In many cases, running a formal auction is simply not practical. Consider the following scenario. You are the patent portfolio manager for a university, and one of your responsibilities is to monetize the patents in the university's portfolio. In most cases, the patented technology is both highly specialized and will require significant development work before it can be truly commercialized. As a result, there are not more than three or four viable acquirers for the rights to any of the individual patents, and any acquirer will need to invest significant additional resources into the technology. You want to run a competitive exchange to encourage the potential buyers to make more generous offers, but you realize that the potential buyers are unlikely to tolerate a formal auction process. The potential acquirers will almost certainly decide to pass on the technology if they have to jump through too many hoops. In that setting, and in so many other similar settings, the patent portfolio manager may decide to run a less formal competitive exchange process.

The formality of a true auction process is not necessary in most cases. Less formal techniques can be equally effective at valuing a set of patent rights if they possess a number of basic elements. Because less formal competitive exchange techniques are more frequently employed by patent right sellers, we examine the issue from the perspective of a seller. There are five basic elements for a sound competitive exchange structure:

1. **Mechanisms for identifying the potential acquirers of the technology:** The patent holder should not assume that the potential acquirers will know the technology is available for transfer. It is up to the patent holder to proactively develop the pool of potential acquirers.
2. **Mechanisms that effectively communicate information about the technology to the potential acquirers:** Poor communication about the technology leads to lower valuations from the potential acquirers. A common refrain from technology buyers is their desire to buy de-risked technology. Better communications provides a clearer picture of the risk associated with the technology. In most cases, the patent holder should prepare marketing materials for the patented technology.
3. **Clear articulation of goals and structure to achieve goals:** The patent holder needs to know what it is looking for and specifically structure the process to get that. Will the purchase price be based on the acquirer's future performance with the patented technology? For example, will the acquirer pay for the patent rights with a running sales royalty license (see Chapter 10)? If the purchase price will be based on future performance, the seller should require potential acquirers to submit business plans that demonstrate how they will commercialize the patented technology. Such business plans will allow the patent holder

to better evaluate each potential acquirer's ability to generate the positive results that are needed to generate license revenue.

4. **Individuals who are capable of evaluating the quality of the various bids:** Acquirer bids are likely to include a lot of information that will need to be evaluated. For example, bids that involve running royalty payments need to be evaluated to determine what their actual value is.

5. **Mechanisms to collect and employ the knowledge generated from past competitive exchanges by the seller:** Patent holders that repeatedly transfer out patented technology can greatly improve their competitive exchange results by collecting information from past negotiations and employing that knowledge in current negotiations.

Pros and Cons of Valuing Patent Rights through Competitive Exchange

There are a number of pros and cons to using the competitive exchange method to value patent rights. Table 8.2 summarizes the strength and weaknesses of this valuation method when used by a rights holder. In sum, competitive exchange is an ideal valuation method when the patent holder is seeking to transfer its patent rights. To help evaluate the quality of various bids, however, the patent holder should also be prepared to conduct additional income, market, or cost method analysis as outlined throughout Chapters 6 through 9.

TABLE 8.2   Strength and Weaknesses of the Competitive Exchange Method When Used by a Patent Holder

Strength	Weaknesses
▪ It determines the maximum price that buyers are willing to pay.	▪ It only works when the patent holder is ready to transfer the patent rights. ▪ It only values patent rights from the acquirers' perspective. The patent rights could be worth more if the patent holder were to maintain and exploit the rights itself. ▪ The ability to determine value is highly dependent on the quality of the competitive exchange structure. ▪ Evaluating the quality of the various bids can be challenging.

COMPARABLE TRANSACTIONS

The second core market method is the comparable transactions method. This method takes a very different approach to valuing an asset than a competitive exchange. Rather than poll the market to determine what buyers are currently willing to pay, the comparable transactions method uses historical precedent to approximate what current buyers would pay based on the assumption that current buyers will act similarly to past buyers (e.g., value things in a similar manner).

Ratio Analysis

One of the most common ways to conduct a comparable transactions analysis is what we will refer to as *ratio analysis*. Mechanically, ratio analysis involves identifying valuation ratios from the prices at which similar assets were sold in the past and then applying that valuation ratio to the asset being valued. Valuation ratios are multiples that are calculated by dividing the price at which the similar asset sold by a relevant economic variable of the asset:[16]

$$\text{Valuation ratio} = \frac{\text{Price at which similar asset is sold}}{\text{Some relevant economic variable of the asset (e.g., forward one-year operating profit from the asset)}}$$

To illustrate this concept, Box 8.3 provides an example of how the comparable transaction method can be used to value a company, which is one of the more common usages of the method.

From a financial analysis standpoint, the same type of ratio analysis can be applied to patents. It requires determining the economic variables that are most relevant to the value of a given patent right and obtaining comparable patent transaction data. Similar to company valuations, the most relevant economic data for patent rights will be, in most cases, future profits and future revenues that can be projected to result from ownership of the patent right. Mechanically, running a ratio analysis for a patent is simple:

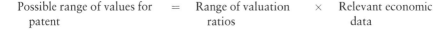

Possible range of values for patent = Range of valuation ratios × Relevant economic data

The difficulty in applying ratio analysis to patent transactions is not the calculation; rather, it is coming up with the comparable data that is needed to feed the calculation (see previous sections). The general dearth of publicly available data about individual patent transactions and the

BOX 8.3: USING THE COMPARABLE TRANSACTION METHOD TO VALUE A COMPANY

First, identify a group of company sales that are comparable to the company being valued (Target). Although none of the comparable transactions will be perfectly comparable, each such transaction should have taken place in the not-too-distant past and ideally would have involved companies (1) from the same (or similar) industry as Target and (2) with similar results, market size, and product profiles as Target.

Second, from the comparable pool, a series of valuation ratios can be calculated. Forward profits and forward sales figures are two of the most common valuation ratios used. For this example, let us assume a pool of seven comparable transactions and that forward 1-year profits is the relevant economic variable:

Enterprise Value of Comparable Company as a Multiple of	Comparable Company						
	A	B	C	D	E	F	G
Forward 1-year profits	$7.4x$	$11.2x$	$6.2x$	$15.0x$	$11.8x$	$10.4x$	$9.8x$

Enterprise Value of Comparable Company as a Multiple of	Summary of Comparable Transactions		
	Range	Average	Median
Forward 1-year profits	$6.2x - 15.0x$	$10.3x$	$10.4x$

Finally, the derived valuation ratios can then be applied to Target's relevant economic data to develop a range of values for Target. Because no company is exactly the same as another, adjustments should be made to the derived valuation ratios to come up with a valuation ratio that is appropriate for Target. For simplicity's sake, let us skip the adjustments and simply assume that Target is much more comparable to the better companies in the comparable pool, but is not as strong as the absolute best company in the pool. The following valuation calculation could then be made:

Possible range of Target's value	$=$	$9.8x$ to $11.8x$	$\times$	Target's forward 1-year profits

comparability problems that accompany data that are available limits the applicability of ratio analysis for patent valuation analysis.

ALTERNATIVES TO THE CORE MARKET METHODS

Given the difficulties involved with the two core market methods, a number of alternative approaches have developed for valuing patent rights that try to approximate what the core methods attempt to reveal. In the absence of accurate information about what the market of technology acquirers have paid, or would pay, for a particular patent right, these alternatives seek to provide insight—although at times that insight can be very unsophisticated and should be used with caution—into how the market is valuing similar technology.

When thinking about the core market methods, it is useful to reflect on the goal of this type of analysis: to determine what buyers would pay (or what sellers would accept) for a given asset. The core market methods do that by seeking what we refer to as revealed preferences (see Figure 8.1). Ideally, the market method measures what a buyer (or seller) would agree to exchange for the *exact same* item, or what we refer to as a *direct, revealed preference*. In that scenario, the market method is informing the valuator how much the market values that specific item. The competitive exchange method is an example of the direct, revealed preference method. There are few examples of direct, revealed preference markets for patents, and those that do exist are far from robust. ICAP Patent Brokerage's patent auction market (see the previous discussion of the Ocean Tomo/ICAP Patent Brokerage auction market) is an example of a direct, revealed preference market. To work around the lack of public and functional direct, revealed preference markets for patent rights, a valuator is likely to use comparable data, or what we refer to as *indirect, revealed preferences*. The most widely used indirect, revealed preference method is the comparable transactions method, which looks at prior, similar transactions to develop valuation ratios that could be applied to the asset being valued. Largely because of the previously mentioned comparability problems, the indirect, revealed preferences needed to conduct a comparable transaction analysis are also very difficult to obtain.

The alternative market methods seek to overcome the problems of the core market methods and still allow for the market to inform the valuator about the value of the patent rights. The remainder of this section focuses on some of the more common alternative market methods for valuing patents.

Shadow Pricing

Sometimes markets communicate valuation information very clearly (comparable transactions method), while other times markets provide more subtle messages. Consider the following scenario. An item exists that is readily measurable (it has a clearly identifiable value), but is not directly relevant for a valuation exercise. That item, however, has something of interest that is hidden inside its identifiable value that is directly relevant to the valuation exercise. How can we extract (or isolate) this hidden information so that it can be used in a valuation?

One method used to extract hidden information that may not be directly measurable itself is to derive the information through logically linking value judgments made for related activities or decisions that may be measurable. This method is referred to as shadow pricing. As the name implies, it involves looking for indirect information (the shadow) of the hidden pricing information that is of interest. Shadow pricing uses a chain of value judgments that logically links the value of any element in the chain to the value to be determined. For example, if one claims that X is more valuable than Y and that Y has a clearly identifiable value of $1,000, one can logically deduce that X has a value of more than $1,000.

One of the best examples of shadow pricing is in putting a value on life. It is often stated that you cannot put a value on a human life, but reality indicates otherwise. Every day we are forced to put a value on life, and other supposedly priceless items, by the decisions that confront us. A decision to drive a car or take an airplane to a distant location, the decision to wear a helmet when riding a motorcycle or a seatbelt when driving a car, or the decision to select one medical treatment versus another all contain information about the decision maker's valuation of life. Government regulations that imply a certain balance of cost versus safety provide a fertile source for shadow prices.[17] For example, when a governmental body enacts a regulation with a predicted effect of a certain number of lives saved and the cost of the regulation to save those lives is known (or can be estimated), an implied value of life can be extracted. For example, suppose that the government proposes a regulation that will cost $100 million to implement and will save 100 lives by reducing cancer-causing chemicals in the workplace. From these facts, we can show that the shadow price of life implicit in this regulation is $1 million. The calculation would be as follows:

$$\text{Minimum value of life} = \frac{\text{Cost of regulation}}{\text{Number of lives saved}} = \frac{\$100 \text{ million}}{100 \text{ lives}} = \$1 \text{ million per life}$$

So, the value of a life, based on this regulatory decision, is worth at least $1 million. Of course, a life may be worth much more. The logic only tells us that $1 million is the minimum implied value of a life based on the facts in this regulatory example.

Shadow pricing can also be used to value patent rights. Two examples of shadow pricing for patent rights are the residual valuation method and the stock price indication method.

Residual Valuation Method   One form of shadow pricing that has received a fair amount attention in the patent valuation literature is the residual valuation method.[18] This method can be employed to determine the market value of a patent right that is held by a publicly traded firm that has one dominant patent right in its intellectual property portfolio, such as a pharmaceutical company that sells a single drug for which it holds the patent rights. In such a case, the patent right can be valued by calculating the firm's residual value after subtracting the value of all the other assets from the firm's market value. Expressed as a formula,

Value of patent right	=	Firm's market value (e.g., market capitalization + takeover premium)[19]	−	Value of firm's tangible assets	−	Value of firm's nonpatent intangible assets (e.g., goodwill, trademarks, copyrights, and trade secrets)

The strength of the residual valuation method is the ease with which it can be expressed into a mathematical formula, which helps to explain why it is so frequently described in the patent valuation literature. In reality, however, there are problems with the residual valuation method that limit its practical application for valuing a patent. To begin with, only a small number of companies fit the requirements needed for running a residual valuation method analysis. Specifically, the company must satisfy three significant requirements:

1. The company must be publicly traded so that a market value can be calculated.
2. The company must have only one major patent.
3. The one major patent is at the core of the company's business model.

The universe of companies that will fit the above profile will never be very large. That universe, however, can be expanded in two ways that make the residual valuation method more meaningful. First, non-public companies that have recently conducted a round of venture capital funding that establishes the market value of the company can also employ the residual valuation method. The second possible expansion is probably the more significant. The residual valuation method is typically discussed as a method for valuing a single patent. It may be that the technique is better suited for valuing a company's overall patent portfolio rather than a single patent. When viewed as a portfolio valuation technique, the universe of companies that fit the profile is greatly expanded:

| Value of firm's overall patent portfolio | = | Firm's market value (e.g., market capitalization + takeover premium) | − | Value of firm's tangible assets | − | Value of firm's nonpatent intangible assets (e.g., goodwill, trademarks, copyrights, and trade secrets) |

Stock Price Indication Method   Similar to the residual valuation method is what we refer to as the stock price indication method. This method is based on the premise that the stock market may have something to say about the value of a publicly traded company's patents. The simplest example of the stock price indication method is when a company's stock price reacts to major news about one of the company's patents. For example, if a company's stock price drops on the release of news that one of the company's patents has been invalidated—and assuming no other major news releases by the company and a relatively calm day in the stock markets—the company's drop in market valuation (which could be measured over multiple days to reduce the risk that investors had an immediate overreaction to the news) could be inferred to be the market's valuation of that patent right.

Absent news events about a particular patent, stock prices can still provide information about patent values. Stock prices can provide a crude and indirect indication of the value of a company's overall patent portfolio. Assuming the company trades on a liquid and relatively efficient stock market, a company's financial ratios can provide insights as to how the market values its patent portfolio. When a company has a significant patent portfolio and better-than-average financial ratios (the company's stock is trading at a price that is higher than its financial performance would normally justify), the market could be indicating its estimate that the patent portfolio has significant value. A number of empirical studies have shown that corporations' market value correlates with their intellectual property assets.[20]

Surrogate Valuation Measures

In many valuation contexts, it can be convenient to use something that is readily observable or measurable to help estimate something that is difficult to observe or measure. Shadow pricing does this by linking the asset that is the focus of the valuation exercise to a revealed market price for another item. It is also possible to extract useful information from observable nonprice data that are revealed by decisions made in the marketplace. We refer to this useful nonprice data as surrogate valuation measures.

One of the most interesting examples of a surrogate valuation measure dates back to eighteenth-century Great Britain. In 1784, William Pitt the Younger, then head of the British government, needed to raise taxes to reduce the national debt. An income tax was rejected as requiring too great an intrusion into private affairs, so a property tax increase was proposed. A property tax solution, however, created its own problem. How could the government quickly and inexpensively value all the property that would need to be taxed? The solution that Pitt employed was one that had a long history in England.[21] Pitt's solution was to employ a Window Tax and use windows as a surrogate measure for property value. The Window Tax was based on the number of windows that a building had. Windows at the time were very expensive. As a result, it was reasoned that more valuable buildings would have more windows than less valuable structures. The number of windows and the building's value were roughly correlated. The advantage of the Window Tax to the tax collector was that windows were easy to count. Not surprisingly, taxed citizens responded to Pitt's increased tax by filling in windows with solid walls to reduce their tax burden. Examples of these blind windows (called Billy Pitt's Pictures) can still be found in Scotland.

In patent valuation, the use of more easily obtained surrogate valuation measures has been suggested as a possible technique to overcome the dearth of readily accessible market price information for patents. A number of academics have noted that surrogate measures derived from publicly available patent data sources (such as the U.S. Patent and Trademark Office and the European Patent Office) can provide useful insights into patent valuations.[22] For example, Bronwyn Hall, Adam Jaffe, and Manuel Trajtenberg published a paper in 2000 noting the increased availability of machine-readable patent data and using that data to uncover a correlation between the number of citations in subsequent patents and the market value of the company owning the observed patents.[23]

In a 2004 article entitled *Valuable Patents*, John Allison, Mark Lemley, Kimberly Moore, and R. Derek Trunkey used a surrogate valuation approach and identified seven characteristics of valuable patents after analyzing an extensive database of patent information.[24] According to the authors' research, patents with the following characteristics tend to be more valuable than ordinary patents:

1. The patent is litigated soon after it is issued.
2. The patent is owned domestically.
3. The patent is issued to individuals or small companies.
4. The patent cites more prior art and is in turn more likely to be cited by other patents than the standard issued patent.
5. The patent prosecution period was longer than for the standard issued patent.
6. The patent contains more claims than the standard issued patent.
7. The patent comes disproportionately from certain industries (e.g., mechanical, computer, or medical device industries).

Because these seven characteristics are measurable inputs, one could develop a seven-factor algorithm that could generate a rough valuation estimate. The use of such surrogate measures (sometimes referred to as factors or indicators) for patent valuation has not only been suggested by academics, but has also been incorporated into some proprietary patent valuation services.[25] These patent valuation services extract information along a number of dimensions that are readily observable (the surrogate measure) and then use that extracted information in a formula to calculate a rough patent valuation. These valuations might be lacking in depth and accuracy, but have the advantage of being instantly available.

Stated Preference Alternatives

For each of the above alternatives, the market provides some type of revealed preference, even if in some cases that revelation is quite subtle. What happens, however, when there is no marketplace to reveal a preference? With patent rights, that scenario is unfortunately very common. In these situations, a stated preference method may be appropriate.

How Stated Preference Methods Work   Stated preference methods ask the decision makers involved in the valuation event, and possibly other relevant individuals, to state their preferences in such a way that an implied value can be extracted from the stated preferences. Stated preference methods are frequently used for difficult valuation problems such as the value of life or the effect of environmental degradation. It is also possible, however, to devise a stated preference methodology for use in patent valuation, particularly within an organization that has expertise in making decisions regarding the relevant patents, the patented technology, and the markets where the patents may be commercially useful. The way stated preference methods work is as the name suggests. Interested parties are asked to state their preferences regarding the relevant valuation data. There are a variety of methods for *making the ask*. Choice experiments,[26] contingent valuation surveys,[27] and prediction markets are all commonly employed techniques for teasing out stated preference data. For the remainder of this chapter, we will focus specifically on the prediction market technique.

Prediction Markets Since 2000, the utility of prediction (or information) markets has been championed as a method to extract useful information regarding an uncertain future event.[28] Employing a betting type of system, participants place wagers on various future outcomes. The participant whose wager prediction comes closest to the actual outcome is rewarded. In the standard information market, the participant buys a type of futures contract on the outcome of a specified event or result. If that event or result comes to pass, the holder of that contract will be rewarded with either real or artificial currency.[29]

In certain circumstances, these markets can outperform both experts and opinion polls. This insight was popularized by James Surowiecki in his book *The Wisdom of Crowds*.[30] The outcome of political elections and sporting events have long been the subject of public wagering with websites such as the Iowa Electronic Markets,[31] InTrade,[32] and Paddy Power[33] providing opportunities to the general public to make predictions with the incentive of a reward for predictions that turn out to be correct. Some prediction markets solicit public participation aimed at specific products or services. Perhaps the best known of them is the Hollywood Stock Exchange, which seeks to glean information about the potential success or failure of movies, television shows, and even the popularity of celebrities.[34]

The characteristics for a successful predictive market are typically cited as including the following:[35]

- **Useful knowledge:** The participants in the market should have some useful experience, insight, or information that is relevant to the decision.

- **Diversity of opinion sources:** The participants bring a diverse set of perspectives, which brings new information to bear on the problem and helps to reduce biases from any one perspective.
- **Independence:** The participants are able to act independently and are not susceptible to manipulation.
- **Sufficient number of participants:** The pool of participants is large enough so that trading is sustainable.
- **Incentive to participate:** The participants have an incentive to take the exercise seriously.

In the patent valuation context, it is possible for a company to establish an internal prediction market that can provide helpful information that can be used to feed various valuation models. Prediction markets can be used to predict product revenues (both amount and timing), operating costs (both amount and timing), litigation risk, potential future opportunities for the patent, and many other useful types of data. There are even organizations that assist companies in setting up and operating an internal prediction market.[36] Companies that reportedly have tapped into internal prediction markets to develop useful information and to assist corporate decision making are Abbott Labs, Arcelor Mittal, AT&T, Best Buy, Chrysler, Chubb, Cisco, Corning, Electronic Arts, Eli Lilly, Frito-Lay, General Electric, Google, Hewlett-Packard, Intel, InterContinental Hotels, Masterfoods, Microsoft, Motorola, Nokia, Pfizer, Qualcomm, Siemens, and TNT.[37] The Google Prediction Market is probably the best documented of these internal prediction markets and has been used to provide management with predictions regarding Google products.[38]

REFERENCES

Akerloff, George. 1970. "The Market for 'Lemons': Quality Uncertainty and the Market Mechanism. *Quarterly Journal of Economics* 84: 488.

Allison, John, Mark Lemley, and Joshua Walker. 2004. "Valuable Patents." *Georgetown Law Journal* 92: 435.

Alpízar, Francisco, Fredrik Carlsson, and Peter Martinsson 2001. "Using Choice Experiments for Non-Market Valuation." *Working Papers in Economics*, no. 52.

Borshell, Nigel. Undated. "Understanding Headline Deal Values: A PharmaVentures Guide to the Interpretation of Deal Terms and Terminology." *PharmaVentures White Paper*. http://files.pharmaventures.com/white_paper_deal_analysis.pdf.

Cherry, Miriam, and Robert Rogers. 2006. "Tiresias and the Justices: Using Information Markets to Predict Supreme Court Decisions." *Northwestern University Law Review* 100: 1141.

Clarkson, Gavin. 2000. "Intellectual Asset Valuation." Harvard Business School Case No. N9-801-192/Rev 10/1/00. Harvard Business School Publishing.

Denton, F. Russell, and Paul Heald. 2003. "Random Walks, Non-Cooperative Games, and the Complex Mathematics of Patent Pricing." *Rutgers Law Review* 55: 1175.

Diamond, Peter, and Jerry Hausman. 1994. "Contingent Valuation: Is Some Number Better than No Number?" *Journal of Economic Perspectives* 8: 45.

Glantz, Andrew. 2008. "A Tax on Light and Air: Impact of the Window Duty on Tax Administration and Architecture, 1696–1851." *Pennsylvania History Review* 15: 18.

Goldscheider, Robert. 2011. "The Classic 25% Rule and the Art of Intellectual Property Licensing." *Duke Law and Technology Review* 6: 6.

Finch, Sharon. 2001. "Royalty Rates: Current Issues and Trends." *Journal of Commercial Biotechnology* 7: 224.

Hahn, Robert. 2004. "Using Information Markets to Improve Policy." AEI-Brookings Joint Center for Regulatory Studies, Working Paper 04-18.

Hanson, Robin. 2007. "Shall We Vote on Values, but Bet on Beliefs?" http://hanson.gmu.edu/futarchy.pdf.

Jarosz, John, Robin Heider, Coleman Bazelon, Christine Bieri, and Peter Hess. Mar. 2010. "Patent Auctions: How Far Have We Come?" *Les Nouvelles*11.

King, Rachel. Sept. 7, 2010. "Companies That Collectively Innovate." *Bloomberg/Businessweek*. www.businessweek.com/technology/content/sep2010/tc2010097_904409.htm.

Layne-Farrar, Anne, and Josh Lerner. Mar. 2006. "Valuing Patents for Licensing: A Practical Survey of the Literature." http://ssrn.com/abstract=1440292.

Milgrom, Paul. 1989. "Auctions and Bidding: A Primer." *Journal of Economic Perspectives* 3: 3.

Milgrom, Paul. 2004. *Putting Action Theory to Work*. Cambridge, UK: Cambridge University Press.

Milgrom, Paul, and Robert Weber. 1982. "A Theory of Auctions and Competitive Bidding." *Econometrica* 50: 1089.

Murphy, William. 2002. "Proposal for a Centralized and Integrated Registry for Security Interests in Intellectual Property." *IDEA* 41: 297.

Omland, Nils. 2011. "Economic Approaches to Patent Damages Analysis." In *The Economic Valuation of Patents: Methods and Applications*, edited by Federico Munari and Raffaele Oriani, 262–287. Cheltenham, UK: Edward Elgar.

Orcutt, John. 2005. "Improving the Efficiency of the Angel Finance Market: A Proposal to Expand the Intermediary Role of Finders in the Private Capital Raising Setting." *Arizona State Law Journal* 37: 861.

Payne, Andrew. Apr. 2006. "Ocean Tomo Patent Auction." www.payne.org/index.php/Ocean_Tomo_Patent_Auction.

Pitkethly, Robert. 1997. "The Valuation of Patents: A Review of Patent Valuation Methods with Consideration of Option Based Methods and the Potential for Further Research." Judge Institute, Working Paper WP 21/97.

Pratt, Shannon, Robert Reilly, and Robert Schweihs 2000. *Valuing a Business: The Analysis and Appraisal of Closely Held Companies.* 4th ed. New York: McGraw-Hill.
Smith, Gordon. 1997. *Trademark Valuation.* Hoboken, NJ: John Wiley & Sons.
Smith, Gordon V., and Russell L. Parr. 1989. *Valuation of Intellectual Property and Intangible Assets.* New York: John Wiley & Sons.
Smith, Gordon V., and Russell L. Parr. 2005. *Intellectual Property: Valuation, Exploitation, and Infringement Damages.* Hoboken, NJ: John Wiley & Sons.
Surowiecki, James. 2005. *Wisdom of the Crowds.* New York: Anchor Books.
Unattributed. Jan. 7, 2007. "A Look at Google's Prediction Market." *Real Time Economics, Wall Street Journal blogs.* http://blogs.wsj.com/economics/2008/01/07/a-look-at-googles-prediction-market/.
United Nations Economic Commission for Europe. 2003. *Intellectual Assets: Valuation and Capitalization.*
Viscusi, W. Kip. 1998. "Rational Risk Policy." 1996 Arne Ryde Memorial Lectures, Oxford University.
Wolfers, Justin, and Eric Zitzewitz. 2004. "Prediction Markets." *Journal of Economic Perspectives* 18: 107.

NOTES

1. Gordon V. Smith and Russell L. Parr, *Intellectual Property: Valuation, Exploitation, and Infringement Damages* (2005), 169.
2. In his book on trademark valuation, Gordon Smith identifies the key ingredients as

   - The existence of an active market involving comparable property
   - Access to price and "deal" information about exchanges of comparable property
   - Arm's length transactions between independent parties

   Gordon Smith, *Trademark Valuation* (1997) 139.
3. Gordon Smith draws a similar conclusion for trademarks. Smith, 139 ("Assembling [the] ingredients [for a market approach] is a bit of a tall order for trademarks").
4. The effect of asymmetric information on markets and the resulting "lemons problem" can be traced to George Akerloff, "The Market for 'Lemons': Quality Uncertainty and the Market Mechanism," *Quarterly Journal of Economics* 84 (1970): 488. Akerloff won the Nobel Prize in economics for this 13-page paper.
5. Nigel Borshell, "Understanding Headline Deal Values: A PharmaVentures Guide to the Interpretation of Deal Terms and Terminology," PharmaVentures White Paper 1 (undated), http://files.pharmaventures.com/white_paper_deal_analysis.pdf; and Finch, Sharon, "Royalty Rates: Current Issues and Trends," *Journal of Commercial Biotechnology* (2001): 7.
6. Item 601(b)(10) of Regulation S-K [17 C.F.R. sec. 229.601(b)(10)].

7. Rule 24b-2 of the Securities Exchange Act of 1934 (17 C.F.R. sec. 240.24b-2) and Rule 406 of the Securities Act of 1933 (17 C.F.R. sec. 230.406).

8. 35 U.S.C. sec. 102.

9. Andrew Payne, "Ocean Tomo Patent Auction" (Apr. 2006), www.payne.org/index.php/Ocean_Tomo_Patent_Auction.

10. John Jarosz, "Patent Auctions: How Far Have We Come?" *Les Nouvelles* 11 (Mar. 2010): 17.

11. Jarosz, 21–22.

12. Jarosz, 15.

13. Jarosz, 15.

14. Jarosz, 15.

15. ICAP Patent Brokerage website, http://icappatentbrokerage.com/auction ("Since April 2006, ICAP Patent Brokerage, and its predecessor organization, Ocean Tomo Transactions, has held 13 live auctions across the United States and Europe resulting in the successful transaction of over $170 million in IP").

16. See Shannon Pratt, Robert Reilly, and Robert Schweihs, *Valuing a Business: The Analysis and Appraisal of Closely Held Companies*, 4th ed., (2000), 226.

17. W. Kip Viscusi, the John F. Cogan, Jr. Professor of Law and Economics and Director of the Program on Empirical Legal Studies at Harvard Law School, is a leading researcher in this area. His research discloses a wide range of implied values of life in various regulatory actions. The values vary widely, but seem to cluster in the $3 million to $7 million range. W. Kip Viscusi, "Rational Risk Policy," 1996 Arne Ryde Memorial Lectures, Oxford University (1998).

18. See, e.g., Gordon V. Smith and Russell L. Parr, *Valuation of Intellectual Property and Intangible Assets* (1989), 204–206; Robert Pitkethly, "The Valuation of Patents: A Review of Patent Valuation Methods with Consideration of Option Based Methods and the Potential for Further Research," Judge Institute Working Paper WP 21/97 (1997), 7–8; F. Russell Denton and Paul Heald, "Random Walks, Non-Cooperative Games, and the Complex Mathematics of Patent Pricing," *Rutgers Law Review* 55 (2003): 1175, 1185–1186; Anne Layne-Farrar and Josh Lerner, "Valuing Patents for Licensing: A Practical Survey of the Literature" (Mar. 2006), http://ssrn.com/abstract=1440292, 8–9.

19. The takeover premium is the additional amount that the acquirer needs to pay to motivate holders of more than 50 percent of the outstanding shares to accept the offer to purchase the company.

20. United Nations Economic Commission for Europe, *Intellectual Assets: Valuation and Capitalization* (2003), 67.

21. The original window tax was introduced in 1696 with amendments and modifications made throughout the next century and a half. Andrew Glantz, "A Tax on Light and Air: Impact of the Window Duty on Tax Administration and Architecture, 1696–1851," *Pennsylvania History Review* 15 (2008): 18.

22. Nils Omland, "Economic Approaches to Patent Damages Analysis." In *The Economic Valuation of Patents: Methods and Applications*, ed. Federico Munari and Raffaele Oriani (2011), 171–182.

23. Bronwyn Hall, Adam Jaffe, and Manuel Tratjenberg, "Market Value and Patent Citations: A First Look," National Bureau of Economic Research, Working Paper No. 7741 (2000).

24. John Allison, Mark Lemley, and Joshua Walker, "Valuable Patents," *Georgetown Law Journal* 92 (2004): 435.

25. See, for example, Pantros at http://www.pantrosip.com/.

26. See, for example, Francisco Alpizar, Fredrik Carlsson, and Peter Martinsson, "Using Choice Experiments for Non-Market Valuation," *Working Papers in Economics* 52 (2001).

27. See, for example, Peter Diamond and Jerry Hausman, "Contingent Valuation: Is Some Number Better than No Number?" *Journal of Economic Perspectives* 8 (1994): 45.

28. Bo Cowgill, Justin Wolfers, and Eric Zitzewitz, "Using Prediction Markets to Track Information Flows: Evidence from Google" (2009), http://www.bocowgill.com/GooglePredictionMarketPaper.pdf; Robert Hahn, "Using Information Markets to Improve Policy," AEI-Brookings Joint Center for Regulatory Studies, Working Paper 04-18 (2004); Justin Wolfers and Eric Zitzewitz, "Prediction Markets," 18 *Journal of Economic Perspectives* 18 (2004): 107; Robin Hanson, "Shall We Vote on Values, but Bet on Beliefs?" (2007), http://hanson.gmu.edu/futarchy.pdf.

29. The Google internal market used an artificial currency called Goobles. The Hollywood Stock Exchange uses HDollars.

30. James Surowiecki, *Wisdom of the Crowds* (2005).

31. http://tippie.uiowa.edu/iem/index.cfm.

32. www.Intrade.com.

33. www.paddypower.com.

34. www.hsx.com/.

35. See, e.g., Surowiecki, 10; Miriam Cherry and Robert Rogers, "Tiresias and the Justices: Using Information Markets to Predict Supreme Court Decisions," *Northwestern University Law Review* 100 (2006): 1141, 1159–1167.

36. Examples include Lumenogic (www.lumenogic.com), Crowdcast (www.crowdcast.com/), and Inkling (http://inklingmarkets.com/).

37. Cowgill et al.; Rachel King, "Companies That Collectively Innovate," Bloomberg/Businessweek (Sept. 7, 2010), www.businessweek.com/technology/content/sep2010/tc2010097_904409.htm.

38. Unattributed, "A Look at Google's Prediction Market," Real Time Economics, *Wall Street Journal* blogs (Jan. 7, 2007), http://blogs.wsj.com/economics/2008/01/07/a-look-at-googles-prediction-market/.

CHAPTER 9

Cost Methods

The final grouping of valuation methods falls under the cost method category. As the name implies, cost methods use some measurable cost to value an asset. Cost methods can be boiled down to this simple statement: The cost of an asset tells you something useful about its value. Despite their simplicity (or more likely because of their simplicity), cost methods tend to be the most widely criticized of the three types of valuation methods. The loudest criticisms focus on cost methods appearing to ignore the fundamental valuation proposition of business assets, which is to generate net economic benefits. The other two methods, on the other hand, do address the fundamental valuation proposition:

- **Income methods** attempt to directly measure the net economic benefits that will flow from an asset.
- **Market methods** attempt to indirectly measure the net economic benefits that will flow from an asset. Presumably, the market participants are trying to measure the future net economic benefits when establishing the market prices that serve as the core for the market methods.

Cost methods do not appear to make any effort to measure future net economic benefits, which makes them an easy target for criticism. What does the cost of an asset have to do with its ability to generate a flow of net economic benefits? Although we do not want to overstate our support for the cost methods—we agree they are the least likely methods to reveal the true value of an asset—we do want to make clear that cost methods can be useful as valuation tools and should not casually be discarded. When used for valuing patent rights, there are two primary cost methods:

1. Cost of development
2. Cost of reasonable alternatives

There is a tendency to lump both of these cost methods together and criticize their validity as useful valuation tools. Such criticisms, however, are overbroad and can be misguided. The cost of reasonable alternatives method, for example, can be a particularly useful valuation tool, as we explain below.

In this chapter, we

▪ Look at some accounting principles that significantly affect the application of cost methods for valuing patent rights.
▪ Explain the two core cost methods and demonstrate how to make practical use of them.

A FEW ACCOUNTING PRINCIPLES

To value a patent right with a cost method, you need information about the costs. To the extent that you are running a historical cost analysis, there is a good chance that you will be relying on financial statements—in particular, the balance sheet—of the company that owns the patent rights being valued. This section examines some of the accounting principles that significantly affect how the cost of patent rights are recorded in a company's financial statements and how a valuator may wish to treat those numbers when running a valuation analysis.

The Cost Principle of Accounting

For most situations, generally accepted accounting principles (GAAP) require that companies record their assets based on the *cost principle of accounting*. In other words, a company's assets are recorded based on the cost the company paid to obtain the asset. It also means that such recorded values generally do not fluctuate based on increases or decreases in (1) the market price of the assets or (2) the actual economic value of the assets to the company. The static nature of the cost principle of accounting tends to cause the accuracy of financial statement asset valuations to become less accurate over time, which is a somewhat ironic outcome. In most cases, the greatest challenge for valuing any given asset is the uncertainty about how that asset will perform in the hands of the acquirer. The longer the acquirer possesses the asset, the more accurate its ability to value the asset should be.

Recording the Initial Cost of a Patent

The cost of a patent will be recorded in a company's financial statements. More specifically, it will typically be recorded in a company's balance sheet (see Box 9.1 for a brief description of the three statements that make up a company's financial statements). Assets that are added to the balance sheet are said to be *capitalized*. Not all costs are capitalized to a balance sheet. Asset purchases that are expected to be used by a company over an extended period of time (more than one year) are capitalized. Asset purchases and other expenditures that will be used up in the given reporting period (typically within 1 year) will be *expensed* to the income statement and not show up as assets on the balance sheet.

BOX 9.1: THE THREE TYPES OF FINANCIAL STATEMENTS

There are three basic financial statements for any company, and each tracks a different financial aspect of the company.

1. A **balance sheet** reports the company's assets, liabilities, and shareholders' equity. Balance sheets adhere to the formula

$$Assets = Liabilities + Shareholders'\ equity$$

   The term *balance sheet* is used because the assets must balance, or equal, the liabilities plus the shareholders' equity. Unlike income and cash-flow statements, a balance sheet does not show the inflows and outflows of assets and liabilities during a specific time period. Rather, a balance sheet provides a snapshot of the company's assets and liabilities on a specific date (e.g., year end, quarter end, or month end).

2. An **income statement** reports a company's revenues and expenses for a specified time period (e.g., for 1 year, quarter, or month). Income statements adhere to the formula

$$Profits = Revenues - Costs$$

   Income statements are also commonly referred to as profit and loss statements because the purpose of such statements is to show the company's profits (if revenues were greater than expenses) or losses (if losses were greater than revenues).

3. A **cash-flow statement** reports the movement of a company's cash for a specified time period (e.g., for 1 year, quarter, or month). This statement shows inflows and outflows of cash and adheres to the formula

$$Change\ in\ cash\ flow = Cash\ in - Cash\ out$$

When a company obtains a patent, it will likely be capitalized to the balance sheet based on the cost of obtaining it. What exactly does "the cost of obtaining it" mean? The first step to understanding the recorded value of a patent is to understand when patent rights are capitalized and at what price. Accounting rules provide two separate treatments for recording the initial cost of a patent, depending on whether the patent rights were internally developed by the company or were purchased from a third party.

Internally Developed Patent Rights   How do companies that create and then patent inventions (Internally Developed Patents) account for this activity? Can a company recognize Internally Developed Patents as an asset on its balance sheet? The answer is kind of, but not really. There are four types of costs associated with Internally Developed Patents:

1. **Research costs:** Research and development consists of two phases: the research phase and the development phase. The costs from the research that lead to the invention are expensed as incurred and not capitalized as an asset.
2. **Development costs:** Under U.S. GAAP, development costs are also expensed as incurred unless a specific exception applies (e.g., development costs for computer software may be capitalized in certain limited circumstances). Under International Financial Reporting Standards, development costs for Internally Developed Patents may be capitalized as assets on the balance sheet. International Accounting Standard 38 provides that development costs for internally generated intangible assets may be capitalized if the company can show, among other criteria, the technical and economic feasibility of the Internally Developed Patents.
3. **Legal expenses and filing fees associated with obtaining the Internally Developed Patent:** These costs are capitalized to the balance sheet as an asset.
4. **Costs to maintain or defend the Internally Developed Patent:** These costs are expensed as incurred.

All told, the initial recorded value of an Internally Developed Patent on a company's balance sheet is likely to be an extremely low number that bears little relationship to the actual economic value of the patent because most of the costs associated with developing the patent are not included.

Purchased Patent Rights   When a company purchases patent rights from a third party (Purchased Patent Rights), the accounting treatment is substantially different. Generally speaking, when a company acquires a Purchased

Patent Right with a useful life of greater than 1 year, the purchase price will be capitalized on the balance sheet as an intangible asset.

Depreciation and Amortization

There are a number of exceptions to the cost principle of accounting (such as mark-to-market accounting for some financial assets), but the biggest exception is the practice of depreciation and amortization.

Depreciating Tangible Assets Tangible assets (other than a few exceptions like land) deteriorate over time or wear out through use and eventually need to be replaced. Depreciation recognizes this gradual deterioration of tangible assets and allows a company to depreciate (or reduce) the recorded value of certain tangible assets over time. For a company to depreciate an asset under U.S. federal tax law, that asset must[1]

- Be owned (not leased) by the company.
- Be used in the active conduct of the company's business or income-producing activity.
- Have a determinable useful life (e.g., "it must be something that wears out, decays, gets used up, becomes obsolete, or loses its value from natural causes"[2]) of more than 1 year.

For depreciable assets, the recorded cost of the asset will be reduced over the asset's anticipated useful life. The depreciated, recorded cost of the asset is frequently referred to as the asset's book value. The depreciation schedule for a given asset (the number of years over which the asset will be depreciated) is determined based on a number of factors such as industry standards and tax and other governmental regulations.

Amortizing Patents Unlike tangible assets, patents do not wear out or decay over time. A piece of machinery, for example, will literally wear out over time from usage, weather erosion, and other physical stress. Apart from physical decay, that machine may also become obsolete as an income-producing asset based on its failure to keep up with technological progress. Patents do not wear out, but do they become obsolete and they do have a finite legal lifetime. As a result, the cost of a patent that is owned and used in the conduct of the company's business should be amortized over its useful life, which may not exceed the remaining life of the patent.

A quick vocabulary lesson is called for here. The terms *depreciation* and *amortization* are related terms with very similar meanings. Both terms describe the writing down of the recorded value of an asset over time to try to

---

BOX 9.2: A PATENT AMORTIZATION EXAMPLE

Acme Electronics purchases a patent for $1 million and estimates its useful life to be 10 years. Acme's accounting treatment for the patent should be

- $1 million cost of patent = capitalized on Acme's balance sheet
- Amortization expense = $100,000 per year for 10 years

---

account for its limited useful life. The big difference between the terms is that depreciation is used to describe the write-down process for tangible assets, whereas amortization is used to describe the write-down process for intangible assets. In other words,

- **Depreciation** is the process of reducing the recorded value of a *tangible* asset over time to approximate the reduction of its useful life.
- **Amortization** is the process of reducing the recorded value of an *intangible* asset over time to approximate the reduction of its useful life.

Patent rights that are capitalized as assets on the balance sheet need to be amortized over the useful life of the patent rights (see Box 9.2). Some intangible assets may not have a limited economic life (such as certain trademarks or trade secrets) and therefore should not be amortized. Patents, however, are not indefinite life intangible assets. For accounting purposes, patent rights are always deemed to have a limited economic life that is not to exceed the shorter of the remaining life of the patent (assuming that maintenance fees will be paid) or the contractual life of the patent rights if the asset holder is a licensee.

COST OF DEVELOPMENT: QUESTIONABLE VALUATION TOOL

Cost-based methods are widely panned by intellectual property valuation experts as being questionable tools for valuing patent rights,[3] with the harshest critics considering them to be almost useless. Although not always stated explicitly, the concern with the cost-based methods is aimed primarily at the cost of development method rather than at the cost of reasonable alternatives method that we will discuss below.

The cost of development method is based on the premise that a patent should be worth at least the amount it cost to develop the patented technology and obtain (and maintain) the patent rights. Expressed as a formula

Minimum value of patent right	=	Cost of developing the technology	+	Patenting and maintenance costs

A party wishing to use the cost of development method to establish the price for transferring a patent right could simply add to the minimum value a reasonable profit margin:[4]

Price of patent right	=	Cost of developing the technology	+	Patenting and maintenance costs	+	Reasonable profit margin

Critiques and Justifications for the Cost of Development Method

Although easy to calculate, the cost of development method has been referred to as "financially naïve"[5] and not grounded in a reasonable financial theory. A patent does not generate value based on its cost. A patent generates value based on its ability to generate future economic benefits. It is not clear what the cost of development indicates about a patented technology's ability to generate future income. On the one hand, there are countless examples (in particular, in the pharmaceutical setting) of patented technologies that were very expensive to develop, but turned out to be commercial failures. On the other hand, there are just as many examples of relatively inexpensive patented inventions that have generated returns that are orders of magnitude greater than the cost of development. The patent system's incentive structure is based on providing the possibility of truly outsized economic returns on invention investments.

To be contrarian, one could make the argument that cost methods do tell us something about the future net economic benefits of a patent. The cost of development typically involves aggregating a series of market-valued decisions, such as buying materials or hiring labor. A cost-method approach that focuses on the historic cost for developing an asset is essentially a series of past market prices. Those individual market transactions were presumably each valued on their ability to generate economic benefits for the acquirer in excess of the acquisition costs. Cost methods therefore tend to be an indirect accumulation of a series of individual market transactions that each indirectly sought to measure a minimum floor of future net economic benefits. It should be pointed out, however, that cost methods do not have much to say about whether that particular accumulation of assets in that particular way turned out as anticipated or whether the purchase decisions added value to the individual assets (in which case the cost methods would undervalue the collection of assets) or detracted from their value (in which case the cost methods would overvalue them).

If the cost of development method is such a questionable tool, why has it persisted as a valuation tool? We think that there are two primary reasons. First, the cost of development method tends to be the least subjective of the valuation methods. Rather than projecting uncertain, future outcomes, the cost of development method employs relatively objective, verifiable numbers through simple equations. An objective number can be derived from the exercise. On the art versus science spectrum, the cost of development methods involves the least art, which helps to explain why it can be popular with accountants and tax officials.

Second, the cost of development method tends to be one of the easiest and cheapest of the valuation methods to employ. With any valuation exercise, picking the appropriate valuation method often involves a trade-off between the cost of conducting the valuation exercise and the precision of that exercise (see Figure 9.1). On that score, the cost of development method tends to score poorly on precision, but highly on cost (it tends to be the least expensive exercise). If one can make an adequate decision with imprecise data, the reduced cost of the less precise cost of development method

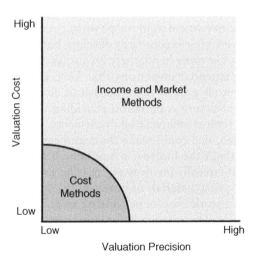

FIGURE 9.1   Cost versus Precision for
Valuation Methods

may support using this more obviously limited methodology. So, what we are left with is an imprecise, but cheap and objective, valuation tool.

Loss Aversion Bias

We will close this discussion of the cost of development with a warning about how it should not be used. Research has shown that people suffer from an economically irrational tendency that is referred to as the loss aversion bias. For most people, the desire to avoid a loss is stronger than the desire to generate a gain. Losing money causes greater psychological pain than gaining money provides psychological pleasure. As a result, there is a human tendency to avoid losses, even when such loss-avoidance decisions are economically irrational. David Genesove and Christopher Mayer's 2001 study of Boston's downtown housing market from the 1990s, for example, showed that listing prices were strongly affected by the purchase price the seller had paid. Rather than choose a list price that predicted what the market would bear, condominium owners who were selling at a loss set significantly higher relative asking prices and were also quicker to withdraw their condominium from the market altogether than were condominium owners who were not selling at a loss.

A patent holder looking to sell a patent should be aware of this loss aversion bias so as to, one hopes, avoid it. The cost of developing the patented technology should be viewed as a sunk cost, and the patent holder should ignore it when setting the price for assigning or licensing the patent.

COST OF REASONABLE ALTERNATIVES: ESTABLISHING A MAXIMUM PRICE

Unlike the cost of development method, the cost of reasonable alternatives method is a very useful valuation technique that we believe is underused by patent decision makers. As we explained in Chapter 5, a patent seldom provides the patentee with complete economic monopoly power over a market. The patentee will have a monopoly to practice the invention, but technical and economic substitutes for the invention will exist in most cases and serve as competitors for the patentee. The patent only prevents competitors from using the invention; the patent does not prevent competitors from using substitute products or services. Determining the cost of reasonable substitutes for the patented technology can provide valuable insights about the underlying value of the patent rights.

In the context of a transaction to transfer patent rights, determining the cost of a reasonable technology alternative should be highly informative for both the patent holder and the potential licensee or assignee. This analysis requires one to calculate what it would cost to develop or acquire an alternative to the patent under consideration.[6] Assuming that the technology acquirer is economically rational, the cost of a reasonable technology alternative should establish an upper limit on the value of the patent rights. An acquirer should not be willing to pay more for the patent rights than it would cost to obtain a reasonable technology alternative.

The cost of reasonable alternatives method can be expressed in the simple formula

Maximum price acquirer should pay for patent rights of income-producing asset	=	Cost of obtaining reasonable technology alternative

This formula assumes a perfectly comparable (or almost perfectly comparable) replacement technology, which may not always be the case. An alternative scenario would be when there is a replacement technology, but such replacement technology is less ideal than the patented technology being valued. In that scenario, the cost of reasonable alternatives method formula should be adjusted as follows:

Maximum price acquirer should pay for patent rights of income-producing asset	=	Cost of obtaining inferior technology alternative	+	Value of reduced productivity or product attributes that comes from using the inferior technology alternative

Some Challenges in Conducting a Cost of Reasonable Alternatives Analysis

Conducting a cost of reasonable alternatives analysis for patent rights can be challenging and tends to be more complicated than for simple, tangible assets. There are a number of reasons for this outcome, most of which stem from the unique nature of patented technologies and patent rights. Determining whether an alternative technology is a reasonable substitute can require significant technical, business, and legal analysis. To illustrate these challenges, let us imagine a complex technological product and a technology acquirer who wants to license a patented technology to serve one function in the overall product. To run a cost of reasonable alternatives analysis, that acquirer will likely need to address the following challenges:

■ **Technical challenges:** Determining whether an alternative technology could replace the patented technology may require extensive testing of alternative technologies or reworking the specifications for the overall product. Such analysis can be both time consuming and expensive.

- **Business challenges:** In addition to determining whether the technology alternative works from a technical standpoint, the acquirer also needs to determine whether that change will affect the market for the overall product. How important are the contributions of the patented technology to the customers of the overall product? Will they notice a change to a replacement technology, and, if so, will they view that negatively?
- **Legal challenges:** Even if a reasonable technology alternative is identified, the acquirer must also determine if the legal rights associated with the alternative are palatable. If the alternative technology is also patented, how comparable are the patent rights? Are the remaining lives of the patents similar? Are there significant encumbrances to the alternative technology patent that may detract from its value? If the alternative technology is not patented, the acquirer needs to assess the potential costs of using nonpatented alternative technology. Will it make defending the market more difficult?

To address these technical, business, and legal challenges, we recommend assembling a group of individuals who collectively have the necessary expertise to conduct a competent valuation. Unlike with commodity-type tangible assets (such as land) where it can be relatively easy to run a cost of reasonable alternatives analysis that allows for a true apples-to-apples comparison (renting space in building A versus building B), the analysis for patent rights will almost always be more complex and subjective. Employing a valuation group with complimentary technical, business, and legal expertise can help to overcome this problem.

Practical Suggestions for Using the Cost of Reasonable Alternatives Method

Both those looking to acquire patent rights and those holding patent rights should consider the uses of a cost of reasonable alternatives analysis. We will now consider such analysis from both points of view.

Acquirers of Patent Rights   When looking to acquire patent rights, the acquirer should, whenever practical, run a cost of reasonable alternatives analysis before making the acquisition. Such an analysis can provide the acquirer with valuable information for improving its negotiating leverage regarding the patent rights. To begin with, such information should help the acquirer to establish a maximum price for the patent rights. If the seller of the patent rights is not willing to transfer the rights below that maximum price, the acquirer should now have a convenient list of alternative suppliers that it can go with. Running a cost of reasonable alternatives method analysis also forces the acquirer to inventory the potential market for technology alternatives. By doing so, it may allow the acquirer to encourage a competitive exchange scenario (see Chapter 8) whereby the various technology providers compete for the acquirer to obtain their specific technology.

Patent Holders Patent holders should also conduct a cost of reasonable alternatives analysis, when practical, before licensing or assigning their rights. The analysis can provide the patent holder with better information about the market for technology alternatives. If the market for alternatives turns out to be thin or nonexistent, the patent holder can be much more aggressive with its licensing or assignment demands. If the market for alternatives turns out to be robust, however, that information may help the patent holder to decide to wrap up the negotiations quickly before the potential acquirer recognizes the extent of the market for alternatives.

REFERENCES

Camerer, Colin, and George Loewenstein. 2004. "Behavioral Economics: Past, Present, Future." In *Advances in Behavioral Economics*, edited by Colin Camerer, George Loewenstein, and Matthew Rabin, 3–52. Princeton, NJ: Princeton University Press.

Denton, F. Russell, and Paul Heald. 2003. "Random Walks, Non-Cooperative Games, and the Complex Mathematics of Patent Pricing." *Rutgers Law Review* 55: 1175.

Department of the Treasury—Internal Revenue Service. Apr. 6, 2011. *Publication 946—How to Depreciate Property*.

Ernst & Young. Jan. 2009. *US GAAP vs. IFRS—The Basics*.

Genesove, David, and Christopher Mayer. 2001. "Loss Aversion and Seller Behavior: Evidence from the Housing Market." *Quarterly Journal of Economics* 116: 1233.

Layne-Farrar, Anne, and Josh Lerner. Mar. 2006. "Valuing Patents for Licensing: A Practical Survey of the Literature." http://ssrn.com/abstract=1440292.

Munari, Federico, and Raffaele Oriani, eds. 2011. *The Economic Valuation of Patents: Methods and Applications*. Cheltenham, UK: Edward Elgar.

Pitkethly, Robert. 1997. "The Valuation of Patents: A Review of Patent Valuation Methods with Consideration of Option Based Methods and the Potential for Further Research." Judge Institute, Working Paper WP 21/97.

Pratt, Shannon, Robert Reilly, and Robert Schweihs 2000. *Valuing a Business: The Analysis and Appraisal of Closely Held Companies*. 4th ed. New York: McGraw-Hill.

Rao, Mohan. 2008. "Valuing Patents and Other Intellectual Property in Licensing Transactions." *PLI/Pat* 923: 527.

Smith, Gordon V., and Russell L. Parr. 2005. *Intellectual Property: Valuation, Exploitation, and Infringement Damages*. Hoboken, NJ: John Wiley & Sons.

Tversky, Amos, and Daniel Kahneman 1991. "Loss Aversion in Riskless Choice: A Reference-Dependent Model." *Quarterly Journal of Economics* 106: 1039.

Walther, Larry. 2010. *PrinciplesofAccounting.com*. www.principlesofaccounting. com/Default.htm.

West, Thomas, and Jeffrey Jones, eds. 1999. *Handbook of Business Valuation*. 2nd ed. New York: John Wiley & Sons.

NOTES

1. Section 179 of the Federal Tax Code; Department of the Treasury, Internal Revenue Service, *Publication 946—How to Depreciate Property* (2009).
2. Internal Revenue Service, *Publication 946*.
3. See, e.g., Anne Layne-Farrar and Josh Lerner, "Valuing Patents for Licensing: A Practical Survey of the Literature" (Mar. 2006), http://ssrn.com/abstract=1440292, 8; F. Russell Denton and Paul Heald, "Random Walks, Non-Cooperative Games, and the Complex Mathematics of Patent Pricing," *Rutgers Law Review* 55 (2003): 1175, 1183; Robert Pitkethly, "The Valuation of Patents: A Review of Patent Valuation Methods with Consideration of Option Based Methods and the Potential for Further Research," Judge Institute, Working Paper WP 21/97 (1997), 8.
4. Layne-Farrar and Lerner, 8.
5. Ibid.
6. Some authors have dubbed this type of calculation the "asset approach" because it envisions substituting another asset of known value for the asset under examination. Thomas West and Jeffrey Jones, eds., *Handbook of Business Valuation*, 2nd ed. (1999), 526.

Patent Valuation in Practice

CHAPTER 10

Pricing Patent Licenses

One of the most critical times for valuing a set of patent rights is when patent rights are being transferred voluntarily. Valuation helps the potential buyer and seller of the patent rights to make a number of informed decisions. Should the transfer take place? If the answer to that question is "yes," when should that transfer take place and what is the ideal method for the transfer? Finally, valuation is needed to price the transfer. Commercial patent right transfers require a price. Determining that price is one of the most important elements (if not the most important element) of the eventual transfer agreement because it is the price that determines each side's eventual profits (or loss) from the deal.

The most common method for transferring patent rights is through some form of license agreement. A patent license is a contractual agreement whereby a licensor grants permission to use a set of patent rights to a licensee during a specified period in exchange for a specified payment. Stated more simply, a patent license serves as a lease of a set of patent rights. Licenses can be grouped into two broad categories, depending on the level of exclusivity the licensor wishes to provide to the licensee. Exclusive licenses are used when the licensor wants to provide patent rights to a single party, and nonexclusive licenses are used when the licensor wants to provide patent rights to multiple parties. Whether exclusive or nonexclusive, a patent license can be tailored in a variety of ways to fit the needs of the parties. The license can cover the entire patent or can be limited in any number of ways. Typical limitations include manner of use limitations, geographic limitations, field of use limitations, and transfer limitations. For a more detailed discussion of exclusive versus nonexclusive patent licenses and the tailoring of patent licenses, see Chapter 2.

In this chapter, we:

- Consider the typical payment structures for patent licenses.
- Examine generally how to price a patent license.

▪ Explore the tendency of parties to gravitate toward less formal valuation techniques and look at some of these less formal techniques.

PAYMENT STRUCTURES

Before attempting to price a particular patent license, it is usually necessary to determine the payment structure for the license. The payment structure can influence the price (and its determination) in a number of ways. This section examines the more common patent license payment structures and explains how such structures can affect the price analysis.

Lump Sum Fees

Lump sum fees are the standard pricing practice for most products or services. A lump sum fee simply means that the buyer pays a specific, fixed price when buying something. For example, if buyer agrees to buy a television from seller for a lump sum fee of $795, buyer will pay that specific, fixed price. Lump sum fees can be complete or partial. A complete lump sum fee means that the payment accounts for the totality of the purchase price. With a partial lump sum fee, the lump sum covers only part of the purchase price and is supplemented with some form of variable fee, such as a running royalty (described below).

In the patent context, lump sum fees go by a number of different names. Fixed fees, up-front fees, down payments, and license issue fees are all commonly used terms.[1] Patent licenses frequently employ partial lump sum royalty payments, but seldom complete lump sums. A survey conducted in 1997, for example, found that 60 percent of patent licenses included partial lump sum fees.[2] A more recent study looked at nearly 3,000 license agreements that were filed with the Securities and Exchange Commission by high-technology and biotech companies from 1994 to 2009 and that included a running royalty provision. This more recent study found that 52 percent of high-technology and 69 percent of biotech licenses included a partial lump sum fee.[3]

Lump sum fees serve a number of positive economic roles in the licensing context. For example, a lump sum fee reduces the licensor's risk in the transaction by reducing the uncertainty of the economic returns that the licensor can expect from the transaction. Lump sum fees also discourage the licensee from *shelving* the license (see later shelving discussion) by requiring the licensee to make a tangible economic investment in the license.

Royalties

Royalties are future payments to compensate the licensor for transferring the patent rights. Royalty payments are most commonly structured as a percentage of the net sales or profits that are actually generated from using the patented technology. Such percentage of generated results royalties are referred to as running royalties (or earned royalties). Royalties can also be structured to be independent of sales or profit results. Examples of independent royalties include minimum royalties, milestone payments, and R&D-funding royalties. Table 10.1 provides a summary of some of the more common forms of patent royalties.

TABLE 10.1 Summary of Common Forms of Patent Royalties

Type	Description	Rationale
Running (or Earned) Royalties		
Running sales royalties	Royalties are calculated as a percentage of the sales generated from using the patented technology.	Provides parties with an intuitively sensible way to deal with patent rights with highly uncertain values. Allows the value of the patent rights to become known through actual performance. Sales royalties tend to be more popular than profit royalties because of the greater complexity involved with calculating profits.
Running profit royalties	Royalties are calculated as a percentage of some form of profitability (e.g., operating profits) generated from using the patented technology.	Provides parties with an intuitively sensible way to deal with patent rights with highly uncertain values. Allows the value of the patent rights to become known through actual performance. Profit royalties are less popular than sales royalties.

(continued)

TABLE 10.1 *(Continued)*

Type	Description	Rationale
Independent Royalties		
Minimum royalties	Used in connection with an earned royalties provision to guarantee the rights holder a minimum amount of revenue from the transaction even if the transferee struggles to sell the patented product.	Reduces the risk for the rights holder that transferee's sales or profit projections are too optimistic. Also helps to prevent transferees from *shelving* the patent rights (i.e., transferee does not intend to use the patent rights, but instead acquires them to block rivals).
Milestone payments	Transferee agrees to pay a set royalty payment upon the occurrence of certain events that show technical progress with the patented technology.	For higher-risk, early-stage patents, milestone payments can be used to reduce the amount of a partial upfront fee. As information that reduces the risk becomes available, the transferee makes payments that would otherwise have been part of the up-front fee.
R&D-funding royalties	A portion of the paid royalties must be used by the rights holder to fund additional research or development that may be needed to further advance the patented invention.	Provides the transferee with confidence that the rights holder will do continuing R&D work.

Sources: Mark Holmes, *Patent Licensing: Strategy, Negotiation, and Forms* (2010); Anne Layne-Farrar and Josh Lerner, "Valuing Patents for Licensing: A Practical Survey of the Literature" (March 2006), http://ssrn.com/abstract=1440292; authors' personal experience.

Running Royalties   When a running royalties approach is used, one of the first issues to resolve is the base against which the royalty percentage will be calculated. Will the royalty percentage be based on sales or profits, and, in either case, how will that base be calculated? Generally speaking, licensing professionals prefer using sales for the royalty base. The preference for a sales royalty base stems from concerns about profit calculations and the greater ability to manage profits through various accounting treatments. This is sometimes characterized as a concern that the licensee will use accounting chicanery to lie about its profits. That characterization may be too strong and is frequently unfair. A more apt description of the potential problem is that a licensor should be concerned about the much greater complexity that goes into calculating profits. There are simply more inputs, many of which involve subjective calls, involved in calculating profits than in calculating sales. Unless the licensor is ready to do all the homework necessary to understand how the licensee will be calculating profits, using sales as the royalty base is a much safer and simpler approach.

Once the parties decide whether to go with running sales royalties or running profit royalties, they next need to define the specific sales or profit measurement. If the parties decide to go with running sales royalties, for example, they need to define which sales measurement will be used for the royalty calculation. The typical sales measurement will be some form of net sales. A common approach is to define net sales as revenues actually received from sales using the patented technology minus transportation costs, taxes (such as sales and value-added taxes), and product returns.[4] In some cases, the parties may opt for a piece rate approach whereby the royalty will be a fixed payment per unit sold.

Although less common, parties occasionally agree to running profit royalties. In the case of running profit royalties, the parties have more choices for how to define the royalty base. Gross margins, operating profits, pretax profits, EBITDA (earnings before interest, taxes, depreciation, and amortization), and net income could all be used. If running profit royalties are to be used, the better approach is to use a profit measurement that is "higher up on the income statement," such as gross margins. As one moves down the income statement, the more one encounters expenses that have little to do with the quality of the patented technology and its economic value and are more likely to be idiosyncratic to that particular licensee. For example, tax strategies, financing, and particular company accounting policies, such as overhead allocation for particular projects, can overwhelm the economic benefit that flows from a patent.

Independent Royalties   In addition to the well-known running royalty strategies, parties also frequently incorporate one or more independent royalty strategies into their licensing transactions. The term *independent royalties* comes from the royalties being independent of sales or profit results. The primary independent royalty strategies are minimum royalties, milestone payments, and R&D-funding royalties.

- **Minimum royalties:** These royalties are used in connection with an earned-royalties provision to guarantee the licensor a minimum amount of revenue from the transaction even if the licensee struggles to sell the patented product.
- **Milestone payments:** The licensee agrees to pay a set royalty payment upon the occurrence of certain events that show technical progress with the patented technology. Sometimes used for pharmaceutical patents, typical milestones include "preclinical tests, applications for clinical testing, and eventual approval."[5]
- **R&D-funding royalties:** A portion of the paid royalties must be used by the licensor to fund additional research or development that may be needed to further advance the patented invention.

Equity Stakes

It is not uncommon for the licensor to accept all or some of the licensee's payments in the form of stock. Instead of paying cash, the licensee issues stock. There are a variety of ways to structure that equity interest, but it will likely involve the licensee issuing one or more of the following securities to the licensor: (1) common stock in the licensee, (2) preferred stock in the licensee, or (3) warrants that entitle the licensor to purchase common or preferred stock at a future date at what should be a favorable price. Equity stakes can be used to pay lump sum fees, running royalties, or independent royalties. The equity-stake option can be particularly attractive to licensees that are cash-poor, earlier-stage start-ups.

Start-up Licensees   High-technology start-up firms are common licensees of patented technology, often licensing the patented technology from universities. These high-technology start-ups, which are created with the intention to grow rapidly and become dominant firms, employ innovations and technological advances to create new products, markets, processes for doing business, and even new industries. One common characteristic that describes most start-ups is a need for more cash to grow the business. Because start-ups are built for rapid growth, they sacrifice near-term profitability so as to generate that growth. At the same time, the financing environment for start-ups tends to be very challenging. Therefore, when a licensor considers licensing its patent rights to a start-up, it frequently faces the following scenario:

- **Start-up positives:** The rapid-growth potential of the start-up may allow it to eventually generate the most sales or profits from the patented technology and therefore the greatest running royalties for the licensor.

■ **Start-up negatives:** The start-up lacks cash to pay a significant lump sum fee and may resist paying cash royalties during the early years of the license. The start-up may need to maintain that cash to grow its business.

One way to address the start-up's cash constraints is to employ equity stakes and structure some of the start-up's payments in the form of stock. Equity stakes can be used to pay up-front fees, earned royalties, or independent royalties. MIT, which commonly licenses its patented inventions to start-ups, provides a successful example of the equity-stake approach and frequently takes equity "in partial lieu of royalties."[6]

Valuing Equity Securities   Employing equity stakes as a payment strategy raises an entirely new set of valuation issues for the parties. If an equity stake is included in the transaction, the parties now need to value more than just the patent rights that are being transferred. The parties also need to determine the value of the equity stake that is included in the transaction (see Box 10.1).

BOX 10.1: VALUING EQUITY SECURITIES

Valuing equity securities is an extensive topic that is beyond the scope of this book. We would, however, like to provide some general thoughts on valuing equity securities. The fundamental goal of the valuation analysis is the same for equity securities as it is for patent rights. In both cases, the goal is to measure the stream of economic benefits that flow to the asset holder and then determine the present value of those benefits. The difference between patent valuation and stock valuation lies principally in where to look for the stream of benefits.

With equity securities, the economic benefits stem from the company's performance. Take, for example, common stock, which represents a percentage ownership in a corporation. Assuming a typical form of common stock, this ownership share entitles the stockholder to a number of rights (both economic and noneconomic), the most significant of which is a residual claim on the corporation's net assets. In plain English, that residual claim means the following:

■ The stockholders do not have direct ownership in the corporation's assets nor are they responsible for the corporation's liabilities. The corporation owns its own assets and is responsible for its own liabilities.

(continued)

(continued)

- The stockholders have an ownership interest in what we refer to as the corporation's *residual* (see Figure 10.1). The residual is the assets that remain upon the liquidation of the corporation after all the corporation's liabilities have been satisfied.
- In addition to waiting for the ultimate liquidation of the corporation, stockholders may also receive a portion of the residual on a current basis if the corporation is solvent and decides to use a portion of its net assets to pay a dividend or buy back outstanding stock.

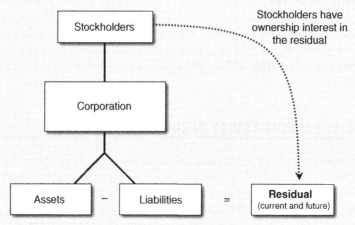

FIGURE 10.1 A Corporation's Residual

This economic right in the corporation's residual drives the value of a stock. Roughly speaking, the value of a stock should be based on the share of the corporation's eventual residual (including future dividend payouts and stock buybacks) represented by the stock, discounted back to the present value. Assuming a healthy growing corporation, the eventual residual should be substantially greater than its current net asset position, which means that much (if not most) of the corporation's eventual residual will be generated in the future by the corporation generating profits. The value of the stock is therefore fundamentally driven by forecasts of the corporation's future profits.

In addition to its role in valuing equity-stake licensing compensation, valuing equity securities also plays an important role in shadow pricing (see Chapter 8).

Select Licensing Scenarios

Developing an optimal payment structure for a patent license can raise a number of specific licensing issues. Shelving, maintaining inventor involvement, and antitrust issues, for example, can be problematic and should be taken into account when structuring the license payments.

Strategies to Avoid Shelving Although running royalty strategies are common, they can be vulnerable to certain types of strategic behavior. From the licensor's perspective, one of the bigger risks with a running-royalty strategy is exposure to shelving, the situation when a firm obtains an exclusive patent license but has no intention of using the patented technology. Instead, the licensee puts aside the invention (shelves it) and uses the acquired patent rights to block competitors from using the technology. Because they have no intention of generating the sales or profits that would trigger payments, licensees wishing to shelve an invention are more than happy to agree to a running royalties structure. If the payment for the exclusive license is entirely based on running royalties, the nonusing licensee could block its competitors from using the technology for free.

When shelving is the probable outcome, the licensor should insist on a complete lump sum fee. If the licensor has competently valued and priced its patent rights, it receives full value with the complete lump sum fee and should be ambivalent (at least from an economic perspective) to whether the licensee shelves the technology. In many cases, however, shelving is not the probable outcome, but instead is only a possible outcome. And what if the licensee is not prepared to pay a complete lump sum fee? What then? In that situation, which describes many possible licensing deals, the licensor could consider alternative scenarios such as supplementing the running royalties with a partial lump sum fee or minimum royalties or the use of a nonexclusive license to competitors to provide a marketplace incentive. Such guaranteed payments and other contractual provisions (such as licensee promising to use the patented technology) should help to dissuade the most serious *shelvers* and will provide the licensor with downside risk protection.

Maintaining Inventor Involvement There is a common misperception about the general maturity of patented technology. An invention that warrants a patent is not necessarily a complete product that is ready for commercialization. On the contrary, many patents require substantial further development for the patented technology to become a viable, commercial product (see Figure 10.2). For earlier-stage technology that requires further development, the parties should determine who will be conducting that further development. Intelligently making that determination requires the parties

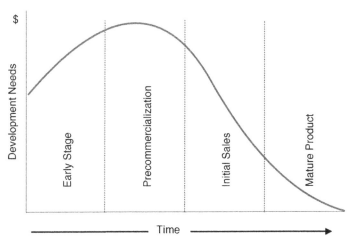

FIGURE 10.2 Patented Technology Can Fall within a Range of Maturity Levels and Development Needs

to conduct a valuation analysis. The parties need to determine who has the best development expertise for the technology and who can conduct the development most cost-effectively.

If the licensor is the more logical party for the further development, the licensee should develop a payment structure that incentivizes that behavior. Including R&D-funding royalties as part of the payment structure is the most obvious choice. With R&D-funding royalties, a portion of the paid royalties must be used by the licensor to fund additional research or development that may be needed to advance the patented invention. R&D-funding royalties can be structured in a variety of ways, such as by tying the payments to defined development milestones. The licensee may also want to consider shifting some of its payments (whether lump sum fees or royalties) from cash to stock. The licensee could make some of its payments in the form of licensee's common or preferred stock. Making the licensor an equity owner in the licensee helps to align the licensor's incentives with the licensee, which should help to encourage, at least partially, the licensor's continued development work.

If the licensee is the more logical party for the further development, the licensor should develop a payment structure that incentivizes that behavior. Assuming a common payment structure whereby the licensor expects to generate the bulk of its payments in the form of sales royalties, the licensor will want to be certain that the licensee does the necessary development work. One possibility is for the licensor to include a lump sum fee and then offer rebates on that lump sum fee as the licensee hits defined development milestones.

In any scenario in which further development is required, the nondeveloping party can also require the developing party to agree in the licensing agreement to do such development. To give the contractual commitments some teeth, the nondeveloping party may want to insist on some type of stipulated damages provision in the licensing agreement that clearly notifies the developing party of the consequences of breaching the commitment.

Licensing and Antitrust Concerns   Patent licensing involves at least one party who plans to use the patent in an effort to generate economic benefits in excess of the acquisition costs. Often these expected economic benefits are to be derived from using the patented technology to reduce competition. It is therefore not surprising that licensing activities can trigger antitrust or competition law concerns. Actions that may benefit an individual patent-wielding competitor can have potentially harmful effects on overall competition and, as such, may be actionable under antitrust laws and draw the unwelcome attention of disgruntled plaintiff competitors or law enforcement authorities from the various states, the federal government, or other governments around the world. Tying a patented technology to nonpatented products to force a purchaser to buy the nonpatented product, acquisition of sufficient patent assets to trigger merger concerns, or using a license to support a price-fixing scheme are all examples of possible competition law problems that can arise.

Extending the Patent License beyond the Patent's Expiration   One fundamental principle in both patent law[7] and antitrust law[8] is that the patent owner cannot engage in practices that exceed the inherent powers in the original patent grant. This restriction includes collecting royalties after expiration of the licensed patent's term for postexpiration use of the patent.[9] As the U.S. Supreme Court said in *Brulotte v. Thys Co.*:

> *A patent empowers the owner to exact royalties as high as he can negotiate with the leverage of that monopoly. But to use that leverage to project those royalty payments beyond the life of the patent is analogous to an effort to enlarge the monopoly of the patent by tieing the sale or use of the patented article to the purchase or use of unpatented ones.*[10]

Along the same vein, courts are hostile to any effort by the patent owner to control the price of unpatented goods even if manufactured by a patented machine or process, or to control the price of unpatented components even if it is combined with a component that may be subject to patent coverage.[11]

Product Price Restrictions   A patented technology can confer on its owner a competitive advantage that allows the patent holder to charge a supra-competitive price in the market, thus allowing the patent holder to earn extra profits on each sale due to this monopoly power. If that patent holder licenses the patented technology to another, is there a way for the patent holder to ensure that these monopoly rents are preserved? One possible an-swer to this question is to include a minimum price restriction in the patent license. The first significant legal examination of this practice occurred in 1926 when the Supreme Court reviewed General Electric's decision to license its competitively superior lightbulbs to Westinghouse in *United States v. General Electric Co.*[12] The patent license required that Westing-house charge a specified price for the lightbulbs (presumably at a price level that maintained the supracompetitive profits for the patented technology). Although the U.S. Supreme Court concluded that General Electric's license did not violate antitrust law, the case has experienced a difficult history ever since and has faced numerous legal challenges from competition enforce-ment authorities[13] as well as court imposed limitations and exceptions.[14] As a result, including a product price restriction clause in a licensing agree-ment is a risky move, especially because the desired results can often be achieved by means that are less likely to draw antitrust scrutiny.

DETERMINING THE PRICE FOR A LICENSE

Once the parties have an understanding of the available pricing options, how should they price a given patent license? What should the parties be trying to accomplish? The flippant answer is that the licensor should be try-ing to charge as high a price as possible, whereas the licensee should be try-ing to pay as low a price as possible. A more useful answer, however, would probably focus on the value of the patent license to the licensor and the licensee. Gordon Smith and Russell Parr explain the value proposition of a patent license as follows:

> *[Value to] the Licensor: The present value of the compensation to be received (typically cash payments) less the present value of the costs that might be incurred to administer the agreement, or income for-gone by electing not to exploit the intellectual property internally.*
>
> *[Value to] the Licensee: The present value of the future economic benefits of exploiting the licensed intellectual*

property less the costs (including payments to the licensor) of doing so."[15]

The value (and therefore the price) of the license stems from the net future economic benefits that flow from the license to each party.

The Pricing Zone

The price of any good should be based on the good's value to both the buyer and the seller. Let us consider a simple example where buyer wants to buy a computer from seller. The price of the transaction should be determined based on the value of the computer to buyer and to seller. For this example, assume that buyer values the computer at $750 and seller values it at $650. Because buyer ascribes a higher value to the computer than seller, a deal should be reached and the price of the computer could be at any point between $650 and $750 (the pricing zone). The key to pricing the computer therefore is accurately determining its value to buyer and seller.

The same pricing principle applies to pricing a patent license. The total price for the license (including lump sum fees and royalties) should be (1) greater than the value of the patent rights to the licensor and (2) less than the value of the patent rights to the licensee. In effect, if the value of the patent license falls within the pricing zone for doing a deal, a transaction makes sense and the parties simply need to figure out how to divide the extra value that is created by the transaction (see Figure 10.3). When royalties are developed intelligently, they are the tangible representation of this value measurement and apportionment. The royalties should measure the licensee's economic benefits from obtaining the patent rights and apportion those benefits between the licensor and the licensee. Any royalty rate within the pricing zone could be a reasonable outcome, although the apportionment could vary greatly, depending on the parties' relative negotiating leverage.

Valuation Methods for a Patent License

No single calculation leads to the perfect price for a patent license. Instead, the parties should work through a general process that identifies the value of the license to the licensor and licensee so as to determine the range of royalties that would be economically reasonable for the transaction. Any of the methods outlined in Chapters 6 through 9 can be used to develop the value boundaries that make up the pricing zone. Income methods (including both discounted future economic benefits (DFEB) analysis and more advanced income methods), market methods, and costs methods can all be used.

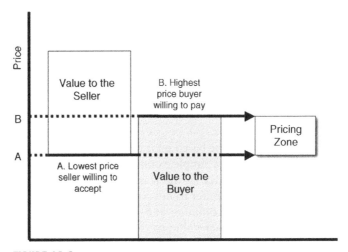

FIGURE 10.3   The Pricing Zone for a Patent License

LESS FORMAL VALUATION TECHNIQUES FOR SETTING ROYALTY RATES

Parties to patent licenses frequently avoid conducting extensive valuation analysis that would allow them to identify the pricing zone intelligently and thereafter choose a proper price. Anecdotal evidence suggests that many parties avoid more elaborate valuation analysis in favor of rules of thumb (or best guesses) to price patent licenses. For example, a Harvard Business School case study found that

> *even organizations that are aware of their intellectual assets tend to choose royalty rates based on a "rule of thumb" rather than rates based on quantitative metrics or analysis of profitability.*[16]

Smith and Parr offer a common explanation for why parties avoid fundamental analysis. They explain, "We often receive the comment that, while our investment analysis techniques make sense theoretically, they are often too difficult to apply because one must make forecasts."[17] Without the will to develop forecasts, income valuation methods—which are the most relevant valuation methods for a licensing transaction—cannot be properly employed, and parties gravitate to less formal techniques. Moreover, the predominance of running royalty rates makes the decision to eschew proper valuation analysis seem less relevant. Running royalties allow parties who are uncomfortable valuing the patent rights to sidestep the problem. Rather than try to value the patent rights at the time of the licensing negotiation precisely, the parties use running royalties to allow the value of the patent rights to become known through actual performance. If the patent rights prove to be valuable in the marketplace, the licensee will pay a high price through greater running royalty payments. If the patent rights prove not to be all that valuable in the marketplace, the price or royalty payments will be low.

There is a fair amount of wisdom to this line of thinking about running royalties. Running royalties allow the licensor and licensee to reach a price in an extremely uncertain environment where the parties may have widely differing views about the ultimate value of the patent rights. Consider the following example. Licensor, a medical device company, has invented a patented device that allows for manipulation of image pixels that make mammograms more easily readable. Licensor believes the patented technology could also be used in the area of satellite imagery and is in talks with Licensee, a satellite imagery company. Licensor and Licensee are considering whether to enter into an exclusive license for the patented technology for the satellite imagery market, but they have very different views about the size of the potential market. Based on Licensor's experience with the patented technology in the medical device market, it believes that this technology will take off in the satellite imagery market and could generate $50 million of net cash flows before the patent expires. Licensee is not as optimistic and believes that the maximum potential cash flows from the technology in the satellite imagery market are $10 million. Both parties are interested in doing the deal, but their estimations of the potential value opportunity are so divergent that reaching a deal would seem to be impossible. Using a running royalty approach, however, could allow the parties to bridge this gap because the eventual price will be based on the actual results rather than their divergent forecasts.

Although running royalties allow the parties to overcome some types of valuation uncertainty, they do not obviate the need for dividing up the potential gains that may flow from the licensing transaction. Let us return to the satellite imagery device patent license. Whether the patented technology generates $50 million, $10 million, or some other amount in net cash flows altogether, the parties need to allocate that net economic benefit between them in some manner. The tendency is to use rather informal techniques to accomplish this. In this section, we review some of the more common informal techniques. In addition, we explain when informal techniques are likely to be an acceptable means for pricing a patent license and when they should be avoided in favor of more elaborate valuation analysis. Specifically, we look at

1. Rules of thumb
2. Industry royalty rates
3. Economic benefit analysis

Rules of Thumb: The 25 Percent Rule

The most well-known rule of thumb for pricing patent licenses is the so-called 25 percent rule, which is generally credited to Robert Goldscheider (see Box 10.2). Application of the 25 percent rule is relatively straightforward. The parties estimate the operating profit that the licensee will generate from the licensing transaction and then devise a royalty rate that results in the licensor receiving 25 percent of those profits. Assuming that the parties agree to use running sales royalties as the payment structure, the 25 percent rule is calculated as follows:

1. Take the estimated operating profit and divide it by expected net sales to arrive at an estimated operating margin.
2. Multiply the estimated operating margin by 25 percent to arrive at the appropriate running sales royalty.

If the parties estimate that licensee's operating margin from the patented technology will be 24 percent from the patented technology, the running sales royalty would be 6 percent. The 25 percent rule can be used

---

BOX 10.2: ORIGINS OF THE 25 PERCENT RULE

The 25 percent rule is frequently traced to a 1959 study conducted by Robert Goldscheider. Goldscheider examined 18 license agreements that had been entered into by a Swiss subsidiary of Philco Corporation (a U.S. manufacturing company) as the licensor. In each case, the license was for 3 years (with a renewal expectation), provided the licensee an exclusive territory, and covered a patented technology and related intellectual property rights. Goldscheider's study found that

the licensees tended to generate profits of approximately 20% of sales, on which they paid royalties of 5% of sales. Thus, the royalty rates were found to be 25% of the licensee's profits on products embodying the patented technology.[18]

to develop the royalty rate for a single-patent product or for a patented technology that will be merely one component among many in a complex array of parts and components. In the more complex setting, the 25 percent rule should not be used to develop a split of the operating profit for the overall product, but instead should be used to develop a split of the incremental economic benefit that stems from that particular patented technology.

Goldscheider explains the theory underlying the 25 percent rule as follows:

> *The licensor and licensee should share in the profitability of products embodying the patented technology. The a priori assumption is that the licensee should retain a majority (e.g., 75%) of the profits because it has undertaken substantial development, operational, and commercialization risks, contributed other technology/intellectual property, and/or brought to bear its own development, operational, and commercialization contributions.*[19]

The 25 percent rule is not popular with most valuation commentators and tends to be treated rather dismissively. It is criticized for its weak theoretical basis and lack of economic rigor.[20] To compound matters, the United States Court of Appeals for the Federal Circuit ruled in *Uniloc USA Inc. v. Microsoft Corp.*[21] that the 25 percent rule may not be used as evidence to prove a reasonable royalty measure of damages without evidence to support its validity (see Chapter 11).

Despite the criticism, we believe that the 25 percent rule should not be dismissed too quickly as a tool for pricing patent licenses in the transactional setting. As long as the parties recognize the 25 percent rule for what it is—namely, an inexact satisfying tool (see Chapter 3)—the rule can be quite useful. As Goldscheider emphasizes when discussing the rule, it is not meant to provide a definitive valuation. Nor does it mean that every negotiation should begin with a 25:75 split and stay there.[22] Instead, the 25 percent rule is meant to provide a potential starting point for a negotiation that can be adjusted upward or downward based on the specific factors of that particular transaction and the parties involved. It serves only modest valuation functions for licensing transactions, but it serves those functions sufficiently well. The 25 percent rule is an allocation tool that forces the parties do two things:

1. Consider the economic benefits that are expected from the licensing transaction.
2. Consciously allocate those benefits.

For a satisficing technique, it is actually quite good. In situations in which there are considerable uncertainties surrounding the future economic benefits, using such an allocation rule can provide an acceptable path to an agreement. We might not recommend the 25 percent rule to determine the price for extremely large licensing transactions that justify more detailed valuation analysis. For smaller licensing transactions that do not warrant detailed valuation analysis, however, the 25 percent rule is not a bad method.

Finally, the 25 percent rule may not be as arbitrary as some commentators would suggest. As a reminder, the function of the 25 percent rule is to provide a starting point for apportioning the licensee's economic benefits from the licensing transaction between the licensee and the licensor. Economic theory does not tell us much about how the parties should apportion the benefit. Any apportionment that falls within the pricing zone is theoretically justified. When two parties have to apportion something and there is no clear justification for favoring one party over the other, a 50:50 split is an appropriate division since both parties are treated equally. The 25:75 allocation naturally flows from that premise as follows:

1. First, the licensor and licensee could split the forecasted economic benefit on a 50:50 basis. In the case of a licensor/licensee apportionment, however, it is likely that the licensee will bear more risk from the transaction and should probably receive better than a 50:50 split. The licensee should probably receive some of licensor's 50 percent, but how much? The licensor and the licensee need to apportion the licensor's 50 percent.
2. If there is again no clear justification for favoring one party over the other, a second 50:50 split is a logical choice. The licensor and the licensee could split the licensor's 50 percent benefit on a 50:50 basis. As a result, the licensor receives 25 percent of the economic benefit and the licensee receives 75 percent (see Figure 10.4).

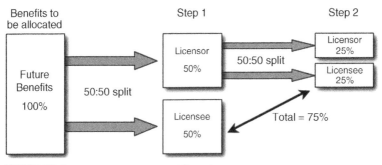

FIGURE 10.4 Arriving at a 25:75 Allocation

To the extent that there are justifications that help to guide the apportionments, the parties should arrive at a different result. If, for example, the licensor has multiple licensees to choose from it may be able to justify a larger percentage of the apportionment, but in the absence of any guidance, the 25:75 split is not illogical.

Industry Royalty Rates

Industry royalty rates are sometimes used as a market-based approach to price a patent license. The parties to a license transaction may use royalty data from prior, comparable transactions in their industry to determine the appropriate royalty rate for their specific transaction. Some of the more common royalty rate sources include Intellectual Property Research Associates, RoyaltySource.com, the Association of University Technology Managers, and the Licensing Executive Society. Such royalty rate sources often provide information on running sales royalty rates and profit rates for a given industry. Box 10.3 provides sample industry royalty rate information. Some royalty source services, such as Intellectual Property Research Associates, also provide royalty information on specific licensing transactions in their database.

Aggregate industry royalty rates provide almost no guidance on how to price an individual patent license. A comparable transaction market method values an asset by looking at the range of prices paid in past or current transactions for similar assets. There are two main requirements for a

BOX 10.3: SAMPLE INDUSTRY ROYALTY RATE INFORMATION

Industry	Running Sales Royalty Rate (late 1980s–2000)			Industry Profit Rates (1990–2000) Weighted Average Operating Margin
	Minimum	Maximum	Median	
Electronics	0.5%	15.0%	4.0%	8.8%
Pharma and biotech	0.1%	40.0%	5.1%	16.4%

Source: Russell Parr, *Royalty Rates for Licensing Intellectual Property* (2007), 47.

comparable transaction market method to provide useful valuation information for a particular patent license:

1. The market transactions used as guidance must be comparable to the license being priced.
2. The market-derived prices must come from a relatively efficient market.

In the case of aggregate industry royalty rates, it is highly unlikely that either requirement is met. First, trying to compare an individual patent to an industry-wide selection of patents is next to impossible. It appears that the distribution of patent valuations is not a normal, or Gaussian, distribution. Instead, patent valuations appear to follow either a power-law or lognormal distribution. At one end of the spectrum will be a large number of patents that will have modest to nonexistent economic value. At the other end of the spectrum will be a much smaller number of patents of enormous value, patents that allow the owner to control multibillion dollar markets. As a result, it is not clear what the median royalty rate for an industry says about a single patent.

Second, the imperfection of most patent markets is well understood. As Massimiliano Granieri and his colleagues explain:

> *This implies that the prices we observe in these markets (royalty rates and fees) might not represent the real 'market' prices. The risk, therefore, is that we use inefficient prices for the valuation of the new license.*"[23]

Economic Benefit Analysis

The last of the less formal methods that we cover is what we refer to as the economic benefit analysis (EBA). In fact, EBA is not really a method; rather, it is more of a process that helps the parties to focus more intently on the rationale for the price that they will end up establishing. In some cases, the EBA process is used in conjunction with a DFEB analysis (see Chapter 6), in particular if the parties want to include significant lump sum fees or minimum royalties. In other cases, EBA will indicate a pricing approach that may not require a formal DFEB analysis. EBA can also include insights from real options theory and other advanced income methods that incorporate the value of future decision opportunities (see Chapter 7).

The EBA process recognizes that there is no single calculation that leads to a proper royalty rate. Instead, EBA encourages a party to a licensing transaction to work through a general process that helps to determine the range of royalties (framed by the upper and lower limits of the pricing zone) that would be economically reasonable for the transaction. This general process can be reduced to a five-step analysis:

1. Identify the benefits that licensee may generate from the licensing transaction.
2. Measure those benefits on a net basis.
3. Determine the value to licensor of not licensing the patent rights to licensee.
4. Consider whether any adjustments should apply.
5. Apportion the benefits between the licensor and licensee.

Identify the Benefits to Licensee The first step in the process is to identify the specific benefits that the licensee will be able to generate from obtaining the patent rights. Typical benefits could include the following:

- Improved profits margins
- Access to new markets
- Increased sales
- Opportunities to sublicense the patent rights
- Improved cross-licensing strength
- Improved technological strength
- Reduced risk of infringement suits

In conducting this first step, it is important to identify each of the potential benefits that can reasonably be expected to flow from the patent rights. Because the licensor will be the party arguing for a higher royalty rate, it is particularly incumbent on the licensor to envision each of the potential uses for the patent rights to be certain that all the benefits are captured in the analysis.

Measure Licensee's Net Benefits Once the licensee's potential benefits have been identified, the valuation methods explained in previous chapters provide the necessary tools to intelligently value those benefits. To illustrate this point, let us consider a few examples that demonstrate how to value some of the more common benefits that flow to licensees. For each of these examples, the probable licensee will be Tech Co., which is a high-technology company that manufactures and sells biomedical devices.

Example 1: Patented invention improves one element of a complex product. In this first example, Tech Co. is considering entering into a 5-year, nonexclusive license for a patented component (Patented Component) that will replace an existing piece of technology (Existing Component) in one of its more complex biomedical devices (Complex Device). The Patented Component will have no effect on the functionality of the Complex Device. The value proposition for using the Patented Component is one of cost savings. Not counting the cost of licensing the Patented Component, its per-unit acquisition cost will be cheaper than the per-unit acquisition cost of the Existing Component currently being used in the Complex Device. In addition, the Patented Component will be easier to install into the Complex Device, which will reduce its overall production costs.

Following the stated assumptions of this example, the value of the Patented Component does not stem from many of the typical patent benefits such as market power or litigation savings. Instead, the value of the Patented Component stems from its ability to reduce the manufacturing costs for the Complex Device. The measurement analysis should therefore focus on that particular benefit. To do that, Tech Co. could generate two 5-year forecasts for the Complex Device. The first forecast (see Table 10.2) would assume continued use of the Existing Component. The second forecast (see Table 10.3) would assume a switch to the Patented Component.

As you can see from Tables 10.2 and 10.3, the switch to the Patented Component would improve Tech Co.'s gross margin from 22.3 percent to 26.4 percent. Because the switch to the Patented Component does not affect overhead expenses, the gross profit margin improvement translates directly to the bottom line and provides a corresponding improvement to Tech Co.'s operating margin. Although not a perfect proxy for the economic benefit that Tech Co. will receive from the Patented Component—because it does not track the benefit all the way through cash flow—it is quite close. Measuring Tech Co.'s economic benefit from the potential patent license is therefore not much more than measuring Tech Co.'s operating margin improvement that would come from using the Patented Component. That insight can then be expressed with the simple equation

Licensee's forecasted economic benefit from the patent rights	=	Forecasted operating margin with patent rights	–	Forecasted operating margin without patent rights

In Tech Co.'s particular situation, its forecasted economic benefits from the Patented Component will be a 4.1 percent operating margin improvement.

Example 2: Single-patent product. In this example, Tech Co. is considering entering into an 18-year, exclusive license for a bundle of patents that belong to the local research university. A professor at the university invented a new biomedical device (the Device) that is protected by a series of patents (the Portfolio), each of which is held by the university. The

TABLE 10.2 Tech Co's First Forecast: Assumes Continued Use of Existing Component

	Year 1	Year 2	Year 3	Year 4	Year 5
Revenue					
Units sold	6,500	6,600	6,650	6,650	6,700
Price per unit	$ 1,100	$1,100	$ 1,100	$ 1,100	$ 1,100
Total revenue	$7,150,000	$7,260,000	$7,315,000	$7,315,000	$7,370,000
Manufacturing Costs					
Cost per unit (excluding costs associated with Existing Component)	$ 700	$ 700	$ 700	$ 700	$ 700
Purchase cost per Existing Component	$ 125	$ 125	$ 125	$ 125	$ 125
Installation cost per Existing Component	$ 30	$ 30	$ 30	$ 30	$ 30
Total manufacturing costs	$5,557,500	$5,643,000	$5,685,750	$5,685,750	$5,728,500
Gross Margin					
Gross profit (total)	$1,592,500	$1,617,000	$1,629,250	$1,629,250	$1,641,500
Gross profit (per unit)	$ 245	$ 245	$ 245	$ 245	$ 245
Gross margin	22.3%	22.3%	22.3%	22.3%	22.3%
Operating Margin					
Total overhead expenses	$1,072,500	$1,089,000	$1,097,250	$1,097,250	$1,105,500
Operating profit	$ 520,000	$ 528,000	$ 532,000	$ 532,000	$ 536,000
Operating margin	7.3%	7.3%	7.3%	7.3%	7.3%

TABLE 10.3 Tech Co's Second Forecast: Assumes Switch to Patented Component

	Year 1	Year 2	Year 3	Year 4	Year 5
Revenue					
Units sold	6,500	6,600	6,650	6,650	6,700
Price per unit	$ 1,100	$ 1,100	$ 1,100	$ 1,100	$ 1,100
Total revenue	$7,150,000	$7,260,000	$7,315,000	$7,315,000	$7,370,000
Manufacturing Costs					
Cost per unit (excluding costs associated with Existing or Patented Component)	$ 700	$ 700	$ 700	$ 700	$ 700
Purchase cost per Patented Component	$ 85	$ 85	$ 85	$ 85	$ 85
Installation cost per Patented Component	$ 25	$ 25	$ 25	$ 25	$ 25
Total manufacturing costs	$5,265,000	$5,346,000	$5,386,500	$5,386,500	$5,427,000
Gross Margin					
Gross profit (total)	$1,885,000	$1,914,000	$1,928,500	$1,928,500	$1,943,000
Gross profit (per unit)	$ 290	$ 290	$ 290	$ 290	$ 290
Gross margin	26.4%	26.4%	26.4%	26.4%	26.4%
Operating Margin					
Total overhead expenses	$1,072,500	$1,089,000	$1,097,250	$1,097,250	$1,105,500
Operating profit	$ 812,500	$ 825,000	$ 831,250	$ 831,250	$ 837,500
Operating margin	11.4%	11.4%	11.4%	11.4%	11.4%

Device is actually quite revolutionary, and there is no existing technology that can replicate what it does. The holder of the patent rights for the Portfolio will therefore be able to pursue the market for the Device with little to no competition for at least a few years. The expectation is that within 3 years, one or more competing technologies will be available for the market and will begin to compete with the Device.

The value proposition in this second example is very different from the value proposition in the first example. With example 1, the value proposition was the patented invention's ability to lower licensee's manufacturing costs and to improve profit margins. With example 2, obtaining the patent rights will open up an entirely new market for Tech Co. But for the Portfolio, Tech Co. would not be able to immediately pursue the market for the Device. As a result, Tech Co.'s economic benefit inquiry should have a very different focus than the inquiry for example 1. With example 2, the focus should be on the entirety of the profits that are to be generated from the Device. Let us start with the initial 3 years of the potential license because Tech Co. forecasts a complete monopoly during that time frame. The economic benefit to Tech Co. could be expressed in the very simple equation

$$
\begin{matrix}
\text{Licensee's forecasted} \\ \text{economic benefit from} \\ \text{the patent rights}
\end{matrix}
=
\begin{matrix}
\text{Forecasted profit} \\ \text{margin from the} \\ \text{patented invention}
\end{matrix}
-
\begin{matrix}
\text{Licensee's typical} \\ \text{profit margin on} \\ \text{new projects}
\end{matrix}
$$

A few points need to be made about this equation. First, this *but for* scenario is not all that common. Although patents are commonly discussed as providing the holder with economic monopoly power (see Chapter 5), that is really the exception. Example 1's scenario of the patented technology providing an incremental improvement to a particular product is a much more common scenario. Technological alternatives make this *but for* scenario relatively rare in practice. We point out this scenario, however, because (1) it does occur on occasion and (2) it tends to be on the minds of patent actors (and sometimes courts and policy makers). By highlighting this calculation, we get the opportunity to both address this specific scenario and provide the useful reminder that it is not a common scenario; therefore, do not overuse this equation.

Second, even when the *but for* scenario does take place, Tech Co.'s economic benefits are less than 100 percent of the profits from the venture. The reason for the reduction is that one should not assume that Tech Co. would do nothing if it did not pursue that opportunity. If Tech Co. did not pursue the opportunity, it would likely invest some of the resources planned for that opportunity in another venture. By pursuing the *but for* opportunity, Tech Co. is forgoing that other venture. To account for that lost opportunity, we suggest subtracting Tech Co.'s typical profit margin on new projects from the profit margin that is expected from the patented invention.

Third, we need to take into account that alternative technologies are expected to begin competing with the Device after 3 years. Such alternative technologies should increase competition in the market for the Device and erode the profit margin. Unless there is something truly exceptional about the Device and its market—such as special barriers to entry—that would allow Tech Co. to defend an above average profit margin for an extended period of time, the profit margin for the Device should erode to something approximating an average profit margin for comparable projects conducted by Tech Co. So, there is a distinct possibility that at some point during the 18-year license, the economic benefit to Tech Co. may be zero. If the profit margin from the Device is less than or equal to the profit margin on Tech Co.'s typical projects, there is no extra benefit generated by the Portfolio's patent rights (see Figure 10.5).

Example 3: Defense against infringement lawsuit. For this example, Tech Co.'s engineering department has developed a component (the Component) for another of its complex biomedical devices. The Component is just one part of the overall device, and Tech Co. never sought to patent the technology. A few years after Tech Co. began using the Component in the device, a third party (licensor) contacted Tech Co. about the Component. Licensor advised Tech Co. that its use of the Component infringed one of licensor's patents and offered Tech Co. the opportunity to license the

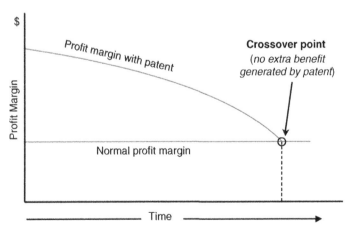

FIGURE 10.5 Crossover Point Where Economic Benefits Drop to Zero

patent. Tech Co. and its attorneys analyzed the infringement claim and concluded that the Component's technology was sufficiently different from the licensor's patent not to constitute infringement. They could not be 100 percent certain, however, that a court would reach the same conclusion. In fact, Tech Co. and its attorneys believe that there is roughly a 20 percent chance that a judge or jury would find that Tech Co. was infringing on the licensor's patent.

With example 3, the value proposition of the license would be its ability to eliminate a potential infringement suit. The value of the patent license to Tech Co. should therefore focus on cost savings from avoiding that lawsuit. This can be done with the formula

Licensee's forecasted economic benefit from the patent rights	=	Forecasted cost of litigation to defend against suit	+	Risk of damages being awarded for infringement	−	Deterrent value on future infringement suits from fighting this suit

Determine Licensor's Not-Licensing Value   Determining the licensee's net benefits from the patent rights should not end the inquiry. The licensee's net benefits only establish one end of the pricing zone. The goal of the EBA process is not simply to determine the maximum price that a licensee may be willing to pay for a license; rather, it is to determine the total economic benefit generated by the licensing transaction so that the amount can be thoughtfully apportioned between the parties. Determining the total economic benefit requires establishing the other end of the pricing zone, which is the value to the licensor of not licensing the patent rights to that particular licensee. We refer to that value as the licensor's not-licensing value (NLV). Establishing the licensor's NLV helps each party to understand the economics of the transaction and its relative leverage in the negotiation better. For the licensor, establishing the NLV helps to determine the following:

- Is licensing the patent rights to that particular licensee the most profitable strategy for the licensor, or should it pursue a different strategy?
- If licensing to that particular licensee is the most profitable strategy, how much more profitable is it than the best alternative (see Box 10.4)? Making that determination helps to inform the licensor on how aggressive it can be when finalizing the royalty rate with the licensee.

BOX 10.4: CONDUCTING A BEST ALTERNATIVE TO A NEGOTIATED AGREEMENT ANALYSIS

In 1981, Roger Fisher and William Ury at Harvard University's Program on Negotiation published their best-selling book, *Getting to Yes: Negotiating Agreement Without Giving In*. In that book, they popularized the concept of the *best alternative to a negotiated agreement* (BATNA). Fisher and Ury recognized, long before the current popularity of behavioral economics, that individuals engaged in negotiations may not always reach an agreement that in hindsight was a good deal for them. The pressure to get it done, the compulsion to reach an agreement, or just that significant time and energy had already been expended could easily lead a negotiation participant to a hasty decision.

One technique that Fisher and Ury suggested to prevent this all-too-natural occurrence was to focus on the BATNA. They took pains to distinguish their BATNA technique from the commonly used bottom-line approach. In a bottom-line approach, the negotiator determines, prior to the negotiations, a position or price that the negotiator will not breach. Although such walk-away positions can help to prevent a really poor agreement, Fisher and Ury note that this method has severe limitations and poses roadblocks to the negotiating parties in trying to construct an acceptable agreement.

Their search for a better approach—one that would help a party to accept agreements that should be accepted and to reject those that should not—led them to propose the concept of BATNA. A BATNA is developed through a three-step process:

1. Creatively and expansively develop a list of actions that can be taken if an agreement is not reached.

2. Winnow that list down to actions that seem the most practical.

3. Tentatively choose the action alternative that seems best.

Fisher and Ury purposefully used the word *tentatively* to emphasize that a BATNA is not to be a static barrier but instead a dynamic position that can be informed by the negotiation process itself. Each offer during the negotiation process is to be judged against the measure of the BATNA. Developing one's own BATNA is only half the story, however. As Fisher and Ury point out, consideration of the other side's BATNA may be even more important. In a particularly cogent example, they tell the story of a community group that is negotiating potential pollution issues with a power company that is building a new power plant. By assessing the power company's BATNA, the community group may come to understand that the best alternative to coming to an agreement with the community group could be either to ignore the group or to just to keep talking with them until such time as the power plant construction is over. Either way, the power company gets the plant built without an agreement with the community group on pollution. Once this original BATNA of the power company is understood, Fisher and Ury suggest that efforts to change the power company's BATNA (perhaps by filing a lawsuit seeking to hold up construction) would greatly facilitate negotiations between the parties.

Establishing the NLV also benefits the licensee. Just as with the licensor, establishing the NLV helps the licensee to better understand its leverage. If the licensor does not have an attractive alternative to consider, the licensee can be more aggressive in negotiations. If the licensor does have an attractive alternative, the licensee may want to be less aggressive in negotiations for fear of losing the licensor to that alternative.

Determining the NLV involves the same two-step process that is used to value the net economic benefits that the licensee expects to generate from the transaction. First, you need to identify the various types of benefits that the licensor may generate by not licensing the patent rights to that particular licensee. Then you need to value each benefit source using the valuation methods explained in previous chapters. Typical NLV benefit sources include the following:

- Practicing the invention exclusively.
- Licensing the patent rights to one or more different licensees.
- Shelving the patent rights.
- Pursuing litigation-based licensing revenues.

Consider Whether to Make Any Adjustments In Chapter 7, we explained the importance of incorporating the value of future decision opportunities that are embedded in a patent into the patent's overall value. Chapter 7 also provided detailed analysis on how to identify and capture the value of those future decision opportunities. Conducting that analysis can be somewhat complex and therefore is unlikely to be done unless the patent license is substantial. What should be done in the other situations when such advanced analysis is not conducted? Should the extra value from the future decision opportunities be left out of the analysis because the parties are not in a position to value it precisely? From the licensor's perspective, this opportunity is an ideal one for a satisficing strategy. Because it is highly unlikely that there is no value at all in such future decision opportunities, the licensor should insist on something. Even if the licensor simply proffers a wild guess about the value of the future decision opportunities, there is now at least a chance that the licensor will receive some additional compensation.

Apportion the Benefits   The final step of the economic benefit analysis is to apportion the benefits of the transaction between the parties. As long as the royalty rate is within the pricing zone, there is no de facto right or wrong answer. Apportioning the benefits is purely a function of leverage and negotiating ability. Parties with greater leverage and better negotiation skills should get a healthier portion of the apportionment.

REFERENCES

Bramson, Robert. 2001. "Valuing Patents, Technologies and Portfolios: Rules of Thumb." *PLI/Pat* 635: 465.

Clarkson, Gavin. 2000. "Intellectual Asset Valuation." Harvard Business School Case No. N9-801-192/Rev 10/1/00. Harvard Business School Publishing.

Cotter, Thomas. 2010/2011. "Four Principles for Calculating Reasonable Royalties in Patent Infringement Litigation." *Santa Clara Computer and High Technology Law Journal* 27: 725.

Degnan, Stephen, and Corwin Horton. June 1997. "A Survey of Licensed Royalties." *Les Nouvelles* 91.

Denton, F. Russell, and Paul Heald. 2003. "Random Walks, Non-Cooperative Games, and the Complex Mathematics of Patent Pricing." *Rutgers Law Review* 55: 1175.

Finch, Sharon. 2000. "Royalty Rates: Current Issues and Trends." *Journal of Commercial Biotechnology* 7: 224.

Goldscheider, Robert. 2011. "The Classic 25% Rule and the Art of Intellectual Property Licensing." *Duke Law and Technology Review* 6.

Goldscheider, Robert, John Jarosz, and Carla Mulhern. 2005. In *Intellectual Property: Valuation, Exploitation, and Infringement Damages*, edited by Gordon V. Smith and Russell L. Parr, 410–426. Hoboken, NJ: John Wiley & Sons.

Granieri, Massimiliano, Maria Isabella Leone, and Raffaele Oriani. 2011. "Patent Licensing Contracts." In *The Economic Valuation of Patents: Methods and Applications*, edited by Federico Munari and Raffaele Oriani, 233–261. Cheltenham, UK: Edward Elgar.

Holmes, Mark. 2010. *Patent Licensing: Strategy, Negotiation, and Forms*. New York: Practising Law Institute.

Kamien, Morton. 1992. "Patent Licensing." In *Handbook of Game Theory with Economic Applications*, vol. 1, edited by Robert Aumann and Sergio Hart, 331–354. North Holland: Elsevier Science.

Katz, Michael, and Carl Shapiro. 1985. "On the Licensing of Innovations." *RAND Journal of Economics* 16: 504.

Layne-Farrar, Anne, and Josh Lerner. Mar. 2006. "Valuing Patents for Licensing: A Practical Survey of the Literature." http://ssrn.com/abstract=1440292.

Merges, Robert. 1999. "The Law and Economics of Employee Inventions." *Harvard Journal of Law and Technology* 13: 1.

Meuller, Janice. 2006. *An Introduction to Patent Law*. 2nd ed. New York: Aspen Law & Business.

MIT Technology Licensing Office Website. No date. Frequently Asked Questions. http://web.mit.edu/tlo/www/about/faq.html#b7.

Orcutt, John. 2009. "The Case Against Exempting Smaller Reporting Companies from Sarbanes-Oxley Section 404: Why Market-Based Solutions Are Likely to Harm Ordinary Investors." *Fordham Journal of Corporate and Financial Law* 14: 325.

Orcutt, John, and Hong Shen. 2010. *Shaping China's Innovation Future: University Technology Transfer in Transition*. Cheltenham, UK: Edward Elgar.

Parr, Russell. 2007. *Royalty Rates for Licensing Intellectual Property*. Hoboken, NJ: John Wiley & Sons.

Romer, Paul M. 1990. "Endogenous Technological Change." *Journal of Political Economy* 98: S71.

Schecter, Roger E., and John R. Thomas. 2004. *Principles of Patent Law Concise Hornbook Series*. St. Paul, MN: West.

Shapiro, Carl. 1985. "Patent Licensing and R&D Rivalry." *American Economic Review* 75: 25.

Smith, Gordon V., and Russell L. Parr. 2005. *Intellectual Property: Valuation, Exploitation, and Infringement Damages*. Hoboken, NJ: John Wiley & Sons.

Thursby, Marie, Jerry Thursby, and Emmanuel Dechenaux. Feb. 2005. "Shirking, Sharing Risk, and Shelving: The Role of University License Contracts." NBER Working Paper No. 11128. http://www.nber.org/papers/w11128.pdf.

Varner, Thomas. Sept. 2010. "Technology Royalty Rates in SEC Filings." *Les Nouvelles*120.

NOTES

1. Massimiliano Granieri, Maria Isabella Leone, and Raffaele Oriani, "Patent Licensing Contracts," in *The Economic Valuation of Patents: Methods and Applications*, eds. Federico Munari and Raffaele Oriani (2011), 236.

2. Stephen Degnan and Corwin Horton, "A Survey of Licensed Royalties," *Les Nouvelles* (June 1997): 91.

3. Varner, Thomas, "Technology Royalty Rates in SEC Filings," *Les Nouvelles* (Sept. 2010): 120 127.

4. See Mark Holmes, *Patent Licensing: Strategy, Negotiation, and Forms* (2010), 4-10.

5. Holmes, 4-6, 4-7.

6. MIT Technology Licensing Office Website, Frequently Asked Questions, http://web.mit.edu/tlo/www/about/faq.html#b7.

7. The patent misuse doctrine is an equitable defense that can be employed to prohibit enforcement of license terms that either expand the patent beyond the terms of its original grant or that have a harmful effect on competition.

8. Even though patent licensing is generally considered procompetitive, the use of a patent can constitute an element of a challenged activity that has anticompetitive effect that is within the scope of the antitrust laws.

9. Delay of royalty payments into the postexpiration period for preexpiration use is permissible, but runs the risk of challenge if misconstrued. *Zenith Radio Corp. v. Hazeltine Research*, 395 U.S. 100 (1969).

10. 379 U.S. 29, 33 (1964), reh'g denied, 379 U.S. 985 (1965).

11. "A patentee may not use the power of his patent to levy a charge for making, using, or selling products not within the reach of the monopoly granted by the Government." *Zenith Radio Corp. v. Hazeltine Research*, 395 U.S. 100, 136 (1969).

12. 272 U.S. 476 (1926).

13. "It has been held per se illegal for a licensor of an intellectual property right in a product to fix a licensee's resale price of that product. . . . Consistent with the principles set forth in section 3.4, the Agencies will enforce the per se rule against resale price maintenance in the intellectual property context." Section 5.2, *Antitrust Guidelines for the Licensing of Intellectual Property*, U.S. Department of Justice and the Federal Trade Commission (1995).

14. *United States v. Line Material Co.*, 333 U.S. 287 (1948); *United States v. New Wrinkle, Inc.*, 342 U.S. 371 (1952); *United States v. Huck Mfg. Co.*, 382 U.S. 197 (1965); *United States v. Univis Lens Co.*, 316 U.S. 241 (1942); *Ethyl Gasoline Corp. v. United States*, 309 U.S. 436 (1940).

15. Gordon V. Smith and Russell L. Parr, *Intellectual Property: Valuation, Exploitation, and Infringement Damages* (2005), 429.

16. Intellectual Asset Valuation, Harvard Business School, Case Study N9-801-192, p. 4.

17. Smith and Parr, 429.

18. Robert Goldscheider, John Jarosz, and Carla Mulhern. In *Intellectual Property: Valuation, Exploitation, and Infringement Damages*, eds. Gordon V. Smith and Russell L. Parr (2005), 411.

19. Goldscheider, Jarosz, and Mulhern, 412.

20. See, e.g., Granieri, Leone, and Oriani, 244–245; Thomas Cotter, "Four Principles for Calculating Reasonable Royalties in Patent Infringement Litigation," *Santa Clara Computer and High Technology Law Journal* 27 (2010/2011): 725, 757; Anne Layne-Farrar and Josh Lerner, "Valuing Patents for

Licensing: A Practical Survey of the Literature" (Mar. 2006), http://ssrn.com/abstract=1440292.
21. 632 F.3d 1292 (Fed.Cir. 2011).
22. Robert Goldscheider, "The Classic 25% Rule and the Art of Intellectual Property Licensing," *Duke Law and Technology Review* 6 (2011): 14.
23. Granieri, Leone, and Oriani, 247.

CHAPTER 11

Patent Infringement Damages

The possibility of massive damages from patent infringement suits is a significant consideration for many patent decision makers. Sizable awards for patent infringement are nothing new, but a recent spate of very large awards has caught the attention of business leaders, politicians, the courts, and academics. Table 11.1 provides the 10 largest damage awards in U.S. federal district court decisions between 1995 and 2009.[1] One of the more striking aspects of this data is that eight of these top 10 damage awards took place in 2007 or later.

The vast majority of patent damage awards, however are orders of magnitude smaller than these top 10 verdicts. During the same 1995–2009 period, the annual median patent damages award (see Figure 11.1) "ranged from $2.4 million to $10.5 million . . . with an overall median award of $5.2 million over the last 15 years."[2] Even taking into account these more modest numbers, the consequences of infringement litigation can be material. Therefore, understanding how patent damage awards are computed is important to intelligent decision making in numerous litigation and nonlitigation patent settings. The potential net returns from bringing a lawsuit as well as the potential net costs from being sued for infringement should factor into a multitude of patent decisions. The well-publicized cross-licensing strategies by Microsoft and Google (see Chapter 5) provide a tangible example of potential damage awards materially motivating patent decisions.

One should not forget that patent litigation damages are not the equivalent of the value of the patent. Although many of the valuation techniques used to help determine infringement damages are the same as those described in earlier chapters of this book, in a patent infringement lawsuit the valuation exercise is to help assess damages (as defined by statute and case law) to the patent holder from the infringing activity. As a consequence, only a portion of the total value of the patent to the patent holder may be at issue in an infringement lawsuit. For example, the lawsuit may cover

TABLE 11.1   Ten Largest Damage Awards in U.S. Federal District Court Decisions, 1995–2009

Damages Award (in Millions)	Year	Defendant	Patented Technology
$1,848	2009	Abbott Laboratories	Arthritis drugs
$1,538	2007	Microsoft	MP3 technology
$521	2003	Microsoft	Internet browser
$432	2008	Boston Scientific	Drug-eluting stents
$388	2009	Microsoft	Software licensing technology
$368	2008	Gateway	Data entry technology
$307	2006	Hynix	Memory chips
$277	2009	Microsoft	Electronic document manipulation technology
$250	2008	Boston Scientific	Balloon-dilation catheters
$226	2007	Medtronic	Spinal implant devices

Source: PricewaterhouseCoopers, "2010 Patent Litigation Study: The Continued Evolution of Patent Damages Law—Patent Litigation Trends 1995—2009 and the Impact of Recent Court Decisions on Damages" (2010).

infringement for only a limited portion of the patent's 20-year life, or the infringement may only have a partial effect on the total profits earned. Patent valuation in such a specialized litigation context is, in many ways, a unique exercise, and the patent value that emerges from this activity is often

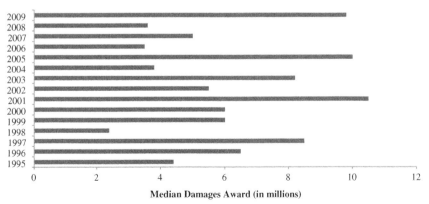

Median Damages Award (in millions)

FIGURE 11.1   Median Damages Awarded in U.S. Federal District Court Decisions, 1995–2009, Adjusted for Inflation and Represented in 2009 U.S. Dollars
Source: PricewaterhouseCoopers, "2010 Patent Litigation Study: The Continued Evolution of Patent Damages Law—Patent Litigation Trends 1995—2009 and the Impact of Recent Court Decisions on Damages" (2010).

more a reflection of the process than a reliable measure of the subject patent's value.

In this chapter, we

- Provide an overview of U.S. law for calculating damages in patent infringement cases.
- Explain the *lost profits* valuation technique and how it is used to compute patent damages.
- Explain the *reasonable royalties* valuation technique and how it is used to compute patent damages.
- Consider a number of additional patent damages matters.
- Provide a *sue or settle* hypothetical.

U.S. LEGAL FRAMEWORK FOR CALCULATING DAMAGES IN PATENT INFRINGEMENT CASES

In the United States, calculating damages in patent infringement cases stems from a single sentence in section 284 of the U.S. Patent Act:

> *Upon finding for the claimant the court shall award the claimant damages adequate to compensate for the infringement, but in no event less than a reasonable royalty for the use made of the invention by the infringer, together with interest and costs as fixed by the court.*[3]

Courts have interpreted section 284 to allow them to fashion patent infringement remedies under two general theories:

1. Lost profits
2. Reasonable royalties

In the past, courts favored the lost profits remedy for patent holders who can demonstrate lost sales, price erosion, or increased costs due to the infringement. When lost profits cannot be proved, the patent holder can recover under a reasonable royalty theory.[4] The reasonable royalty approach establishes the patent holder's minimum damages recovery as indicated by the statute's language "in no event less than a reasonable royalty." Unlike some European countries, the United States does not include a restitution (or unjust enrichment) option for calculating patent damages (except in the case of design patents). The U.S. approach focuses on compensating the patent holder for its losses rather than requiring the infringer to disgorge its ill-gotten profits (see Box 11.1). Under this compensatory theory, damage awards seek to put the patent holder in the same economic position it would have been in had the infringement not occurred. The lost profit and reasonable royalty theories go about calculating the patent holder's compensatory damages in different manners, as discussed later.

BOX 11.1: INFRINGER'S PROFITS NOT RECOVERABLE IN THE UNITED STATES EXCEPT IN THE CASE OF DESIGN PATENTS

The restitution option for patent damages was abolished in the United States by the 1946 amendment to the U.S. Patent Act. Prior to the amendment, the U.S. Patent Act expressly permitted the patent holder to recover an infringer's profits. In *Aro Mfg. Co. v. Convertible Top Replacement Co.*,[5] the U.S. Supreme Court confirmed that the 1946 amendment eliminated recovery of infringer's profits. In the decision, the court explained that

> *the present statutory rule is that only "damages" may be recovered. These have been defined by this Court as "compensation for the pecuniary loss [the patent holder] has suffered from the infringement, without regard to the question whether the [infringer] has gained or lost by his unlawful acts."*[6]

For design patents, however, an infringer's profits are recoverable. Design patents may be used for a design that is ornamental and primarily nonfunctional. Section 289 of the U.S. Patent Act provides:

> *Whoever during the term of a patent for a design, without license of the owner, (1) applies the patented design, or any colorable imitation thereof, to any article of manufacture for the purpose of sale, or (2) sells or exposes for sale any article of manufacture to which such design or colorable imitation has been applied shall be liable to the owner to the extent of his total profit, but not less than $ 250, recoverable in any United States district court having jurisdiction of the parties.*[7]

Among the three main types of intellectual property—patents, copyrights, and trademarks—patents are unique in not allowing recovery of the infringer's profits.

The big exception to the compensatory approach under U.S. law is a limited right to treble damages. The U.S. Patent Act's section 284 provides that "the court may increase the damages up to three times the amount found or assessed."[8] Although the statute does not specify when the treble damages provision should be applied, courts have largely limited these enhanced damages to cases of "willful infringement."[9] See Box 11.2 for a history of patent damages provisions under the U.S. Patent Act.

BOX 11.2: HISTORY OF PATENT DAMAGES PROVISIONS UNDER THE U.S. PATENT ACT

Date	Statute	Damage Provisions
1788	U.S. Const. art. 1, § 8, cl. 8	Congress shall have the power to "promote the Progress of Science and useful Arts, by securing for limited Times to Authors and Inventors the exclusive Right to their respective Writings and Discoveries."
1790	Patent Act of 1790, ch. 7, sec. 4, 1 Stat. 109	The infringer "shall forfeit and pay . . . such damages as shall be assessed by a jury"
1793	Patent Act of 1793, ch. 11, sec. 5, 1 Stat. 318	Patentee entitled to "at least three times the price, for which the patentee has usually sold or licensed to other persons, the use of the said invention."
1800	Patent Act of 1800, ch. 25, sec. 3, 2 Stat. 37	"The price, for which the patentee has usually sold or licensed to other persons, the use of the said invention" language replaced with "three times the actual damage sustained by the patentee."
1819	Patent Act of 1819, ch. 19, sec. 1, 3 Stat. 481	Federal courts authorized to act in both equity and law. This permitted "two remedies to the owner of a patent whose rights had been infringed, and he had his election between the two: he might proceed in equity and recover the gains and profits which *(continued)*

		the infringer had made by the unlawful use of his invention, the infringer in such a suit being regarded as the trustee of the owner of the patent as respects such gains and profits; or the owner of the patent might sue at law, in which case he would be entitled to recover, as damages, compensation for the pecuniary injury he suffered by the infringement, without regard to the question whether the defendant had gained or lost by his unlawful acts, — the measure of damages in such case being not what the defendants had gained, but what the plaintiff had lost." *Birdsall v. Coolidge*, 93 U.S. 64 (1876)
1836	Patent Act of 1836, ch. 357, sec. 14, 5 Stat. 117	"Whenever, in any action for damages . . . a verdict shall be rendered for the plaintiff . . . it shall be in the power of the court to render judgment for any sum above the amount found by such verdict as the actual damages sustained by the plaintiff, not exceeding three times the amount thereof, according to the circumstances of the case, with costs."
1861	Patent Act of 1861, ch. 88, 12 Stat. 246	Duty to mark (added in Patent Act of 1842, 5 Stat. 543, 544) or actual notice to infringer required for recovery of damages.
1870	Patent Act of 1870, ch. 230, sec. 59, 16 Stat. 198	"Power is given to the court . . . to enter judgment for any sum above the amount of the verdict, not exceeding three times the amount of the same, together with costs; but the jury are strictly limited in their finding to the actual damages which the plaintiff has sustained by the infringement." *Birdsall v. Coolidge*, 93 U.S. 64 (1876)

(continued)

1897	Patent Act of 1897, ch. 15, 29 Stat. 692	Courts of law given the power to grant injunctions in patent cases and to allow recovery of both the infringer's profits and the patentee's damages.
1922	Patent Act of 1922, ch. 58, sec. 8, 42 Stat. 392	Amendment to Patent Act codifying the evolving case law that permitted the award of a "reasonable sum" (i.e., a reasonable royalty) where actual damages or loss of profits were probable but not readily calculable.
1946	Patent Act of 1946, ch. 726, 60 Stat. 778	The current damage section adopted: "damages adequate to compensate for the infringement, but in no event less than a reasonable royalty for the use made of the invention by the infringer, together with interest and costs as fixed by the court." Disgorgement of infringer's profits deleted from the act and subsequently interpreted by the Supreme Court as eliminating recovery of infringer's profits as damages in *Aro Mfg. Co. v. Convertible Top Replacement Co.*, 377 U.S. 476, 505 (1964).
1952	Patent Act of 1952, ch. 29, sec. 284, 66 Stat. 792 (codified at 35 U.S.C. § 284)	Patent act codified into Title 35. Damage provisions appear in sec. 284, which is the current applicable damages statute.

LOST PROFITS

Lost profits provide a theoretically sensible approach to calculating patent damages. The most fundamental right that comes with a patent is the right to exclude others from "making, using, offering for sale, or selling the invention."[10] Although the primary remedy for an exclusionary right is an injunction (see Box 11.3), an injunction can only provide prospective relief starting from the time it is granted. The patent holder is also entitled to

BOX 11.3: "LEVERAGE OF AN INJUNCTION"[11]

The Patent Act of 1897 (29 Stat. 692) specifically empowered the courts of law hearing patent infringement cases to grant injunctions. Since that time, the potential for injunctive relief has been an important consideration in patent infringement litigation. It should therefore come as no surprise that an injunction against further infringement is the "normal" remedy[12] for patent infringement and is the first remedy listed in the U.S. Patent Act:

> *The several courts having jurisdiction of cases under this title [35 USCS Sects. 1 et seq.] may grant injunctions in accordance with the principles of equity to prevent the violation of any right secured by patent, on such terms as the court deems reasonable.*[13]

Injunctive relief is recognized as an effective method to exclude future patent infringement. Although a permanent injunction is no longer automatic after *eBay, Inc. v. MercExchange, LLC,*[14] a permanent injunction still generally follows an infringement verdict. It is the threat of a preliminary injunction and its effect on the negotiating positions of the parties that can cause controversy, particularly if the subject patent covers only a minor component of the total product.

relief for the period prior to the injunction taking effect. Although an injunction allows the patent holder to regain the benefit of its contractual bargain with the government that is provided by the patent, a lost profits remedy provides the patent holder with the economic benefits it should have earned if the infringement had not occurred.

What Are Lost Profits?

The patent holder is entitled to the additional profits that would have been earned in a hypothetical world where infringement did not occur. The patent holder needs to model the effect of the infringing behavior on its profits. This modeling typically entails looking at the effect of the infringement on four aspects of the patent holder's business:

1. **Lost sales:** Did the infringement cause a reduction in the patent holder's sales of the patented product?

2. **Price erosion:** Did competition from the infringer reduce the price of the patent holder's sales of the patented product?
3. **Increased costs:** Did lost sales of the patented product prevent the patent holder from benefiting from production cost savings?
4. **Collateral sales:** Did lost sales of the patented product prevent the patent holder from making collateral sales of other products or services? Did the infringer sell a single product that included both the patented product as well as other noninfringing components? Did the infringer sell a series of separate but related infringing and noninfringing products?

To collect any of these lost profits, the patent holder must prove with reasonable probability that the infringer caused the lost profits. Courts frequently discuss this concept in "but for" terms. The patent holder must prove that it is more likely than not that the alleged lost profits would have been earned "but for" the infringement.

Panduit Test and Its Relaxation

One of the leading cases for establishing this "but for" causation is *Panduit Corp. v. Stahlin Brothers Fibre Works, Inc.*[15] *Panduit* provides four factors that a patent holder must prove to recover damages based on lost profits:

1. Demand for the patented product.
2. Absence of acceptable noninfringing substitutes.
3. Patent holder's manufacturing and marketing ability to exploit the demand.
4. The amount of profit patent holder would have made.

Panduit does not provide the exclusive test for establishing lost profits.[16] Over the years, court interpretations of *Panduit* have relaxed its standards and have demonstrated that other paths exist for establishing lost profits. Having said that, *Panduit* does remain the most cited approach and provides a useful framework for establishing generally what a patent holder must show to collect lost profits.

Panduit's first factor—demand for the patented product—is seldom an issue during litigation.[17] Demand can be demonstrated, for example, by introducing the infringer's sales as evidence of market demand for the patented product.[18] Sales by the infringer show that there were buyers who wanted at least some version of the patented product.

Panduit's second factor—absence of acceptable noninfringing substitutes—tends to be the most challenging for patent holders to prove.

If acceptable noninfringing substitutes exist, how do we know that the patent holder would have made the sales in the absence of the infringer? The customers may have purchased the substitutes instead. The patent holder can satisfy the second factor by proving "either that (1) the purchasers in the marketplace generally were willing to buy the patented product for its advantages, or (2) the specific purchasers of the infringing product purchased on that basis."[19]

The infringer will try to counter by showing that acceptable alternatives were available that possessed the key qualities of the patented product or that the features of the patented product were not material to the purchasers' decisions. If strictly interpreted, the second factor suggests that lost profits may only be recovered in a "two-supplier market" that is composed of only the patent holder and the infringer.[20] Subsequent court decisions, however, have relaxed the second factor and made clear that lost profits can be recovered in a multisupplier market. In *State Industries Inc. v. Mor-Flo Industries Inc.*,[21] for example, the court allowed the patent holder to use a market share analysis to satisfy the second factor. One commentator described the effect of *State Industries* as follows:

> *After* State Industries, *that [second] prong can be read as absence of noninfringing substitutes that would have totally absorbed all of the infringer's sales, or as absence of noninfringing substitutes that were so desirable that the [patent holder] cannot prove he or she would have made any sales against them. In this way, the second prong precludes recovery only where noninfringing substitutes completely account for the infringer's sales.*[22]

Panduit's third factor—manufacturing and marketing capacity—requires the patent holder to show that it had the capacity to make the additional sales that are the basis of the lost profits calculation. If the patent holder did not have sufficient capacity at the time of the infringing sales, the patent holder will be allowed to show that it had the ability to expand its capacity through reasonable means (such as subcontracting) to meet the increased demand.[23]

Panduit's fourth factor—amount of lost profits—is not a causation factor at all, but instead requires the patent holder to prove the lost profits with sufficient certainty. Once the patent holder has established the infringer caused the injury, the exact quantification of the injury is somewhat relaxed. To describe the extent of this relaxation, courts use statements such as "the amount of lost profits awarded cannot be speculative but the amount need not be proven with unerring precision."[24]

Calculating Lost Profits

A patent holder suing for lost profits is entitled to lost incremental profits.[25] In other words, the patent holder is not required to include its fixed costs in its profit calculation. The United States Court of Appeals for the Federal Circuit has explained this approach as follows:

> *The [incremental profits] approach recognizes that it does not cost as much to produce unit N + 1 if the first N (or fewer) units produced already have paid the fixed costs. Thus fixed costs—those costs which do not vary with increases in production, such as management salaries, property taxes, and insurance—are excluded when determining profits.*[26]

When suing for lost sales, that means the patent holder is entitled to

$$\text{Lost profits} = \text{Revenues from lost sales} - \text{Variable costs}$$

Beyond the court's guidance on the incremental profit issue, neither the U.S. Patent Act nor the courts have mandated specific valuation techniques for proving lost profits. A patent holder is free to use any reasonable methods and assumptions that it believes will help it to prove its lost profits with sufficient certainty. As we discussed above, patent holders seeking to recover lost profits tend to focus their analysis on four aspects of their business:

1. Lost sales
2. Price erosion
3. Increased costs
4. Collateral sales

In this section, we will provide some guidance on how a patent holder may wish to approach each of these avenues for demonstrating a lost profit.

Actual Lost Sales The most obvious basis for the patent holder's lost profits is lost sales of the patented product that were caused by the infringement. How many additional sales would the patent holder have made of its patented product "but for" the infringement? A typical starting point for that analysis is to identify the infringer's sales and determine what percentage of those sales the patent holder would have made absent the infringement.[27]

Two-Supplier Market In a two-supplier market (the patent holder and the infringer are the only suppliers for the product), there is a rebuttable presumption that the patent holder would have made all the infringer's sales if the patent holder can show that it had sufficient manufacturing and marketing capabilities.[28] It is only a presumption, however, and it can be overcome by the infringer. In one case, for example, the infringer was able to show that its infringing product was sufficiently cheaper in price and different in features (the patent holder sold a high-end product, whereas the infringer sold a cheaper product) that its customers probably would not have purchased the patent holder's product.[29] In a 2009 case, a court noted with approval an expert's opinion that started with a 100 percent capture rate for a two-supplier market, but reduced the capture rate to 90 percent based on the expert's experience that "there are always at least some customers of the patent infringer who would have been unwilling to buy from the patentee for reasons completely unrelated to the product itself."[30]

Multisupplier Market: Market Share Approach   True two-supplier markets tend to be rare. The more common scenario is the multisupplier market, where there are other suppliers that also serve the market targeted by the patented product. In a multisupplier market, the patent holder cannot simply presume that it would have captured the infringer's sales. To address the difficulties involved with trying to prove lost sales in a multisupplier market, the courts developed the *market share approach*. In the *State Industries* case, the court held that the patent holder can demonstrate the sales it would have made "but for" the infringement by demonstrating its market share in the product.[31] Lost sales can therefore be calculated by multiplying the infringer's sales by the patent holder's demonstrated market share:

Lost sales   =   Infringer's sales   ×   Patent holder's market share percentage

To prove market share, the patent holder must employ a reasonable method that is based on "sound economic proof of the nature of the market."[32] To develop a dynamic, or evolutionary, estimate of the patent holder's market share, a valuator may want to consider using a Markov chain (see Chapter 7).

Price Erosion   Basic economics tells us that when competition in a market for a good or service increases, the price of that good or service will decrease (see Figure 11.2). As a result, the infringer's sales do more than just divert sales away from the patent holder. The infringer's sales can also depress the price that the patent holder is able to charge for the patented product.[33] If the infringement is sufficiently widespread, the market price for the patented technology could be driven down to its marginal cost. If the price were reduced to the marginal cost, the patent holder's lost profits from diverted sales would be zero unless price erosion was included in the

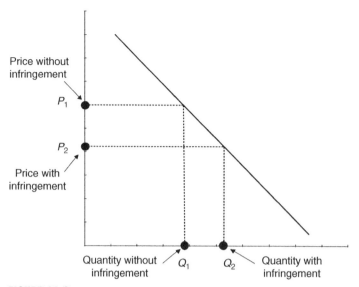

FIGURE 11.2 Increased Competition Causes Price Erosion and Quantity Accretion

analysis. Courts can include the effect of this price erosion in the patent damages award.

One issue that economists note frequently, but that may not be well understood by courts, is the corresponding *quantity accretion* that comes with price erosion.[34] If the price of a given product is lowered and the demand remains constant, the unit sales for that product will increase.

To illustrate the potential effect of price erosion and quantity accretion on lost profits, consider the following scenario: An infringer diverted 10,000 unit sales of the patented product, and the resulting price erosion reduced the patented product's per-unit incremental profit from $100 to $20. If the patent holder were to be awarded lost profits from actual lost sales without considering price erosion, the patent holder's award would be $200,000. That number would fail to capture the extent of the patent holder's actual lost profits. On the other hand, if the court were to account for price erosion but not adjust for quantity accretion, the award would be $1 million. That $1 million would overestimate the patent holder's actual lost profits because the patent holder would not have been able to sell 1,000 units at $100 per-unit incremental profit absent infringement.

Increased Costs Infringing sales can also have an effect on the cost side of the patent holder's ledger. Infringing sales can increase the patent holder's costs in a few ways. First, by diverting sales away from the patent holder, the infringer may have prevented the patent holder from experiencing the positive effects that come from economies of scale. The patent holder, for example, may not have been able to benefit from volume discounts on supply contracts or efficiency improvements that would have resulted if sales volumes were higher.

The *learning curve effect* provides a further example of cost savings that may have been lost due to the infringer's activities. Learning curve (and experience curve) effects (see Box 11.4) express the mathematical relationship between the accumulated output of a product and the unit costs of the product. It is a well-recognized economic principle that efficiency and productivity improves the more a task is repeated; the improvements tend to be the greatest in the early stages of the task and then slow over time. The relationship is generally expressed in terms of a percentage decline in costs for each doubling of output. For most standardized industries, 10 to 30 percent learning curve effects are common.[35] The unit cost declines of 10 percent and 30 percent for each doubling of output are generally described as 90 percent and 70 percent learning curves. By diverting sales, the infringer may have slowed the patent holder's ability to benefit from the learning curve effect, which then causes the patent holder to operate at a higher cost structure than expected absent infringement. Figure 11.3 charts the unit costs for 80 percent and 70 percent learning curves for a series of cumulative outputs. Referring to this figure, a company with an 80 percent learning curve effect that has a cumulative output of 120,000 units will have unit costs of $81. With a cumulative output of 240,000 units, the unit cost would drop to $73. The harm to the patent holder would be even greater if the industry has a 70 percent learning curve effect. In that situation, the

---

BOX 11.4: LEARNING CURVES AND EXPERIENCE CURVES

"Learning" curve and "experience" curve effects are related but slightly different concepts.[36] Learning curve effects were first observed in the manufacture of aircraft prior to World War II[37] and have been subsequently documented in a large number of industries.[38] It has been suggested that learning curve effects are even more pronounced in knowledge and technology intensive industries.[39] The effect has also been retroactively applied to analysis of historical manufacturing data.[40] To be precise, the term *learning curve* effect applies to the decline in manufacturing costs as output increases, whereas the term *experience curve* effects is slightly broader and is used to describe the decline in total costs as output increases.

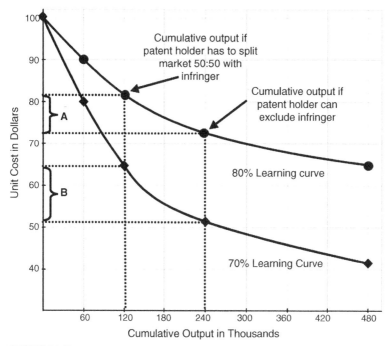

FIGURE 11.3 Learning Curve Effect

patent holder could expect unit costs of $49 after 240,000 units of cumulative output if it did not have to share the market with the infringer.

On a more straightforward note, the infringer's activities may have increased the patent holder's costs by motivating the patent holder to increase advertising, selling, and distribution expenses so as to cope with the increased level of competition.[41]

Entire Market Value Rule In addition to lost profits from diverted sales of the patented product, the patent holder may also be entitled to damages for certain sales of unpatented products. Under the *entire market value rule*, a patent holder can collect lost profits from sales of unpatented products "that are not part of the patented product at all, but that are sold in connection with the patented good and therefore likely would have been sold by the patentee if the patentee rather than the infringer had made the sale of the infringing good."[42] There are two classic scenarios in which the entire market value rule may apply:

1. The infringer sells a single product that includes both the patented product as well as other noninfringing components.

2. The infringer sells a series of separate but related infringing and noninfringing products.

When the patented and unpatented components are embodied in a single product, the entire market value rule allows the patent holder to base its lost profits on the sale of the entire product if the patented component is the basis for customer demand for the product. When the patented and unpatented components are not embodied in a single product but instead are sufficiently related to create a functional unit, the entire market value rule may nonetheless apply.[43] To calculate lost profits on the basis of the "functional unit," the patent holder must show that the patented product was the basis for customer demand for the functional unit of products. See Box 11.5 for a recent application of the entire market value rule in the functional unit scenario.

BOX 11.5: JUICY WHIP: THE DISPENSER PLUS THE SYRUP

Juicy Whip was the holder of a beverage dispenser patent. The beverage dispenser stores the beverage syrup and water separately and mixes them just before dispensing. The dispenser features a transparent bowl that creates an attractive impression and was found to help induce beverage sales.

Juicy Whip obtained a decision against Orange Bang and others for infringing its dispenser patent. Juicy Whip sought to prove lost profits damages that included lost profits from lost syrup sales. The district court did not allow Juicy Whip to recover damages from syrup sales. In a 2004 decision, *Juicy Whip, Inc. v. Orange Bang, Inc. et al.*,[44] the Court of Appeals for the Federal Circuit reversed and ruled that there was a sufficient "functional relationship" between the dispenser and the syrup to allow Juicy Whip to attempt to prove lost profits from lost syrup sales. The court stated:

> *The dispenser and the syrup are in fact analogous to parts of a single assembly or a complete machine, as the syrup functions together with the dispenser to produce the visual appearance that is central to Juicy Whip's [dispenser] patent. Despite some limited interchangeability—other syrups may be used in Juicy Whip's dispenser and, likewise, other dispensers could use Juicy Whip's syrups—the two items do "function together*

> *to achieve one result." The dispenser needs syrup and the syrup is mixed in a dispenser. Such is indeed a functional relationship, and a functional relationship between a patented device and an unpatented material used with it is not precluded by the fact that the device can be used with other materials or that the unpatented materials can be used with other devices. . . . Accordingly, we . . . remand this sticky issue for further proceedings to allow Juicy Whip to prove lost profits on its syrup sales.[45]*

Apportionment The doctrine of apportionment tends to come up in scenarios in which the patent holder seeks to apply the entire market value rule. If the patent holder's patent covers the entire product sold by the infringer, the lost profit base will be the totality of the infringing product sales. If, however, the patent covers only a part of the infringing product (such as an improvement to, or a component of, the product), the patent's value in the sales must be apportioned unless the entire market value rule applies. The entire market value rule developed as an exception to the apportionment doctrine[46] and appears to have pushed the doctrine into the background.[47] As a result, the apportionment doctrine is now used as a defense to the entire market value rule.[48]

REASONABLE ROYALTY

Until 1915, U.S. courts largely rejected the reasonable royalty method for calculating patent damages.[49] In the 1889 case of *Rude v. Westcott*,[50] for example, the Supreme Court held that

> *in order that a royalty may be accepted as a measure of damages against an infringer, who is a stranger to the license establishing it, it must be paid or secured before the infringement complained of; it must be paid by such a number of persons as to indicate a general acquiescence in its reasonableness by those who have occasion to use the invention; and it must be uniform at the places where the licenses are issued.*

Absent this evidence, the patent holder was limited to nominal damages. The Supreme Court finally permitted a reasonable royalty method in 1915 with its decision in *Dowagiac Manufacturing Co. v. Minnesota Moline Plow Co.*[51] The *Dowagiac* decision was codified into the Patent Act of 1922, and reasonable royalties have been authorized as a recovery method for patent infringement ever since.

Increased Popularity of the Reasonable Royalty Method

Patent litigators have traditionally thought of lost profits as the ideal patent damages remedy, with reasonable royalties serving only as a fallback when lost profits cannot be proved. The general preference for lost profits is not surprising, because that method would encompass any market power (see Chapter 5) that comes from excluding competitors from the market.[52] Recent empirical data, however, shows that the theoretical preference for lost profits does not translate to recent practice. In a 2010 report, PricewaterhouseCoopers found that the reasonable royalties method has become the "predominate measure of damages" for patent infringement cases.[53] For infringement cases that awarded damages, 75 percent of the awards were based on the reasonable royalty method from 1995 to 2001 and 78 percent were based on the reasonable royalty method from 2002 to 2009.[54] There are a number of reasons for the recent dominance of the reasonable royalty method:

- Proving the causation requirements that are required to obtain lost profits can be challenging.
- Calculating lost profits with sufficient certainty can be difficult.
- To collect lost profits, the patent holder needs to manufacture and sell the patented product in such a manner that it could have made the sales to the purchasers of the infringing product. Because they do not manufacture and sell products, nonpracticing entities (NPEs) (see Chapter 5) are generally not able to recover under the lost profits method,[55] and because NPEs bring a substantial percentage of the patent infringement lawsuits, it is not surprising to see an increase in the reasonably royalty method.
- Court interpretations of the reasonable royalty method have rendered it more generous to patent holders (see the discussion below).

The popularity of the reasonable royalty method does not appear to be a temporary trend. Instead, it appears to be a systemic change in the way that patent holders approach their infringement litigation.

Reasonable Royalty Method Calculates Compensatory Damages, but from a Different Perspective than Lost Profits Method

Like lost profits, reasonable royalties are meant to compensate the patent holder for its losses and place it in the same economic position it would have been in had the infringement not occurred. The difference between the compensatory approach of the lost profits method and the reasonable royalty method is the *idealized patent holder* who is expected to use the method. For the lost profits method, the idealized patent holder is a manufacturer that is practicing the invention. For the reasonable royalty method, the idealized patent holder is an NPE, which significantly changes the focus of the valuation analysis. Mark Lemley explains:

> *What it takes to "make the patentee whole" is very different if the patentee's only interest is in licensing the patent than if the patentee's interest is in excluding competition and maintaining a monopoly price. Thus, reasonable royalty case law properly inquires into what the marketplace would actually pay for rights to the technology, bearing in mind that the licensee has to make a profit as well. By contrast, it is not only possible but common that lost profits will exceed the defendant's gains from infringement.*[56]

A reasonable royalty seeks to determine an amount that a person desiring to practice the invention as a business proposition would be willing to pay as a royalty and yet still be able to generate a reasonable profit.[57] In effect, the inquiry requires determining the value of the patent to the patent holder and the infringer and identifying a royalty that falls within that range. The resulting royalty may be in the form of a "lump sum" royalty or the more traditional running royalty rate (see Chapter 10).[58]

Section 284 of the U.S. Patent Act provides that the patent holder's damages shall be no less than a reasonable royalty, but it does not explain how that reasonable royalty is to be calculated. Determining what constitutes a reasonable royalty has therefore been left to the courts. There are two common approaches applied by courts:

1. Hypothetical negotiation
2. Analytical method

Hypothetical Negotiation and the *Georgia Pacific* Factors

The most commonly employed technique for making the reasonable royalty determination is the use of a "hypothetical negotiation" fiction. The court may calculate a reasonable royalty by "postulating a hypothetical negotiation between a willing licensor and licensee at the time infringement commenced."[59] In the 2009 *Lucent Technologies, Inc. v. Gateway, Inc.*

case, the Court of Appeals for the Federal Circuit explained the purpose of the hypothetical negotiation as follows:

> *The hypothetical negotiation tries, as best as possible, to recreate the ex ante licensing negotiation scenario and to describe the resulting agreement. In other words, if infringement had not occurred, willing parties would have executed a license agreement specifying a certain royalty payment scheme.*[60]

The 1970 case of *Georgia-Pacific Corp. v. United States Plywood Corp.*[61] provides the most common framework for determining the hypothetical negotiation's outcome. *Georgia-Pacific* provides 15 factors for a court to consider when determining the reasonable royalty.

1. The royalties received by the patentee for the licensing of the patent in suit, proving or tending to prove an established royalty.
2. The rates paid by the licensee for the use of other patents comparable to the patent in suit.
3. The nature and scope of the license, as exclusive or nonexclusive; or as restricted or nonrestricted in terms of territory or with respect to whom the manufactured product may be sold.
4. The licensor's established policy and marketing program to maintain his or her patent monopoly by not licensing others to use the invention or by granting licenses under special conditions designed to preserve that monopoly.
5. The commercial relationship between the licensor and licensee, such as whether they are competitors in the same territory in the same line of business or whether they are inventor and promoter.
6. The effect of selling the patented specialty in promoting sales of other products of the licensee, the existing value of the invention to the licensor as a generator of sales of his nonpatented items, and the extent of such derivative or convoyed sales.
7. The duration of the patent and the term of the license.
8. The established profitability of the product made under the patent, its commercial success, and its current popularity.
9. The utility and advantages of the patent property over the old modes or devices, if any, that had been used for working out similar results.
10. The nature of the patented invention, the character of the commercial embodiment of it as owned and produced by the licensor, and the benefits to those who have used the invention.
11. The extent to which the infringer has made use of the invention and any evidence probative of the value of that use.

12. The portion of the profit or of the selling price that may be customary in the particular business or in comparable businesses to allow for the use of the invention or analogous inventions.
13. The portion of the realizable profit that should be credited to the invention as distinguished from nonpatented elements, the manufacturing process, business risks, or significant features or improvements added by the infringer.
14. The opinion testimony of qualified experts.
15. The amount that a licensor (such as the patentee) and a licensee (such as the infringer) would have agreed upon (at the time the infringement began) if both had been reasonably and voluntarily trying to reach an agreement; that is, the amount which a prudent licensee—who desired, as a business proposition, to obtain a license to manufacture and sell a particular article embodying the patented invention—would have been willing to pay as a royalty and yet be able to make a reasonable profit and which amount would have been acceptable by a prudent patentee who was willing to grant a license.

Established Royalties   Some commentators view *established royalties* as a third theory for determining patent damages, along with the lost profits and reasonable royalty method.[62] Others treat established royalties as one of the *Georgia-Pacific* factors (the first factor) and a part of the hypothetical negotiations to establish a reasonable royalty. Regardless of where it is classified, an established royalty is one that other licensees have actually paid to the patent holder for the infringed patent. Generally speaking, it is the infringer who will argue for the court to apply an established royalty. The infringer will seek to use the established royalty to prevent the patent holder from obtaining a reasonable royalty that is higher than what it has previously obtained in the marketplace.[63]

Convincing a court to find and employ an established royalty can be challenging. For prior licenses to prove an established royalty, the licenses must be: "(1) paid or secured before the infringement began; (2) paid by a sufficient number of persons to indicate the reasonableness of the rate; (3) uniform in amount; (4) not paid under threat of suit or in settlement of litigation; and (5) for comparable rights or activity under the patent."[64] Satisfying the established royalty criteria is not easy, and "few courts have found an established royalty."[65] When an established royalty is demonstrated, courts may nevertheless decide to award the patent holder a reasonable royalty above the established royalty,[66] but courts are unlikely to award a reasonable royalty below the established rate.[67]

Estimating the Outcome from the Hypothetical Negotiation   Assuming that a definitive, established royalty has not been demonstrated, the court will be the ultimate arbiter for deciding how the hypothetical negotiation would have turned out. This hypothetical construct causes many philosophical problems and is the subject of much criticism,[68] but the underlying goal of the exercise is to approximate the royalty upon which the parties would have agreed to in an arm's-length negotiation if they had been willing licensors and licensees just before infringement began. In theory, it means that the patent holder and the infringer should both benefit from the license agreement.

Georgia-Pacific's 15 factors are not the exclusive method for determining the outcome of the hypothetical negotiation, but they are the most popular. In any particular case, the court is not constrained to only the *Georgia-Pacific* factors nor is it required to consider them all. It does not appear that any case has relied on all 15 factors.[69] A 2002 study of 93 reasonable royalty awards between 1990 and 2001 found that each of the factors was cited a significant number of times as being considered in rate determination (see Figure 11.4).

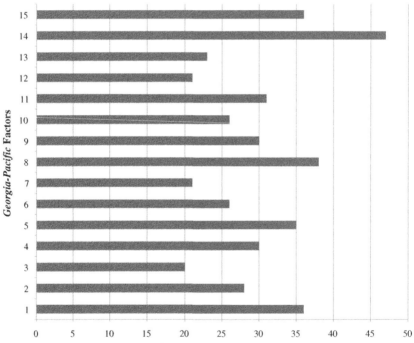

Number of Cases Citing That *Georgia-Pacific* Factor as Part of the Royalty Rate Determination

FIGURE 11.4   *Georgia-Pacific* Factors in District Court Decisions, 1990–2001
Source: Michele Riley, "A Review of Court-Awarded Royalty Rates in Patent Infringement Cases (1990–2001)," in *Intellectual Property: Valuation, Exploitation, and Infringement Damages*, eds. Gordon V. Smith and Russell L. Parr (2005), 712.

One of the more prominent concepts to run through the *Georgia-Pacific* factors is the availability of substitutes. Namely, what substitute products are available to the infringer and what substitute opportunities are available to the patent holder?[70] From the infringer's (licensee's) perspective, the presence or absence of comparable substitute products should be a primary determinant of the price it would be willing to pay for a license. As Michael Keeley explains:

> *The maximum amount a licensee would be willing to pay for a license is the benefit it receives compared to its next-best alternative. If perfect substitutes are available at no cost, then the licensee would be willing to pay nothing and the patent would be of no value. On the other hand, if the substitutes are not perfect or have costs, the maximum amount the licensee would be willing to pay is the incremental profits it could make by selling the patented product compared to the next-best alternative plus the cost (if any) of acquiring the next-best technology.[71]*

The availability of substitute products shows up in a number of the *Georgia-Pacific* factors:[72]

- Factor 1: Available substitutes should depress the patent holder's established royalties.
- Factor 2: Available substitutes should depress the infringer's existing licensing fees for comparable patented products.
- Factor 8: Available substitutes will reduce the patent's market power and thereby reduce its profitability.
- Factors 9 and 10: Available substitutes will reduce the unique advantages and benefits conveyed by the patent.

From the patent holder's (licensor's) perspective, the focus should be on the availability of substitute opportunities other than licensing to the infringer. Those substitute opportunities, more than anything else, should determine the price that the patent holder would demand to grant a license. Assuming that the patent holder is a profit maximizer, it should consider the opportunity costs of granting a particular license.[73] Depending on the patent holder's particular situation, granting a license can impact its profitability in a number of ways, including the following:

- **Diverted actual sales:** Licensee sales may divert sales of the patented product by the patent holder or its other licensees. The patent holder would want to charge a royalty that offsets the effect of those lost sales.

■ **Price erosion:** Increased competition from the licensee could also cause price erosion (see the previous discussion) in the patented product. To reduce the price erosion problem, the patent holder "could charge the licensee a sufficiently high per unit royalty to ensure that the licensee did not price below the optimum level. (A per unit license fee increases the licensee's marginal cost which would cause it to raise its price.)"[74] If the infringer did not charge the optimum per unit price, the "quantity accretion" effect (see the previous discussion) should be accounted for.

■ **Increased costs:** Diverted sales may cause the patent holder to operate at an artificially high cost structure (see the previous discussion), which should be accounted for in the royalty rate.

■ **Diverted collateral sales:** Licensee sales of the patented product may also divert patent holder's ability to sell unpatented products under the same types of scenarios discussed previously. Once again, the patent holder should be expected to capture this economic effect in any agreed royalty rate with the licensee.

A number of the *Georgia-Pacific* factors focus on these opportunity-cost concerns for the patent holder. Specifically, factors 3, 4, 5, 6, 8, 11, and 12 largely focus on the importance of exclusivity to the patent holder and the economic effect of the infringer violating that exclusivity.

Analytical Approach

The leading alternative to the hypothetical negotiation is the so-called *analytical approach*. This approach attempts to measure the excess profits that the infringer earned on the infringing product based on the patented technology and to apportion those excess profits between the patent holder and the infringer.[75] There are two steps in this method:

1. Calculate the excess profits:

Excess profits = Profit earned on infringing – Infringer's usual
                   devices   profit

2. Apportion the excess profits between the patent holder and the infringer.

In addition to being used as a stand-alone technique, the analytical approach can also be used to determine the outcome of the hypothetical negotiations method.[76]

Rules of Thumb

Rules of thumb have been used from time to time as evidence of how to apportion the profits between the patent holder and the infringer under the hypothetical negotiation or the analytical approach. The most well known of these rules of thumb is the 25 percent rule (see Chapter 10). This rule seeks to apportion between the parties the operating profit that resulted from the patent. Assuming no special factors that favor one party receiving a greater share of the profits, the 25 percent rule suggests that the parties would have agreed to a 25:75 operating profit split, with the licensor receiving the 25 percent. For example, if the infringer's use of the patent generated $20 million in operating profit, the patent holder would be entitled to $5 million.

In *Uniloc USA Inc. v. Microsoft Corp.*,[77] the Court of Appeals for the Federal Circuit held

> *as a matter of Federal Circuit law that the 25 percent rule of thumb is a fundamentally flawed tool for determining a baseline royalty rate in a hypothetical negotiation. Evidence relying on the 25 percent rule of thumb is thus inadmissible under* Daubert *and the Federal Rules of Evidence, because it fails to tie a reasonable royalty base to the facts of the case at issue.*[78]

As a result, the 25 percent rule is no longer admissible evidence for apportioning profits between the patent holder and the infringer without evidence that supports its validity, and the same can probably be said for other potential rules of thumb.

Apportionment

As with lost profit awards, the apportionment doctrine also applies to reasonable royalty awards. See the earlier general discussion of the apportionment doctrine.

Expanding Reasonable Royalty Damages

Beginning with the 1978 *Panduit* decision, the trend in reasonable royalty decisions has been to expand the remedy beyond simply determining a commercially reasonable royalty. These expansions have increased the potential damages that may be sought under the reasonable royalty measure and increased its popularity among plaintiffs. Three of those enhancements are (1) the *Panduit* kicker, (2) applying the entire market value rule to reasonable royalty cases, and (3) rejecting the infringer's need to make a profit.

***Panduit* Kicker**   In *Panduit*, the court explained that determining a reasonable royalty after infringement is not the equivalent of ordinary royalty negotiations among truly willing patent holders and licensees. If the reasonable royalty were limited to a purely commercial rate in all settings, there would be times when that rule would incentivize infringement. The court wrote:

> *Except for the limited risk that the patent owner, over years of litigation, might meet the heavy burden of proving the four elements required for lost profits, the infringer would have nothing to lose, and everything to gain if he could count on paying only the normal, routine royalty non-infringers might have paid. . . . The infringer would be in a "heads-I-win, tails-you-lose" position.*[79]

In the case before the *Panduit* court, the patent holder spent $400,000 in attorney fees over 13 years of litigation to receive a $44,709.60 trial court award. The infringer, on the other hand, was able to generate $1,788,384 in sales. Noting the injustice to the patent holder, the court stated:

> *On the date a patent issues, a competitor which made no investment in research and development of the invention, has four options: (1) it can make and sell a non-infringing substitute product, and refrain from making, using, or selling a product incorporating the patented invention; (2) it can make and sell the patented product, if the patent owner be willing, negotiating a license and paying a reasonable (negotiated) royalty; (3) it can simply take the invention, running the risk that litigation will ensue and that the patent will be found valid and infringed; or (4) it can take a license under option (2) and thereafter repudiate its contract, challenging the validity of the patent. Determination of a reasonably royalty, after election of option (3), cannot, without injustice, be treated as though the infringer had elected option (2) in the first place.*[80]

The *Panduit* court vacated the trial court's award with instructions that allowed the award to be increased. The *Panduit* decision was pre-Federal Circuit, but the United States Court of Appeals for the Federal Circuit has since formally adopted the *Panduit* kicker to award damages that exceed a reasonable royalty so as to compensate the patent holder for the infringement.[81] A leading treatise on patent damages summarizes the status and boundaries of the *Panduit* kicker as follows:

> *The* Panduit *kicker should not be considered available as a way to award attorney fees or enhanced damages for willful infringement*

when the stringent standards for those two awards have not been met. . . . It is within the discretion of a court to reach a reasonable royalty determination in excess of what the hypothetical willing licensor and licensee might have agreed. However, that enhancement must be through application of the Georgia-Pacific factors and other factors mentioned. Federal Circuit precedent would indicate any enhancement of a damages award must be based on a finding of willful infringement or bad faith.[82]

Entire Market Value Rule   Expansion of the entire market value rule from a lost profits' doctrine to a reasonable royalties doctrine has been one of the more controversial issues in patent damages awards (see Box 11.6). The rule's expansion can be traced to a dicta statement in *Rite-Hite Corp. v. Kelley Co.* when the Court of Appeals for the Federal Circuit said that "courts have applied a formulation known as the 'entire market value rule' to determine whether such components should be included in the damage computation, whether for reasonable royalty purposes . . . or for lost profits purposes."[83] The statement was dicta because *Rite-Hite* involved lost profits rather than a reasonable royalty measure. Since the *Rite-Hite* case, however, the Court of Appeals for the Federal Circuit has permitted the entire market value rule to be used to establish reasonable royalties in a number of cases.[84] To apply the entire market value rule to a reasonable royalty measure, the patent holder must prove the same elements as in a lost profits case. Namely, the patent holder must prove two things:

1. The patented and unpatented components are embodied in a single product or are sufficiently related to create a functional unit.
2. The patented feature constitutes the basis for customer demand.

If the entire market value rule is found to apply, the patent holder can collect a reasonable royalty based on the entire value of the single product or functional unit, as the case may be.

BOX 11.6: INCREMENTAL ECONOMIC VALUE ANALYSIS

The entire market value rule is one of the more controversial patent damages doctrines, with its spread to the reasonably royalty measure drawing particular criticism. One reason for this criticism may be the

(continued)

(*continued*)
doctrine's largely "binary" nature. Either the doctrine is satisfied and the patent holder can collect damages from collateral sales, or it is not satisfied and the patent holder is not allowed to collect damages on collateral sales.

An on-off approach is not, however, well grounded in economic theory. Take the example of a single product that contains patented and unpatented components. Any patented feature can be associated with a potential change in customer demand for the product. If the patented feature is the *sole* reason that the product is selected by the customer over alternatives, the incremental economic value is 100 percent. In other words, without the patented feature, the demand for the product would be zero. At the other end of the spectrum, a patented feature may add nothing to customer demand, and the incremental economic value of such a patented feature would be zero. The range of possibilities, however, can be anywhere from 0 to 100 percent with most scenarios involving an incremental economic value of greater than 0 but less than 100 percent.

Almost by definition, patent holders that are allowed to calculate their damages based on the entire market value rule are overcompensated. Their incremental economic value will likely be less than 100 percent, but they are allowed to collect damages as if it is 100 percent. On the other hand, patent holders that are denied use of the entire market value rule are likely being undercompensated because their incremental economic value is likely to be greater than 0. If patent damages more accurately reflected the incremental economic value of the patented product, some of the controversy surrounding when and how to apply the entire market value rule could be alleviated. One has to wonder whether the development of the entire market value rule as an on-off rule stems from its label as the "entire" market value rule. If the doctrine had received a more moderate name, such as the "collateral sales doctrine," it may have developed differently

Infringer Profit Not Required   In theory, the patent holder's reasonable royalty award should be limited by a requirement that the infringer make a profit from the hypothetical negotiation. In *Georgia-Pacific*, the court explained that "the very definition of a reasonable royalty assumes that, after payment, 'the infringer will be left with a profit.'"[85] The Court of

Appeals for the Federal Circuit, however, has rejected the infringer profit requirement and has specifically stated that "there is no rule that a royalty be no higher than the infringer's net profit margin."[86]

ADDITIONAL PATENT DAMAGES MATTERS

The damages award in a patent infringement lawsuit is determined at the trial level by either a jury or a judge. Although appeals to higher courts are common in patent litigation, appeals regarding the damages awarded by the lower court have a difficult path to success. The damages amount is a question of fact as opposed to a question of law.

Appealing a Patent Damages Award

To appeal a question of fact, a litigant must demonstrate to the appellate court that clear error was made by the lower court judge by a preponderance of the evidence.[87] The U.S. Supreme Court has said that "a finding is 'clearly erroneous' when although there is evidence to support it, the reviewing court on the entire evidence is left with the definite and firm conviction that a mistake has been committed."[88] Figure 11.5 provides a summary of judicial standards of review for patent litigation. For patent damages that are determined by a jury, the burden is even higher. The appealing litigant must show that the jury's conclusion was, in the words of the Court of Appeals for the Federal Circuit, "grossly excessive or monstrous, clearly not supported by the evidence, or based only on speculation or guesswork."[89]

These high standards of review mean that the appellate court is going to give great deference to the damages determination made at the trial court level, which makes reversal or modification on appeal less likely. Litigants therefore need to pay particular attention to the damages issue at the trial court level.

Prejudgment Interest

The U.S. Patent Act's section 284 allows plaintiffs to recover prejudgment interest. In 1983, the U.S. Supreme Court clarified that prejudgment interest should "ordinarily be awarded" as part of the patent holder's adequate compensation.[90] The interest rate that courts have applied covers a range of possibilities, from the U.S. treasury bills rate at the low end through the prime lending rate or even the interest rates the patent holder paid for loans during the infringement period.

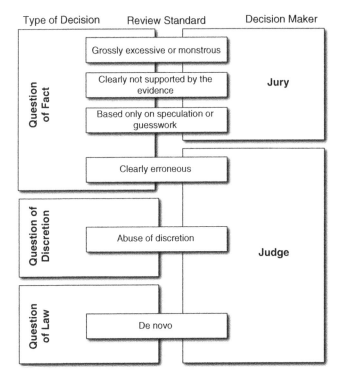

FIGURE 11.5   Judicial Standards of Review for Patent Litigation

Enhanced Damages

Patent damages, whether lost profits or a reasonable royalty, focus on compensating the patent holder for losses. The U.S. Patent Act's section 284 permits a court to "increase the damages up to three times the amount found or assessed." Courts have largely limited these enhanced damages to cases of "willful infringement,"[91] which can be described as "blatant disregard of the patentee's rights."[92] Willful infringement requires a relatively high showing by the patent holder. If the infringer did not know of the patent until sued or if the infringer reasonably believed that the patent was invalid or not being infringed, the court is unlikely to find that willful infringement occurred.[93]

Attorney Fees

Litigation costs are one of the major expenses involved with a patent lawsuit. As a result, the possibility to recoup those expenses can be a significant factor

TABLE 11.2   Median Patent Infringement Litigation Costs, 2011

	Patent Infringement Suits		
	Less than $1 Million at Risk	$1 Million to $25 Million at Risk	More than $25 Million at Risk
Median total costs for litigation	$650,000	$2.5 million	$5.0 million

Source: Law Practice Management Committee of the American Intellectual Property Law Association, "Report of the Economic Survey 2011" (2011).

when making litigation decisions. Table 11.2 provides the median total cost of litigation for patent infringement suits as reported by the American Intellectual Property Law Association based on its economic surveys. These total costs include "outside legal and paralegal services, local counsel, associates, paralegals, travel and living expenses, fees and costs for court reporters, photocopies, courier services, exhibit preparation, analytical testing, expert witnesses, translators, surveys, jury advisors, and similar expenses."[94]

The U.S. Patent Act's section 285 provides that "the court in exceptional cases may award attorney fees to the prevailing party." Although this statement would appear on its face to treat both prevailing plaintiffs and defendants equally, the case law that has developed appears to favor patent holders. A successful patent holder may be eligible for attorney fees under section 285 by showing willful infringement, although willful infringement will not always result in an award for attorney fees. For the successful accused infringer, obtaining attorneys requires a higher showing. Courts have awarded attorney fees to successful accused infringers when the patent holder's behavior could be characterized as inequitable conduct or pursuit of frivolous litigation.

ANSWERING THE SUE OR SETTLE QUESTION

Throughout this book, the foundational perspective is that of the decision maker. In the patent litigation context, one of the most important decisions is whether to settle the dispute out of court or proceed to trial. The vast majority of filed lawsuits are settled prior to trial, and this percentage is even higher if one includes settlement of threatened but unfiled claims. One valuation technique that is particularly well suited for this decision is the decision-tree technique that was introduced in Chapter 4. That technique involves constructing a decision tree that captures the various assessments regarding uncertainty and risk and combines them with assessments regarding possible outcomes.

The beauty of the technique is that it disassembles a complex problem into more approachable elements—particularly the risks and uncertainties—that can be more easily assessed. Once this step is done, the elements are reassembled in a logically consistent manner so that a decision can be calculated based on the various inputs and assumptions. In the litigation context, this decision incorporates the damage calculations, but it also includes consideration of important additional elements such as uncertainty and other potential costs and benefits not included in the damages.

Patent Holdings versus Apollo Hypothetical

To illustrate how to conduct the analysis for a sue or settle (or settle or defend) decision tree, consider the following hypothetical example. Patent Holdings holds a patent that is used in mobile communication devices. Apollo Corporation manufactures and sells mobile phones and has received a letter from Patent Holdings that claims that Apollo is infringing on one of Patent Holdings' patents. The letter includes a demand that Apollo pay a lump sum royalty payment of $100,000. Apollo needs to decide whether or not to pay the royalty payment.

Using these facts together with some estimates regarding probabilities, potential damages and expected costs, a basic decision tree can be developed to assist Apollo with its decision (see Figure 11.6). The tree captures four possible uncertain future events:

1. Summary judgment outcome
2. Trial outcome
3. Decision to appeal
4. Appeal outcome

Of course, a much more elaborate tree could be constructed, but this basic tree helps illustrate the utility of the technique. In constructing the tree, the following assumptions regarding the uncertainties were made:

- The probability that Apollo wins at the summary judgment level is 75 percent.
- The probability that Apollo wins at trial is 90 percent.
- The probability that Patent Holdings appeals an adverse trial outcome is 20 percent.
- The probability that Apollo appeals an adverse trial outcome is 80 percent.
- The probability that the appellate court will overturn the trial court is 10 percent.

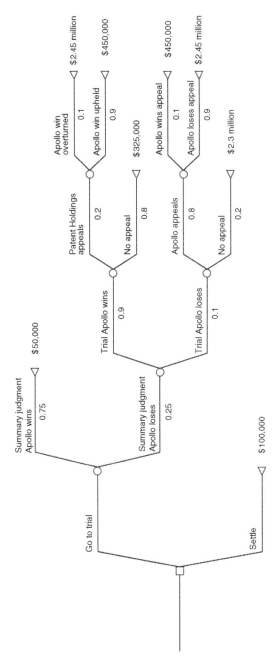

FIGURE 11.6 Basic Decision Tree for Apollo's Settle or Defend Question

- The tree also incorporates certain cost assumptions for Apollo (again simplified for illustration purposes): The cost to litigate to summary judgment is $50,000, the costs to litigate through trial is an additional $250,000, the amount of damages if Patent Holdings wins at trial is $2,000,000, and the cost to prosecute any appeal is an additional $150,000.

This decision-tree scenario has been deliberately shortened to make the problem more accessible (not to mention to better permit the tree's display in this book). Were it a nonhypothetical decision tree, the number of decision and uncertainty nodes could be significantly increased to better reflect the full complexity of the situation facing the litigants. Even with a condensed decision tree, however, important insights can be gleaned to improve the decision-making process.

When this tree is rolled back (see Figure 11.7), the technique informs the decision maker that the expected monetary value of a decision to go to trial is $181,750. Because the cost of the settlement offer is $100,000 and Apollo is seeking to minimize expenditures, the rational decision to minimize costs is to pay the $100,000 demand.

The decision tree makes obvious what is already intuitively known by those who are forced to participate in this type of settle or defend exercise in the real world. Even with a high chance of success on the merits—75 percent probability of winning at summary judgment and 90 percent probability of winning at trial—it still makes economic sense for Apollo to pay the $100,000 settlement offer.

The Importance of Putting on the Other Person's Shoes

Before finalizing its decision to settle or defend, however, Apollo should run the decision analysis from Patent Holdings' perspective.[95] Seeing the decision from the other party's perspective can provide the decision maker with very valuable insights. Figure 11.8 shows a decision tree for Patent Holdings' decision to sue Apollo for infringement or settle. Because Patent Holdings has a number of licensees (potential and actual) for the contested patent in addition to Apollo, the potential costs to Patent Holdings should it lose the Apollo infringement suit could be significant. For purposes of this exercise, assume that those loses would be $5 million in potential royalties and settlements. The tree assumes that the attorney fees are the same as those facing Apollo, and the uncertainty probabilities are the same as with the earlier decision trees.

When this new decision tree is rolled back (see Figure 11.9), some interesting insights emerge. Patent Holdings has much more to lose from a bad

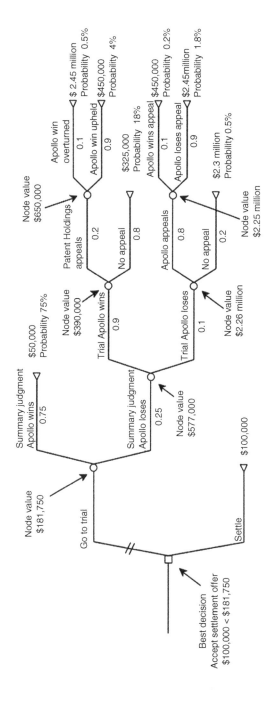

FIGURE 11.7 Rolled-Back Decision Tree from Apollo's Perspective

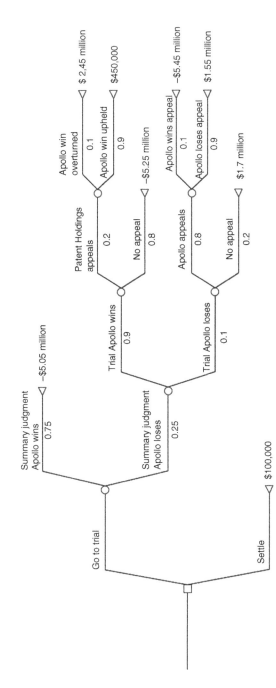

FIGURE 11.8 Decision Tree from Patent Holdings' Perspective

304

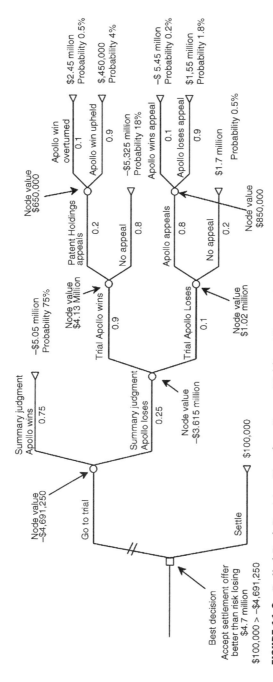

FIGURE 11.9 Rolled-Back Decision Tree from Patent Holdings' Perspective

outcome than Apollo. From the rolled-back decision tree, it appears that from Patent Holdings' perspective any settlement would be better than the potential to lose more than $5 million. Because much of this $5 million would be in the form of forgone earnings and not actually out-of-pocket costs, it may make sense from a business strategy point of view for Patent Holdings to gamble that Apollo will view the situation solely from its own perspective and pay the settlement and that other companies will do the same. If Apollo does the above assessment, however, it should now have powerful ammunition in settlement negotiations to force Patent Holdings down to a mere nuisance value settlement payment. Apollo should call Patent Holding's bluff and demonstrate a firm resolve in defending against the lawsuit.

REFERENCES

Abernathy, William, and Kenneth Wayne. Sept.–Oct. 1974. "Limits of the Learning Curve." *Harvard Business Review*.

Butler, Bryan. 2011. *Patent Infringement Compensation and Damages*. New York: Law Journal Press.

Cauley, Richard. 2009. *Winning the Patent Damages Case*. New York: Oxford University Press.

C. K. Coughlin, Inc. 1973. HBS Case Study 9-174-083.

Durie, Daralyn, and Mark Lemley. 2010. "A Structured Approach to Calculating Reasonable Royalties." *Lewis and Clark Law Review* 14: 627.

Freedman, David. Nov.–Dec. 1992. "Is Management Still a Science?" *Harvard Business Review*.

Ghemawat, Pankaj. Mar.–Apr. 1985. "Building Strategy on the Learning Curve." *Harvard Business Review*.

Hirschmann, Wilfred. Jan.–Feb. 1964. "Profit from the Learning Curve." *Harvard Business Review*.

Janicke, Paul. 1993. "Contemporary Issues in Patent Damages." *American University Law Review* 42: 691.

Keeley, Michael. 1999. "Estimating Damages in Patent Infringement Cases: An Economic Perspective." www.cornerstone.com/pubs/xprPubResultsCornerstone.aspx?xpST=PubRecent.

Law Practice Management Committee of the American Intellectual Property Law Association. 2011. "Report of the Economic Survey 2011."

Lemley, Mark. 2009. "Distinguishing Lost Profits from Reasonable Royalties." *William and Mary Law Review* 51: 655.

Love, Brian. 2007. "Patentee Overcompensation and the Entire Market Value Rule." *Stanford Law Review* 60: 263.

McCune, Connor. 2011. "IP Leveraging and Learning/Experience Curve Effects." Univ. of New Hampshire Law Student White Paper Series (copy on file with authors).

Meuller, Janice. 2006. *An Introduction to Patent Law*. 2nd ed. New York: Aspen Law & Business.

Morin, Michael. July–Aug. 2005. "Processing Grain: Lost Profits Damages and Some Practical Considerations for the Patent Litigator." *IP Litigator*.

Opderbeck, David. 2009. "Patent Damages Reform and the Shape of Patent Law." *Boston University Law Review* 89: 127.

Pincus, Laura. 1991. "The Computation of Damages in Patent Infringement Actions." *Harvard Journal of Law and Technology* 5: 95.

Pretty, Laurence. 2011. *Patent Litigation*. New York: PLI Press.

PricewaterhouseCoopers. 2010. "2010 Patent Litigation Study: The Continued Evolution of Patent Damages Law—Patent Litigation Trends 1995—2009 and the Impact of Recent Court Decisions on Damages."

Riley, Michele. 2005. "A Review of Court-Awarded Royalty Rates in Patent Infringement Cases (1990–2001)." In *Intellectual Property: Valuation, Exploitation, and Infringement Damages*, edited by Gordon V. Smith and Russell L. Parr, 706–722. Hoboken, NJ: John Wiley & Sons.

Schecter, Roger E., and John R. Thomas. 2004. *Principles of Patent Law, Concise Hornbook Series*. St. Paul, MN: West.

Seaman, Christopher. 2010. "Reconsidering the Georgia-Pacific Standard for Reasonable Royalty Patent Damages." *Brigham Young University Law Review* 1661.

Spence, A. Michael. 1981. "Competition, Entry, and Antitrust Policy." In *Strategy, Predation, and Antitrust Analysis*, edited by Steven Salop, 45–88. Report by the Federal Trade Commission Bureau of Economics and Bureau of Competition.

Valenti, Paola Maria. 2011. "Economic Approaches to Patent Damages Analysis." In *The Economic Valuation of Patents: Methods and Applications*, edited by Federico Munari and Raffaele Oriani, 262–287. Cheltenham, UK: Edward Elgar.

Werden, Gregory, Lucian Beavers, and Luke Froeb. 1999. "Quantity Accretion: Mirror Image of Price Erosion from Patent Infringement." *Journal of the Patent and Trademark Office Society* 81: 479.

Werden, Gregory, Luke Froeb, and James Langenfeld. 2000. "Lost Profits from Patent Infringement: The Simulation Approach." *International Journal of the Economics of Business* 7: 213.

NOTES

1. Note that the landmark $873 million patent damage award against Polaroid took place in 1991, before the 1995–2009 timeframe for Table 11.1.
2. PricewaterhouseCoopers, "2010 Patent Litigation Study: The Continued Evolution of Patent Damages Law—Patent Litigation Trends 1995—2009 and the Impact of Recent Court Decisions on Damages" (2010), 7.
3. 35 U.S.C. sec. 284.

4. See *Panduit Corp. v. Stahlin Bros. Fibre Works, Inc.*, 575 F.2d 1152, 1157 (6th Cir. 1978) ("When actual damages, e.g., lost profits, cannot be proved, the patent owner is entitled to reasonable royalties.").
5. 377 U.S. 476 (1964).
6. 377 U.S. 476, 507 (1964).
7. 35 U.S.C. sec. 289.
8. 35 U.S.C. sec. 284.
9. See, e.g., *In re Seagate Tech.*, 497 F.3d 1360 (Fed. Cir. 2007).
10. 35 U.S.C. sec. 154.
11. This quotation was used to describe a situation in which a patent holder could use the threat of injunction to extract royalties from an alleged infringer to which the patent holder could not recover otherwise. *Odetics, Inc. v. Storage Tech. Corp.*, 185 F.3d 1259, 1272 (CAFC 1999).
12. Mark Lemley, "Distinguishing Lost Profits from Reasonable Royalties," *William and Mary Law Review* 51 (2009): 657.
13. 35 U.S.C. sec. 253.
14. 547 U.S. 388 (2006).
15. 575 F.2d 1152 (6th Cir. 1978).
16. See Paul Janicke, "Contemporary Issues in Patent Damages," *American University Law Review* 42 (1993): 709.
17. Roger E. Schecter and John R. Thomas, *Principles of Patent Law, Concise Hornbook Series* (2004), 335; Janicke, 700.
18. *Gyromat Corp. v. Champion Spark Plug Co.*, 735 F.2d 549, 552 (Fed. Cir. 1984) ("The substantial number of sales . . . of infringing products containing the patented features is compelling evidence of the demand for the product.").
19. *Standard Havens Prods., Inc. v. Gencor Indus., Inc.*, 953 F.2d 1360, 1373 (Fed. Cir. 1991).
20. Paola Maria Valenti, "Economic Approaches to Patent Damages Analysis," in *The Economic Valuation of Patents: Methods and Applications*, ed. Federico Munari and Raffaele Oriani (2011), 363.
21. 883 F.2d 1573 (Fed. Cir. 1989).
22. Janicke, 704.
23. See *Bio-Rad Lab v. Nicolet Instrument Corp.*, 739 F.2d 604 (Fed. Cir. 1984).
24. *Bio-Rad Lab v. Nicolet Instrument Corp.*, 739 F.2d 604, 616 (Fed. Cir. 1984).
25. *Paper Converting Machine Co. v. Magna-Graphics Corp.*, 745 F.2d 11 (Fed. Cir. 1984).
26. *Paper Converting Machine Co. v. Magna-Graphics Corp.*, 745 F.2d 11, 22 (Fed. Cir. 1984).
27. Bryan Butler, *Patent Infringement Compensation and Damages* (2011), 5-21.
28. See *Del Mar Avionics, Inc. v. Quinton Instrument Co.*, 836 F.2d 1320 (Fed. Cir. 1987).
29. *Bic Leisure Products, Inc. v. Windsurfing International, Inc.*, 1 F.3d 1214 (Fed. Cir. 1993).
30. *Haemonetics Corp. v. Baxter Healthcare Corp.*, 593 F.Supp.2d 303, 306 (D. Mass. 2009).

31. 883 F.2d 1573, 1578 (Fed. Cir. 1989).
32. *Grain Processing Corp. v. Am. Maize-Prods. Co.*, 185 F.3d 1341, 1350 (Fed. Cir. 1999); see also *Ericsson, Inc. v. Harris Corp.*, 352 F.3d 1369, 1377–1378 (Fed.Cir. 2003).
33. See, e.g., *In the Matter of Mahurkar Double Lumen Hemodialysis Catheter Patent Litigation*, 831 F.Supp. 1354 (N.D. Ill. 1993).
34. Gregory Werden, Lucian Beavers, and Luke Froeb, "Quantity Accretion: Mirror Image of Price Erosion from Patent Infringement," *Journal of the Patent and Trademark Office Society* 81 (1999): 479.
35. Pankaj Ghemawat, "Building Strategy on the Learning Curve," *Harvard Business Review* (Mar.–Apr. 1985).
36. For a more complete discussion, see William Abernathy and Kenneth Wayne, "Limits of the Learning Curve," *Harvard Business Review* (Sept.–Oct. 1974).
37. Wilfred Hirschmann, "Profit from the Learning Curve," *Harvard Business Review* (Jan.–Feb. 1964).
38. These industries range from facial tissue to computer chips; see Ghemawat.
39. A. Michael Spence "Competition, Entry, and Antitrust Policy," in *Strategy, Predation, and Antitrust Analysis, Federal Trade Commission*, edited by Steven Salop (1981). One way of summing up the learning curve effect is that practice makes perfect. In information-age industries where flexibility and willingness to change are present, the benefits of learning curve effects should be significant. In addition, some have argued that the more complex the undertaking the greater the rate of learning; see Hirschmann. As a consequence, in high-risk, high-reward winner-take-all markets, any incremental benefits, such as those from a learning curve effect, may be sufficient to determine the winner. Another author claims that "self-organizing systems are learning systems." David Freedman, "Is Management Still a Science?" *Harvard Business Review* (Nov.–Dec. 1992).
40. Application of learning curve analysis to the production of Model T and Model A automobiles by Abernathy and Wayne. The authors also discuss the dangers of strategic reliance on learning curve effects.
41. Valenti, 268–269.
42. Lemley, 660.
43. *Rite-Hite Corp. v. Kelley Company*, 56 F.3d 1538, 1550 (Fed.Cir. 1995):

    The unpatented components must function together with the patented component in some manner so as to produce a desired end product or result. All the components together must be analogous to components of a single assembly or be parts of complete machine, or they must constitute a functional unit. Our precedent has not extended liability to include items that have essentially no functional relationship to the patented invention and that may have been sold with an infringing device only as a matter of convenience or business advantage.

44. 382 F.3d 1367 (Fed.Cir. 2004)
45. 382 F.3d 1367, 1372–1373 (Fed.Cir. 2004).

46. See, e.g., *Velo-Bind, Inc. v. Minn. Mining & Mfg. Co.*, 647 F.2d 965 (9th Cir. 1981).
47. See Brian Love, "Patentee Overcompensation and the Entire Market Value Rule," *Stanford Law Review* 60: (2007): 269.
48. Bryan Butler, *Patent Infringement Compensation and Damages* (2011), 2-28.
49. Christopher Seaman, "Reconsidering the *Georgia-Pacific* Standard for Reasonable Royalty Patent Damages," *Brigham Young University Law Review* (2010): 1668.
50. 130 U.S. 152 (1889).
51. 235 U.S. 641 (1915).
52. Lemley, 655.
53. PricewaterhouseCoopers, 12.
54. Ibid.
55. Seaman, 1675.
56. Lemley, 661.
57. *Panduit Corp. v. Stahlin Bros. Fibre Works, Inc.*, 575 F.2d 1152, 1157-1158 (6th Cir. 1978).
58. *Uniloc United States v. Microsoft Corp*, 2009 WL 691204 (D.R.I. March 16, 2010).
59. *Minco, Inc. v. Combustion Engineering, Inc.*, 95 F.3d 1109, 1119 (Fed. Cir. 1996).
60. 580 F.3d 1301, 1325 (Fed. Cir. 2009).
61. 318 F.Supp 1116 (S.D.N.Y. 1970).
62. See, e.g., Butler, chap. 3.
63. Richard Cauley, *Winning the Patent Damages Case* (2009), 39.
64. Butler, 3-4.
65. Ibid.
66. *Nickson Industries Inc. v. Rol Manufacturing Co.*, 847 F.2d 795 (Fed. Cir. 1988).
67. Butler, 3-8.
68. For example, some have argued that *Georgia-Pacific* provides so many factors that could be considered and balanced that the test provides little to no practical guidance to the jury. Daralyn Durie and Mark Lemley, "A Structured Approach to Calculating Reasonable Royalties," *Lewis and Clark Law Review* 14 (2010): 631. Other common criticisms focus on the hypothetical negotiation's assumption that (1) there is an equilibrium point at which the parties would have reached a licensing agreement, when in fact that may not have been the case, and (2) the parties have perfect information at the time of the negotiation, including information about the future.
69. *Dragan v. L.D. Caulk Co.*, 1989 WL 1333536, ∗9 (D.Del. Apr. 21 1989), aff'd, 897 F.2d 538 (Fed. Cir. 1990).
70. See Michael Keeley, "Estimating Damages in Patent Infringement Cases: An Economic Perspective" (1999), http://www.cornerstone.com/pubs/xprPubResults-Cornerstone.aspx?xpST=PubRecent 10.
71. Ibid.
72. Ibid.
73. Ibid.

74. Ibid.
75. See *Lucent Technologies, Inc. v. Gateway, Inc.*, 580 F.3d 1301, 1324 (Fed.Cir. 2009).
76. Butler, 4-28.
77. 632 F.3d 1292 (Fed.Cir. 2011).
78. 632 F.3d 1292, 1315 (Fed.Cir. 2011).
79. *Panduit Corp. v, Stahlin Bros. Fibre Works, Inc.*, 575 F.2d 1152 (Fed.Cir. 1978).
80. 575 F.2d 1152, 1158–1159 (Fed.Cir. 1978).
81. *Mahurkar v. C.R. Bard, Inc.*, 79 F.3d 1572, 1580-1581 (Fed.Cir. 1996); *Maxwell v. J. Baker, Inc.*, 86 F.3d 1098, 1110 (Fed.Cir. 1996).
82. Butler, 4-35– 4-36.
83. 56 F.3d 1538, 1549 (Fed.Cir. 1995). Mark Lemley explains that that it is not clear that the Federal Circuit had ever applied the entire market value rule to decide a reasonable royalty case before the *Rite-Hite* decision. Lemley, 662.
84. See, e.g., *Bose Corporation v. JBL, Inc.*, 274 F.3d 1354 (Fed.Cir. 2001).
85. *Georgia-Pacific Corp. v. United States Plywood Corp.*, 318 F.Supp 1116, 1122 (S.D.N.Y. 1970).
86. *State Indus., Inc. v. Mor-Flo Indus., Inc.*, 883 F.2d 1573, 1580 (Fed.Cir. 1989); see also *Mars, Inc. v. Coin Acceptors, Inc.*, 527 F.3d 1359, 1374 (Fed.Cir. 2008) ("we reject Coinco's argument that a reasonable royalty can never result in an infringer operating at a loss.").
87. Fed. R. Civ. P. 52(a).
88. *United States v. United States Gypsum Co.*, 333 U.S. 364, 395 (1948).
89. *Brooktree Corp. v. Advanced Micro Devices, Inc.*, 977 F.2d 1555, 1580 (Fed. Cir. 1993).
90. *General Motors Corp. v. Devex Corp. et al.*, 461 U.S. 648 (1983).
91. See, e.g., *In re Seagate Tech.*, 497 F.3d 1360 (Fed. Cir. 2007).
92. Schecter and Thomas, 344.
93. Schecter and Thomas, 344–345.
94. Law Practice Management Committee of the American Intellectual Property Law Association "Report of the Economic Survey 2011" (2011), 35.
95. A classic Harvard Business School case study (C.K. Coughlin, Inc. HBS Case Study 9-174-083 [1973]) illustrates the importance of performing the decision analysis from the other side's perspective. This case study was one of the first to illustrate the utility of the decision-tree method for making patent litigation decisions.

CHAPTER 12

Unlocking the Potential
Value within Patents

The transition from an industrial, goods-based economy to an entrepreneurial, knowledge-based one has reshaped the fabric of the global economy over a relatively short timeframe. Land, buildings, and machinery are being supplanted by intellectual property—in particular, patents—as the most influential assets in this new economy. As with any rapid systemic change, this shift in economic focus creates substantial new opportunities. The increased recognition of patents as a significant business asset, for example, has led entrepreneurs, firms, and investors to seek alternative methods for extracting value from patents. These emerging practices are helping to create new economic potential for patents.

Valuable assets, including patents, possess what can be referred to as *potential* value.[1] Potential value is untapped capital-generation potential that exists within a given asset and that can be alienated from the asset without alienating the asset itself. Stated more plainly, one can think of assets as having two types of qualities:

1. **Intrinsic qualities:** The essential qualities of the asset are its intrinsic qualities. For a business asset, it is the essential qualities that allow it to generate streams of future economic benefits. Take, for example, a commercial building. It generates streams of future economic benefits for the building owner through a number of intrinsic functions, such as providing office space for the owner, generating rent from tenants, and selling advertising space on the side of the building. Patents possess intrinsic qualities for generating streams of future economic benefits. Chapter 5 provided an overview of these intrinsic qualities, which revolve around the ability to exclude others from practicing the invention covered by the patent.

2. **Capital-generation qualities:** Most valuable assets also have a dormant ability to generate capital that is separate from the intrinsic qualities. Rather than using the asset's intrinsic qualities to generate future economic benefits, simply owning the asset brings with it an ability to generate investment capital without having to actually sell the asset.

Secured financing provides one of the most common examples of the potential value in assets. Asset owners are able to leverage the value of their assets by using them as collateral to obtain loans on terms that are much more favorable than could be obtained without collateral. Land, buildings, and machinery have long been used as loan collateral and have helped to increase debt-market efficiency and dramatically expand investment capital availability. Economist Henry de Soto has written extensively on the potential value in assets. To help illustrate the concept, de Soto uses the analogy of a mountain lake and its potential energy.

> *We can think about this lake in its immediate physical context and see some primary uses for it, such as canoeing and fishing. But when we think about this same lake as an engineer would be focusing on its capacity to generate energy as an additional value beyond the lake's natural state as a body of water, we suddenly see the potential created by the lake's elevated position. The challenge for the engineer is finding out how he can create a process that allows him to convert and fix this potential into a form that can be used to do additional work. In the case of the elevated lake, that process is contained in a hydroelectric plant that allows the lake water to move rapidly downward with the force of gravity, thereby transforming the placid lake's energy potential into the kinetic energy of tumbling water. This new kinetic energy can then rotate turbines, creating mechanical energy that can be used to turn electromagnets that further convert it into electrical energy. . . . Thus an apparently placid lake can be used to light your room and power the machinery in a factory.*[2]

The potential energy from the mountain lake is very similar to the potential value that exists within assets. The potential energy or value does not flow simply from the intrinsic qualities of the mountain lake or asset, but instead flows primarily from an extrinsic process that unlocks an otherwise dormant, additional benefit. The commercial exploitation of an asset's potential value takes place within a complex environment that requires numerous human-made legal and financial institutions to exist and function properly. The quality of these institutions will play a large role in the potential value that can be extracted from a given asset. Returning to the mountain lake analogy, human-made devices and processes are needed to capture the mountain lake's potential energy. Moreover, using different devices or processes can dramatically change the energy output—more efficient hydroelectric turbines, for example, will produce more electricity— even though the mountain lake itself remains the same. The same principle applies to assets and potential value. Different legal and financial institutions may generate vastly different potential value from the very same asset.

For today's businesses, patents are frequently more relevant and valuable than traditional land, building, and machinery assets. In theory, patents should be one of the richest sources for potential value and investment capital, which is particularly important when one considers that firms with valuable patent assets should be among the most entrepreneurial of firms. As economist Joseph Schumpeter noted more than a half century ago, a healthy economy is a dynamic organism that is constantly in a state of change and renewal. Schumpeter described the process as one of *creative destruction* whereby competition and innovation constantly revolutionize the economy from within—"incessantly destroying the old one, incessantly creating a new one."[3] By seeking innovations to render their competitors obsolete, entrepreneurial firms create new products, markets, processes for doing business, and even new industries. Established competitors, as well as entire industries, that cannot keep pace with the innovations and increased competition are forced out of business, thereby causing a constant renewal of the economy. In short, the continuous creation and growth of entrepreneurial firms is one of the most important factors for the success of an economy.

Access to investment capital is critical to the creation and growth of entrepreneurial firms. So, it would be ideal if entrepreneurial firms were able to efficiently unlock the potential value of patents to access investment capital to grow their businesses. To compound matters, the speed of knowledge and innovation is accelerating. Paradoxically, although the new economy is knowledge-based, its speed of change is such that the value of that knowledge to its owner may be short-lived. In some industries, product life cycles are shrinking from years to months. Many patents must be exploited increasingly rapidly if their holders are to reap a commercial return. The ability to exploit that opportunity, however, may depend on raising adequate investment capital in a timely manner.

Unfortunately, the potential value within patents remains a largely untapped resource. That fact is slowly beginning to change. In particular, two practices are emerging to help patent owners tap into the potential value of their patents. They are the use of patents as collateral to secure loans and the securitization of patents.

In this chapter, we

- Explain the critical role that institutions and the law play in unlocking the potential value of patents.
- Analyze the emerging methods for extracting potential value from patents.
- Explain the intersection between traditional valuation analysis and these emerging practices.

KEEPING PACE WITH ECONOMIC CHANGES

History is replete with examples of how legal institutions have evolved to accommodate shifts in economic activity. Thousands of years ago, our ancestors made the leap from a culture and economic system based on hunting and gathering to one of domesticated animals and planned agriculture. The control and use of land became the primary source of wealth creation in agricultural societies. Societal institutions evolved over time to recognize the preeminent role of land. The law, for example, developed the rules of ownership and transfer for this important asset. Societies that developed institutions that were responsive to this new fixed-agricultural economy flourished in a manner not possible in the hunter-gatherer economy that preceded it.

Another major transformation began less than 300 hundred years ago as the Industrial Revolution swept out of England to eventually encompass the globe. The wealth creation assets shifted to the means of production. Wealth depended not on how much land a person owned, but on the ownership of the means of mass production of tangible goods and the resources necessary to feed the industrial machine. Institutions again evolved to accommodate the new society. Corporation laws were created to limit the liability of investors and allow a firm's management to be separated from its ownership. Labor laws developed to address the needs of a new class of worker, and consumer protection laws helped to increase consumer confidence and the growth of impersonal markets for goods. As firms grew more powerful, competition laws were implemented to set the permissible rules of marketplace behavior.

Today, we are in the midst of another transformation that is testing the existing institutions that were developed to serve the needs of the industrial age. The information age, and the increasing importance of knowledge assets, such as patents, has brought new challenges to traditional areas of the law and created new issues. As we will explain throughout this chapter, evolving institutions and legal solutions are critical for patent owners to extract the potential value from their patents.

PATENTS AS COLLATERAL FOR SECURED LOANS

Secured loans are probably the oldest method to extract value from an illiquid asset. Cuneiform records demonstrate that credit arrangements were common all the way back in ancient Mesopotamia to help to finance the burgeoning agricultural economy along the Tigris and Euphrates rivers. Four thousand years later, playwright William Shakespeare made the pledge of a "pound of flesh" to secure a loan the centerpiece of his *Merchant of Venice.*

A secured loan involves lending money, the repayment of which is backed by assets that are owned by the borrower. Security agreements are the mechanisms that drive secured loans. In a security agreement, the debtor grants the creditor a security interest in an asset offered as collateral. If the debtor defaults on the loan, the creditor is able to gain ownership of the pledged asset. Although security interests are enforceable between the parties to the agreement, creditors wishing to defend against competing third-party interests must notify the general public of their security interest in the debtor's collateral. In the United States, under the Uniform Commercial Code's (UCC) Article 9 system, the creditor's public notification is known as *perfection.* A perfected security interest assures creditors priority over subsequent third-party claims to the collateral.

The security aspect of secured loans helps to increase the economic efficiency of the lending process dramatically (see Figure 12.1). One of the biggest challenges in the lending function revolves around the debtor's ability to repay the loan. As the risk that the debtor will default increases, the

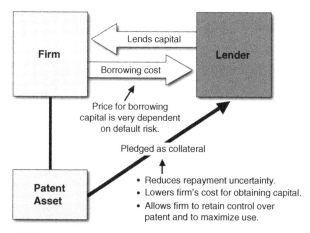

FIGURE 12.1 Efficiency of Secured Lending Process

interest rate charged by the creditor needs to increase correspondingly to compensate the creditor for this nonrepayment potential. Debtors can therefore substantially reduce their cost of capital if they can reduce, or eliminate, this nonrepayment concern. Providing collateral to secure the loan provides an ideal solution for debtors. At the same time, the secured loan process allows the debtor to retain title to and maximize the value of these collateral assets. All told, the secured lending process allows for a lower cost of investment capital while maintaining ownership of assets with the parties who are best able to exploit their value.

For the secured lending process to work, debtors must be able to pledge assets. Historically, collateral has taken the form of tangible assets such as land, buildings, and machinery. State rules and procedures governing creditor interests in these agricultural- and industrial-age assets are well established. Creditors are experienced at valuing traditional tangible assets, drafting mortgages and security agreements encompassing these assets, and properly perfecting the resulting security interests. Judicial treatment of conflicts involving multiple creditors having security interests in the same tangible asset is relatively clear-cut and consistent. As a result, most creditors are comfortable with the certainty of security agreements used to secure loans that are backed by tangible assets.

When patents serve as the collateral for a secured loan, the certainty of the security arrangement and its ability to protect a creditor's financial interests is greatly reduced. Any individual secured loan system poses two important concerns for creditors: (1) Who owns (or has ownership claims to) the collateral, and (2) what is the value of the collateral? Patents pose particular problems under both concerns.

Ownership Concern: Who Owns the Patent?

A creditor wishing to take a collateral interest in a patent will want to ensure that the debtor owns the patent. This ownership concern has two distinct parts:

1. The creditor has to determine with some certainty that the debtor is the actual owner of the patent being used as collateral.
2. The creditor needs to determine if there are prior pledges or transfers against the patent that could interfere with the creditor taking control of the collateral should default occur.

The ownership problem was solved for land by the evolution of formal registries of deeds that provide public documentation and notice of ownership as well as potential future claims of ownership. The legal system, in turn, gives force to the system by defining what rights and obligations arise from various recording activities. The UCC system—specifically its Article 9—was designed to provide a similar function for loans collateralized by tangible goods. For patents and other forms of intellectual property, the legal and financial systems are still working to develop reliable methods to address the ownership concern.

Original Ownership and Assignments Determining original ownership is not particularly difficult for patents because the government creates the property through a well-documented grant (see Chapter 5). Tracking assignments, however, can be a little more challenging. An assignment is patent parlance for the sale of a patent (see Chapter 2). Each assignment needs to be tracked to determine if the current patent holder has proper title in the patent. The current holder will need to be able to construct a chain of title that shows each assignment from the original patent to the current ownership (see Chapter 5).

Each assignment should be recorded with the patent office and therefore be easy to prove. In the United States, however, such recordation is optional and not mandatory. Moreover, the U.S. Patent and Trademark Office (PTO) does not confirm the accuracy of the assignment, so an inaccurate assignment could be recorded. Assignees, however, do have a substantial incentive to properly record the assignment, as the U.S. Patent Act provides that "an assignment, grant or conveyance shall be void as against any subsequent purchaser or mortgagee for a valuable consideration, without notice, unless it is recorded in the Patent and Trademark Office within three months from its date or prior to the date of such subsequent purchase or mortgage."[4]

Pledges and Liens Tracking pledges and liens on a patent can be even more difficult than determining original ownership. In 1992, the American Bar Association established a task force to examine security interests in intellectual property. That task force observed that

> the current state of the law governing security interests in intellectual property is unsatisfactory. There is uncertainty as to where and how to file, what constitutes notice of a security interest, who has priority, and what property is covered by a security interest. This area of the law is further complicated by the fact that both federal and state laws impact on these issues.[5]

Although a handful of cases have helped add some order to the situation for patents, the general observation still rings true today.

To protect its interest in collateral, a creditor needs to establish a valid claim against the collateral that will take precedence over other potential claimants. To do so, an asset encumbrance system needs to have a public notice element so that the lender can determine if there are prior pledges against the property that could interfere with the lender taking control of the collateral should default occur. Likewise, a creditor taking a security interest in an asset of a debtor must give notice to the public that the asset is now encumbered by their security interest so as to ensure priority of that interest over subsequent third parties. Chapter 5 provides a basic overview of the U.S. law regarding security interests in patents. In brief, there is some uncertainty as to where and how to file notice of encumbrances, what constitutes notice, who has priority, and what property is covered by a security interest.

Tracking Assignments, Pledges and Liens   Despite some confusion with the law, one of the biggest obstacles to creditors resolving the ownership issue for patents stems from a much simpler problem. Mechanically, how does a creditor track assignments, pledges, and liens on a patent that could detract from the creditors' rights to the patent in the event of a default? The difficulties in performing the necessary examination of the various assignments, pledges, and liens regarding patents has led to some innovative solutions. One such innovation is described in Box 12.1.

Valuation Concern: What Is the Patent Worth?

Assuming that the creditor is able to get comfortable with the patent ownership issue, the creditor must then confront the valuation issue. How much is the patent worth? In the event of a default by the debtor, will the patent rights be worth enough money to cover any unpaid amounts?

Valuation Mechanics   The mechanics of the valuation should be no different than the mechanics discussed throughout this book. The valuator needs to prepare properly for the valuation (see Chapter 5) to understand the legal rights that make up the patent being valued:

- What exactly is being valued: the invention, the patent rights, or both?
- What are the specific legal characteristics of the patent rights being valued?
- How will the patent rights be used? (Different usages can generate very different values for a patent.)

BOX 12.1: PORTAL FOR INTELLECTUAL PROPERTY RIGHTS

In 1999, the Whittemore School of Business and Economics at the University of New Hampshire, the University of New Hampshire School of Law (then known as the Franklin Pierce Law Center), and the University of Maine School of Law received a grant from the PTO to explore the existing structural obstacles to leveraging the value of intellectual property in secured transactions in the United States. The research team found that the absence of a nationwide system to easily determine the ownership of, and any preexisting security interests in, intangible assets increased the uncertainty surrounding patents (and other intellectual property assets) as collateral. This uncertainty increased investor risk, which translated into higher costs of capital for entrepreneurs and small businesses.[6]

The team made a recommendation that a one-stop search page "portal," accessible via the web, that could access individual state UCC filing systems as well as the federal assignment databases maintained by the PTO and the Copyright Office would be a significant improvement. This centralized and integrated security-interest perfection information system would use a centralized web server using a customized common gateway interface, or CGI, script program that interacts with the database engine for each state's UCC filing system and for the federal intellectual property assignment databases to provide the search criteria and receive the search results. This portal or gateway approach allows each database (state or federal) to maintain independence and sovereignty over its own information.

In 2001, a follow-on cooperative agreement with the PTO was undertaken to begin implementing the proposed system as a proof-of-concept project. The project would include the federal patent-assignment database maintained by the PTO and the state UCC Article 9 database systems of three states: New Hampshire, Maine, and Massachusetts. This project was successfully completed and is now being introduced to actual UCC database users through the New Hampshire secretary of state's office as part of the UCC system maintained by the state. The short-term objective of this ongoing project is to obtain feedback from actual users in the financing and legal fields to improve the portal, to add access to additional state UCC Article 9 databases, and eventually to add in the trademark and then copyright assignment databases maintained by the federal government.

(continued)

(continued)

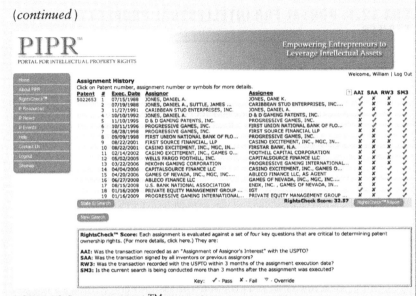

FIGURE 12.2   RightsCheck^{TM} Example

One innovation of the PIPR system is the RightsCheck^{TM} software feature that was developed to quickly and easily confirm patent ownership. It is the only software product that analyzes risk associated with the transfer of patent ownership rights. Currently, two RightsCheck modules are available: Patent Rights Search, which searches the federal patent assignment database; and Security Interest Search, which allows users to search the UCC Article 9 electronic database notice systems in participating states. Figure 12.2 provides an example of a RightsCheck performed on a patent.

Once the preparatory work is completed, the valuator can employ one or more of the valuation methods discussed earlier in Chapters 6 through 9. Depending on the specifics of the patent rights that are to be valued, the valuator can employ one or more of the income, market, or cost methods. Collateral-focused valuations can have a few differences from more standard valuations. Two of the bigger differences are (1) precision may be less important in collateral-focused valuations and (2) there is a need to manage valuation fluctuations over time.

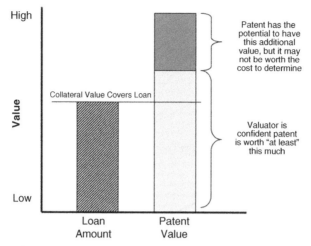

FIGURE 12.3 Precision May Be Less Important in Collateral-Focused Valuations than in Standard Valuations

The precision issue stems from the creditor not needing the exact value of the patent rights. Instead, the creditor simply needs to know that the value of the patent rights is sufficient to cover any unpaid amounts if the debtor defaults on the loan (see Figure 12.3). For example, let us assume the following:

- The creditor wants collateral to cover a $50,000 loan, and the debtor pledges a particular patent.
- The creditor's valuator conducts an analysis of the patent. The valuator is confident that the patent is worth "at least" $150,000 and could be worth up to $500,000.

In this scenario, the creditor may not need to incur the costs of further valuation analysis to try to provide more precision to its analysis on whether the patent is worth more than $150,000. Depending on the cost of the further analysis and the importance of the excess value to the creditor's risk analysis of the debtor, such additional analysis may not be necessary.

The issue of patent valuations fluctuating over time can be more complicated. Patents tend to have greater valuation-fluctuation profiles than many of the asset classes that are commonly accepted by creditors as collateral, such as real estate. To be more specific, many patents have a

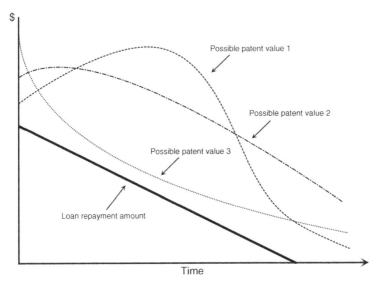

FIGURE 12.4 Declining Patent Values and the Effect on Loan Collateral

heightened risk for a declining valuation, including extremely rapid declines. The risk of a declining valuation stems from a number of factors:

- The shelf-life for new technology can be very short.
- The limited duration of a patent creates a date certain when the patent rights will have zero value.
- The risk of possible invalidation hangs over many patents.

A creditor wanting to accept a patent as collateral needs to value that patent in a manner that tracks value over the life of the loan. Just because the patent's value exceeds the loan amount on day one of the loan does not mean that it will exceed the repayment amount at year 5 when the default could occur. Figure 12.4 graphically demonstrates how a creditor needs to track the potential value decline for patent assets with the declining repayment amount of the loan. Although the patent valuations fluctuate wildly in Figure 12.4, the valuations always exceed the loan repayment amount and therefore should be fine.

Managing the Value Decline Risk   Creditors are not completely helpless to the value decline risk. In fact, creditors have certain tools at their disposal to actively mitigate the risk. One possible tool is patent validity insurance. First developed by Swiss Re New Markets in 1999, patent validity insurance can provide a degree of downside risk protection for secured-loan creditors. A patent validity insurance policy indemnifies the policy beneficiary for amounts lost if the patent is later invalidated. Specific insurance coverage varies, but some features of the insurance protection that are relevant to a creditor include the following:

- Legal costs incurred in defending a patent infringement claim.
- Legal costs in bringing an action for a declaration of noninfringement.
- A discretionary coverage for a single, lump sum payment in the event that the patent is declared invalid.

Although patent validity insurance would appear to have potential, the market for this insurance product remains small and weak.[7] In a study of the feasibility of possible insurance schemes against patent litigation risk, the European Commission found a low level of demand for patent validity insurance (at least at current premium levels) and few insurers that were interested in offering this insurance product based on current demand.[8]

SECURITIZING PATENTS

Another emerging method to convert patent assets into investment capital is through an asset-backed securitization technique. Asset-backed securitization is a financial tool that is frequently used to separate and reassign cash flows from illiquid assets. Asset-backed securitization vehicles can be traced to the 1960s when they were used to monetize credit card receivables. Mortgage-backed securitization vehicles emerged in the 1980s, and the first intellectual property–backed securitization vehicles were sold in the 1990s.

Even though asset-backed securities have had a profound effect on the financial world, there is no widespread understanding of this increasingly important process. The concept is simple to describe, but can be devilishly hard to execute. Any asset that generates a cash flow can form the basis for the securitization process. One of the most common assets used in this manner is the residential mortgage, and its securitization has transformed real estate financing. Obtaining a mortgage was once a geographically discrete process that involved a local lending bank and a borrowing homeowner from the same locale.[9] The emergence of mortgage-backed securities lowered the lending risk and allowed home loans to become a national, rather than a local, industry. The lower risk and standardization of mortgage loans lowered the cost of borrowing, which has made homeownership accessible to a much broader percentage of the public.

Asset securitization is the process by which assets with an associated cash flow are pooled and converted into instruments (securities) that may be offered and sold more freely in the capital markets. A typical securitization transaction involves three main actors:

1. The **originator** is the pretransaction owner of the cash flow-producing assets. The originator sells these assets to a special-purpose vehicle.
2. The **special-purpose vehicle (SPV)** purchases the cash flow-producing assets from the originator. To pay for these assets, the SPV sells security interests (typically bonds) to investors. The cash flow from the assets (coupled with the possible proceeds from an asset sale) is then used to repay the bonds. If structured properly, the SPV structure will shield the originator from liability if the SPV is not able to repay the bonds.
3. The **investors** are the purchasers of the bonds (or other security interests) issued by the SPV.

Figure 12.5 provides a diagram of this basic process.

The resulting asset-backed securities should be significantly more liquid than the underlying assets. Because the resulting securities are a form of contract, they can be tailored in an almost infinite number of ways. This tailoring allows for the securitization structure to isolate specific benefits and risks. Certain investors, for example, may only want to invest in a particular patented technology and avoid having to invest in the overall company that owns the patented technology. Asset securitization has another important benefit. It makes diversification easier and thus lowers investor risk. By pooling the cash flow receivables for a number of assets, the risk of nonpayment becomes more predictable. For example, credit card receivables became less risky when consolidated and bundled together in a so-called financial wrapper.

Emergence of Intellectual Property Asset Securitization

The promise of intellectual property as a securitizable asset class has not escaped the attention of intellectual property holders or the capital markets. On the one hand, intellectual property assets are ideal for the securitization process. Many intellectual property assets have the following general characteristics:

- They are illiquid.
- They can provide a rich source for cash flows, typically from licensing payments.
- They can benefit from the risk isolation aspects of asset securitization because different investors may be interested in different elements of the intellectual property assets.
- They can benefit from the risk reduction that comes from pooling.

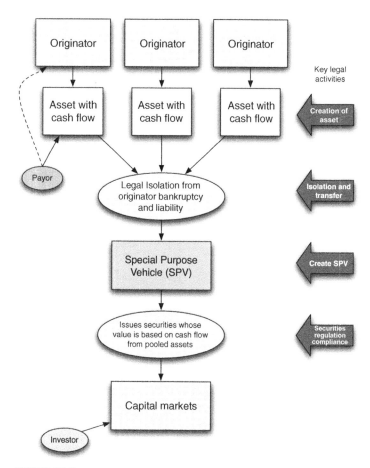

FIGURE 12.5   Basic Asset Securitization Process

On the other hand, uncertainty regarding ownership (particularly potential lien creditors) and complications in making the valuation determinations have caused the capital markets to proceed cautiously with intellectual property asset securitization products.

There are two paths to transforming intellectual property into a financial asset suitable for securitization (see Figure 12.6). One possible path involves a loan to the intellectual property owner with the intellectual property serving as collateral. This method brings up the complications previously discussed regarding the perfection of security interests

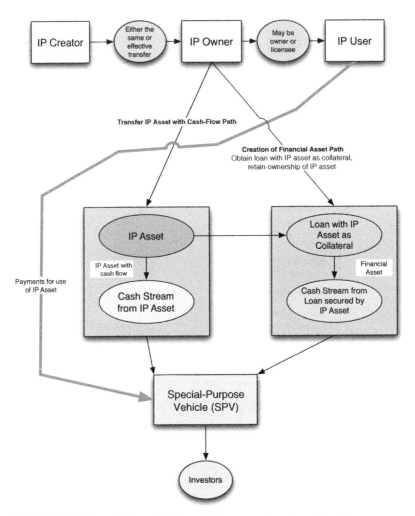

FIGURE 12.6   Two Paths to Intellectual Property Asset Securitization

in intellectual property. The attraction is that the investor (or, more accurately, the SPV set up for the investor) does not have to hold, and manage, the intellectual property asset, but instead merely holds and manages the rights to collect the cash flow. The second possible path involves the transfer of the intellectual property to the SPV, but this path, too, has potential complications relating to standing to bring a lawsuit and recovery of lost profits.

Examples of Intellectual Property and Patent Securitization Deals

Although some film studios had securitized the future cash flows from their film catalogues in the early 1990s and a few companies had securitized trademarks, the Bowie Bond deal in 1997 is often marked as the beginning of the real interest in intellectual property asset securitization.[10] The Bowie Bond issuance, which sold for $55 million and paid a 7.9 percent annual return, was backed by publishing and recording copyrights to 287 David Bowie songs. Copyright royalties from those songs provided the cash flow to pay the bond's principal and interest obligations. The Bowie Bonds were quickly followed by a number of copyright securitization deals that mimicked the structure of the Bowie Bond deal (see Table 12.1).

Since that time, intellectual property asset securitization deals have grown beyond copyright deals to include some patent securitization deals (see Table 12.2). The following patent securitization deals are summaries of four of the higher-profile ones.

Zerit Deal   The first recorded patent securitization deal took place in 2000 when Royalty Pharma AG securitized the royalty stream from a drug called Zerit®. Yale University obtained a patent in 1995 for a technology that treated HIV. Yale transferred the patented technology to Bristol-Myers Squibb (BMS) through an exclusive license, and BMS used the technology as the basis for Zerit. In exchange for the exclusive license, BMS agreed to pay Yale running royalties (see Chapter 10) based on Zerit's commercial success. In 2000, Yale assigned its patent rights (including its right to future

TABLE 12.1   Select Early Music Copyright securitization Deals

Year	Issuance	Amount	Securitized Copyright Assets
1997	Bowie Bonds	$55 million	Publishing and recording rights to 287 David Bowie songs
1998	Motown Hit Machine Bonds	$30 million	Share of publishing rights to 312 songs held by songwriters Edward Holland, Brian Holland, and Lamont Dozier
1999	James Brown Bonds	$30 million	Publishing and recording rights and performance royalties to 750 James Brown songs

Sources: Duff & Phelps Credit Rating Co., Asset-Backed Securities—DCR Comments on Music Royalty Securitizations (Sept. 1999); The Pullman Group LLC website.

TABLE 12.2 Select Patent Securitization Deals

Year	Original Patent Owner	Amount	Patent
2000	Yale University	$100 million	Single patent for HIV treatment drug
2003	Various pharmaceutical companies	$225 million	Portfolio of patents for 13 drugs
2004	Motorola	$50 million	Motion Picture Experts Group patents
2005	Emory University	$525 million	Single patent for HIV treatment drug

Zerit royalties) for $100 million to an SPV formed by Royalty Pharma. To come up with the $100 million, the SPV issued $115 million of debt and equity securities. The deal structure included collateral in addition to the patent, and the SPV purchased an insurance policy in the event that Zerit royalties were lower than forecasted. It turns out that the royalties were significantly lower than projected: Zerit sales from 2001 through 2003 were roughly $850 million lower than analysts' projections. The SPV was required to prepay the debt securities in 2002 "after breaching covenants for three consecutive reporting periods."[11]

Royalty Pharma's $225 Pool of Pharmaceutical Patents In 2003, Royalty Pharma brought the second major patent securitization deal to market. For this next deal, the SPV held patent royalty interests in 13 drugs: Genentech's and Biogen Idec's Rituxan®, Celegen's Thalomid®, Eli Lilly's and Johnson & Johnson/Centocor ReoPro®, Centocor's Retavase, Chiron's TOBI®, Novartis' Simulect®, Roche's Zenapax®, Ligand's Targretin Capsules®, Memorial Sloan Kettering's Neuprogen/Neulasta, Organon's Variza®, GSK and Adolor's Entereg®, Pfizer's lasofoxifenev and Wyeth's bazedoxifene.[12]

Royalty Pharma judged that one of the problems with the Zerit deal was the single-patent structure of the deal. This next deal was purposefully structured to involve a portfolio of drugs. For this second deal, the SPV issued $225 million of variable funding notes and "was rated AAA by both Moody's and Standard & Poor's largely because of the insurance of the deal by MBIA Insurance Group."[13] Interestingly, 4 of the 13 drugs were still product candidates in the final stages of FDA approval at the time of the deal and did not yet have a track record of established royalties.

Motorola/GE Capital Deal In June 2004, Motorola transferred a portfolio of noncore patents to GE Commercial Finance for an up-front fee of

$50 million.[14] GE created a special purpose entity to hold and service the portfolio that involved two GE entities: GE Capital, which came up with the money, and GE Licensing, which provided the expertise and did the structuring work. This GE special-purpose entity collected an undisclosed percentage of royalties over the coming years. The transaction was structured as a sale/license-back deal because Motorola wanted to keep using many of the patents transferred. For those more speculative patents in the portfolio, namely those without a current cash flow stream, GE and Motorola agreed to equally share any royalties that might arise from these patents.[15]

Emory University Deal　　Another deal involving a major research university is illustrative of how the concept has spread. In July 2005, Royalty Pharma and Gilead Sciences completed a deal with Emory University, purchasing the patent royalties on worldwide net sales of the HIV drug emtricitabine, also known as Emtriva®. Emory University received a one-time payment of $525 million.

The Future of Patent Securitization Deals

It is not difficult to envision patent securitization becoming a more significant financial product in the future. Although patent-backed deals remain a distant third to copyright- and trademark-backed deals, there are reasons to believe that the market for patent-backed deals will grow over time. There are a number of standard explanations for the limited market for patent-backed deals. One of the more common explanations is the "significant asset complexity and high up-front costs"[16] that are required to structure a patent-backed deal. We are skeptical that the complexity or cost rational truly explains the lack of patent-backed deals. That explanation was likely valid in the early 2000s when the first deals were being structured, but by now the techniques for structuring these deals is no longer unknown. Such deals may be more complex and expensive to structure than a simple credit-card receivables securitization deal, but we doubt that they are so complex and expensive as to explain the current low volume of deals.

A much more likely explanation for the lack of deals is the valuation difficulty they pose. As companies and investors become more comfortable with valuation techniques for patents, however, substantial growth in patent-backed securitization deals should follow. Notice that we did not say that the problem was an inability to value the underlying patent assets. It is useful to remember that the quality of a valuation exercise (whether for a patent or otherwise) is always a function of (1) the wisdom of the valuation method chosen, (2) the quality of the data that is available to feed the valuation method, and (3) the ability of the valuator to interpret the results of the valuation exercise.

The basic techniques for valuing patents are now fairly well understood (see Chapters 6 through 9). It is possible that better techniques will emerge for determining specific aspects of a patent (such as the real option value embedded in a given patent; see Chapter 7). For the most part, however, perfectly adequate methodologies for valuing patents are known. What is challenging about valuing patents is not a matter of methodology, but instead is a matter of developing sufficiently accurate inputs to feed the methodologies and to interpret the results of the exercise. Most of the current research on patent valuation has been conducted by economists and financiers who tend to focus primarily on the methodology part of the valuation equation. At some point, patent holders and investors will understand the diminishing returns from that quest. More energy should be devoted to developing more accurate cash flow projections and more transparent markets, which is exactly what investors do with other types of assets.

As Voltaire once wrote, "Perfect is the enemy of the good."[17] There will never be an ability to value perfectly the patent assets that may be the subject of a securitization deal, but that is no different from the inability to perfectly value credit receivables or residential mortgages (which commonly serve as assets for securitization deals). The difference in the ability to value patents assets when compared to credit card receivables or residential mortgages is simply one of degree. They all can be valued, but the accuracy of the cash flow projections for the credit card receivables and residential mortgages are less complicated and more predictable than those for a patent. It is simply a difference in certainty. The valuation for the patent assets will be less certain. When properly framed, markets know how to deal with uncertainty. Uncertainty is treated as a cost, and investors lower the price that they will pay for an asset based on the level of uncertainty. The greater the uncertainty, the lower the price investors will pay.

Not all patents, however, possess the same level of uncertainty regarding their ability to generate cash flows. Some patents, such as successful pharmaceutical patents for drugs with little competition, have relatively certain cash flows, whereas others have very uncertain cash flows. To the extent that the uncertainty surrounding the future cash flows can be identified, investors in the market can assess and take that risk in exchange for a level of compensation. We believe that there are already two obvious opportunities where patent securitization can yield extra value and should become more prevalent. First, patents with highly certain future cash flows can be the source for patent securitization deals in much the same way that other certain cash flow assets are used in securitizations. In that setting, the patent owners that decide to securitize their patents can generate the same types of benefits as other asset owners that create securitization structures. Namely, the patent owners can turn illiquid assets into liquid ones, receive balance sheet relief, and diversify their risk portfolio. Those benefits can be worth a substantial amount of money, which can be used to provide a more favorable price to the securitization investors. Markets do a splendid job of facilitating these types of exchanges and allocating the risks and rewards between the parties.

The second opportunity is for patents with highly uncertain future cash flows. Start-up companies in need of cash or universities that are poorly equipped to evaluate the uncertainty surrounding their patents, for example, could be ideal candidates for patent securitization deals that are more deeply discounted. Uncertainty is acceptable as long as it is identified. What markets and investors do not like is unexpected surprise: cash flows that are wildly optimistic, overstated competitive advantages to be derived from the patent assets, or unrealistic sales and earnings projections.

One last element that should help to facilitate growth in patent securitization deals will be the emergence of market intermediaries to help with information gathering and analysis for, and monitoring of, the patent securitizations deals. One reason for the success of public securities markets is the development of numerous market intermediaries such as research analysts, institutional investors, rating agencies, and public auditors. When such intermediaries begin to develop around the patent securitization market, it will be a clear sign of the maturity of that market and its ability to release the inherent potential value of patent assets.

REFERENCES

Business Wire. Apr. 22, 1999. "Swiss Re Develops Patent Validity Insurance for the Patent and License Exchange." www.allbusiness.com/company-activities-management/company-structures/6678581-1.html#ixzz1WeX0HHI5.

CJA Consultants Ltd. June 2006. *Patent Litigation Insurance: A Study for the European Commission on the Feasibility of Possible Insurance Schemes against Patent Litigation Risks—Final Report.*

Comptroller of the Currency–Administrator of National Banks. Nov. 1997. *Asset Securitization, Comptrollers Handbook.*

Damron, James, and Joseph Labbadia. 1999. "Asset-Backed Securities—DCR Comments on Music Royalty Securitizations." Duff & Phelps Credit Rating Co.

de Soto, Hernando. 2000. *The Mystery of Capital—Why Capitalism Triumphs in the West and Fails Everywhere Else.* New York: Basic Books.

Edwards, David. No date. "Patent Backed Securitization: Blueprint For a New Asset Class." Internet whitepaper. www.securitization.net/pdf/gerling_new_0302.pdf.

Geithner, Timothy, François Gianviti, Gerd Haeusler, and Teresa Ter-Minassian. June 2003. "Assessing Public Sector Borrowing Collateralized on Future Flow Receivables." *International Monetary Fund Report.*

Gollin, Michael. 2008. *Driving Innovation: Intellectual Property Strategies for a Dynamic World.* New York: Cambridge University Press.

Hillery, John. June 2004. "Securitization of Intellectual Property: Recent Trends from the United States." *Washington|CORE LLC.*

Janger, Edward. 2004. "Threats to Secured Lending and Asset Securitization: Panel 1: Asset Securitization and Secured Lending: The Death of Secured Lending." *Cardozo Law Review* 25: 1759.

Jarboe, Kenan, and Roland Furrow. 2008. "Intangible Asset Monetization: The Promise and the Reality." Athena Alliance Working Paper no. 3.

Munari, Federico, Maria Odasso, and Laura Toschi. 2011. "Patent-Backed Finance." In *The Economic Valuation of Patents: Methods and Applications,* edited by Federico Munari and Raffaele Oriani, 309–336. Cheltenham, UK: Edward Elgar.

Murphy, William. 2002. "Proposal for a Centralized and Integrated Registry for Security Interests in Intellectual Property." *IDEA* 41: 297.

Nikolic, Aleksandar. 2009. "Securitization of Patents and its Continued Viability in Light of Current Economic Conditions." *Albany Law Journal of Science and Technology* 19: 393.

Odasso, Christina, and Mario Calderini. 2009. "Intellectual Property Portfolio Securitization: An Evidence Based Analysis." Paper presented at Copenhagen Business School 2009 Summer Conference.

Ruder, David. 2008. *Strategies for Investing in Intellectual Property.* Washington, DC: Beard Books.

Schumpeter, Joseph. 1950 (republished in 1976). *Capitalism, Socialism, and Democracy.* 3rd ed. New York: HarperPerennial.

Task Force on Security Interests in Intellectual Property, American Bar Association Business Law Section. June 1, 1992. *Preliminary Report.*

Ward, Thomas. 2001. "The Perfection and Priority Rules for Security Interests in Copyrights, Patents, and Trademarks: The Current Structural Dissonance and Proposed Legislative Cures." *Maine Law Review* 53: 391.

Ward, Thomas. 2009. *Intellectual Property in Commerce.* 9th ed. St. Paul, MN: West.

NOTES

1. This discussion of potential value was motivated by a discussion of potential value that economist Hernando de Soto included in his 2000 book, *The Mystery of Capital—Why Capitalism Triumphs in the West and Fails Everywhere Else.*
2. de Soto, 44–45.
3. Joseph Schumpeter, *Capitalism, Socialism, and Democracy,* 3rd ed. (1950), 83.
4. 35 U.S.C. sec. 261.

5. Task Force on Security Interests in Intellectual Property, American Bar Association Business Law Section, *Preliminary Report* (June 1, 1992), 1.
6. The citation for this initial report is William Murphy, "Proposal for a Centralized and Integrated Registry for Security Interests in Intellectual Property," *IDEA* 41 (2002): 297.
7. CJA Consultants Ltd., *Patent Litigation Insurance: A Study for the European Commission on the Feasibility of Possible Insurance Schemes Against Patent Litigation Risks—Final Report* (June 2006), 14.
8. CJA Consultants Ltd (June 2006), 14–15.
9. Jimmy Stewart's portrayal of George Bailey in the classic movie *It's A Wonderful Life* epitomizes the old mortgage system. On a side note, the film is a Christmas classic in the United States largely due to the failure to protect its intellectual property rights. The copyright on the 1946 film was not renewed in 1974, and the lapse in copyright permitted the film to be repeatedly shown on television. Twenty years later, in 1994, after the film had become a hot commodity, NBC was able to secure the exclusive rights to the film.
10. The association of Bowie Bonds with intellectual property asset securitization may be unfortunate because the bonds eventually sunk to junk bond status.
11. John Hillery, "Securitization of Intellectual Property: Recent Trends from the United States," *Washington|CORE LLC* (June 2004): 28.
12. Hillery, 31–32.
13. Ibid., 31.
14. Some of the patents in the portfolio involve the technology underlying standards of the Moving Picture Experts Group.
15. Based on interviews conducted by a former University of New Hampshire law student and research assistant, Julia Siripurapu, with Leo Cook, General Counsel of GE Licensing. Interview conducted January 4, 2006.
16. Federico Munari, Maria Odasso, and Laura Toschi, "Patent-Backed Finance," in *The Economic Valuation of Patents: Methods and Applications*, eds. Federico Munari and Raffaele Oriani (2011), 328.
17. *"Dans ses écrits, un sàge Italien / Dit que le mieux est l'ennemi du bien."* Voltaire in *La Bégueule*.

CHAPTER 13

Valuation in Patent-Based Tax-Planning Strategies

Tax-planning strategies can provide firms with a significant competitive advantage. Cost-effectively reducing a firm's tax liabilities increases its profitability and thereby provides the firm with greater net resources to pursue its business strategies or reward its owners. Not surprisingly, tax consequences drive a firm's decision making in many contexts. Firm managers are constantly looking for tax strategies that will help to minimize the firm's overall tax burden. Employing a patent-based tax-reduction strategy requires a firm to make numerous decisions, and valuation should play a major role in each of those decisions. Valuation helps to identify potential tax-reduction strategies, to evaluate the costs and benefits from the strategies, and to choose between competing strategies. Adequately valuing the patent rights is also a necessary compliance element for these strategies. Finally, if the tax-reduction strategy is structured correctly for a group of patents, the reduced tax burden associated with profits generated from those patents will increase the patents' overall value.

Intellectual property assets, including patents, have become an increasingly popular focus for tax-reduction strategies. When developing these strategies, patents provide three key advantages over corporeal assets such as land, factories, vehicle fleets, or warehouses full of physical products as follows:

1. **Patent transfers are largely invisible to taxing authorities.** If Microsoft were to decide to move its corporate headquarters from Redmond, Washington, to some new location, it would be an overt and obvious event. Every relevant taxing authority would be on notice of the event and would be able to determine for itself the tax ramifications of the transaction. If the taxing authority disagreed

with Microsoft's tax characterization of the transaction, it could challenge that characterization and possibly require a greater tax payment. If Microsoft decides to transfer billions of dollars of intellectual property rights to a jurisdiction with lower taxes—which it did, as discussed later in this chapter—such transaction could easily be missed by taxing authorities. Because tax-reduction strategies frequently operate in a gray area of permissibility, the relative invisibility of patents can be a very attractive feature for tax strategists.

2. **Governments will lower taxes to attract capital, and patents are a particularly attractive target for such efforts.** Governments have long used tax strategies as a carrot to attract capital. Frequently referred to as *tax competition*, a taxing jurisdiction will lower its effective tax rate for particular types of capital or economic activities to attract more of that activity into the jurisdiction. Governments, for example, have long used tax breaks to encourage companies to locate high-employment factories in their jurisdiction. With governments increasingly understanding the critical role that innovative, technology-based companies play in promoting sustained economic success, their motivation to develop tax incentives to attract those particular companies has also increased. Companies with more patent assets tend to be more innovative and successful, so it is not surprising if government tax strategies focus on attracting patents into their jurisdictions.

3. **There is an ease in moving patents.** For governments to use favorable tax treatments to compete for capital, that capital must be relatively mobile. The more mobile the capital, the more likely that the tax treatment will determine where a firm will locate that capital. Patents are extremely mobile assets and can be moved inexpensively from one jurisdiction to another in the blink of an eye. If another location provides a more attractive tax treatment for income generated from a firm's patent assets, it is relatively easy to move the assets to that more favorable location.

In this chapter, we

- Provide examples of patent-based tax-reduction strategies to illustrate the concept.
- Explain transfer pricing and its role in structuring tax-reduction strategies.
- Explain how to determine transfer prices for patent rights.

EXAMPLES OF PATENT-BASED
TAX-REDUCTION STRATEGIES

In 1993, the global pharmaceutical firm Merck engaged in a complicated set of transactions involving its patents to two blockbuster cholesterol-lowering drugs. In this section, we will examine those transactions as well as review the growth of such patent-based tax-reduction strategies.

Merck's Tax-Reduction Strategy for Its
Two Patents

Our summary of the 1993 Merck strategy for two patents is based largely on a 2006 *Wall Street Journal* investigative report on the matter,[1] coupled with a few press releases and news stories. We have not had the luxury of analyzing the structure in detail, nor have we had access to internal company documents. Like most tax-planning strategies, this one remains a company trade secret that has never been fully disclosed.

Merck needed funds to complete its $6 billion acquisition of Medco, a prescription-benefit management firm. To help fund the transaction and also to provide significant tax savings, Merck's investment bankers and lawyers developed a strategy that involved transferring Merck's patents for its highly successful cholesterol-lowering drugs Zocor® and Mevacor® to a Merck-controlled, off-balance-sheet Bermuda limited partnership. The Bermuda partnership licensed these patents back to Merck in exchange for royalty payments. The royalty payments lowered Merck's U.S. income (and taxes) and shifted the income to Bermuda and the Merck-controlled partnership. The key to the structure was finding an outside partner that could absorb the taxable income. Merck found a midsized British bank that contributed several hundred millions of dollars in cash to purchase a minority interest in the Bermuda partnership. That contribution, along with much of the royalty payments, found its way back to Merck through loans to other Merck subsidiaries.

This structured transaction, which involved numerous subsidiaries and complicated contractual arrangements, helped Merck to generate considerable tax savings between 1993 and 2001 as the structure moved profits from Zocor and Mevacor out of the United States and off of Merck's books. The 2006 *Wall Street Journal* report estimated the savings to be in the neighborhood of $1.5 billion in U.S. federal taxes.[2] Sometimes, though, a hugely profitable business arrangement can attract unwanted attention. In 2004, the U.S. Internal Revenue Service (IRS) informed Merck (and a number of other companies using similar transactions and arrangements) that it was challenging the strategy. The IRS asserted that the arrangement was not a legitimate partnership, but instead a loan agreement that did not qualify for the income transfer or expense write-offs claimed by Merck. In February 2007, Merck agreed to settle a number of tax disputes with the IRS, including the Zocor/Mevacor arrangement, which resulted in an aggregate payment to the government "of approximately $2.3 billion in federal tax, net interest and penalties."[3]

A $2.3 billion settlement with the IRS would seem to provide a strong disincentive for Merck and other companies to pursue this type of aggressive tax strategy in the future. It turns out, however, that the Zocor/Mevacor arrangement may have been a profitable one for Merck even taking into account the sizable IRS settlement (see box 13.1). When one factors in the uncertainty of the IRS successfully challenging the strategy, the pursuit of such a strategy would appear to be manifestly advantageous.

BOX 13.1: WAS THE ZOCOR/MEVACOR ARRANGEMENT WORTH IT?

Businesses make calculated decisions about risk versus benefit every day. When one examines the Merck dispute with the IRS over the Zocor/Mevacor arrangement, one can argue that the decision to use the challenged structures and transactions was a profitable business decision despite the $2.3 billion settlement. Before continuing, we need to stress that the following valuation analysis is based on approximate numbers. It has been estimated that Merck saved $1.5 billion from the Zocor/Mevacor arrangement. We cannot confirm the accuracy of that amount. In addition, Merck's $2.3 billion settlement with the IRS included the settlement of a number of disputes in addition to the Zocor/Mevacor arrangement. Neither the IRS nor Merck ever disclosed the percentage of the settlement that was attributable to the Zocor/Mevacor arrangement. Recognizing these information limitations, we can still conduct a satisficing valuation analysis (see Chapter 3) of the arrangement. To run our analysis, we have made the following assumptions:

- Merck saved $1.5 billion.
- The $1.5 billion was spread out evenly from 1993 to 2004.
- Discount rate was 7 percent.

Based on those assumptions, Merck generated a substantial net present value gain even with the massive $2.3 billion settlement payment.

Year	Tax Savings That Year	Net Present Value of the Savings
1993	$125,000,000	$301,859,273
1994	$125,000,000	$283,435,937
1995	$125,000,000	$266,137,030
1996	$125,000,000	$249,893,925
1997	$125,000,000	$234,642,183
1998	$125,000,000	$220,321,299
1999	$125,000,000	$206,874,459
2000	$125,000,000	$194,248,318
2001	$125,000,000	$182,392,787
2002	$125,000,000	$171,260,833
2003	$125,000,000	$160,808,294
2004	$125,000,000	$150,993,703
2005	$ 0	$ 0
2006	$ 0	$ 0
Total savings to Merck		$2,622,868,041

If our assumptions are correct, Merck earned more than $300 million from the Zocor/Mevacor arrangement after the taking into account the $2.3 billion settlement. The chart demonstrates a net positive value given the assumptions used. It assumes that there was a 100 percent chance that the arrangement would be challenged by the IRS and a substantial settlement would result. If one goes a step further and uses a decision tree to assess the situation that includes an assessment regarding the probability of challenge at less than 100 percent, the value of the decision becomes even more favorable to Merck. In the decision tree in Figure 13.1, we inserted a 75 percent probability that the arrangement would be challenged by the IRS and lead to the eventual settlement. This assumption, of course, is arbitrary, but it illustrates the point. A lower probability would make the original decision even more valuable.

(continued)

(continued)

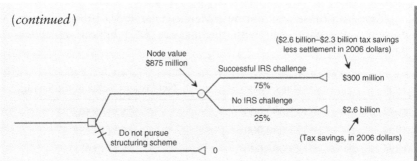

FIGURE 13.1 Decision-Tree Analysis of the Zocor/Mevacor arrangement

In this basic decision tree, the value of the upper branch is $300 million, which is the same number calculated in the net present value chart. The lower branch value is the net present value of the $2.6 billion in tax savings that were reportedly earned by Merck during the life of the scheme. By this rudimentary estimate and using a 75 percent probability that the scheme would be successfully challenged by the IRS, the value of the decision to pursue the scheme increases to roughly $875 million. If the probability of successful challenge by the IRS were increased to 90 percent, the net present value of the decision would still be about $530 million.

It certainly appears that it was a good business decision by Merck, even assuming the large settlement cost and a very high probability of successful challenge by the IRS.

Intellectual Property–Based Tax-Reduction Strategies Are Not Slowing

Merck is by no means alone in this type of strategic structuring of intellectual property rights and obligations to reduce tax liabilities. At the time that Merck was settling its dispute with the IRS, companies such as Dow Chemical, GE, and GlaxoSmithKline were reported to have similar arrangements with important patents. Moreover, the IRS's well-publicized settlement with Merck does not appear to have slowed intellectual property–based tax-reduction strategies. If anything, the strategies have simply become more sophisticated and potentially even more lucrative.

The growth of intellectual property–based tax-reduction strategies has not escaped notice at the IRS despite some successful (from the IRS's point of view) settlements. In 2006, then IRS commissioner Mark Everson remarked, "Tax issues associated with the transfer of intangibles outside the United States have been a high risk compliance concern for us and have seen a significant increase in recent years. Taxpayers, especially in the high technology and pharmaceutical industries, are shifting profits offshore."[4]

These tax-reduction strategies are not limited to exploiting income tax differences between countries. These strategies can also be used to exploit income tax differences between states. Microsoft provides a good example of a company that has reportedly arranged its intellectual property portfolio to achieve both domestic and international tax benefits. On the domestic side, Microsoft established a Nevada intellectual property holding company in 2001 called Round Island, LLC, to benefit from Nevada's favorable intellectual property tax treatment. Nevada does not tax royalty income on intellectual property. Microsoft transferred significant intellectual property assets, including various patent rights, into this Nevada intellectual property holding company, which then charged intellectual property royalties to Microsoft's operations in other states. Those royalty payments could then be expensed and thereby reduce the state profits (and state income taxes) of Microsoft's other operations. The reduced profits from those other operations were attributed to Round Island, which were not taxable in Nevada because they were royalty income on intellectual property. Microsoft merged out Round Island in November 2009 and presumably has come up with a new arrangement to manage its domestic tax liabilities.

Microsoft has also used an international intellectual property holding company strategy to reduce tax liability. Microsoft reportedly saved billions of dollars in taxes, including roughly $500 million from its 2005 tax bill, through the use of two Irish subsidiaries,[5] Round Island One and Flat Island, which licensed Microsoft software in Europe, the Middle East, and Africa. Per a *Wall Street Journal* report, Round Island One controlled "more than $16 billion in Microsoft assets . . . [and generated] gross profits of nearly $9 billion in 2004."[6] The report went on to explain that Round Island paid less than $17 million in taxes. Flat Island reported a profit of $800 million in 2004 and paid no taxes. Overall, Microsoft reported a decrease in its worldwide effective tax rate from 33 percent to 26 percent, with roughly half of that improvement coming from "foreign earnings taxed at lower rates."[7] In 2006, Microsoft applied to the Irish Companies Office to reregister both its Round Island One and Flat Island subsidiaries as companies with unlimited liability. Unlimited liability companies in Ireland have no obligation to publicly disclose their accounts, and any further information about the potential tax benefits of these operations is now hidden from public view.

More recently, Google was reportedly able to slash $3.1 billion off its U.S. federal tax liability for the 3 years from 2007 to 2010. It first moved certain intellectual property assets to Ireland and Holland, and then it moved profits from worldwide operations first through an Irish company (Google Ireland Holdings) and then through a Dutch entity, eventually ending up in a holding company in tax-friendly Bermuda.

TRANSFER PRICING

A complex (and expensive) multicountry and multiple entity structure is not always necessary to enjoy the types of tax benefits discussed above. A simple structure of two entities in different tax situations can deliver tax relief. The key is using the power of transfer pricing to shift income. One thing that all these tax saving structures and transactions have in common is that they involve transfer pricing. As the economy becomes increasingly global in scope and companies and individuals carry on trade that spans various taxation borders, the potential effect of transfer pricing to the various participants grows. According to a group of experts assembled by the United Nations, transfer pricing "is probably the most important tax issue in the world."[8]

Transfer pricing, as the name suggests, refers to the price at which an asset or service is transferred within an organization or between related organizations or individuals. It differs from true market pricing because transfer pricing, by definition, does not involve independent participants in an arm's length transaction. As such, transfer pricing is ripe for manipulation by the buyer and seller. Developing a justifiable transfer price therefore tends to be one of the most significant determinants in the overall success of a patent-based tax-reduction strategy. A transfer price valuation that is properly conducted can yield an effective and legal arrangement, whereas an improper or overly aggressive valuation can lead to costly challenges from taxation authorities.

How Transfer-Pricing Structures Can Lower Taxes

The basic objective in a transfer-pricing scheme is to shift a business organization's income from higher-tax jurisdictions to a lower-tax jurisdiction. This shift is typically accomplished through a parent company's subsidiaries (see Figure 13.2). A subsidiary in a lower-tax jurisdiction will sell (or license) some asset or service to the parent company's subsidiaries in higher-tax jurisdictions. This arrangement results in an extra expense for the subsidiaries in the higher-tax jurisdiction, which in turn lowers the amount of taxable income earned in those jurisdictions. Correspondingly,

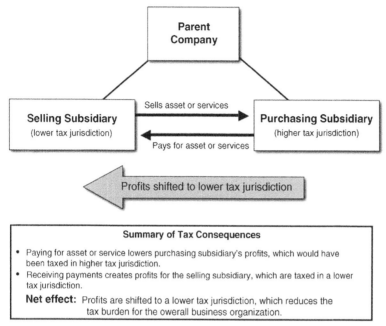

FIGURE 13.2 Basic Transfer-Pricing Structure

the entity in the lower-tax jurisdiction has now generated revenue from the transfer, which increases the taxable income earned in the lower-tax jurisdiction. Because the income has been shifted from a higher- to a lower-tax jurisdiction, the net result is a lower overall income tax liability for the consolidated business organization.

Arranging a Patent-Based Transfer-Pricing Structure

Intellectual property assets, including patents, are particularly well suited for transfer-pricing structures. The idea is to transfer the bulk of the business organization's valuable intellectual property assets to a subsidiary (an intellectual property holding company) located in a lower-tax jurisdiction (see Figure 13.3). The intellectual property holding company will then license the intellectual property assets to the organization's operating subsidiaries and thereby transfer a portion of the operating subsidiaries' taxable income to the intellectual property holding company's lower-tax jurisdiction.

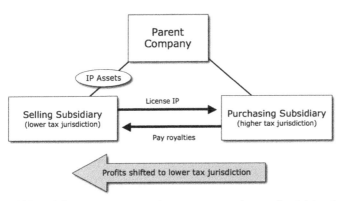

FIGURE 13.3 Basic Intellectual Property–Based Transfer-Pricing Structure

Once the basic intellectual property–based transfer-pricing structure is established, its tax-reduction role is not limited solely to transfer pricing. The intellectual property holding company can also be used to license the organization's intellectual property to third-party customers outside the parent company's home jurisdiction and allow the organization to earn that taxable income in a lower-tax jurisdiction (see Figure 13.4). The actual

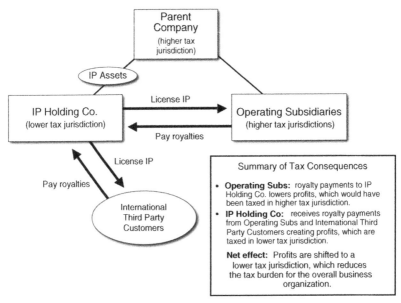

FIGURE 13.4 Slightly More Detailed Diagram of Basic Intellectual Property–Based Transfer-Pricing Structure

structure will typically end up being much more complicated than what we have shown in Figure 13.4. Actual structures frequently involve multiple subsidiaries performing the basic function of the intellectual property holding company, and such subsidiaries may be located in multiple jurisdictions around the world. Loan and dividend payments are then layered over the basic structure to transfer funds throughout the business organization. Much of this added complexity is motivated by a desire to repatriate the aftertax profits to an entity in the organization that can best use the extra funds, but without triggering substantial new tax obligations.

Early History of Intellectual Property–Based Transfer-Pricing Structures

One of the first widespread international uses of intellectual property–based transfer-pricing structures to reduce tax liabilities can be traced to the 1970s, when a number of companies transferred various intellectual property rights to Puerto Rican subsidiaries to take advantage of U.S. and Puerto Rican tax laws at the time. The transfer could be structured such that income that was subsequently earned from royalties was not taxed in either the United States or Puerto Rico.[9]

A very public example of this early Puerto Rican strategy involved the pharmaceutical company Eli Lilly and its patent for the drug Darvon. Darvon, the trade name of propoxyphene hydrochloride, has since been removed from the U.S. market due to potential cardiac toxicity, but at the time was seen as a promising new class of potentially nonaddictive synthetic analgesics and was widely prescribed for pain relief. Eli Lilly had developed Darvon in the United States and had deducted the related research and development costs as business expenses on its U.S. federal income tax returns. Lilly then transferred the Darvon patents (U.S. Patent 2,728,779 and subsequent improvement patents used to make Darvon-N) to one of its subsidiaries in Puerto Rico that also manufactured the drug for worldwide distribution. The Darvon patent allowed Eli Lilly to effectively exclude competitive pharmaceutical products, and profits from Darvon sales were substantial. The use of the Puerto Rican subsidiary to transfer some of these profits from the relatively high-tax United States to lower-tax Puerto Rico eventually led to litigation between Eli Lilly and the IRS.[10]

In its 1985 opinion, which ran more than 200 pages, the U.S. Tax Court found that the transfer of the patents was permissible but the transfer prices used by Eli Lilly to allocate income and expense deductions among the parent and subsidiary companies needed to be adjusted to reflect "arm's length prices." The structure was not problematic, but the prices used for the transfer-pricing transactions were. One important point made by the U.S.

Tax Court that lies at the heart of the ongoing efforts by companies to strategically structure patent rights and obligations to lower tax burdens is that "taxpayers have the right so to arrange their affairs that their taxes shall be as low as possible."[11] A taxpayer "is not obliged to pursue a course of action giving rise to a greater tax liability if another is open which will give rise to a lesser liability."[12]

DETERMINING TRANSFER PRICES FOR PATENT RIGHTS

There is nothing illegal about shifting income to a lower-tax jurisdiction via a transfer-pricing structure as long as the transfer prices are fair and reflect the true economic realities of the transaction. The problem is that what the structuring party may believe to be fair can be disputed by taxing authorities. Tax-reduction strategies frequently involve uncertainty in two areas:

1. Uncertainty that taxing authorities will audit the transaction.
2. Uncertainty that taxing authorities will successfully challenge some element of the transaction.

When it comes to transfer-pricing structures, the element that is most likely to be challenged is the fairness of the transfer prices used in the transaction.

When tax authorities challenge the fairness of transfer prices, it can be expensive for the company taxpayer. In 2006, global pharmaceutical company GlaxoSmithKline agreed to pay the IRS $3.4 billion to settle a transfer-pricing case. The IRS had alleged that Glaxo had underpaid its U.S. taxes dating back to 1989. The $3.4 billion settlement, which was the largest payment ever made to the IRS to settle a tax dispute, could have been even worse. Glaxo reportedly estimated "that the matter could have cost it as much as $15 billion."[13]

Transfer-Pricing Rules and Regulations: Section 482 Overview

For U.S. tax law purposes, section 482 of the U.S. Internal Revenue Code and its resulting regulations provide the primary governance for pricing related-party transactions. Section 482 is a two-sentence provision that appears relatively innocuous on its face. Section 482 states:

In any case of two or more organizations, trades, or businesses (whether or not incorporated, whether or not organized in the United States, and whether or not affiliated) owned or controlled directly or indirectly by the same interests, the Secretary [of the Treasury or her delegate] may distribute, apportion, or allocate gross income, deductions, credits, or allowances between or among such organizations, trades, or businesses, if he determines that such distribution, apportionment, or allocation is necessary in order to prevent evasion of taxes or clearly to reflect the income of any of such organizations, trades, or businesses. In the case of any transfer (or license) of intangible property (within the meaning of section 936 (h)(3)(B)), the income with respect to such transfer or license shall be commensurate with the income attributable to the intangible.

From these two sentences has arisen an immense body of law. More than a hundred pages of current regulations (the Regulations) have been promulgated under section 482, and entire books have been written on the details and complexities of complying with section 482 and the Regulations.[14] It is not our intention to sort through all of the intricacies of section 482. Our goal for this chapter is much more modest. We wish simply to explain the basic function of section 482, its application to patent rights, and the guidance it provides for pricing related-party transfers of intangibles.

Purpose of Section 482

Section 482 traces its roots back to the early decades of the twentieth century. Congress became aware of companies using controlled businesses to strategically shift income to lower-tax jurisdictions during the 1920s[15] and answered with section 45 of the Revenue Act of 1928, which eventually became section 482 with the adoption of the Internal Revenue Code of 1954. Section 482 allows the IRS to reallocate the income, deductions, credits, or allowances between controlled entities to prevent tax evasion or to reflect more accurately the income of the combined organization. The purpose of section 482 is to place "a controlled taxpayer on a tax parity with an uncontrolled taxpayer by determining the true taxable income of the controlled taxpayer."[16]

The Arm's Length Standard and Comparability

Section 482 and the Regulations determine true taxable income, in most cases, by applying an arm's length standard to the prices charged in the related-party transactions.[17] Related-party transfer prices satisfy the arm's length standard if they are consistent with the prices that would have been charged if uncontrolled entities had engaged in the same transaction. The arm's length standard seeks to employ an impartial market-based valuation technique. Ideally, parties seeking to develop a transfer price would identify perfectly identical transactions that had been willingly and independently negotiated by unrelated parties. The price from these perfectly identical, independent transactions would then serve as the transfer price for the related-party transaction.

In reality, perfectly identical, independent transactions are extremely difficult to locate. The Regulations recognize this problem and get around it by embracing comparability analysis. The arm's length standard can be satisfied by referring to comparable, independent transactions under comparable circumstances. Comparability analysis is, by definition, a subjective exercise that is susceptible to manipulation. One of the reasons for the voluminous nature of the Regulations is their attempt to address the problems of subjectivity and the potential for manipulation. The Regulations try to implement the arm's length standard by providing permissible pricing methods, defining the parameters of comparability, and explaining how comparability relates to the various pricing methods. If the taxpayer can demonstrate that its transfer prices fall within a reasonable range based on the arm's length standard, the IRS will not reallocate income between the taxpayer's controlled entities.

Best Method Rule

The Regulations provide a number of acceptable methods (see below) for developing transfer prices that comply with the arm's length standard. Because of the inherent subjectivity and potential for manipulation that comes with comparability analysis, however, the Regulations require the taxpayer to employ the *best method*. There is no strict priority between the acceptable methods, and no one method is presumptively deemed more reliable than another. Instead, the best method rule requires that for a taxpayer to comply with the arm's length standard, the taxpayer must employ the method that provides the most reliable measure of what an arm's length transaction would generate. The Regulations go on to explain that a particular method will qualify as the best method "only if the comparability, quality of data, and reliability of assumptions under that method make it more reliable than any other available measure of the arm's length result."[18] The Regulations also provide a number of examples that help to illustrate tangibly how to apply the best method rule.[19]

Pricing Intangible Assets under Section 482

The Regulations endorse a number of specific methods that a taxpayer can use to demonstrate that its transfer prices comply with the arm's length standard. Different methods apply depending on whether the related-party transaction involves tangible or intangible property. Because we are addressing patent-based tax-reduction strategies, the intangible property pricing methods will be the focus of this section. Patents, inventions, formulae, processes, designs, patterns, or know-how are all included within the definition of intangibles.[20]

Intangible Property and the Super Royalty Provision   Developing arm's length prices for related-party transfers of intangible assets can be particularly challenging. In 1986, Congress adopted the so-called super royalty provision in response to some of the challenges. The super royalty provision stems from the second sentence of section 482, which was added by the Tax Reform Act of 1986. The second sentence of section 482 states:

> *In the case of any transfer (or license) of intangible property (within the meaning of section 936 (h)(3)(B)), the income with respect to such transfer or license shall be commensurate with the income attributable to the intangible.*

This second sentence was accompanied by new methods for demonstrating that a related-party transfer of intangible property complies with the arm's length standard and a periodic adjustment power for the IRS. The super royalty provision arose out of concerns that U.S. companies were not able to adequately demonstrate compliance with the arm's length standard for transfers of intangible assets to foreign subsidiaries.

As a general rule, there tends to be less comparable transaction data for intangible assets than for tangible assets, which makes comparability analysis more problematic. The difficulty in generating an arm's length price is most severe for so-called *super intangibles*[21] (extremely high-profit intangibles such as certain pharmaceutical patents) that generally have no comparable transactions to consider. Companies with super intangibles seldom, if ever, transfer them to uncontrolled entities. The complete lack of comparable transactions coupled with the uncertainty that surrounds super intangibles in their early stages creates an environment that could be exploited by U.S. companies. They could transfer their super intangibles to low-tax foreign jurisdictions for a single, lump sum payment or recurring royalty rate that understated the true value of the super intangible. In each case, the effect would be to deprive the United States of rightful tax revenue.

It is not inappropriate to shift future profits to the low-tax foreign jurisdiction. It is inappropriate, however, to avoid U.S. taxes on the profit that should have been generated from the transfer of the super intangible to the foreign subsidiary by underpricing that transfer.

The super royalty provision inserts a *commensurate with income* standard for intangible property that allows the IRS to make periodic adjustments under section 482 to the transfer price charged for the intangible property.[22] The super royalty provision reduces the ability of U.S. companies to underprice transfers of intangible assets because the IRS has the ability to revisit the transfer price to make sure that it reflects the income that the intangible asset is actually generating in the marketplace.

Acceptable Methods for Pricing Intangible Assets   Subject to the arm's length standard, the best method rule, the comparability requirement, and the commensurate with income standard, the Regulations expressly permit three methods for pricing intangible assets:

1. The comparable uncontrolled transaction method (CUTM)
2. The comparable profits method (CPM)
3. The profit split method (PSM)

If the taxpayer can demonstrate that some other method (an unspecified method) generates a better arm's length result, the Regulations also permit the use of such method.

Comparable Uncontrolled Transaction Method   The CUTM[23] evaluates whether the transfer price for an intangible asset satisfies the arm's length standard by considering the "amount charged in a comparable uncontrolled transaction."[24] The advantage of this method is that if such a comparable transaction can be found, it will provide a market-derived valuation based on the decisions of a willing and independent buyer and seller and thus avoid the messiness of attempting a more elaborate valuation calculation with the accompanying uncertainty and risks coupled with the myriad assumptions that may be involved.

If there exists an uncontrolled transfer of the "same" intangible under the same, or substantially the same, circumstances as the related-party transaction that is being priced, the CUTM will generally be the best method for pricing the related-party transaction. The circumstances of the uncontrolled transaction will be considered substantially the same as the related-party transaction "if there are at most only minor differences that have definite and reasonably ascertainable effect on the amount charged and for which appropriate adjustments are made."[25]

If substantially similar uncontrolled transactions cannot be identified, the CUTM allows the taxpayer to resort to a comparability analysis. The taxpayer may use uncontrolled transactions that involve the transfer of "comparable intangibles under comparable circumstances."[26] The Regulations provide detailed guidance for determining the comparability of the intangible and the circumstances of an uncontrolled transaction. For the intangible from an uncontrolled transaction to be considered comparable to the intangible in a related-party transaction, both intangibles must

- Be used in connection with similar products or processes within the same general industry or market.
- Have similar profit potential.

The Regulations explain that the most reliable method for measuring profit potential is by "directly calculating the net present value of the benefits to be realized (based on prospective profits to be realized or costs to be saved) through the use or subsequent transfer of the intangible, considering the capital investment and start-up expenses required, the risks to be assumed, and other relevant considerations."[27] The Regulations go on to explain that the need to reliably measure profit potential "increases in relation to both the total amount of potential profits and the potential rate of return on investment necessary to exploit the intangible."[28] When the taxpayer cannot obtain the information needed to make the net present value calculations and the need to reliably measure profit potential is low, comparison of profit potential may be based on the following comparable circumstances factors:

- The terms of the transfer.
- The stage of development of the intangible in the market in which the intangible is to be used.
- Rights to receive updates, revisions, or modifications of the intangibles.
- The uniqueness of the property and the period for which it remains unique.
- The duration of the license, contract, or other agreement, and any termination or renegotiation rights.
- Any economic and product liability risks to be assumed by the transferee.
- The existence and extent of any collateral transactions or ongoing business relationships between the transferee and transferor.
- The functions to be performed by the transferor and transferee.[29]

Comparable Profits Method   The CPM[30] evaluates whether the transfer price for an intangible asset satisfies the arm's length standard in a very different manner than the CUTM. Whereas the CUTM examines comparable transactions, the CPM focuses on comparable objective measures of profitability (profit-level indicators). The basic idea under the CPM is to look at profit-level indicators from uncontrolled taxpayers that engage in similar business activities to the related-party transaction and under similar circumstances. These profit-level indicators are meant to show the profit rate for comparable businesses conducting comparable transactions to the related-party transaction. That profit rate can then be applied to the related-party transaction to determine the transfer price that would generate such profit rate.

Specifically, the CPM provides that an arm's length result may be shown by calculating the operating profit that the *tested party* would have earned on the related-party transaction if its profit level indicator were equal to a comparable operating profit.[31] The tested party is the participant in the related-party transaction whose operating profit attributable to that transaction "can be verified using the most reliable data and requiring the fewest and most reliable adjustments, and for which reliable data regarding uncontrolled comparables can be located."[32] The result is that the tested party tends to be the least complex of the controlled taxpayers and tends not to own valuable intangible property or unique assets that distinguish it from potential uncontrolled comparables.

The CPM's methodology is familiar to those who conduct financial ratio analysis. What the section 482 labels as a profit level indicator (see Box 13.2) is nothing more than a ratio that measures relationships between profits and costs incurred or resources deployed. This ratio is derived from uncontrolled taxpayers that engage in similar business activities to the related-party transaction and under similar circumstances. If there are differences between the tested party and an uncontrolled comparable that would materially affect the reliability of the ratio, adjustments should be made that are explained in the Regulations. Once the ratio is finalized, the transfer price is determined by calculating the transfer price that is needed to yield that ratio. For example, if the relevant ratio is operating profit to sales and the comparable uncontrolled taxpayers produce an operating profit to sales ratio of 3 percent, the transfer price would be the price that forces the tested party's operating profit to equal a 3 percent operating profit to sales ratio. In reality, however, the comparable uncontrolled taxpayers would not generate a single ratio. Each uncontrolled taxpayer is likely to have a slightly different ratio, and the group of comparables collectively provides a range of ratios. The Regulations provide detailed instructions on how to determine and utilize the range.[33]

BOX 13.2: PROFIT-LEVEL INDICATORS EXPLAINED

Profit-level indicators are defined as "ratios that measure relationships between profits and costs incurred or resources employed."[34] Whether a particular profit-level indicator is appropriate for determining a particular transfer price depends on a number of factors, including the following:

- The nature of the activities of the tested party.
- The reliability of the available data with respect to uncontrolled comparables.
- The extent to which the profit level indicator is likely to produce a reliable arm's length income determination for that particular tested party.

The Regulations specifically state that two profit-level indicators may provide a reliable basis for comparing operating profits:

1. **Rate of return on capital employed:** Rate of return on capital employed is the ratio of operating profit to operating assets. This indicator is particularly relevant when operating assets play a greater role in generating operating profits for both the tested party and the uncontrolled comparable.

2. **Financial ratios:** Financial ratios that measure relationships between profit and costs or sales revenue can be used. They are more sensitive to functional differences than a rate of return on capital employed, so greater comparability analysis is required when using a financial ratio analysis. Specific financial ratios that may be appropriate include ratio of operating profit to sales and ratio of gross profit to operating expenses.

In addition, if the taxpayer can demonstrate that other profit-level indicators provide a more reliable measurement of the income the tested party would have earned in an arm's length transaction, the Regulations also permit the use of such other profit-level indicators.[35]

Profit Split Method The final specified method is PSM,[36] which tries to ascertain the arm's length price for a related-party transfer by valuing the economic contributions of each of the parties to the transaction and then allocating the operating profit or loss from the activity among the parties in accordance with the relative value of each controlled taxpayer's contribution. The Regulations require that such relative value be determined "in a manner that reflects the functions performed, risks assumed, and resources employed by each participant in the relevant business activity."[37] The allocation of operating profit or loss is intended to imitate the division of profit or loss that would have resulted if the parties had not been related. Once the profit split is determined, the transfer price is calculated by using the transfer price that is needed to yield that profit split for the controlled taxpayers.

The Regulations allow for two distinct PSM approaches for developing the profit split. One is the comparable PSM, and the other is the residual PSM.

Under the comparable PSM,[38] a profit split is derived by reference to the allocation of operating profits between uncontrolled taxpayers in similar transactions and activities. The derived operating profit split from these uncontrolled transactions is then used to split the operating profits between the related parties in the related-party transaction.[39]

In reality, the comparable PSM appears to be seldom, if ever, used.[40] To begin with, the reliability of the comparable PSM is dependent on a number of factors that tend to greatly limit the potential field of meaningful comparables. Two of those factors are the degree of consistency between the controlled and uncontrolled taxpayers in accounting practices and the reliability of the available data on the allocation of costs, income, and assets between the relevant business activity and the participants' other activities.[41] Even when comparables can be identified, the financial data needed to run a Comparable PSM analysis tend to be confidential, proprietary information that cannot be obtained.

The residual PSM[42] attempts to isolate the residual pool of profits that specifically results from the unique intangible that is the subject of the related-party transaction. The idea is to clear away the routine contributions that tend to be easier to price and then attempt to divide the residual profit. The residual PSM is frequently used in more complex transactions where both sides to the related-party transaction are contributing valuable intangibles.[43] The residual PSM involves a two-step process, as follows:[44]

1. Allocate a sufficient level of operating income to each of the related parties in the transaction to provide compensation for routine contributions to the related-party transaction (e.g., tangible property contributions that are included in the transaction, distribution and marketing services, or other services).[45] Identifying the routine contributions requires a functional analysis of the functions performed, risks assumed, and resources employed. The compensation rate for the routine

contributions is determined based on comparable uncontrolled tax-payers performing comparable activities.

2. Allocate the residual profits (i.e., the profits that remain after the step 1 profit allocation) among the related parties based on the relative value of their nonroutine contributions to the transaction.[46] If the nonroutine contributions stem from contributions of nonroutine intangible property, the relative value of such contributions may be measured in a number of ways. The Regulations expressly approve the following techniques:

   ■ Referring to external market benchmarks that reflect fair market value of each intangible.
   ■ Estimating the capitalized cost of developing the intangible minus an appropriate amount of amortization based on the useful life of each intangible.
   ■ Calculating the amount of actual expenditures in recent years if the intangible property development expenditures of the parties are relatively constant over time and the useful life of the intangibles contributed by each party is approximately the same.

The residual PSM is more frequently used for determining transfer prices than the comparable PSM. A May 2011 Working Draft of the United Nations Practical Manual on Transfer Pricing for Developing Countries provides the following comparison of the residual PSM and the comparable PSM:

> *The residual profit split method is more used in practice than the [comparable] approach for two reasons. First, the residual approach breaks up a complicated transfer pricing problem into two manageable steps. The first step determines a basic return for routine functions based on comparables. The second step analyzes returns to often unique intangible assets based not on comparables but on relative value which is, in many cases, a practical solution. Secondly, potential conflict with the tax authorities is reduced by using the two-step residual approach since it reduces the amount of profit split in the potentially more controversial second step.*[47]

Unspecified Methods The Regulations also permit the use of unspecified methods if the taxpayer can demonstrate that another method generates a better arm's length result. This practice is consistent with the current preference for a flexible best method approach and provides the possibility for more creativity on the part of the taxpayer in developing a valuation for any specific transaction that best reflects its economic realities.

Advance Pricing Agreements

To reduce some of the risk and uncertainty surrounding related-party transfer-pricing structures, the taxpayer can try to enter into an advance pricing agreement (APA) with one or more government tax authorities. An APA is a contract that the taxpayer enters into with the tax authority to obtain pre-approval for the transfer-pricing methodology it intends to use for a related-party transaction. The taxpayer agrees to use a specified methodology for a given transaction in a given time period in exchange for the tax authority agreeing not to seek any transfer-pricing adjustments.

Although obtaining an APA can reduce the taxpayer's uncertainty about its transfer-pricing methodologies, it can also raise other uncertainties. Requesting an APA puts the taxpayer's related-party transaction on the tax authority's radar, which entails its own set of uncertainties and risks. For straightforward arrangements that have little controversy surrounding them, the need to engage in the APA process is probably not beneficial. On the other hand, where a novel or controversial structure is contemplated, an APA may provide welcome clarity. The APA process also affords the taxpayer the opportunity to propose more creative approaches to the transfer-pricing problem that are not contemplated by the current regulations. As long as the suggested approach is reasonable and the taxpayer can convince the tax authority of the validity of the proposed method, an APA can assure the taxpayer that the tax authority will not be a source of prosecutorial uncertainty during the covered time period. That can be particularly true when the taxpayer's structure involves multiple taxing authorities throughout the world. Each separate tax authority may have a very different view on the proper allocation of income from the related-party transaction, which can cause the uncertainty to grow exponentially. In these situations, an APA that embraces a transfer-pricing method that is acceptable to multiple taxing authorities could be worth the effort.

REFERENCES

Ad Hoc Group of Experts on International Cooperation in Tax Matters. June 26, 2001. "Transfer Pricing: History, State of the Art, Perspectives." *United Nations Document* 2: ST/SG/AC.8/2001/CRP.6.

Bonano, William. Feb. 1999. "Transfer Pricing for Intangible Property under Section 482." *International Tax Bulletin—Pillsbury Winthrop Shaw Pittman LLP Tax Page.*

Devereux, Michael, Ben Lockwood, and Michela Redoano. 2002. "Do Countries Compete over Corporate Tax Rates?" Warwick Economic Research Paper No. 642.

Drucker, Jesse. Sept. 28, 2006. "How Merck Saved $1.5 Billion Paying Itself for Drug Patents: Partnership with British Bank Moved Liabilities Offshore; Alarmed U.S. Cracks Down—'The Art of Tax Avoidance.'" *Wall Street Journal*.

Drucker, Jesse. Oct. 21, 2010. "Google 2.4% Rate Shows How $60 Billion Lost to Tax Loopholes." *Bloomberg*.

Eicke, Rolf. 2008. *Tax Planning with Holding Companies: Repatriation of US Profits from Europe: Concepts, Strategies, Structures*. The Netherlands: Kluwer Law International.

Feinschreiber, Robert. 2001. *Transfer Pricing Handbook*. 3rd ed. Somerset, NJ: John Wiley & Sons.

Finfacts Team. Mar. 9, 2006. "Microsoft to Hide Irish Tax Haven Data of Subsidiaries That Have Saved It Billions of Dollars in US Taxes." *Finfacts Ireland Business News*.

Hizengrath, David. Sept. 12, 2006. "Glaxo to Pay IRS $3.4 Billion—Tax Settlement Is Biggest in Agency's History." *Washington Post*.

Internal Revenue Service Press Release. Feb. 14, 2007. "Merck Agrees to Pay IRS $2.3 Billion." www.irs.gov/newsroom/article/0,,id=167773,00.html.

King, Elizabeth. 2008. *Transfer Pricing and Corporate Taxation: Problems, Practical Implications and Proposed Solutions*. New York: Springer.

Lent, Robert. 1966. "New Importance for Section 482 of the Internal Revenue Code." *William and Mary Law Review* 7: 345.

New York Times. Nov. 17, 2005. "American Ingenuity, Irish Residence."

Sartori, Nicola. 2009. "Effects of Strategic Tax Behaviors on Corporate Governance." http://works.bepress.com/nicola_sartori/1.

Simpson, Glenn. Nov. 7, 2005. "Irish Subsidiary Lets Microsoft Slash Taxes in U.S. and Europe: Tech and Drug Firms Move Key Intellectual Property to Low-Levy Island Haven Center of Windows Licensing." *Wall Street Journal*A1.

Smith, Gordon V., and Parr, Russell L. 2005. *Intellectual Property: Valuation, Exploitation, and Infringement Damages*. Hoboken, NJ: John Wiley & Sons.

Working Draft of the United Nations Practical Manual on Transfer Pricing for Developing Countries. May 2011. www.un.org/esa/ffd/tax/documents/bgrd_tp.htm.

Wright, Deloris. 1993. *Understanding the New U.S. Transfer Pricing Rules*. Chicago, IL: Commerce Clearing House.

NOTES

1. Jesse Drucker, "How Merck Saved $1.5 Billion Paying Itself for Drug Patents: Partnership with British Bank Moved Liabilities Offshore; Alarmed U.S. Cracks Down—'The Art of Tax Avoidance,'" *Wall Street Journal* (Sept. 28, 2006).
2. Drucker.
3. Internal Revenue Service Press Release, "Merck Agrees to Pay IRS $2.3 Billion" (Feb. 14, 2007), www.irs.gov/newsroom/article/0,,id=167773,00.html.

4. Mark Everson, Written Testimony before Senate Committee on Finance on Compliance Concerns Relative to Large and Mid-Size Businesses (June 13, 2006), www.irs.gov/newsroom/article/0,,id=158644,00.html.

5. Glenn Simpson, "Irish Subsidiary Lets Microsoft Slash Taxes in U.S. and Europe: Tech and Drug Firms Move Key Intellectual Property to Low-Levy Island Haven Center of Windows Licensing," *Wall Street Journal* (Nov. 7, 2005), A1; New *York Times* "American Ingenuity, Irish Residence" (Nov. 17, 2005).

6. Simpson, A1.

7. Ibid.

8. Ad Hoc Group of Experts on International Cooperation in Tax Matters, "Transfer Pricing: History, State of the Art, Perspectives," *United Nations Document* 2 (June 26, 2001): ST/SG/AC.8/2001/CRP.6.

9. Deloris Wright, *Understanding the New U.S. Transfer Pricing Rules* 14–15 (1993).

10. *Eli Lilly and Co. v. Commissioner*, 84 T.C. 996 (1985). Other cases challenging similar structures were *GD Searle & Co. v. Commissioner*, 88 T.C. 25 (1987) and *Bausch and Lomb v. Commissioner*, 91-1 USTC P. 50,244,933 Fed .2d 1084 (2d Cir. 1991).

11. *Eli Lilly and Co. v. Commissioner*, 84 T.C. 996, 1120 (1985).

12. *Eli Lilly and Co. v. Commissioner*, 84 T.C. 996, 1120 (1985).

13. David Hizengrath, "Glaxo to Pay IRS $3.4 Billion—Tax Settlement is Biggest in Agency's History," *Washington Post* (Sept. 12, 2006),.

14. See, e.g., Robert Feinschreiber, *Transfer Pricing Handbook*, 3rd ed. (2001); and Robert Cole, contributing author and ed., *Practical Guide to U.S. Transfer Pricing*, 3rd ed. (2006).

15. See Robert Lent, "New Importance for Section 482 of the Internal Revenue Code," *William and Mary Law Review* 7 (1966): 345, 346.

16. Income Tax Reg. sec. 1.482-1.

17. Income Tax Reg. sec. 1.482-1.

18. Income Tax Reg. sec. 1.482-8(a).

19. Income Tax Reg. sec. 1.482-8(b) and sec. 1.482-8T.

20. Income Tax Reg. sec. 1.482-4(b)(1).

21. Wright, 503.

22. Income Tax Reg. sec. 1.482-4(f)(2).

23. Income Tax Reg. sec. 1.482-4.

24. Income Tax Reg. sec. 1.482-4(c)(1).

25. Income Tax Reg. sec. 1.482-4(c)(2)(ii).

26. Income Tax Reg. sec. 1.482-4(c)(2)(ii).

27. Income Tax Reg. sec. 1.482-4(c)(2)(iii)(B)(1)(ii).

28. Income Tax Reg. sec. 1.482-4(c)(2)(iii)(B)(1)(ii).

29. Income Tax Reg. sec. 1.482-4(c)(2)(iii)(B)(2).

30. Income Tax Reg. sec. 1.482-5.

31. Income Tax Reg. sec. 1.482-5(b)(1).

32. Income Tax Reg. sec. 1.482-5(b)(2).

33. Income Tax Reg. sec. 1.482-5(b)(3) and sec. 1.482-1(e)(2).
34. Income Tax Reg. sec. 1.482-5(b)(4).
35. Income Tax Reg. sec. 1.482-5(b)(4)(iii).
36. Income Tax Reg. sec. 1.482-6.
37. Income Tax Reg. sec. 1.482-6(b).
38. Income Tax Reg. sec. 1.482-6(c)(2).
39. Income Tax Reg. sec. 1.482-6(c)(2)(i).
40. Wright, 111.
41. Income Tax Reg. sec. 1.482-6(c)(2)(ii)(C).
42. Income Tax Reg. sec. 1.482-6(c)(3).
43. *Working Draft of the United Nations Practical Manual on Transfer Pricing for Developing Countries* (May 2011): 63, www.un.org/esa/ffd/tax/documents/bgrd_tp.htm.
44. Income Tax Reg. sec. 1.482-6(c)(3)(i).
45. Income Tax Reg. sec. 1.482-6(c)(3)(i)(A).
46. Income Tax Reg. sec. 1.482-6(c)(3)(i)(B).
47. *Working Draft of the United Nations.*

About the Authors

William J. Murphy is a Professor of Law and Chair of the Commerce and Technology Law Graduate Program at the University of New Hampshire School of Law (formerly the Franklin Pierce Law Center, one of the top schools of intellectual property in the country). Murphy cofounded UNH Law's Intellectual Property Valuation Institute and currently serves as its director. After law school, Murphy served as an antitrust trial attorney for the Federal Trade Commission's Bureau of Competition before continuing his education at the Harvard Business School. During business school, he was a contributing founder of an educational software company and a global pharmaceutical clinical trials company. He has taught graduate and undergraduate courses at Harvard in the Extension and the Radcliffe Seminars Programs, and in the College of Management at the University of Massachusetts Boston. He has been a Visiting Professor of Economics at Dartmouth College and a Fulbright Scholar at University College Cork, Ireland. He was the founding partner of the intellectual property boutique law firm Frankel, Murphy and Ogden before joining the faculty at UNH Law. He is the author of *R&D Cooperation among Marketplace Competitors* (Quorom, 1990). Murphy earned a JD degree from Pennsylvania State University's Dickinson School of Law, and he holds master and doctorate degrees from Harvard University's Graduate School of Business.

John L. Orcutt is the Associate Dean for Faculty Research and a Professor of Law at the University of New Hampshire School of Law. Orcutt cofounded UNH Law's Intellectual Property Valuation Institute and its International Technology Transfer Institute (which is a specialized research and consulting center that seeks to help countries throughout the world foster economic development by improving the flow of publicly funded innovations from universities and research institutes into the commercial sector). Orcutt is the author of *Shaping China's Innovation Future: University Technology Transfer in Transition* (Elgar Publishing, 2010). Before coming to UNH Law, Orcutt worked as a technology investment banker with Robertson Stephens in Silicon Valley and as a capital markets attorney with

Shearman & Sterling in its New York and Paris offices. Orcutt earned a JD degree from the University of California at Berkeley.

Paul C. Remus is a shareholder of the law firm of Devine, Millimet & Branch, P.A. in Manchester, New Hampshire. Remus concentrates his intellectual property practice in prosecuting patent applications, drafting noninfringement opinions, and licensing technology. He also mediates disputes involving intellectual property and is on the U.S. District Court Mediation Panel List. Remus also represents both companies and venture capitalists in private placements and other financings involving intellectual property. Remus is the first New Hampshire intellectual property lawyer listed in *Super Lawyers*, is also listed in Woodward/White's *Best Lawyers in America* in the field of Intellectual Property, and is the founder and past chairman of the Intellectual Property Section of the New Hampshire Bar Association. He also rows competitively and refuses to wear a tie. Remus earned a JD degree from the University of Michigan.

Index

379

Printed and bound by CPI Group (UK) Ltd, Croydon, CR0 4YY

23/04/2025

14660921-0003